DARIUS B. MOON
THE HISTORY OF A MICHIGAN ARCHITECT 1880-1910

James MacLean

SoloVerso Press
Publisher

Copyright © 2015 James V. MacLean

First Published in the United States of America in 2015
by
James V. MacLean, Lansing MI, 48915

For more information visit www.soloverso.com

ISBN-13: 978-0692574850
ISBN-10: 0692574859

All rights reserved. No part of this publication may be reproduced, distributed, or transmitted in any form or by any means, electronic or mechanical methods, including photocopying, recording, or any information storage and retrieval systems, without the prior permission in writing of both the copyright owner and the publisher.

Printed in the United States of America

Typeset and Designed by Jodi Miller

TABLE OF CONTENTS

Preface 1
Acknowledgements 5
A Life 7
1880 15
1881 23
1882 28
1883 40
1884 41
1885 42
1886 47
1887 48
1888 51
1889 65
1890 67
1891 82
The Chicago Interlude 1891-1893 93
1894 94
1895 104
1896 124
1897 132
1898 132
1899 148
1900 150
1901 159
1902 167
1903 206
1904 249
1905 268
1906 297
1907 303
1908 329
1909 371
1910 382
After 1910 396
Appendix A 403
Appendix B 410
Bibliography 411
Index 416

PREFACE

O. Friend Howe Residence, 321 W. Hillsdale, Lansing, MI

Like many historical studies, this book had its genesis in a question. One evening when working at the Reference Desk at the Capital Area District Library, a caller asked a simple question, "Was a home located at 321 W. Hillsdale the Madison Bates double house designed by Darius Moon?" The home was scheduled for demolition but there was some interest in preserving the home if it was designed by Moon. After a few hours of working on the question, I determined that the home was not the Madison Bates double house, but a home owned by O. Friend Howe. But it raised an interesting question; just what structures did Darius B. Moon design? The records in regards to buildings Moon designed were sketchy and incomplete. As a researcher I was intrigued and decided to pursue it. I began what I thought would be a fairly quick project to determine what structures Moon designed. I was so wrong! Five years later, with eyes now ruined from reading countless reels of microfilm and tracking down endless leads, I have finished. This study is limited to those buildings that Moon worked on between 1880 and 1910. I was made aware that another researcher was working on the Moon buildings prior to 1880. Tragically, Charles Leap died before he finished his research. I decided to maintain my focus on the years 1880-1910 and not expand it; simply it would have been too large a project to do otherwise. [1]

---

[1]   This study of the Darius Moon buildings has taken some interesting twists. There is a business block in Red Cloud, Nebraska that has the name Moon chiseled on the front gable; it was brought to my attention by a traveler who felt this was as a Darius Moon building. It was not; the building was owned by Senator John W. Moon, who was from Michigan and for a time lived in Red Cloud. Senator John W. Moon's name would resurface again when I discovered that the National Register of Historic Places listed a home in Bay View, Michigan as being designed by Darius Moon. It was not, the cottage was designed for Senator John W. Moon, but not by Darius Moon. I would like to thank Mary Jane Doerr for her research on the home, her work *Bay View; An American Idea* is the definitive work on Bay View Michigan. I would also like to thank the Joyce Terhune at the Webster County Historical Museum for the information on the Moon building in Red Cloud Nebraska.

This journey has led to meeting some interesting people like other professionals who enjoy much like I do the challenge of research. I have met several genealogists who have spent countless hours researching their family's history. In some instances, I have been able to help them in their search, but in most cases, they provided far more to my research then I to them. Oh yes I have bored quite a few people. I learned that when writing a book you are no fun at parties or any social situation. Innocently a person will ask "What's new!" The result on my part is an unwarranted offensive of remarks on local architecture, which leaves the victim looking for polite way to flee. Man, am I boring! I would like to take this time to apologize to my colleagues who listen to me ramble on about Moon and, unlike other people, could not walk away.

AN IMPORTANT NOTE ABOUT SOURCES

The information derived for this work has its basis in three lists that were developed at different times and outline the structures for which Darius Moon acted as a contractor or designer. None of the lists spell out exactly what structures Moon designed or those where his role was contractor and in some instances he may have served as both. The first is a listed developed by Audrey Gould, Moon's granddaughter. This resource is compiled from Moon's diaries and is titled "Since the Yr. 1888 All of the Following Bldgs. I Made Plans For." The inventory does contain some structures that were built prior to 1888, which is peculiar given the title of the work. There are several challenges with the Gould list. First there are several odd spellings of names, for example Henry Kositchek is spelled Henry Kosichek and Jacob Stahl is Jake Stables. There also is the question of just what type of structure did Moon designed for his clients. For example, the list contains just the name, Frank Nice; did Moon design a home, a building or remodel a structure for Frank Nice? One important fact to remember is that even though Moon drew up plans for a structure, the plans may not have been accepted or the building/home may not have been built. One fact that cannot be ignored is that the Gould list was compiled from Moon's personal diaries; it is the closest to a primary source document that has been discovered.

The second list, is a catalog of buildings which was used to form the basis for the third list. The veracity of the second list is difficult to determine. The list is part of the Reedy Collection at the Forest Parke Library and Archives. No mention is made by Reedy of her having access to the Moon diaries nor are any notes in Reedy's hand of the diaries' contents. The majority of the notes in this collection are in David Caterino's hand writing. It is possible that the notes for the second list were disposed of when the third list Reedy/Caterino Inventory of Moon Buildings was created. In the writing of this book the second list is used sparingly, deference is given to the Gould list first and the Reedy/Caterino inventory of Moon Buildings second, while this second list is used sparingly.

The third list which I believe was developed by Diana Reedy and David Caterino, is far more extensive. I have titled the third list the Reedy/Caterino Inventory of Moon Buildings. Was the Reedy/Caterino research based upon correspondences with Audrey Gould? This unfortunately is unknown. David and Diana are deceased and Mrs. Gould is in the twilight of her life and verification is now not possible. The list may have been created using the Moon diaries which are mentioned in the text of the Biography of Moon that is on the first page of the work. The problem is we can only speculate as to the sources used to create the list. During the course of this book I will cite the Gould list and the Reedy/Caterino list in regards to the individual structures. If the building was on neither list, the source for the information will be listed. At this point in time the Moon diaries are lost and it should be noted that the Gould family has been very supportive of this project.

Moon's own work *Michigan in the Fifties*: My Father's Family and A True Story, has extensive information on Moon's childhood and early life until 1893 when he returns to Lansing from Chicago. It is unfortunate that Moon stopped his account in 1893. It would have been interesting to have his views on the growth of Lansing. *Michigan in the Fifties* has an unusual layout; the first section is titled My Father's Family and is an account of the Moon family's move to Michigan from New York, a genealogy of the families that traveled to Michigan and an account of his early years in Delta Township. The second section is labeled Number One, A True Story and consists of stories from Darius' youth. It is followed by A True Story Volume Two, which recounts Moon's teenage years, his early work as a carpenter and his time in Chicago. There is a final chapter, Further Recollections of Darius Moon's *Michigan in the Fifties*, which reverts to telling stories of his childhood and teenage years. Together they present a fascinating account of Moon's early life and are quite revealing in the family problems which developed and the challenges Moon faced in his journey to become an architect.

In the Nineteenth century and the majority of the Twentieth century the source for information in any community was the local paper. Lansing was fortunate to have two local papers between 1880 and 1910, as well as two Ingham County papers. The papers were a wealth of information on the development of Lansing. In many instances they verify the Gould or Reedy/Caterino lists. In other cases they recount buildings that Moon designed that were previously unknown. Much like today, newspapers contain errors. With the pressure to get the newspaper to press words are misspelled or locations are incorrectly listed. In the course of this book only the most egregious mistakes in the newspaper articles will be corrected and those modifications will be marked by brackets.

SOME NOTES ON THE TEXT

When including address the modern street number is given first and the older street number is in parentheses.

The earliest image that could be located is included no matter the quality; current photographs are used when no earlier images exist. The cost of construction is based upon the dollar figure given at that time. For a conversion to current prices see the website Measuring Worth, http://www.measuringworth.com which gives a realistic view of the value of the United States dollar.

ABBREVIATIONS

ICD	Ingham County Democrat
ICN	Ingham County News
DFP	Detroit Free Press
LJ	Lansing Journal
LJW	Lansing Journal Weekly
LR	Lansing Republican
LRW	Lansing Republican Weekly
SR	Lansing State Republican
LSJ	Lansing State Journal

ACKNOWLEDGEMENTS

Writing a book is never an easy task. Besides the hours of research that producing a book entail, there is also the responsibility of chasing down endless leads, many of which were dead ends. Over the years I have received assistance in answering research inquires from a variety of people. I would like to acknowledge the following people for their assistance with my queries: Timothy Bowman for his genealogy assistance, Linda Peckman for helping me bounce ideas back in forth on the location of Moon's first home in Lansing, Jamie Ellis, Doug Johnson for is knowledge and good humor in answering my questions on editing images, Linda Koch at the Allegan Public Library who I asked the same question twice and who answered both times with professionalism and grace, Jill Shepard, Senior Executive Assistant at the Michigan Millers Mutual Insurance Company whose research on the insurance company's archive was invaluable, Sherry Owens of the Pascagoula Public Library Mississippi, Christine McCullough, Julie Mannino who answered many questions on who was buried where, Mary Jane Doerr who knowledge of Bay View Michigan is unsurpassed, Diane Hawkins of the Hastings Public Library, Amanda Sheets, Ed Busch who helped to solve the mystery of what happened to Herbert M. Rogers, Kris Rzepczynski who is invaluable resource to the people of Michigan and David Kositchek one of the most engaging people I have met on this journey. If I have overlooked anyone I am deeply sorry.

There are several organizations that aided in my research and for whose assistance I am grateful: the people at Environmental Data Resources for their permission to use the Sanborn Map Images contained within this work and the staff at the State of Michigan Office of Financial and Insurance Regulation who provided timely answers for my questions on the genealogy of local financial institutions, very quickly I might add.

A special mention must be given to these four people and the Reference Staff at the Capital Area District Library. Win Stebbins whose extensive knowledge of early Lansing business history and the development of Roaring Brook Michigan are priceless. Win Stebbins for is help in many areas, David Votta the master of all things historic in Lansing. Rodney Jewett who knows more about the history of Ingham County, Michigan then any person I have ever met. Finally, Craig Whitford a good friend who offered direction and advice when it was needed and listened to me blather on about all things Moon. He had no choice and he couldn't outrun me. Thanks Craig for listening and for everything. Elizabeth Breed, who read the manuscript several times and offered many suggestions and corrections to the text. Finally I need to thank the Reference staff at the Capital Area District Library: Eunice, Anne, Matt, Mari, Jim, Dennis, Jolee, and finally Regina, who is the only person who has survived sharing an office with me. Thanks for the encouragement.

This work is dedicated to Audrey Gould without whose work we would have no beginning. David Caterino and Diana Reedy without whose pioneering efforts in local history so much of Lansing's past would have been lost. Finally, as always, my parents John and Elizabeth Mac Lean who I miss everyday.

One final note, any mistakes/omissions in the text are mine and mine alone. Please contact me if any images have been used without permission. It is best to consider this book as a starting point and it is my hope that it helps to uncover more information about Darius B. Moon the man as well as the architect.

Many of the contained in this book are from the Stebbins Collection located in the Forest Parke Library and Archives, Lansing Michigan others were graciously furnish by a variety of people and their names noted in the appropriate place. Every attempt was made to find the earliest image of the buildings in this work, alas that was not always possible and several modern photographs are included.

Organization

The book is organized chronologically based upon the dates provided by the Gould List, more on the later. Where the building dates are in conflict with the Gould List, the anomaly will be noted.

Cover Image: The Stebbins' Cottage Roaring Brook, Michigan courtesy of Mark Rudd

The 1904 City Directory Advertisement for Darius Moon's Architectural firm

"I have always tried to be the master of everything I done, that is, I always tried hard to do the very best I was capable of doing. And it's always been my motto, that if another man could do a job of work better then I could, I wanted to know how he done it. And because of that trait people call me a crank."

Darius B. Moon

A LIFE

Darius B. Moon was born in Cattaraugus County, New York on January 24, 1851 to David Sands Moon and Mary (née Wiltse) Moon. In what must have been a shock to his family, Sands decided to sell his farm and other interests in New York and purchased 80 acres of undeveloped land in Delta Township, Eaton County Michigan in 1853.[2] Just why Sands decided to relocate his family to an undeveloped homestead in Michigan is unknown. It may have been a chance to build a life for his family that offered unlimited potential or a restlessness in Sands Moon that was part of his personality that arose again and again. In 1862 Sands Moon enlisted in the Union Army and while marching from Traverse City, Michigan, died in Allegan County in 1864. Darius had a difficult if almost nonexistent relationship with his father. In fact he states that "The Father had never been much interested in any of the children" and earlier that "Father was stern, and all of us children seemed to cringe and shrink from him." Sands Moon had a certain amount of wanderlust in his soul, and gave in to it ignoring his responsibility to a wife and nine children. Moon's beloved mother Mary was the opposite of her husband. Mary is described in glowing terms by Darius; "Mother was all goodness, and it always seemed so nice to have her near us." Mary Moon kept the family together making sure the chores were completed and seeing to the needs of the youngest children. Mary Moon passed away on August 29, 1901. Darius's relationship with his brothers and sisters is harder to gauge. Upon the death of his father, his mother allowed his older brothers Andrew and Robert to take control of their father's assets; both sons would marginalize their mother and exploit the land while using their siblings as a source of free labor. As Darius describes "The three younger boys never had any playspells while living on the old farm, the older brothers kept them at work every day in the week but Sundays." The extended version of Darius's description of his early life is heart rending. However it was not all hardship. Like for many young adults there were times of amusement. When his was sixteen, Darius attended the Michigan State Fair which at that time was held on the site of what would become the Grand River Plant of Oldsmobile. Darius tells us about the great fun he, his friends and his brother Rufus had at the fair. Rufus, or Ruff as Darius referred to his older brother, had a little too much fun and was a little worse for wear with the beer he had consumed. The eight mile walk home was a bit much for Ruff and as Darius describes it "…got a bit funny and sleepy and we could not get him to walk." so Darius and his companions laid Ruff to sleep in a cornfield and set up camp for the night. The next morning Ruff was found sitting next to the fence of the cornfield wondering what had happened and how he got there. Ruff would never tell his mother what happened and he never took another drink from that day forward. Mary was teetotaler and none of the children drank, except Darius who would have the occasional beer.

Young Darius grew up wanting more from life. His exploration of the township as a boy awakened something in him. In a sense it may have been what his father, Sands had sought; that there was more to life then the soul crushing work as a farmer. Moon related a story of his leaving the homestead. One day while working with his older brother Martin in the cornfield, Darius decide that he was done with the life of a farmer. He symbolically threw his hoe in a nearby swamp and set out to begin a new life. Darius began his new life as a carpenter working for $15.00 a month for a builder named Peter S. Wright. He worked from sunrise to sunset six days a week, and on Sunday he would return home to spend time with his mother and siblings. On Monday he would return to working as a carpenter. Moon would spend three years learning the building trade. Then in 1871 Darius left the employ of Wright and began to work independently with his first job netting him a profit of $300. With that money he loaned $200 to a local farmer and enrolled in Lansing Commercial College were he received a practical business education. He studied in the winters of 1871-1872 and, in the warmer months, continued his work as a contractor; it must have been a grueling pace. In 1877 Darius moved to Lansing to work as a contractor and more importantly to wed. On February 8, 1877 Darius Moon married Miss Ellen M. Sprague, a local school teacher. The couple would have four children, Florence, Dell B., Princess E. and Mary Ellen Moon.[3]

---

2   Darius Moon's father went by this middle name Sands.
3   Moore 1717 and Past 450.

In 1889 Moon gives up contracting to devote his time to being an architect. An interesting side note to Moon's life at this time is that he sat on a jury that would hear the case of Flossie Martin, who was accused of being an prostitute in a house of ill fame, the notorious Gate House on East Michigan avenue. The home was raided, and city officers found unmarried men and women in bed together. Justice John H. Chase and Prosecuting Attorney Arthur D. Prosser both felt that enough evidence was present for a conviction, but that did not happen and Miss Martin was acquitted by a hung jury. It is unknown how Moon voted in the trial but quite a ruckus was created by the exoneration.[4]

In February 1891 Moon left Lansing for Chicago. The reason he gives in *Michigan in the Fifties* was that his business was slow. He would leave his wife and children at home and live the bachelor life again, and from his own description, he did. What we do know from Moon's account of his time in Chicago is that he liked to have a good time; he was one of the boys who liked to have an occasional beer with his co-workers and in one instance appropriated a case of beer from two of his acquaintances. Maybe it was something in his genes; the last gasp of his father; Sands Moon's blood in his veins. But it was not all fun. This was a perfect time for an architect to refine his skills with the building boom in Chicago which was a result of the 1893 World's Columbian Exposition, also known as the Chicago World's Fair. What is known is that Moon lived and worked in Rogers Park just north of Chicago. Moon's own account is sketchy. The reader never learns the name of the company that Moon works for, nor the location of the buildings he designed in Chicago and the surrounding areas.[5]

Upon his return from Chicago at the end of the fair in 1893, Moon's business began to grow. He landed several important commissions that showcased his talents. His work for Sparrow, Stahl, Brown and Brooks cemented his place as an up and coming architect in Lansing; he was no longer building farm houses and barns. Not only was Moon an architect but he was also an inventor. In 1899 along with Cyril Blatt, a farmer and later a confectioner, they designed and patented the 'Combined Match Safe and Cigar Tip Cutter'; however no one has ever acted upon or purchased the patent.[6]

---

4 See *SR* 5/1/1891. On April 30, 1891 a jury of six men, Fayette M. Howe, D.B. Moon, J.A. Bowen, Charles Thenen, John B. Voiselle and William S Sellers, deadlocked over the guilt of Flossie Martin three jurors for a guilty verdict and three jurors for an acquittal.
5 Moon Part I 35, Part II 38
6 Patent number: 655171.

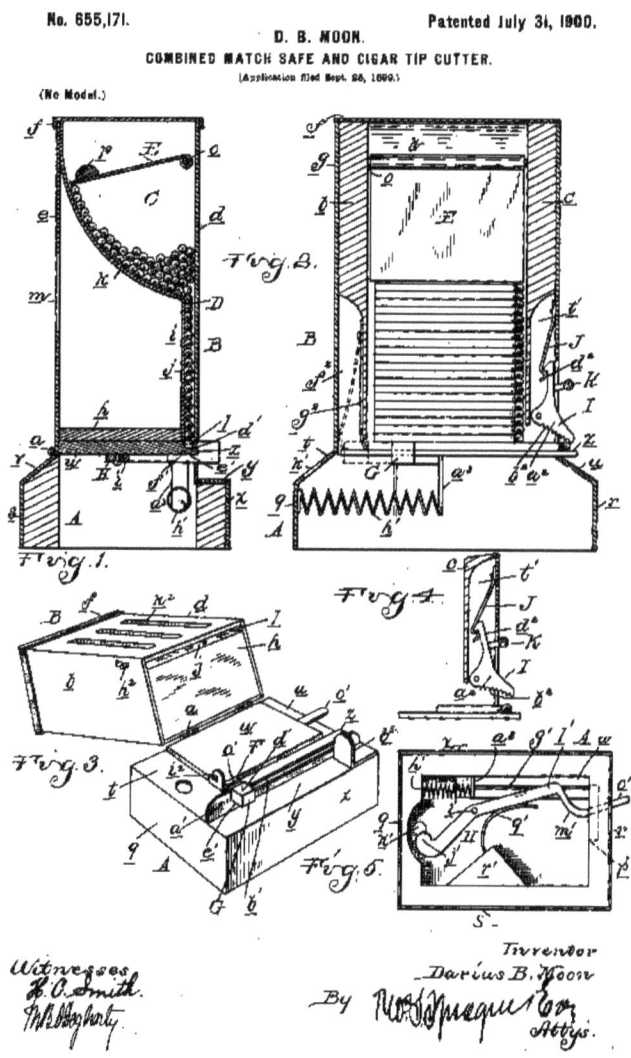

Patent drawing for Moon's Combined Match Safe and Cigar Tip Cutter

In May of 1901 Moon moved his office from his home to the Dodge Block, 225 N Washington Avenue, Suites 5-6. It was unusual that Moon only worked with two other people during his career. At this time he employed Clyde M. Douglas as a draftsman. Douglas had previously worked for R. Arthur Bailey, another Lansing architect. In 1905 Douglas would leave Lansing for Chicago and was employed in the office of Walter B. Griffin a well know architect who was awarded the contract for the design of Australia's new capital city, Canberra. Douglas undoubtedly worked on many of these drawings. After Griffin departed for Australia, Douglas became the Superintendent of Buildings and Grounds at the University of Chicago, a position he held until his death in 1917. Clyde M. Douglas was the son of John M. Douglas a man Moon designed a home for in 1882.[7]

---

7   See the *Ingham County News* 3/6/1919 for Clyde Douglas' death. For information on the Douglas family see the *South Haven Daily Tribune* 4/10/1913.

The nameplate on the gate from Moon's office

Darius Moon worked for a time with an assistant named Raymond W Spice. Raymond was born in May of 1887 the son of William W. and Harriet E. (née Bacon) Spice. Harriet was the daughter of Dr. John H. and Helen Bacon. In December of 1885, William and Hattie moved to St. Ignace, Michigan where William became the manager of the Russell Hotel. Within a short period of time Raymond would be orphaned, his mother passed away in 1897 and his father would die of pneumonia on November 26, 1898 in St. Ignace. Raymond was sent to live with his grandmother, Mrs. Helen Bacon, in Lansing. Spice worked with Moon from 1907-1911. They must have made an interesting team. Dell B. Moon, Darius' son, had no interest in becoming an architect; he was drawn to the skilled trade side of the building profession, becoming a respected plumber. Darius Moon was at ease with Spice and made him a partner in the architectural firm. Aside from Clyde Douglas, who was employed as draftsmen, Moon worked alone. This is the only instance of Moon having a partner during his long career. Moon must have seen something in young Spice that he respected. Raymond later moved to Los Angeles, California and from his draft registration record from World War I, it is known that he worked as a structural engineer. By 1923 Spice was secretary of the Davidson Construction Company, later in life he would be a consulting engineer. On January 24, 1914 he married Miss Ailene Cauthorn; the couple would have one child Mary S. Spice. Raymond W. Spice died in 1968 in Los Angeles and is buried at Wee Kirk o' the Heather, Forest Lawn, Glendale, California.[8]

---

[8] SR 11/26/1898. Most of Raymond's life has been reconstructed using *Familysearch.org* and *Ancestry.com*. Dr. J.H. Bacon, Raymond's grand father who was a surgeon with the 14th Michigan Cavalry and later with the 16th Michigan Infantry died on March 13, 1871.

Moon's office in the Dodge Block, Moon is pictured far left

In the background of the above photograph, there are architectural drawings hanging on some of the walls showcasing some of the buildings Moon designed. The wonderful advantage of a scanned image is the ability to pull out details in the photograph that were previously unavailable. In the center of the photograph below the framed image, is a drawing of the Turner Dodge home. Many other images have also been pulled from this photograph. What is intriguing are the photographs just to the left of the young lady. There are eighteen images that are just too small from which to pull a*NY*thing useful, these would be crucial to the study of Moon's work. Over her shoulder is a sketch of the Olds' home. Just above Raymond Spice who is working at the drawing board in the right of the photograph, is a picture of the clubhouse Moon designed for J.H. Moores. During the time Moon & Spice worked together they moved their office from the Dodge block to the Tussing building. The young lady in the photograph may be one of Moon's daughters. Yes, the man sitting to the left of the image, framed by the doorway is Darius Moon.

Darius B. Moon

On August 29, 1900 the woman who had played such a crucial part in Darius' life, Mary Wiltse Moon died. The formidable and beloved woman who held the Moon family together after the death of Sands Moon was no more. The majority of Darius' work *Michigan in the Fifties* is devoted to the role his mother played in the every day life of the family. After the death of Sands Moon she raised seven children on an underdeveloped farm in Eaton County. In 1903 the Moon family suffered another personal tragedy just before Christmas, Mary Ellen Moon, the youngest child, died of congestion of the brain, which is an increased volume within one or more blood vessels of the brain. The effect on the family must have been devastating. Darius, who had over twenty-five commissions for buildings during this period had immersed himself in his architectural work. He was a devoted father and the death of Mary undoubtedly greatly affected him.

Unlike many historic figures, we know more about Darius' early life than we know about his later years. Darius remained a popular local architect until about 1915, at which time there was a dramatic decline in the number of commissions he received. There were no longer any large projects offered to him, however many of his former patrons remained loyal. He designed several buildings for Lucien Driggs. Moon's later plans became rather formulaic, although his design for the Clarence H. Palmer house at 1514 Osborn and the home for Dr. Charles W. Ellis at 1710 Moores River Drive demonstrated his understanding of contemporary architecture.

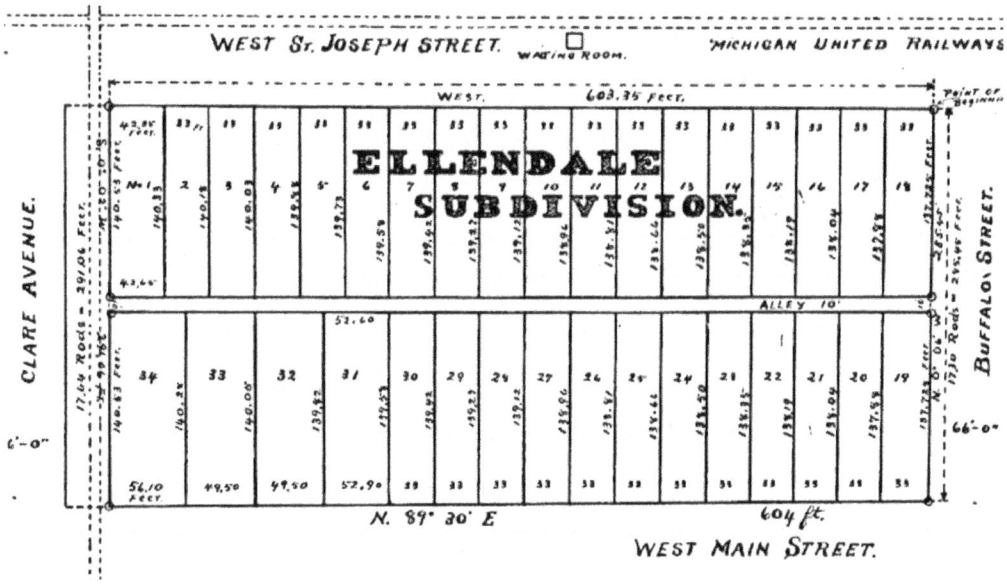

Ellendale Subdivision 1917

Being a realist Moon understood he could not depend on architectural commissions as his only means of support so early in his life Darius and his wife Ellen began to invest in real estate. Although their holdings were not large they did manage to accumulate a number of properties. In fact in 1917, Darius along with his son Dell created the Ellendale Subdivision on Lansing's west side. Ellendale, named in honor of Darius' wife was located between St. Joseph Street and West Main Street, between Buffalo Street and Clare Avenue. Alas like many of Moon's works it was destroyed by the construction of I-496.

Moon's 1891 City Directory Advertisement
Oddly the image is of the Main Building at the University of Michigan

Ellen M. Sprague, Darius Moon's adored wife, was born in Onondaga Township, Ingham County, Michigan in 1849. Her mother, Manervy (née Sherd) Sprague died during childbirth. Her father Molton (Moulton) Sprague passed away much later on February 6, 1861 in Dewitt Michigan. On the back of John and Catherine Sherd's grave stone at the Aurelius Center Cemetery, Ingham County, Michigan, is this notation, "Manervy wife of Molton Sprague 1831-1849." In Darius Moon's biographical sketch, in Moore's History, "In 1877 Mr. Moon was married to Miss Ellen M. Sprague, who was born in Onondaga township, Ingham County, Michigan, daughter of Molton Sprague. The mother of Mrs. Moon died when she was born and her father when she was still an infant, and she was reared in the home of Horace L. Olcott, a pioneer builder of Lansing." It seems that Moulton Sprague, overcome by his wife's death, placed Ellen (Minerva) with the Olcott family.

The 1860 Census lists that Moulton Sprague was postmaster in Dewitt, Michigan and remarried with one child, Minerva E. Sprague, age 11. In the 1860 Census Horace and Electra Olcott (Alcott) are listed as living in Lansing with two children, Ellen M. age 10 and Frances G. Olcott (Alcott) age 1. But in the 1870 Census the Horace Olcott (Alcott) household consists of his wife Electra, Ellen Sprague, a schoolteacher age 20 and Frances age 11. It is interesting that Ellen's surname changed during that ten year time period and that Minerva E. Sprague disappears from the historic record. It seems that Ellen M. Sprague was listed twice in the 1860 Census, once as Minerva E. Sprague and once as Ellen M. Olcott (Alcott). The image of Darius Moon and Ellen Sprague's marriage certificate confirms that Ellen's middle name was Minerva. Ellen may have disliked her given name and reversed her middle name with her given name, the Olcott's were the perfect couple to raise Ellen Sprague. Horace and Electra Olcott had eight children of which seven died as infants and only their daughter Francis survived to adulthood. In Electra's obituary Ellen Moon is described as her adopted daughter. In a 1913 article on the building of the first Capitol in Lansing, Ellen referred to Horace Olcott as being her father. Horace was a stone mason who came to Lansing in 1847 to work on the new capitol building; he supervised the construction of the Female College, the Second National Bank Building, and the homes of D.L. Case and James Turner. In 1864 he left Lansing and purchased a farm in Delta Township. It may have been through Olcott and his background in construction that Moon met his future wife. Horace's wife Electra was born Electra Neal on January 30, 1818 at Lysander, New York. She married Horace in 1839 and settled in Lansing. After Horace's death on April 5, 1877 she moved to Grand Ledge, Michigan where she remained until her death on April 13, 1896. Moon had this to say about Horace, "At one time before I was married, when I was hanging around the girl's home, and her foster father was an old redheaded Irishman had this to say to me after some of my criticism. Dry he says, if you should ever get to heaven, the first thing you will say to Saint Peter, that throne ain't plumb. And I can still hear him laugh, while he took a fresh chew of tobacco." It may be worth noting that at Horace's funeral in 1877, over 80 carriages were present the largest ever at the time in Delta Center; Horace must have been quite a man.

After his retirement in 1923 Darius tinkered about the house, wrote an account of his early life in Michigan and wrote poetry. He became a far different person than the man who once stared down Henry Gibbs at a meeting of the Lansing School Board. On Wednesday afternoon March 21, 1934 Ellen M. Moon, the most important person in Darius' life passed away at the home that they both loved. Darius B. Moon a man who rose from difficult circumstances to become Lansing's favorite architect died peacefully at his home at 116 S. Logan Street on Friday March 25, 1939. The funeral service was held at Estes-Leadley Funeral Home and officiated by the Reverend D. Stanley Coors. Late on the evening of March 28, 1939 under a cold and overcast sky, Darius Bartlett Moon was laid to rest at Deepdale Cemetery next to his beloved wife Ellen.[9]

---

9   For Ellen M. Moon see the *LSJ* 3/22/1934 for Darius B. Moon see the *LSJ* 3/26/1939.

1880

GEORGE E. KING, BARN

Watertown Township, Clinton County, Michigan

"Lively work. D.B. Moon of this city recently built a barn for George E. King of Watertown, 36 by 48 feet with 20 feet posts. In just 30 days from the commencement of the job the building is ready to be painted" (*LR* 5/22/1880).

Alonzo Holly, 6130 Mt. Hope, Delta Township, Eaton County, MI

Early in Moon's career he built several barns in Delta Township, Michigan. The image of Alonzo Holly's barn is one of the few surviving images the style of barn that Moon built or designed. In all likelihood the barn Moon built for George King in Watertown Township resembles the structure built for Holly. Moon had a tendency to recycle designs. An example of this reuse of plans is Moon's design for the Krause home in Clinton County, Michigan and the Emery Wells home in Eaton County, Michigan.

Born in Niagara County, New York on April 18, 1837 to David and Electra (née McKey) King, George E. King had lost both of his parents by the age of eight. At the age of fifteen George came to Lansing and found employment with James I. Mead working as a clerk in his store. A year later George left for Wisconsin to take a position which must have been extremely lucrative because when he returned to Michigan in 1855, he purchased forty acres of land in Clinton County, Section 15, Watertown Township, the north east corner of Francis and Howe Roads. On December 17, 1857 George married Miss Susan Smith the daughter of Jonas and Lucinda Smith. After the wedding George was again offered a job in Wisconsin where the couple lived for two years. Upon their return to Michigan, George developed the forty acre farm he purchased earlier. The couple would have one child, Frank Smith King who was born on December 23, 1859. George would serve as Township Clerk for seven years and was the Highway Commissioner for one year. George E. King passed away on April 2, 1909, following a stroke. His wife Susan died at the home of her granddaughter Mrs. John Stoll on April 29, 1920 after an illness that left her blind and invalid.[10]

MORGAN HUNGERFORD HOUSE

602 W. Ionia, Lansing, MI

---

10 *Clinton Republican* 4/8/1909 and *Portrait and Biographical Album of Clinton* 946. For Susan King's death see *Clinton Republican* 5/6/1920.

"New Buildings. —...M. B. Hungerford, one of the most enterprising farmers, is erecting a handsome residence on the corner of Ionia and Pine Street. It is of red brick with stone trimmings, and will be finished in the natural woods of Michigan. D.B. Moon of this city is the architect of all the above buildings, also the builder of the Timmerman residence, and has the contract for the woodwork of Mr. Hungerford's dwelling. James Hilliard doing the mason work" (*LR* 11/30/1880).

The Morgan Hungerford House is a striking cross gable Victorian home. The features that are intriguing about the residence are the two second floor porches, the Italianate features surrounding the entrance porch and the double entry doors help to make this home one of the treasures of Lansing. Notice the two story bay window in the photograph below, and how Moon merged the brackets between the first and second floor. There is also a second floor porch above the side entrance which is original to the structure and not a later addition unlike the first floor door on the west side of the home under the second floor porch. The home is still standing in 2015 although it has been heavily modified.

A side view of 602 W. Ionia, Lansing, MI

Morgan B. Hungerford was born in Novi, Michigan on February 20, 1832 to Benjamin and Eliza (née Burch) Hungerford. When he was fifteen his parents returned to Henderson, New York where Morgan attended the local public schools. When Morgan was twenty-one he returned to Michigan to teach school near South Lyon. Morgan is listed in the 1860 census as married to Harriet Hungerford, who was born in New York in 1831. This is all the information that has been uncovered on Morgan's first wife Harriet. In 1867 he moved to Lansing, where he managed the Van Dyne farm and his own 120 acre farm located just south of Michigan Avenue about where Sexton High School is located today. After the death of Harriet, Morgan married Mrs. Antoinette Bowser in 1865. She was born Antoinette Chubb on June 29, 1835 in Lyons, Michigan. At the age of 22 Antoinette married the Rev. Aaron Bowers in 1857, and unfortunately the good Reverend passed away in 1861. Antoinette moved to Lansing in 1867 with her new husband Morgan, and the couple settled in Lansing Township, just on the outskirts of the city of Lansing. In 1881 'the family took up their residence at the beautiful home, corner of Ionia and Chestnut streets'. Ten years later, Morgan's wife, Antoinette died of Bright's disease at their home on July 13, 1891. Morgan married again on April 25, 1894 to Mrs. Angeline E. Haze Smith in Lansing, Michigan. Mrs. Smith was the daughter of Dr. William H. Haze, a former Mayor of Lansing. Earlier in her life she married Dr. Harvey Smith of Detroit; the couple had one child, Harvey. After the death of her husband and son, Mrs. Smith retuned to Lansing with her late son's four children who she adopted and raised with the help of her new husband. Morgan was an ardent prohibitionist and a member of Central Methodist Church and served as a trustee for the church. As Morgan's physical condition declined he traveled to California with his wife in the hopes that the climate would be beneficial to his health. Morgan must have sensed that the end was near and he returned to Lansing on March 7, 1904. Morgan B. Hungerford died at the home of his brother-in-law on March 21, 1904, his wife Angeline was at his bedside.[11]

JAMES TIMMERMAN HOUSE

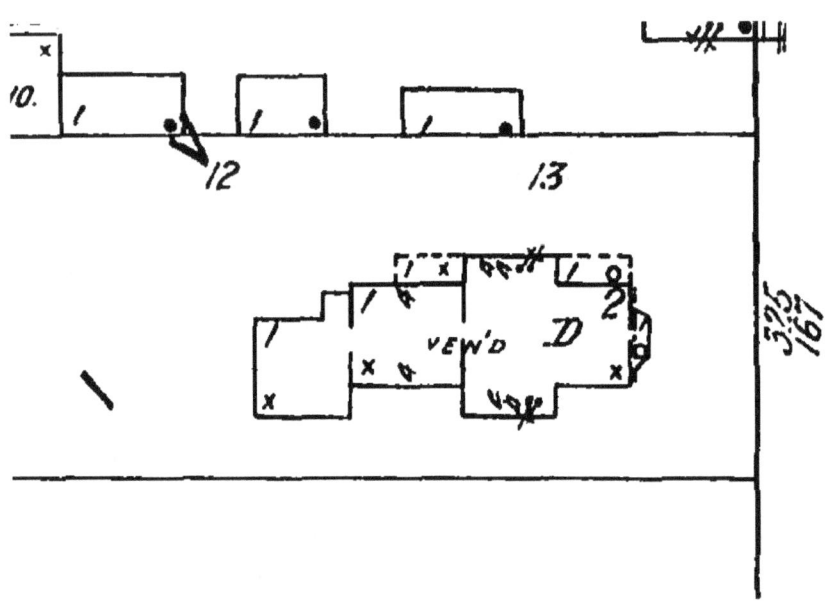

325(167) N. Larch, Lansing, MI

"New Buildings. — ...James Timmerman, republican supervisor of Watertown, Clinton County, is erecting a fine brick residence on Larch Street in this city.... D.B. Moon of this city is the architect of all the above buildings, also the builder of the Timmerman residence" (*LR* 11/30/1880).

James Timmerman's home was located at 167 N. Larch Lansing, Michigan; the address would change in 1906 to 325 N Larch as a result of the renumbering of the streets. No image survives of the home but the above Sanborn image tells us that the home had certain physical characteristics. The home was two stories in height, had a bay window at the front of the home and a side entry porch. From the above image the home was in all likelihood a cross gable T house. The ells of both sides of the home are of equal size resulting in the floor plan that resembles the shape of a cross.

---

11   For Morgan Hungerford see *SR* 3/21/1904. For Antoinette Hungerford see *SR* 7/13/1891. Angeline Smith Hungerford died July 28, 1923, see *LSJ* 7/28/1923.

There is little on the life of James Timmerman. He was born in New York in 1824 and was married to Adelia and the couple had one daughter, Susan Maria, who married Merton H. Smith in Lansing on March 17, 1873. In 1882 after the death of his wife Adelia, James retired from farming and moved to Lansing where he built his home at 325 N. Larch. At the age of 58, James married Miss Estella A. Greenough in Leslie, Michigan on September 3, 1884. The only account that we have of the Timmerman's in Lansing relates to James' second wife, Estella. "Mrs. E.A. Timmerman of 167 Larch street north has had an experience which it will be well for the neighbors to observe and profit thereby. During the night or early morning a rather small mongrel dog killed 15 fowl, most of them choice Leghorns, Plymouth Rock and Mincokas." James Timmerman would pass away at his home on May 2, 1895.[12] The home was torn down in 1971.

LANSING FRACTIONAL DISTRICT #4 SCHOOL

St Josephs & Waverly, Lansing, MI

"New Buildings. — The new schoolhouse in Lansing fractional district No. 4 is nearly completed. It is built of red brick with artificial stone trimmings, and is a neat and commodious structure. Choat & Martin are the contractors…. D.B. Moon of this city is the architect of all the above buildings" (*LR* 11/30/1880). "Fractional School House No. 4, west of the city on St. Joseph st. was completely gutted by fire last evening. The fire was caused by a defective chimney" (*SR* 4/21/1888).

The above image has long been cited as the Lansing Fractional School that Moon designed. Unfortunately all the evidence seems to suggest it is not. The *State Republican* article from April 21, 1888 states that the school house was gutted by fire. The image itself has the date June 7, 1910. The use of the term 'gutted' suggests that

---

12   *SR* 5/3/1895 and the *Ingham County News* 5/9/1895. James' wife Adelia predeceased him; she died on October 29, 1882. For the fowl story see the *SR* 5/15/1897.

the interior of the structure was destroyed but the exterior structure was intact. It is entirely possible that the structure was renovated after the fire and not torn down and rebuilt. No mention of a new schoolhouse being erected has been located, nor has any account of the schoolhouse being salvaged been discovered.

WILLIAM W. MATTHEWS HOUSE

1130 W. Michigan, Lansing, MI

There are three possibilities for the Bill Matthews home in 1880. William W. Matthews was a local contractor who came to Lansing in 1870 at the age of twenty-three. In January of 1877 he purchased Lot 18 Block 3 in J.M. French's subdivision from John M. French and Wife for $275.[13] Two homes were built on this lot 1128 W. Michigan and 1130 W. Michigan.

---

13 See Ingham County Register of Deeds. Liber 63 p. 550.

1128 W. Michigan, Lansing, MI

The home at 1130 W. Michigan seems to be the best possibility of being a Moon designed home. The other home at 1128 W. Michigan is of a later design. Both houses have been torn down and there is little information about either home. The 1878 City Directory has William Matthews living on Michigan Avenue west of Logan Street and in the 1883 City Directory he is living at 1203(1023) W. Ottawa Street.

1203(1023) W. Ottawa, Lansing, MI

The property at 1203(1023) West Ottawa was purchased by Anna C. Matthews in August of 1881 for $540 from Mrs. Sarah Moses.[14] The purchase price was quite high for an empty lot; the average price for a lot on the outskirts of Lansing at this time was about $200. There may have been some type of residence on the lot at that time. Just what home Moon designed for William W. Matthews is unknown. Images of all three homes are presented because it is possible that the date on the Gould list is incorrect. Both 1130 W. Michigan and 1203 W. Ottawa fit the style of home Moon was designing at this time. It is also important to remember that Matthews was a contractor and would have been familiar with Moon's work. Plus they were neighbors.

William W. Matthews came to Lansing in 1870 and worked as a builder and contractor in the city for many years. William married Miss Anna C. Perry and they had four children, John S., William C., Beryl and Maud Irene Matthews. William W. Matthews passed away on July 23, 1937.[15] From the Gould inventory of Darius Moon Buildings, listed as "Hse Bill Matthews, 1880".

---

14   See Ingham County Register of Deeds. Liber 79 p. 270.
15   *LSJ* 7/26/1927.

1881

MARK GARRETT HOUSE

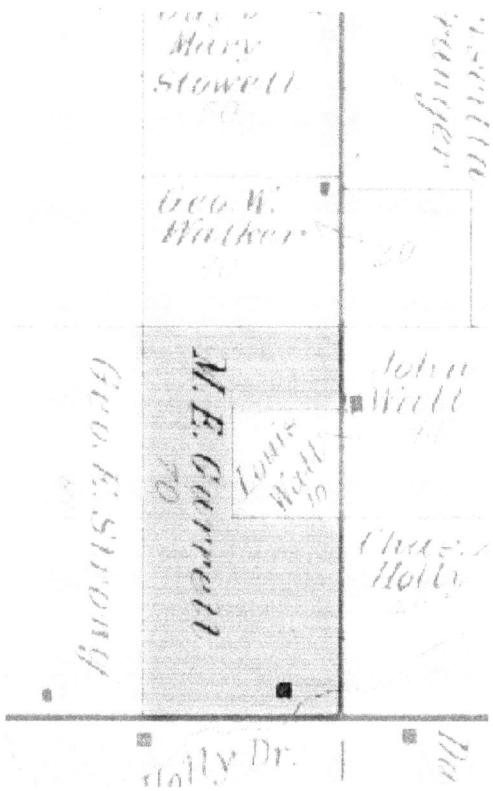

Delta Township, Eaton County, MI

The above image shows the location of the farm owned by a M.E. Garrett, in Delta Township, Eaton County, Michigan located on the NW corner of Creyts Road and Mt Hope Highway (County 14).

Only a smattering of information could be located on Mark E. Garrett who was born in Michigan in 1852, the son of John and Louisa Garrett. At some point John and his wife settled in Delta Township, Eaton County, Michigan. On February 1, 1878 Mark would marry Miss Charlotte (Mollie) E. Ames, who unfortunately died on March 4, 1901 in Maple Rapids, Michigan as a result of complications from surgery to remove a cancerous tumor. The couple would have one child, Raymond M. Garrett. After the death of his first wife Mark married Miss Mae C. Welch, the daughter of William and Lucy Welch on November 16, 1906. An active member of his church at Delta Center, Mark had been a member of the choir for more then 45 years. Mark E. Garrett would die at his home on November 30, 1935, survived by his wife Mae and son, Raymond.[16] From the Gould inventory of Darius Moon Buildings, listed as "Hse Mark Garrett, 1881".

---

16   *LSJ* 12/2/1935. Mae would live almost 30 years as a widow, dying on December 23, 1964, see *LSJ* 12/24/1964.

WILLIAM DANN HOUSE

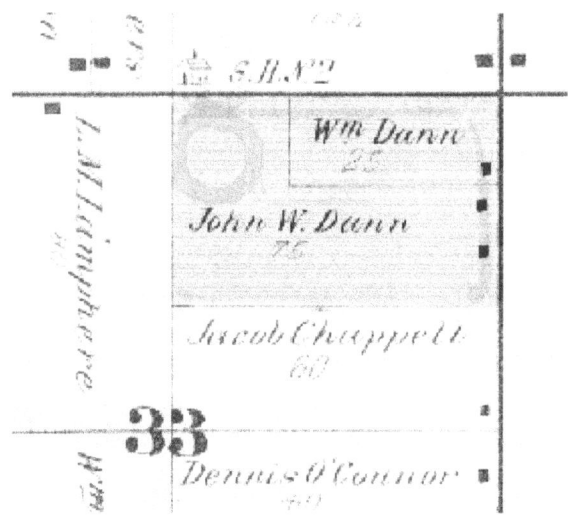

Delta Township, MI

There are two possibilities for the location of this home, William Dann and his son John W. Dann. Both father and son had farms located next to each other as can be seen on the 1895 Atlas of Eaton County. The name Wm. Dann appears along with that of his son, J.W. Dann (County 14). Their properties would have been located on the southwest corner of Millett Highway and Canal Road in Delta Township, Eaton County, Michigan. Neither home is standing and just which home Moon designed is unknown.

William Dann was an early settler in Delta Township; he was born in Lincolnshire, England on January 22, 1816. In the fall of 1854 William immigrated with his family to the United States and settled in Lorain County, Ohio. Later in September of 1860 his wife Mary (née Jickells) and the mother of John and Rosa, died. Six years later William sold his farm in Ohio and moved to Eaton County to live near his son John. In 1863 William would marry Miss Sarah Foster, who died in January of 1903; there were no children from William's second marriage. William would remain near his son until his death on December 10, 1902. In his obituary he is referred to as "Grandpa" Dann and he was survived by his son John W. Dann and a daughter Mrs. Rosa Foster of Cadillac, Michigan.[17]

William's son, John W. was born in Lincolnshire England on May, 6 1849 and came with his father when he immigrated to Ohio and worked as a farm laborer. In 1866 his father purchased 80 acres of land in Delta Township in Section 33, where he worked with his father to clear and improve the land. William was described as a man with a limited education, who through back breaking work became a successful farmer and an active member of the community; he was Vice President of the Eaton County Agricultural Society, a member of the Grange, a member of the Directorate of the Farmers' Mutual Insurance Company of Eaton and Barry Counties and a Director of the Michigan Mutual Cyclone, Tornado & Windstorm Company. On February 26, 1871 William married Miss Abigail Cecelia Joslin, daughter of James and Sarah Joslin. William and Abigail had two children: a son, Lewis J. and a daughter Mary. John W. Dann died at his home on June 6, 1918 after a long illness.[18] From the Gould inventory of Darius Moon Buildings, listed as "Hse Will Dan, 1881".

---

17   *Grand Ledge Independent* 12/19/1902.
18   *Grand Ledge Independent* 6/14/1918 and *Past and Present of Eaton County* 258.

WILLIAM BOYLAN HOUSE

4911 Clark Road, Watertown Township, Clinton County, MI

This is a striking farmhouse; the one story structure with the modern bay window must be an addition to the original structure. The windows on the home have a semi-surround lintel, not plain and not ostentatious, unlike those one would find in the city and they lend a simple beauty to the home. The porch adds to the structure, the slight arch at the top of the segmented column lends lightness to the porch.

William Boylan, a prominent farmer and resident of Clinton County was born July 5, 1830 in Greene County, Pennsylvania and was the son of James and Mary (née Winget) Boylan. William came to Michigan with his parents in 1849 and settled in Washtenaw County, Michigan. On March 23, 1853 William married Miss Fannie C. Fitzsimmons; the daughter of Thomas and Eliza (née Waters) Fitzsimmons. William and Fannie would have four children: Hattie, May, Lulie and Florence, who predeceased her parents. A diehard Republican, William served as Justice of the Peace in Watertown Township in 1872 and 1878. In 1864 William purchased the farm on Clark Road and spent several years clearing the land of its timber and improving the property. On June 30, 1905 Fannie C. Boylan died at her home on Clark Road. Less then two years later her husband William, who was living with his daughter Mrs. May Ainslee, died on Sunday February 17, 1907 devastated over the loss of his wife Fannie.[19] From the Reedy/Caterino inventory of Moon buildings.

---

19   *LJ* 2/18/1907 and *Portrait and Biographical Album of Clinton* 540.

GEORGE SUTLIFF HOUSE

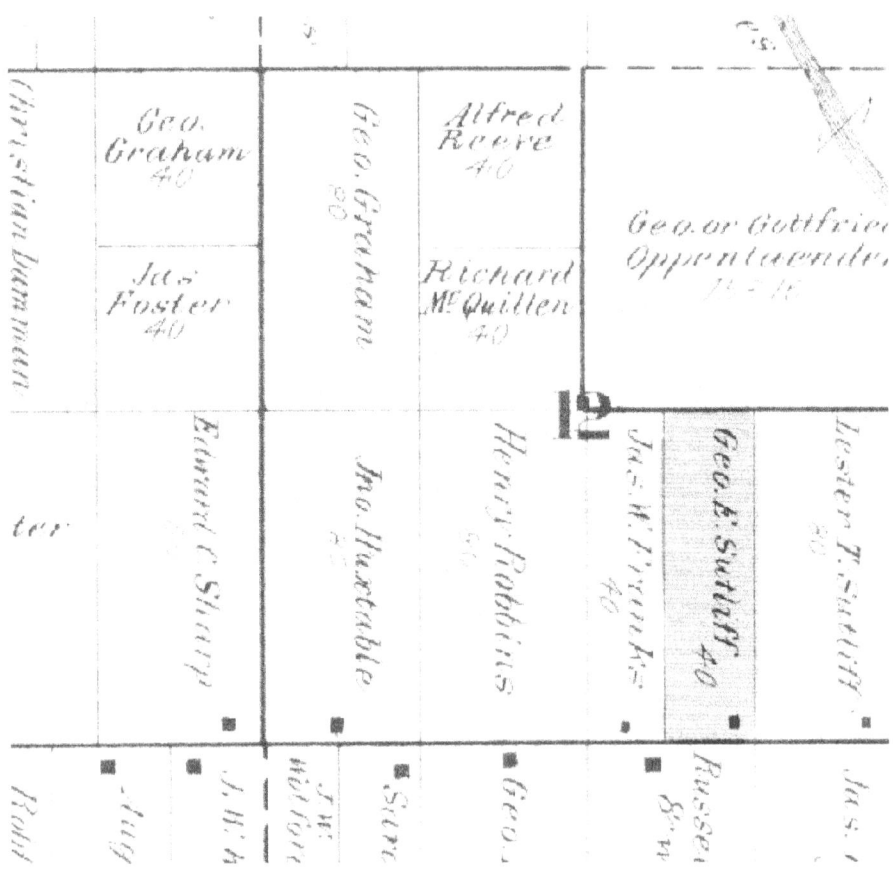

Delta Township, Eaton County, MI

Delta Township News-"George Sutliff has the walls for his new house raised" (*LR* 6/21/1881).

George Sutliff's property was located north of Saginaw Highway about where the Tuffy Muffler shop is today at 4210 W Saginaw. George E. Sutliff came to Lansing in 1853, with his parents Lester T. and Betty Sutliff and settled on a farm on West Saginaw in Delta Township, Eaton County Michigan. He attended school in old Benton House School in Lansing, which later would be the site of R.E. Olds' home. On January 27, 1872 George married Miss Prelia E. Carey; there were no children from the marriage. George E. Sutliff died at his home, 520 W. Ionia in Lansing on March 2, 1926. His wife Prelia would pass away in 1929.[20] From the Reedy/Caterino inventory of Moon buildings.

---

20   *LSJ* 3/2/1926.

BENJAMIN F. HAMIL HOUSE

7730 W. Cutler Road, Riley Township, Clinton County, MI

The Hamil residence is one of the finest examples of an Italianate farmhouse which is still standing in Clinton County, Michigan. The simple hip roof design and the striking wraparound porch make this an appealing home. Moon seemed to have specialized in ornate porches. The capitals of the Italianate porch columns extend outward and help to support the eave of the porch which is a detail that Moon never used again. The addition on the back seems to be Second Empire in design. Notice the tall narrow windows with the elaborate crowns and the decorative brackets on the overhanging eaves. This is a farm house which states to visitors that the owner was a person of substance. Notice the elaborate iron work cresting at the flat of the hipped roof. The home is still standing in 2015.

Benjamin F. Hamil was born September 11, 1824 in Monroe County, New York, the son of Isaac and Bethiah (nee Barrett) Hamil. The family would move to Ashtabula County, Ohio and a year after moving to Ashtabula, Benjamin's father died. His mother moved the family to Oakland County Michigan where Benjamin worked as a farm hand for $12 a month to support his mother. On New Years Day 1842 Benjamin married Miss Amanda C. Johnson. The couple would have four children, William, Sarah, Silas and Charles R. Hamil, none of the children survived their parents. In 1846 Benjamin moved to Clinton County and settled on a piece of Government land, Section 4 in Watertown Township where Benjamin worked for many years to develop a farm. Later he purchased forty acres of land on Section 33, Riley Township where this home was constructed in 1881. He died in 1902 at the age of 82 and was buried in the Wacousta Cemetery.[21] After Benjamin's death, Amanda, who was an invalid, was cared for by the Cronkite family until her death on April 3, 1904.[22] From the Reedy/Caterino inventory of Moon buildings.

---

21   See *LJ* 1/23/1902 and (*Portrait and Biographical Album of Clinton and Shiawassee Counties* 406).
22   See *Clinton Republican* 4/7/1904 and 4/14/1904.

1882

HARRY BAUMGRAS HOUSE

515 Liberty, Lansing, MI

The home is a front gabled with two attractive twists, the dip in the front gable [a clipped gable] and the asymmetrical wing. It's the porch that confuses the researcher, as it is almost western. Notice the brackets supporting the bay window and the Italianate brackets at the top of the bay window. The home was torn down in 1987.

515 Liberty, Lansing, MI

Born in New York City on September 24, 1840 Henry Baumgras came to Lansing in 1864. Baumgras was an artist, woodcrafter, taxidermist and naturalist, an interesting combination of talents for one man. When the Michigan State Capitol building was completed, Henry Baumgras was employed to work on the interior decorations. Later he partnered with Martin Rohrer and established the firm Baumgras & Rohrer, which specialized in decorating and painting. Henry was an accomplished artist who left many oil paintings and drawings of the Lansing area and was a talented taxidermist whose large collection of stuffed animals included many examples of the birds and other wildlife that inhabited the forests around Lansing. Henry had little time for politics or politicians; he refused all offers to take a more active role in local government, choosing only to serve on the Lansing Board of Education for two terms.

Henry Baumgras 1840-1910

Henry was married to Mary Annah, who was the mother of his six children, Lydia, Estella, Daniel, Frederick, Josephine and Henry P. Baumgras. His wife Mary would pass away on August 7, 1880 at the age of forty. On December 11, 1882 Henry married Mrs. Francis C. (née Pigot) Watts. Francis was born in Market Drayton, England on December 11, 1820. She came to America in 1841 and settled in Medina, New York; later she would move to Canada. She married John E. Watts, who passed away in 1877; the couple had no children. After her marriage to Henry in 1882, Frances raised Henry's children as her own and is described as a kind-hearted and devoted step-mother. Frances passed away at her home on April 3, 1903 at the age of 82. Henry Baumgras died at the home of his daughter, Estella on October 3. 1910, Henry was a remarkable and talented man, whose artistic works are now lost to history.[23] Henry's sister Elizabeth was married to Philip Krause of Gunnisonville, for whom Moon also designed a home. From the Reedy/Caterino inventory of Moon buildings.

MARY WELLS HOUSE

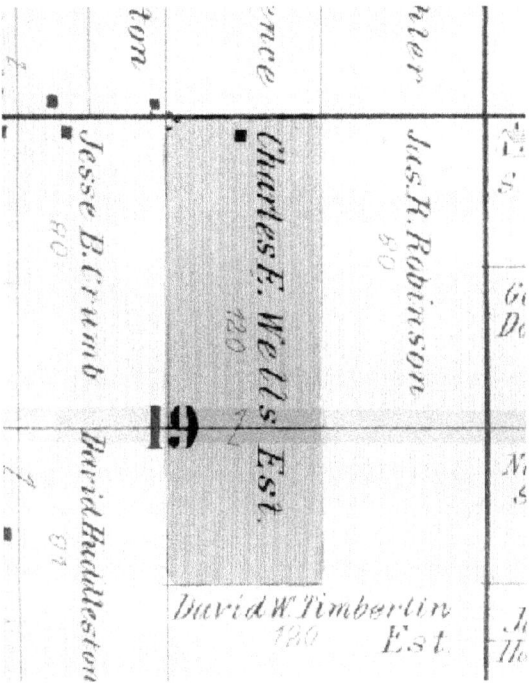

Delta Township, Eaton County, MI.

The Delta Township plat map in 1873 has Charles E. Wells owning 120 acres in Section 19 Delta Township, southwest side of E. St Joseph Highway and Nixon Road. There was no home present on the property (Lake 13). The 1896 plat map has the same property listed as being owned by the Charles E. Wells estate with a home on the property. Given the location on the Eaton County plat maps this could be the home at 6628 E. St Joseph, however, the township records that this home was built in 1900. This may not be correct. The home below is a simple ell home; a style which was common in rural areas and the type of home Moon had built many times.

---

23 For Mary Baumgras see *LRW* 8/11/1880. For Frances see *LJ* 4/4/1903. For Henry see *LJ* 10/4/1910 and *SR* 10/4/1910. Henry's last name Baumgras, is also listed at Baumgrass, in his obituary in the *State Republican* his last name is written as Baumgrass, while in the *Lansing Journal* his last name is spelt Baumgras.

6628 E. St Joseph Highway, Eaton County, MI

Mary Nixon Wells was born in Delta Township on August 8, 1849, the daughter of John and Jane (née Jackson) Nixon. At the age of 24 she married Charles E. Wells who owned the farm adjacent to the Nixon family homestead. Charles was the older brother of Emri J. Wells, for whom Moon would also design a home. Charles would die on December 26, 1876 and Mary would live the remainder of her life as a widow. The marriage produced three children, Albert Wells, Myrtle Wells Simpson and Frank Wells who stayed with his mother. Mary would spend her entire life on the family farm dying there at the age of 71 on November 30, 1911.[24] From the Reedy/Caterino inventory of Moon buildings.

---

24 *Grand Ledge Independent* 12/8/1911.

JOHN M. DOUGLAS HOUSE

730 W. Ionia or 734 W. Ionia, Lansing, MI

There is a John M Douglas listed in the 1883 Lansing City Directory as living at 732 W Ionia and working as a driver for the American Express Company. The problem is that there is no 732 W. Ionia listed in the City Directories after 1883 nor is there a 732 W. Ionia on the Sanborn maps. The best candidates are 730 and 734 W. Ionia. These are unadorned gabled ell homes. Both have interesting features; the home at 730 W. Ionia has a simple porch pediment which resembles an aspect that would be repeated in Moon's later work. The house at 734 W. Ionia has a half circle window on the facing of the front gable. Based upon Moon's later work it seems that the residence at 730 W. Ionia most resembles a Moon designed home.

John M. Douglas was born in Lansing, Michigan on March 11, 1855 to John A. and Angelina (née Merton) Douglas. On September 20, 1876 he married Miss Clara J Pierson in Onondaga, Michigan. The couple would have two children, Ethelyn L., and Clyde [Willard] M. Douglas; Clyde would later work for Moon as a draftsman. In the 1880 Census John is listed as a painter living on Allegan Street, with his wife and young daughter. While in Lansing John worked as a painter and decorator, a trade he would practice for the rest of his life. By 1898 the family had moved to South Haven, Michigan where John worked for John A. Hagerman as a painter. John was a large man, and is described as having a "sturdy build and having weighed over 200 pounds since coming to South Haven, it is hard to realize that he has weighed as high as 275 pounds while at Lansing". He also moonlighted as a policeman, express driver and a hotel clerk. In 1907 Douglas formed a partnership with Martin Van Slyke and established Doug and Van Painting and Decorating Company. After his divorce from Clara, John married Elizabeth B Voorhees on June 22, 1905.[25] John M. Douglas passed away in South Haven on April 9, 1913 at the age of 58 from pernicious anemia.[26] From the Reedy/Caterino inventory of Moon buildings, Douglas House 1882.

---

25 Clara Douglas married Frank E. Starkweather on April 29, 1906 in Leslie Michigan. Clyde M. Douglas, her son by John would pass away at her home in Leslie on February 27, 1919.
26 *South Haven Daily Tribune* 4/10/1913.

PETER OLIVER HOUSE

1100 W. Michigan, Lansing, MI

Peter Oliver was born on February 25, 1850 in Lynn, Ontario to George and Rebecca Oliver. He came to Michigan in 1865 and worked as a carpenter. In 1874 he married Miss Sarah Clow and they had one child, Arthur W. Oliver, who died in 1930. Peter would work as a farm laborer for several years in Clinton County, moving to Lansing in the late 1880s where he would work as a carpenter and later as a contractor. Following Sarah's death on February 20, 1882, Peter would marry Lizzie Biddecomb who passed away in 1932. Later in life Peter would work in the Biological Division of the Michigan Department of Health. Peter Oliver died at his home on May 23, 1939 and was survived by two grandchildren: Earl Oliver of Lansing and Mrs. A.H. McGeachy of Eaton Rapids.[27]

It is recorded in Peter's obituary that he built his home 50 years ago which would place the date of construction at some time in 1888. J.M. French's subdivision plated in 1870 was one of the earliest developed areas of western Lansing. The home built by Oliver was one of the last surviving homes originally built in French's subdivision. A simple center gable home, the structure has many interesting features. The original entrance porch is the side porch closest to MLK (Logan), the entrance with the small porch and pediment was a later addition. Notice how this later porch masks the bay window and diSRupts the façade of the house. Unfortunately the home was torn down in 2009. From the Reedy/Caterino inventory of Moon buildings.

---

27   *LSJ* 5/24/1938.

JOHN HENDERSON HOUSE

326 Harrison, Grand Ledge, MI

In his work The Grand Ledge Works of Darius Moon, Haueter places the date of construction of the John Henderson house as 1888. In his research he discovered no documentation to prove that Moon designed this home. Haueter believed that Moon planned the home or at least parts of the home based upon the Reedy/Caterino inventory. It is odd that the Henderson home and Griswold homes do not appear on the Gould inventory of Darius Moon Buildings; it may be that Moon acted as the contractor for the home. This would be the type of structure that would be expected early in Darius Moon's career. Haueter points out that many "stock" items were used for the interior ornamentation and that the exterior is rather plain. To John L. Henderson, with his background as a painter/decorator the interior work would have been very important to him, even though he had a limited budget. In a sense Moon was the perfect architect/contractor for this home as Moon's hands-on approach undoubtedly saved Henderson money. It is also quite possible that Henderson either knew Moon or had worked with him before (Haueter 12).

The residence is an example of a cross gable home with a small side entry porch; notice the bay window with Italianate details. The siding on the gable with the saw-tooth element and the pent roof over the window are intriguing details. What is interesting about this home is the porch. Moon throughout his career paid particular attention to a porch's features. The Tuscan style columns on the porch lend a simple grace to the structure.

John L. Henderson was born in Michigan in July of 1860, the son of Joseph and Harriet Henderson. On October 11, 1885 John married Miss Roanna Murray in Grand Ledge, Michigan; they had one child Leroy J.

Henderson. John worked as a painter and decorator his entire life. In 1908 he sold his home in Grand Ledge to John H. Brunger and moved to Lansing to work as painter/decorator. After the death of his wife Roanna, John married Marguerite M. (?). He eventually moved to Florida, finally settling in Hillsborough County where he died in 1949. This home is still standing in 2015. From the Reedy/Caterino inventory of Moon buildings.

EDWARD P. GRISWOLD HOUSE

216 E. Jefferson, Grand Ledge, MI

David S Haueter, in his paper The Grand Ledge Works of Darius Moon uncovered that Ionia, Michigan architect Claire Allen designed the home for the Griswold's while Moon acted as the contractor. Haueter also places the year of construction as 1887.[28] In 1885 Florence Griswold purchased the lot on which the home would be built. After her husband, Edward died in 1890 Florence would sell the home in 1891 to Mrs. Harley Tinkham for $2,500.

The Queen Anne style home has a gable center with a false second floor gable, which when viewed straight on from the street blends with the roof line. The porch is the strongest feature of the home with the turned posts; the spindle frieze and the sunburst carving on the pediment give the home an ornateness that is not present in the rest of the exterior structure. What is odd are the three windows on the upper façade. What was their purpose architecturally? Usually windows are stacked in a symmetrical pattern; these windows seem out of place with the style of the home.

---

28   *Grand Ledge Independent* 6/24/1887, 12/16/1887 and Haueter 12. Architect Claire Allen later relocated to Jackson Michigan and become a prominent Michigan architect.

Edward P. Griswold was an up and coming young man in Grand Ledge who was engaged in the dry goods business. He was the manager of the Griswold Dry Goods Store, owned by George Griswold. Born in 1849 in Batavia, New York, Edward married Miss Florence T. Case on August 3, 1872 in Plainwell, Michigan; the couple would have one child, Louise. Later for some unknown reason, Edward decided to leave his family and job to go prospecting in the state of Washington. Edward P. Griswold died near Tacoma, Washington on February 14, 1890, leaving a wife and young daughter in Grand Ledge, Michigan. The body of Edward was brought home and was buried in Allegan, Michigan.[29] Later, Edward's daughter Louise married Orien S. Cross on July 27, 1905, and fortunately that turned out all right. The last record we have of Edward's wife Florence is in the 1930 Census; she is listed as a boarder living in Asheville, North Carolina. The home is still standing in 2015. From the Reedy/Caterino inventory of Moon buildings.

DUBOIS HOUSE AND BARN

Riley Township, Clinton County, MI

In 1896 there was an I.T. Dubois in Riley Township (Isaac F. DuBois). His home would have been located at the northwest corner of Francis and Chadwick roads, and nothing remains of the house or the barn. There were many other people with the family name of DuBois in Clinton Country in this time period. However, none of them had a home in Riley Township.

---

29 *Grand Ledge Independent* 2/21/1890.

CHARLES E. NASH HOUSE

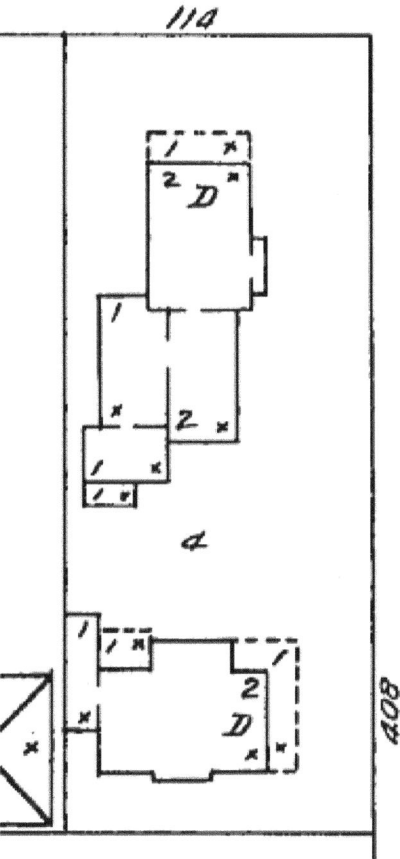

120 (114) S. Walnut, Lansing, MI

Charles E. Nash's home was located at 120 (114) S Walnut. Unfortunately the home was torn down between 1908 and 1913 as a result of the construction of the First Church of Christ Scientist. The last resident of the home before it was torn down was Edwin H. Porter and his wife Emily, Charles Nash's daughter. There is no surviving image of 120 S. Walnut.

Charles E. Nash was born on February 18, 1819 in Smithfield, Madison County, New York. He came to Lansing in 1858 to work in the Michigan Land Office as a clerk. Charles would marry Miss Mary Jackson in Adrian, Michigan on February 11, 1873. The couple had two daughters Hattie [Harriet] and Emily [Berta]. Later in life he was involved in local real estate market. Charles E. Nash died at his home on April 24, 1891; Charles' daughter, Emily would marry Edwin H, Porter, who would later have a home designed by Moon.[30] From the Reedy/Caterino inventory of Moon buildings, 1882.

---

30   SR 4/24/1891.

PHILIP KRAUSE HOUSE

1841 E. Clark Road, DeWitt Township, Clinton County, MI

Built in 1882 and located at 1841 E Clark Road, Dewitt Township, this typical brick farmhouse has some interesting details, foremost are the carved stone lintels for the windows. The exterior of the home is almost an exact duplicate of the Emery Wells home at 7146 E Mt Hope in Eaton County, Michigan, located about twenty miles away from the Krause home.

Philip T. Krause was a pioneer settler of Gunnisonville, Michigan, who died at his home, 1107 Seymour Lansing, Michigan on March 6, 1915. Philip was born in Michigan in 1840 and married Miss Elizabeth P. Baumgras on December 27, 1866 in Lansing, Michigan; Elizabeth was Henry Baumgras' sister. Philip and Elizabeth would have six children: Katherine, Louis P., Herman P., Eugene J., Matilda and Clara B. Krause. Their father, Phillip acquired his father's homestead from his siblings and "…he afterward built a good, neat brick residence and substantial outbuildings, thus making a well improved farm" (Daboll 299).

Philip continued farming until 1899, when he retired and purchased a home at 1107 Seymour Street in Lansing. Reverend I.T. Weldon and Reverend F.M. Cottrell conducted Philip's funeral service at the Gunnisonville church; both Reverends were former pastors of First Methodist Episcopal Church of Lansing of which Philip T. Krause was a member. The pallbearers were Edward Smith, J.J. Hayden, Andrew and Arthur West, James Gunnison and Boyden Hubbard; burial was at Gunnisonville Cemetery.[31]
From the Reedy/Caterino inventory of Moon buildings. The home is still standing in 2015.

---

31 *LSJ* 3/8/1915, Philip's name is also listed as Kraus. It is unclear if the Krause's have five or six children, the 1880 Census lists Louis but not Matilda, while later works exclude Louis and list Matilda.

LORENZO JUDSON HOUSE

St. Joseph Hwy, Oneida Township. Eaton County, MI

The home was located on St. Joseph Highway just west of Royston Road across from the Grand Ledge Country Club (County 13). Lorenzo Judson was born in Medina County Ohio on May 19, 1849, to Warren and Roxy (née Raymond) Judson. At the age of twenty-one he came to Michigan and one year later married Miss Susan Waldo on October 4, 1871 in Grand Ledge, Michigan. After the wedding he purchased 80 acres of land in Section 24, opposite his farter-in-law's, Silas Waldo homestead. After clearing the land Lorenzo built a "commodious brick structure". He lived his entire life on his farm and raised five children, Mark, Nellie, Mabel and Mary, and Florence who predeceased her father by twenty years. Lorenzo Judson died suddenly at his home at the age of 63 on Monday February 26, 1912.[32] It is interesting that on the atlases from this period the property was in his wife's family name Waldo. Susan Judson would pass away on June 11, 1927. From the Reedy/Caterino inventory of Moon buildings.

---

32 *LSJ* 2/27/1912 and *Past* 401.

1883

STEVE MILLER HOUSE

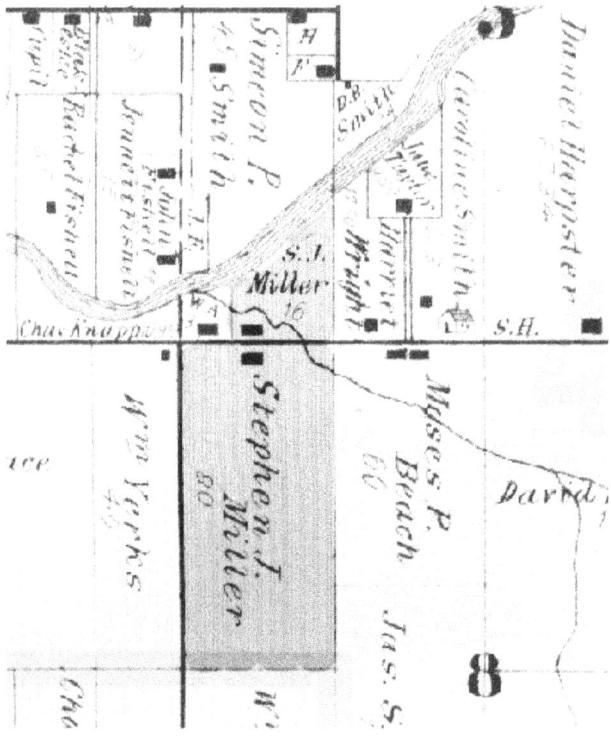

W. Willow Highway, Delta Township, Eaton County, MI

"At one time while I was building a house for Steve Miller near Grand Ledge" (Moon Part II 28). The home would have been located on the south east corner of Nixon Road and Willow Highway, the site now owned by the Grand Ledge School District (County 14). The house no longer stands and no other information has been located on this home.

Stephen J. Miller was born in Williamsburg, Massachusetts on April 15, 1827 to Stephen and Hannah (née Jenkins) Miller, one of eight children that the couple raised. At the age of 12 he moved with his parents to Mesopotamia, Ohio, where on December 30, 1847 he married Miss Olive Lepper; the couple would have four daughters, Emma A., Olive, Helen and Laura. Both Helen and Laura died in 1893. Miller was one of the original Forty-Niners; he traveled overland to California and worked in the goldfields for several years. He retuned to Ohio and in June of 1854 he moved to Michigan and purchased the land in Delta Township, where he remained his entire life. After suffering a series of strokes, Steve Miller died at his home on August 16, 1908 at the age of 81.[33]

---

33   SR 8/17/1908 and the *Grand Ledge Independent* 8/21/1908.

1884

EMRI WELLS HOUSE

7146 E. Mt Hope, Delta Township, Eaton County, MI

Notice the similarities between this home and the Philip Krause house on Clark Road which Moon designed in 1882. Except for the locations of the chimneys these homes are almost identical. The surrounding window lintels and small attic window are nice features of this residence. Notice the wrap around porch with the Tuscan style columns.

Emri [Emery] J. Wells was born June 28, 1842 in Pennsylvania, the son of Thurston and Artemesia (née Fisher) Wells. On July 3, 1863 he married Amy Rachel Lewis. They had four children: Birdsie, Artemesia, Hayes Earl, and a son, who died in infancy. Emri served in the Union Army during the Civil War with the 12th Michigan Infantry Regiment, Company D. which fought at the Battle of Shiloh and the Siege of Vicksburg. A successful farmer for many years, Emri divorced his wife Amy to marry his lover Mrs. Orpha Wilson Gilmore on December 12, 1901 in Ithaca, Michigan. Mrs. Gilmore was at one time the proprietress of a house of ill fame located at 413 William Street in Lansing, Michigan. On the night of September 9, 1899 the home was raided and Mrs. Orpha Wilson Gilmore was arrested along with her 'daughters' Bertha and Josie. Orpha was convicted of operating a house of prostitution on July 11, 1900 and served eight months in the Detroit House of Corrections.[34] Emri waited for her release and the couple married and moved to St. Louis, Michigan where Emri lived the remainder of his life. He died on January 11, 1920. Emri's body was returned to Delta Center for burial.[35] The residence is still standing in 2015. From the Reedy/Caterino inventory of Moon buildings.

---

34   *LJ* 9/11/1899, *SR* 9/11/1899, *SR* 9/13/1899, *SR* 9/20/1899, *SR* 9/23/1899, *ICN* 7/12/1900, *ICD* 7/12/1900 and People 252: 473.
35   *Grand Ledge Independent* 1/16/1920 and *LSJ* 1/13/1920. Orpha C. Wells died in Lansing on 12/20/1923, *LCN* 12/21/1923.

1885

WALTER PRATT FLATS

1100 W. Ottawa, Lansing, MI

The Gould inventory of Darius Moon Buildings indicates that Moon designed a set of flats for Walter Pratt in 1885. The use of the term flats presents a problem. The use of the expression flats usually denotes an apartment or suite of rooms on one floor forming a residence. A flat has its own street entrance, whereas an apartment can only be entered from inside the building. A flat is not a double house, or as they are referred to today, a duplex. There are two street entrances for the home at 1100 W. Ottawa and, for example, in the 1908 City Directory there are two separate listings for the residents, Charles W. Nichols and Walter C. Pratt. The Lansing City Assessor's records shows this home was built in 1887, so everything seems to fit. On the night of August 1, 1892 the *State Republican* records that Walter Pratt's home on West Ottawa Street was burglarized although nothing was taken. In the 1894 City Directory Pratt is listed at 913 W. Ottawa Street. The conflict with the addresses may be because the streets were renumbered twice before 1906. None of the other properties owned by Walter Pratt had multiple residences on the lot.

Carriage House, 1100 W. Ottawa, Lansing, MI

From the surviving records it seems that Walter rented the house to Darwin J. Benjamin, Shipping Clerk, at the Board of Auditors and then reoccupied the property in 1906. The 1100 W. Ottawa address changed through the years and at one time it was listed as 218 N. Logan. A picture of the home's carriage house is seen above, it is one of the few still standing in Lansing, and is included due to its architectural significance. Many people drive by this house and never notice this outstanding building.

Notice the sunburst detail over the window.

The home is a graceful Queen Anne style residence which has been painstakingly restored and the image does not do justice to the structure. The two double bay windows with overhanging dormers as well as the irregular roofline suggest all the traits of a Queen Anne home. The recessed porches on both the first and second floor are an interesting feature. The plain stick columns are not original as the columns and frieze on the porch would have been much more elaborate. What is curious are the Italianate style brackets supporting the overhanging dormers; they seem out of place. The carriage house, which still stands on the property, is Gothic in appearance with a square pattern motif in the center gable which Moon never used again in any of his designs.

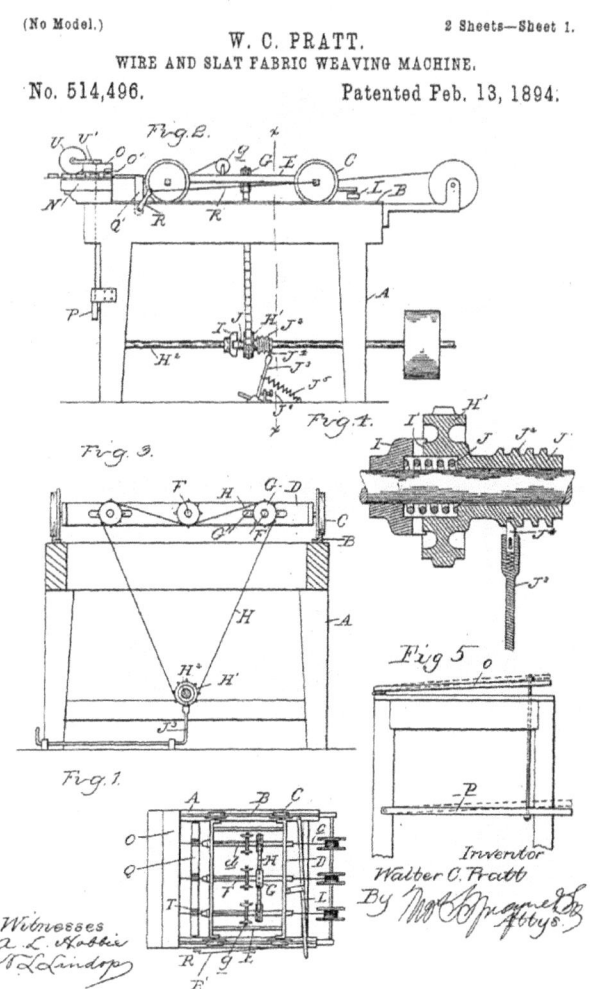

Walter C. Pratt's Patent

An inventor and an early entrepreneur in Lansing, Walter C. Pratt was born in Fort Wayne, Indiana, on April 27, 1853. He came to Lansing in 1871, where he first worked with Professor William James Beal to manufacture carriages. Later he was employed by William J. and Charles W. Holmes, wagon makers. In 1894 Walter perfected his machine for weaving baskets, the W.C. Pratt Wire and Slat Fabric Weaving Machine and concentrated on the production of woven wire baskets.[36] In 1902 Walter established a basket factory in the Lapham & Longyear Plant on East Michigan Avenue. After selling his basket manufacturing business due to declining health, Walter devoted his time to developing his inventions. On November 11, 1874 he married Florence E. Dickerson of Hudson, Michigan; the couple had one child, Beulah, who would later marry Charles W. Nichols. Walter C. Pratt passed away at his home on October 18, 1931.[37] From the Gould inventory of Darius Moon Buildings, listed as "Walter Pratt Flats, 1885".

---

36 See the *SR* 8/2/1894 for a description of the Basket Making device.
37 *LSJ* 10/19/1931 and *Lansing Capital News* 10/19/1931. For the establishment of Pratt's factory see *LJ* 11/20/1902. For the weaving device see United States Patents Numbers 514496, 600269 and 725989.

EDWARD C. SHARP HOUSE

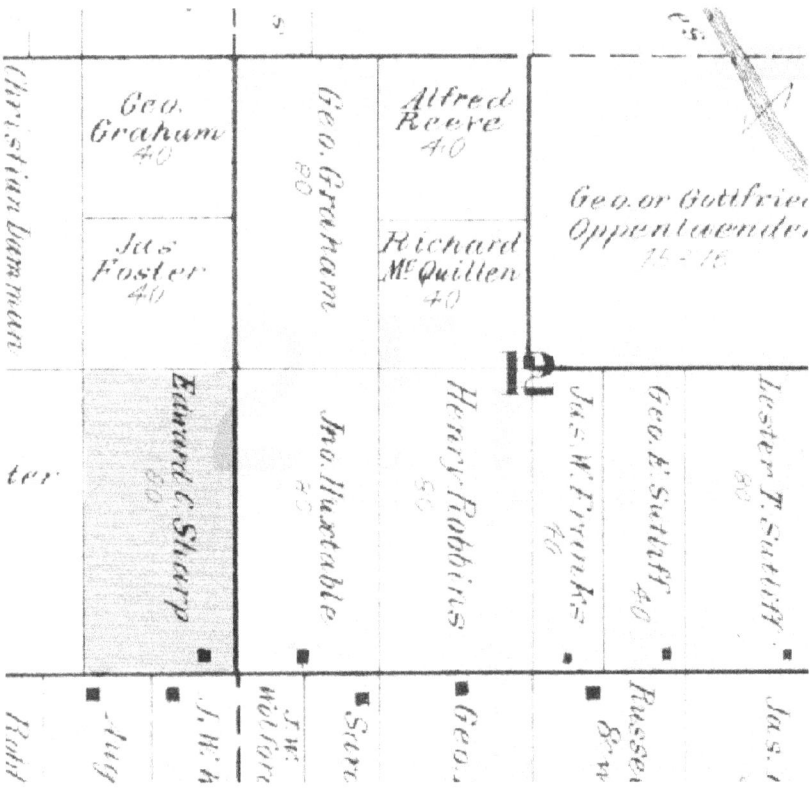

Elmwood Road and Saginaw Hwy, Delta Township, Eaton County, MI

Edward C. Sharp was born in Lansing, Michigan on August 31, 1855. At the age of two his parents moved the family to Eaton County where Edward would remain his entire life. Edward married Miss Ida May Tuck on April 15, 1885. Edward C. Sharp died at his home on W. Saginaw Road on August 2, 1942 and was survived by three sons, William and Clarence of Lansing, Christopher of Grand Ledge, and two daughters, Mrs. Frankie M. Potter and Mrs. Lolo L. Bengry (Bengrie) both of Lansing. Edward's wife Ida predeceased him in 1928.[38] Edward was the brother of John J. Huxtable, who lived just east of his farm. Edward Sharp's farm would have been located on the northwest corner of Elmwood Road and Saginaw Highway. The home no longed stands. From the Reedy/Caterino inventory of Moon buildings.

---

38 *LSJ* 8/3/1942.

1886

JOHN HUXTABLE HOUSE

5000 Block W. Saginaw, Delta Township, Eaton County, MI

The Huxtable home strongly resembles the houses Moon designed and built for Krause and Wells. It is a simple ell style residence. This style home was meant to be functional but not ornate. As with both the Krause and Wells homes you can see the ornate stone lintels and the wraparound porch. The simple round window on the gable end seems to be a trademark of the style of home Moon was designing at this time. The addition on the back seems to have been added later based upon the style of windows.

John Huxtable's home would have been located in the 5000 block of W. Saginaw, just east of his brother's Edward C. Sharp home. There is a notable tendency for neighbors of family members to recommend Moon's services to their relatives or friends. John James Huxtable was a lifelong resident of Eaton County, born in Delta Township in February of 1859, the son of James and Elizabeth Huxtable. John J. Huxtable would spend his entire life living on the farm where he was born. John would marry Minnie Lazell the daughter of Uriah and Lucy (née Nichols) Lazell on February 28, 1888. On March 18, 1924 while he was at the home of his son-in-law Joseph G. Creyts, John committed suicide with a shotgun in the cellar of the home; he had been unwell for quite some time. He was survived by his wife, Minnie, four daughters, Mrs. Maud H. Stackman of Grand Ledge, Mrs. Jessie I. Creyts of Delta Township, Mrs. Marion McMillen of Grand Ledge and Miss Florence Huxtable of Mason.[39] The residence has been torn down. From the Reedy/Caterino inventory of Moon buildings.

---

[39] *Lansing Capital News* 3/19/1924 and *LSJ* 3/19/1924

1887

FRANK MOORE'S HOUSE

Frank I. Moore House, 929 (917) N. Washington, Lansing, MI

Just which Frank Moore, Moon designed a home for in 1887 is a bit of a mystery. There are two candidates, Frank I. Moore and Frank W. Moore, both of whom were prominent Lansing residents. In 1878 "F. I. Moore, city assessor, this week sold his residence on Larch street, 1st ward, to Henry Mulliken, for $900. Mr. Moore at once removed to the gothic building on Washington avenue, nearly opposite Henry Mosely premises" (*LRW* 7/5/1878).

"Frank I. Moore, city assessor, has bought off a New York gentleman lot 2 of block 44, west side of Washington avenue, and now occupies it as his residence" (*LRW* 7/19/1878). This would be 927 N. Washington Avenue. This would lead one to believe that Frank I. Moore could be effectively ruled out as the one for whom Moon designed a home in 1887 because there was already a home on the lot at 927 N. Washington. However, "The house of Frank I. Moore is being moved on the railway track today and causes a tie up in the system" (*SR* 5/6/1887). The original home that was located at 927 N. Washington was moved off the lot in 1887. So it is possible that the home that once stood at 927 N. Washington was designed by Darius Moon in 1887. Frank I. Moores' home will be covered in the 1900 section of this work.

Frank W. Moore's House, 1221 N. Grand River, Lansing, MI

The other possibility is that Moon designed a home for Frank W. Moore the owner of a coal and wood business in Lansing. In 1887 Frank W. Moore moved into his new home at 1221 N. Grand River [1217 Seymour] and there is no mention in either newspaper as to who the architect was. According to the City Assessor's office, the home at 1221 N. Grand River was built in 1886. The Frank W. Moore's residence is an Italianate style structure which resembles the Benjamin F. Hamil House on Culter Road in Riley Township, Clinton County. Notice how the brackets are spaced along the soffit in pairs. There are limestone lintels over the windows and the front is a different style from the rest of the home. The porch has Tuscan type columns and a plain frieze, far different from the majority of the homes designed in the Italianate style.

Frank W. Moore's House, 1221 N. Grand River, Lansing, MI

Frank Wesley Moore was born in Chester Hill, Hampden County, Massachusetts on September 9, 1851 the seventh child of W.E. and Lucretia Moore. Frank came to Lansing in 1870 with his brother Harrison and founded a coal and wood business which he operated until 1920, when he sold it to Hall-Higgins Fuel and Supply Company. As a young man Frank W. Moore was active as a volunteer fireman, when the most advanced piece of equipment the fire department owned was a hand pump. He was a member of the Franklin Avenue Presbyterian Church and at one time or another he held every office within the church except that of Pastor. On November 19, 1879 Frank married Miss Clara Frances Keith; the couple had one child Earl V. Moore.

A quick side story about their son Earl, "Yesterday, Earl B[V] Moore, son of F.W. Moore of 1217 Seymour street, was kicked in the face by a colt while playing in front of his father's house. Earl is but 3½ years old and the force of the kick stunned him but broke no bones. His condition is much improved today and it is expected he will be well soon" (*SR* 8/29/1894).

```
BEST GRADES OF ANTHRACITE AND BITUMINOUS COAL          TWO YARDS

                        F. W. MOORE

                       COAL, WOOD, COKE

         SOMERS COAL—Our Push
         Yards on L. S. & M. S. and P. M. Rys.
            Office 200 Washington Ave. N.          LANSING, MICH.
               218 Franklin Ave. E.
```

Frank W. Moore advertisement

Frank W. Moore died on June 13, 1926 in Lansing and was survived by his wife Clara and son Earl V. Moore. Earl Moore would go on to become the Director of the University School of Music in Ann Arbor, after whom the Earl V. Moore Building, in Ann Arbor, Michigan is named. So all in all, that colt's kick did little damage. Mrs. Clara Francis Moore was born in Prescott, Massachusetts on October 17, 1853 the daughter of Oliver and Hattie (née Sears) Keith. The family would move to Lansing in 1866 where her father would work as the Overseer at the state Reform School. Clara's brother was Fred C. Keith who Moon designed a home for in 1908. Mrs. Moore was active in the North Presbyterian Church and for 70 years was a leader in the women's organization of the church. When her mounting health problems compelled her to stop attending meetings of the church's Women's Society, the group decided to rename the society in her honor, the Clara F. Moore Circle. After suffering a broken hip two days before her 90th birthday her health began to deteriorate and just 12 days later Mrs. Clara F. Moore died at her home. [40]

The home at 1221 N Grand River is still standing. From the Gould inventory of Darius Moon Buildings, listed as "Frank Moore, 1887".

1888

This is an important year for Darius Moon and it is best told in his own words. "Building the farmers house was the start of the boys contracting, he followed it every year for 18 years to 1888. He built farm and city houses, a church the year he was 21 years of age, besides a large timber frame barn for a farmer. And in after years, he built any and all kinds that would give him work, and in one year he built 26 houses. And many of them were fine brick houses that will show for themselves now [1932]. During all those years of hard work, he had been studying to make his dream come true, the dream to be an architect. And in the year of 1888 his first building was the Fifth Ward School building in Lansing, Michigan. The date stone in the front brick wall is dated 1888 his plans for that building were chosen by the school board as the best of ten plans that was submitted in a competition by other architects. He opened an office in 1890 and followed his chosen profession up to the year 1923 a period of 35 years, then retired" (Moon Part I 15).

---

40   For Frank W. Moore see *LSJ* 6/15/1926 and *Lansing Capital News* 6/15/1926. For Clara F. Moore see *LSJ* 10/29/1943.

FIFTH WARD SCHOOL

FIFTH WARD SCHOOL.

137 N. Larch, Lansing, MI

In 1887 the Lansing School Board decided to solicit plans for a new brick school building for the Fifth Ward with a total cost of $8000. A total of nine plans were submitted by architects from across the country, the only named architects besides Moon, were John B. Tarleton of Detroit and Clare Allen of Ionia. The building of the Fifth Ward School, later to be known as the Larch Street School developed into quite a saga. On April 5, 1888 the school board officially selected the plans of Darius Moon for the new school building. This would be the first large scale project for Moon and had the possibility of making or breaking his career. Problems started almost immediately. After requesting sealed bids from contractors the school board discovered that all of the bids came back higher than the budgeted amount of $8,000. The plans were reworked by the building committee and new bids were solicited from contractors. Finally on May 31, 1888 ground was broken for the new school. The following articles regarding the tale of the building of the Fifth Ward School are reproduced below; they make for very interesting reading and give a sense of Moon's personality and professionalism.

OFFICE OF THE BOARD OF EDUCATION
Lansing MICH, August 27, 1888

"Mr. Jones submitted the following resolution: Resolved, By the Board of Education of the City of Lansing, that the clerk of this board be and he is hereby instructed to notify D.B. Moon, the architect of the Fifth Ward school building, that unless the full detail plans of the said building are furnished complete to this Board by next Wednesday evening at 8 o'clock that he will be discharged from further service as the architect and superintendent or overseer of said building, from said hour, and that the President of this Board be and he is hereby instructed to procure a competent architect to complete the detail plans of said building. Yeas 10 Nays 0" (SR 8/28/1888).

HERE'S A LONG HOLIDAY
May be no School Sessions on the East Side for Weeks Yet

"There can be no school sessions in the Fifth ward before the first of next January - perhaps. That is the opinion to-day of several members of the Board of Education, most of whom ascribe the slowness of which the new building is creeping skyward as due wholly to the failure of Architect Moon to have his plans prepared on time. "We have dillydallied along all summer," said one, "until, as stated yesterday in the Journal, we had decided to discharge Mr. Moon off-hand if he did not have the roof plans ready by 8 o'clock this evening."
"And the Board meant it?"
"Every word of it. Forbearance has ceased to be a virtue. We have been delayed all along by his slowness, and it will prove highly expensive as well as annoying. His failure to have the details prepared when the contract was let will doubtless cause the contractors to present large bills for extras."
"Are Mr. Moon's plans complete now aside from the roof?"
"No there are lots of details of the inside work that have not been provided for. The workmen have been delayed more or less on pretty nearly everything. The boards made a mistake in employing Mr. Moon at the outset, but we are going to rectify it as far as possible and right away too."
"I want to say just this much," said another member, "and that is that Moon has made an admirable superintendent. He has pinned the contractors to exactly what he wanted done, and has compelled them to take down partially completed work and change it to suit the specifications."
"What will you do for a school building until the new structure is completed?"
"Oh, perhaps we can use the old building again, though it is in bad shape and has an insufficient foundation."
"Mr. Moon states that the plans for the roof were in the hands of the builder last Saturday night, the board being unaware of this when it ordered him to produce them by to-night or quit. He alleges that the work has not been delayed at all by dilatory actions on his part, but rather because the contractors failed to get their material on hand in time and because he compelled them to do certain portions of the work over again. He believes that this has created some ill feeling against him in some quarters" (LJ 8/29/1888).

"Architect D.B. Moon, of the Fifth ward school building, states that the School Board is premature in the action taken Monday evening. The plans and specifications were furnished at the time specified, and the fault lies with the contractors and not with him. The work was not being done according to the plans and he stopped them. The work was afterward resumed through the Board, but not with his consent, as the construction was not in accordance with his ideas" (SR 8/29/1888).

137 N. Larch, Lansing, MI

SOMEONE MUST GO
Contractor Gibbs Takes a Hand in the Fifth Ward Muddle

"One of the two men interested in the Fifth ward school house must go, "said Contractor Henry Gibbs to The Journal, this afternoon, "and it will be either the architect or myself. I will not do another stroke of work under the present conditions. The statements made by the architect yesterday are utter falsehoods, and I want the taxpayers to know just who has caused the delay. Look here."
Mr. Gibbs pulled a drawing from under his buggy seat and unrolled it before the reporter.
"That," he continued, "is the detailed plan Mr. Moon says he submitted to me last Saturday. Now what details are there in it? For instance, there are ten hips and ten valleys in the roof, and not one of them is shown. Why you couldn't even build a pair of stairs from that drawing. I am going to drive to the member of the board who is a practical mechanic, and ask him what he thinks of that for a detailed plan. I have been under a disadvantage for two months owing to this delay, and it has reached a point where nothing more can be done" (*LJ* 8/30/1888).

THE DOVE OF PEACE
IT SETTLES DOWN UPON THE NEW FIFTH WARD SCHOOL BUILDING AT LAST
WORK WILL RESUME AT ONCE
A Satisfactory Compromise Effected — A Lively Session of the Board of Education.

"A Special meeting of the Board of Education was held last night, and the members, Henry Gibbs, the contractor for the new Fifth ward school building, said several things in a crisis, decided away. The gist of

Mr. Gibbs argument was that matters had come to a focus so far as he was concerned. He could not and would not continue the building under the superintendency of Mr. Moon.

He had been delayed repeatedly on his estimate and after three members of the board had assured him that the windows were to be finished the same as the High School building Mr. Moon brought specifications that made each window foot up 88 cents more. As there were 41 windows it made a decided difference and in addition Mr. Moon insisted on a system of wainscoting that would cost the builder $35 extra. All of this and much more did Mr. Gibbs say, while superintendent Moon sat nearby in silent placidity that even Mr. Gibbs last remark that he feared Moon would do him some wrong if he was continued in the work did not greatly disturb.
"How can he do you any wrong?" enquired S.L. Kilbourne.
"If you were a mechanic you would find out," was Mr. Gibbs tart reply. "To continue under Mr. Moon would be unbearable for me and my workmen as well."
The upshot of the lively session was that a committee was directed to confer with Mr. Gibbs and his bondsmen to-day, and if no satisfactory arrangements could be made a special meeting would be held to-night to make arrangements to complete the building at once. The consultation with the bondsmen — Alfred Wise and H.J. Havens — and Mr. Gibbs was held this forenoon and a compromise satisfactory to Mr. Gibbs was effected. The latter is scouring the city this afternoon for carpenters with which to push the work. Mr. Moon will be retained in his present position" (*LJ* 9/5/1888).

Henry Gibbs was well known in Lansing. Gibbs was born in St. Albans, Vermont on April 18, 1815, and at the age of 15 moved with his parents to Monroe County, New York, where he worked with his father as a carpenter. In 1838 Henry moved to Eagle, Michigan where he worked as a builder, constructing one of the first framed school houses in Clinton County, Michigan. By 1847 Henry was working in Lansing as a carpenter on the old State House under the supervision of Henry Jipson. Later in 1856 Gibbs's moved to Watertown Township, Clinton County, Michigan where he served as Justice of the Peace. Gibbs returns to Lansing in 1873 where he established himself as a contractor and in 1874 he was elected a member of the Lansing School Board from the Fifth Ward and served until 1885. In 1875 Henry Gibbs acted as the superintendent of construction for the new Lansing High School Building. Gibbs was a respected contractor who also worked on the Downey House, the State Office Block, Plymouth Congregational Church, St. Paul's Episcopal Church, Park Baptist Church and many other structures. Henry Gibbs died in Lansing on March 15, 1897.[41]

Just what caused this conflict between Moon and Gibbs? Moon was very proud of the design he created for the Fifth Ward School. From the accounts given above it would seem that the contactor was not following Moon's architectural plans. Gibbs was also the contractor on Lansing High School, which has been described as a 'white elephant' of a building. The high school project was plagued by cost overruns and less than stellar workmanship by the contractor. Factors that undoubtedly influenced Darius Moon, including slipshod work by a contractor, was not going to happen in a building he designed. Moon always seemed to be involved in the day-to-day building of his projects and given the injuries suffered from previous falls on the job site demonstrates that Moon was a hands on architect. Moon must have been a pain in the backside of the contractor as well as a resource of knowledge. What is telling is that Samuel Kilbourne, a member of the school board at this time would a short while later employ Moon to design a home for him. Undoubtedly, Kilbourne saw something in the young architect that he admired.

---

41   *SR* 3/16/1897 and *LJ* 3/16/1897.

137 N. Larch, Lansing, MI

A MODEL SCHOOL HOUSE
The New Fifth Ward Building will be Ready for Occupation Monday

"The finishing touches are to-day being given to the new Fifth ward school building, and Monday morning it will be ready for occupancy. The structure is one of the most attractive and substantial in the city, and for comfort and convenience no better school building can be found in the State. Contractor Gibbs evidently intended it a monument to his declining days, and it will stand a lasting credit to his skill.
The structure is two stories high, with basement and covers and area 42x68 feet. A large hall way runs through the building on the first floor, and to the right and left of this are well lighted and splendidly ventilated school rooms 24x32 feet in dimension. The second floor is also divided into two school rooms, each 24x39 feet. All the departments are supplied with cloak rooms and a teacher's room for storing their private property. The floors throughout the building are constructed of hard maple, and the rooms are beautifully finished in white pine, highly polished in oil. The doors at the main entrance and those leading into the vestibules swing both ways, a plan to be highly commended. The building is heated and ventilated by the Smead system, with which the readers of THE JOURNAL are quite familiar. Every school room is supplied with ten small registers and one large register which enables the teacher to regulate of the room at her pleasure. The closets are located in the basement and are constructed on the dry method. The blackboards and other equipments are all of the latest and most serviceable kind. Apparently, the cost of the building is about $10,000, a sum a trifle in advance of the estimate, but the money has been well expended and will redound to the credit of those who have had the matter in charge. It is a model school" (*LJ* 1/5/1889).

The double-winged Fifth Ward School was an impressive example of the Lansing School District willingness to embrace progressive architecture. The surrounding lintels and stone work over the half circled windows on the third floor lend a powerful appearance to the building. The center steeple, which must have held a school bell, is imposing especially when it is noted that the roof of the school was red. Notice the roughhewn stone foundation with the subtle arched windows which were later removed and covered with a hip roof as seen in the above image. Oddly enough the much ballyhooed Smead heating system failed in the first week of use in January, and by 1892 needed to be modified. The bell tower was later removed and the building was torn down in 1954-1955. From the Gould inventory of Darius Moon Buildings, listed as "Fifth Ward School Building, 1888".

BENJAMIN F. DAVIS HOUSE

528 S. Washington, Lansing, MI

"While working on B.F Davis's new house, Wednesday afternoon, D.B. Moon stepped on a piece of loose scantling and fell through the floor, the scanting following, hitting him on the head and tearing his ear in two. The ear was sewed together" (*SR* 9/6/1888).

"Mr. B.F. Davis has moved into his elegant new House on Washington avenue south" (*LJ* 3/22/1889).

Benjamin F. Davis was a respected member of the Lansing community and his house was a graceful addition to South Washington Avenue. The Davis home was one of the most beautiful houses in Lansing, one of many that some time ago lined South Washington Avenue. A who's who of Lansing's rich and famous once lived in this area. The homes of Edward Sparrow, James Potter, R.E. Olds, and many others once made South Washington Avenue the premier address in Lansing. Unfortunately all their homes are lost to history.

Sunburst Motif on 528 S Washington

The Davis home was a mixture of several architected features. The multiple bay windows, the striking turret, with its conical dome, the sunburst motif on the pediment over the porch, over the entrance a centered second floor porch, the multiple gables and the rough stone foundation all point toward a Queen Anne Style structure. What is of interest is the flat upper roof and the imposing center chimney all interesting features not normally seen in a Queen Anne design. Philip A. Siebert, in his paper B.F. Davis Mansion, described the structure as "Victorian Carpenter Gothic".[42] If you look closely at the upper part of the roof you can see the metal cresting detail which ends at each gable with a finial which is an eye appealing finish to the home. Moon was mixing several architectural styles in his design and in many cases this could be disastrous. In this instance Moon successfully mixed the styles and designed a winner. The house is simply stunning and would pave the way for Moon's other design commissions.

Benjamin F. Davis 1844-1934

Benjamin F. Davis was born in Elba, New York on October 14, 1844, to William F. and Mary Maria (née Hague) Davis. In the fall of 1853 the family moved to Lansing where William purchased a small farm in the southeast area of the city and built a home on Cedar Street.[43] Benjamin would attend school at the Michigan Agricultural College until 1864 when ill health compelled him to withdraw. After working for

---

42   Siebert 1-2. Siebert also mentions that an original drawing of the structure by Moon had been discovered. The current location of the drawing is unknown.
43   The home is still standing at 521-523 Torrance Court while the old barn has been converted into a home and stands at 525-527 Torrance Court.

the Quartermasters Department in Washington, D.C. for three years, Davis returned to Lansing and began a stave and lumber business which he operated until 1881. He then founded the Lansing Wheelbarrow Company, which became the Lansing Company. In 1886 he organized the City National Bank, served as the treasurer of the Michigan Agricultural College. He was also instrumental in the formation of many of Lansing's early companies and served on the Board of Directors of numerous Michigan corporations.

An image of the Davis house in the 1970s

On May 18, 1875 Davis married Miss Eva [Delia Olivia] Sparrow, sister of Edward Sparrow. Miss Eva Sparrow was born in Ireland on September 10, 1853, and was six years old when she came to Lansing with her mother and five siblings. She attended the Michigan Female College under the tutelage of Misses Abby and Delia Rogers. She was a talented artist and many of her paintings and those of other artists decorated her home on South Washington Avenue. Eva was a supporter of the Lansing Industrial Aid Society where she acted as a benefactor and a teacher to the less fortunate. While visiting a friend, Mrs. Ella Burnham Palmer in Chicago, Eva was struck down with what was diagnosed as congestion of the brain. Dr. Nathan S. Davis past president of the International Medical Congress was summoned, but there was little he could do to stop the progression of the attack. Eva passed away at 1:30 am on Wednesday January 22, 1890 leaving two children, Bessie and Edith Eve.[44] The home burned in the 1970s just as the Historical Society of Greater Lansing was fighting for its preservation.

In Moon's 1904 City Directory advertisement B.F. Davis is listed as one of the gentlemen for whom he had designed a home.

From the Gould inventory of Darius Moon Buildings, listed as "B.F. Davis Residence, 1888".

---

44   See the *LJ* 1/22/1890 and *LJ* 1/27/1890.

GEORGE DAYTON APARTMENTS

400-416 N. Larch, Lansing, MI

The Gould list notes that Moon did some type of work for George Dayton in 1888. There are several options for these flats/apartments, 400-416 N. Larch Street, 601-613 W. Michigan Avenue and 600-614 W. Michigan Avenue.

"Geo. M. Dayton is breaking ground for flats at the corner of Clark and Shiawassee streets" (*LJ* 3/13/1889). This must be a misprint as Clark never crosses Larch Street; the writer must have meant Larch, not Clark.

"Geo. L. Dayton is erecting eight handsome flats on the corner of Larch and Shiawassee streets" (*SR* 8/27/1889). "George M. Dayton has nearly completed on Larch street a fine brick apartment house containing eight dwellings and one on Shiawassee street containing three dwellings" (*SR* 11/19/1889). The apartment building on North Larch was torn down in March of 1954 after they were condemned by the city.[45]

---

[45] *LSJ* 2/24/1954.

400-416 N. Larch, Lansing, MI

Between 1888 and 1892 George Dayton built several structures, an eight unit brick apartment house on Larch Street and an apartment house on Shiawassee Street in 1889. Dayton later traded the apartment house on Shiawassee Street for the S.S. Olds farm. In 1890 Dayton built two sets of French flats on each side of Michigan Avenue and Pine Street, eight new houses on Saginaw Street in 1892, and finally the construction of thirteen brick flats on the northwest corner of Capitol Avenue and Shiawassee Street in 1892. The flats on the corner of Capitol Avenue and Shiawassee Street were designed by Lansing architects Edwyn Bowd and Earl Mead. (*SR* 4/18/1892)

601-613 W. Michigan, Lansing, MI

"Geo. M. Dayton has purchased a large block of property on each side of Michigan avenue, corner of Pine street, and has broken ground for two blocks of brick French flats" (*SR* 9/18/1890).

"Frank Nichols broke ground this morning for George M. Dayton's block of seven stone-fronted flats, to be built at the corner of Pine street and Michigan avenue" (*SR* 4/16/1891).

600-614 W. Michigan, Lansing, MI

Images of all three sets of flats are included because of their similarities. Because the Gould list is unclear on the number of flats/apartments or their location, Moon may have designed all three sets of French flats for Dayton. Dayton would later trade two of the Michigan Avenue flats to a party from White Cloud, Michigan for general dry goods stock valued at $9000 and another to George W. Frary for the inventory of his clothing store valued at $4000. This was typical of Dayton who was continually trading real estate after it was developed for other properties or a store's inventory.[46] In June of 1892 Dayton would sell one of these terraces on West Michigan Avenue to E.W. Edwards for $4500. This was a remarkable sum for that time and would represent about $120,000 in today's money using the Consumer Price Index. This number would be higher if other factors were considered.[47] Dayton had built eight sets of flats on the north side of Michigan Avenue and seven flats on the south side. The flats at 600-614 W. Michigan Avenue are of special interest because they are immediately adjacent to the John O. Black residence that Moon designed.

---

46   There are many instances of this type of trading by Dayton, see *SR* 4/11/1892 for an example.
47   *SR* 6/16/1892 for the value of a dollar see http://www.measuringworth.com/uscompare/.

John O. Black House, 618 W. Michigan, Lansing, MI

On March 1, 1920 Darius purchased the West 11 feet of Lot 4 and the East 11 feet of Lot 5 in Block 104, 618 W. Michigan Avenue from John O. Black for $1. The property Moon purchased abutted the townhouse at 614 W. Michigan Avenue. In 1915 Moon designed a home for J.O. Black his son-in-law; it could be that Moon designed the French style flat on Black's 22 foot wide lot on West Michigan Avenue to mimic the Dayton flats.[48] The structure at 618 W. Michigan was built in 1917-1918. In the above image of 618 W. Michigan you can see that the building blends with 614 to a certain point. However, the difference in the brick work, the style of the porch and the stonework of the pillars that support the lower porch are evident. Does this mean Moon designed the flat at 600-614 W. Michigan? No, but it does support that scenario and if that is correct, it lends credence to the theory that Moon designed all three sets of flats for Dayton in 1888.

George M. Dayton was born in Eaton County on April 3, 1843 to Samuel and Lucinda (née Phillips) Dayton. As a young man George moved to Lansing to engage in the real estate profession. Early in his life he married Miss Sarah Brown and the couple would have two daughters: Edna E. and Bettie A. Dayton. George had extensive property holdings throughout Ingham County. Oddly George engaged in a long running feud with Jacob Stahl over another set of terrace homes Dayton built on N. Capitol Avenue and Shiawassee Street. It seems that Stahl purchased the north set of terraces at a foreclosure sale, with the understanding that Dayton would repurchase the property from Stahl. Dayton never did, and continued to occupy the property, much to Stahl's chagrin. What followed was an eight year court battle that was finally settled by the Michigan Supreme Court in 1903. George M. Dayton died on November 6, 1912 at his home in Lansing, Michigan, a man who built over 50 terrace homes in Lansing of which none survived.[49]
From the Gould inventory of Darius Moon Buildings, listed as "George Dayton apts, 1888".

---

48 Florence Moon married John O. Black after her divorce in 1913 from Charles E. Day, who she had married in 1907. After the death/divorce of John Black, Florence married John W. Hallett.
49 *LSJ* 11/6/1912. For the end of the Dayton v. Stahl case see the *SR* 3/6/1903.

1889

SAM KILBOURNE HOUSE

112 E. Main, Lansing, MI

Sam Kilbourne had extensive property holdings in Ingham County, but this was the home that Kilbourne occupied. The city directories and Sanborn maps bear out that this is the right house, although the city assessor seems to disagree, and their records state that the house was built in 1860 with an addition added in 1915. The porch's columns and banister seem to suggest a home that was more striking than the one we see in the above image, covered in asbestos shingles. Don't be fooled by this image as this was a very large home that extended quite a ways back on the property. There was also another large structure present on the back of the property.

Samuel Kilbourne 1839-1925

Sam Kilbourne was a member of the Lansing Board of Education that hired Darius Moon to build the Fifth Ward School and it is doubtful that he would have employed an architect that he did not respect. Samuel A. Kilbourne was an important figure in Lansing history. Born near Toronto on April 15, 1839, Samuel's father Joseph H. Kilbourne brought his family to Meridian Township where he purchased a large tract of land from Chief Okemos.[50] Joseph was a member of the 1847 State House and was instrumental in bringing the Capitol to Lansing. For a time Samuel was educated at home and later by Reverend Richard Taylor. In 1854 he attended Albion College, and three years later entered the Michigan Agricultural College when it

---

50   Joseph H. Kilbourne left Canada because of his participation in the Upper Canadian Rebellion.

opened, becoming one of the first students. At the age of 21, Samuel entered the University of Michigan to study law and after graduation he returned to Lansing to set up a practice. He served as Deputy Clerk of the Michigan Supreme Court, he was also a member of the Lansing Board of Education. The City Attorney and an assistant to the Prosecuting Attorney, in 1874 he was elected to the State Legislature as a Democrat and remained active in the party the rest of his life. In 1862 Samuel married Miss Louisa F. Burchard, daughter of John W. Burchard, one of the first settlers in Lansing Township. Louisa died in 1873 and only one child from the marriage survived, Mary L. Kilbourne, who later married James Harris. Samuel remarried in 1874 to Miss Cornelia W. Truax who would pass away on December 1, 1898. Two years later Samuel would marry Mrs. Carrie M. Crosby Hyatt on December 19, 1900. Samuel A. Kilbourne passed away at the state hospital in Kalamazoo, Michigan on June 11, 1925.[51] In 1925 Samuel Kilbourne lived at 501 S. Capitol Avenue in a home designed in 1902 by Darius Moon for Samuel Kilbourne's mother-in-law Mrs. Louise H. Crosby. From the Gould inventory of Darius Moon Buildings, listed as "Sam Kilbaurn Hse, 1889". The home was torn down in 1954.

ELMER A. PATCH HOME

1113 W. Michigan, Lansing, MI

On June 11, 1889 Moon sold to Elmer A. and Carrie E. Patch Lots 2-3 of Assessor's Plat No. 8.[52] The house on Lot 2, 1109 W. Michigan was built in 1908. While the home on Lot 3, 1113 W. Michigan was built in 1890. The selling price $550 was quite high for an unimproved lot outside of the city and may indicate that a home was present on the lot when Moon sold the property to Patch. Or that Moon agreed to provide a set of plans in the sale price and to act as the contractor? Patch was a carpenter by trade and would have been familiar with Moon's work and they lived just around the corner from each other. Moon divided property into three lots and sold Lots 2-3 before he lost Lot 1 to George Murray to foreclosure.[53]

---

51 *LSJ* 6/12/1925 and *Lansing Capital News* 6/12/1925.
52 The description of the property is a simplification, this area of Lansing was not plated until 1926, the actual description follows; In 1882 Ellen Moon acquired in the SE ¼ of Section 17 The SE ¼ of Section 17 a 3 ½ -rod wide parcel (57.75 feet N.-S. x 165 feet EW), being 41.25 feet (2 ½ rods) S. of the centerline of Michigan Avenue and 33 feet (2 rods) W. of the centerline of Logan Street.
53 Murray acquired the mortgage the entire parcel in a foreclosure sale by public auction in 1890. Since Moon had sold off the western portion to Patch, Murray also acquired property held by Moon in Eaton County. The mortgage foreclosure was for $3,900 and included a large parcel in Sec 35, T4N - R3W, Delta Township, Eaton County, Michigan. The legal description follows: The parcel was the E½, SW¼ and that part of the E½, NW ¼ lying SE'ly of the centerline of Lansing Rd. and a smaller adjoining piece in the SE ¼ lying along the west side of the Grand River. The property is currently owned by the Nature Way Association. Surveys completed by Jack N. Owens, PS.

The property Moon sold to Patch June 11, 1889 would have two homes built on the lot, the one at 1109 W. Michigan was built in 1908 and is a rather plain home and built after the Patch's moved. The residence at 1113 W. Michigan was built in 1890 and has many characteristics of a Moon home. Elmer Patch and his wife move to Tampa, Florida where Carrie E. died on January 24, 1918 and Elmer died on April 17, 1930. It seems the couple had at least three children die at an early age one at the home at 1113 W. Michigan in 1890. Orlo Stanley (d. 1884) Charles Elmer Patch, Clarence L. Patch, Unnamed child (d. 1890) and Eva Patch.

1890

WILLIAM C. BROWN HOME

1003 N. Washington, Lansing, MI

"MesSRs. WB Stone and CO have bought the Kimball property at the corner of Washington Avenue and Kilbourne street. They intend to erect some first class convenient tenement houses" (*LRW* 9/19/1883). The W.B. Stone Lumber Company was owned by William C. Brown and William B. Stone and that the property was purchased almost ten years before the home was built. William Brown in the 1884 City Directory is listed as living at 1009 N. Washington Avenue.

"W.C. Brown will erect a $3,000 residence at the corner of Washington avenue and Kilbourne street" (*LJ* 6/13/1890).

This is one of the few Queen Anne style homes with some Italianate features that exist in Lansing today. The carved stonework over the windows, the quoins stone work at the corners which is brought out by the dark paint easing the pattern of the brick work, the pyramid capped tower with the small gable on the front with a planter below the window, and the sun porch with the second floor porch make this a visually appealing structure. Notice the stone work over the windows that are set off by the choice of the paint color; the home's original color was red brick and sandstone.

> **BROWN LUMBER CO.**
> ===== DEALERS IN =====
> **ROUGH AND DRESSED LUMBER**
> ===== MANUFACTURERS OF =====
> SASH, DOORS, AND ALL KINDS INTERIOR FINISH
> MILL AND YARDS: MICHIGAN AVE. EAST

Brown Lumber Company advertisement from the 1909 Oracle

The home at 1003 N. Washington was built in 1891 by William C. Brown co-owner of the Brown Lumber Company. William Clark Brown was born on March 29, 1848 in McHenry County, Illinois, the son of James and Jane (née Clark) Brown. He came to Lansing in 1876 and entered the lumber trade and was President of the Brown Lumber Company with his brother Arnold J. Brown as a partner. Brown was a member of the Concatenated Order of Hoo-Hoo a fraternal organization and was on the board of control for the Michigan Retail Lumber Dealers' Association. In Greenville, Michigan on October 25, 1874 William married Miss Margaret A. Cleveland; the couple would have one child, a daughter, Jane Ida Brown. After the death of his first wife, William married Miss Helen Moots, the daughter of Henry and Anna (née Leadly) Moots on September 27, 1887 in Dewitt, Michigan. The couple would have one child, Helen. William C. Brown died at home on November 5, 1909 of Bright's disease.[54] Less than two years later in June 1911, Mrs. Helen Brown, a passenger in an electric automobile driven by her daughter Helen was injured after Miss Helen lost control of the vehicle at Moores Park and the automobile ended up in the Grand River. Only Mrs. Brown was injured. Miss Helen and the other passenger, Miss Roberta Woodworth were fine. Mrs. Brown's health rapidly deteriorated and she died at her home on Friday February 16, 1912.[55] The home was later purchased by Lawrence Price. The residence was given by Price's heirs to St. Lawrence Hospital in 1931; later in 1935 the home was sold to Bernard Lavey of Lavey Funeral Home. The building is still standing after being restored following a devastating fire in 1982. The home was placed on the National Register of Historic Places in 1984.

In Moon's 1904 City Directory advertisement Wm. A. [C.] Brown is listed as one of the gentlemen for whom he had designed a home. From the Gould inventory of Darius Moon Buildings, listed as "William Brown Hse-Lansing, 1895".

---

54   *LJ* 11/6/1909.
55   *LSJ* 2/16/1912.

MRS. FRED BERTCH HOME

532 S. Grand, Lansing, MI

The Gould list has Moon designing two homes for a Mrs. Fred Bertok [Bertch] at some point in his career; the only possibility is Mrs. Fred Bertch in 1890. One was a home at 532 S. Grand Street which served as the Bertch's principle residence and the second was a double house listed at 526-528 S. Grand. No other information on the double house at 526-528 S. Grand has been located. The house at 532 S. Grand was a beautiful structure with an ornate double decker porch, slim and delicate columns, and a gable motif on the gable of the upper porch. There is a small dormer and the stick work arches over the gable make this an appealing home. Moon's skill as an architect had developed; he was beginning to incorporate other architectural elements into his work.

532 S Grand Avenue detail

Fredrick W. Bertch was born in Germany in 1844, and at the age of six came with his parents to Buffalo, New York. In 1861 Fredrick moved to Lansing and established a meat market at 333 S. Washington. Bertch believed in the value of Lansing property as an investment and had quite extensive real estate holdings throughout the city. He was active in both civic and Masonic affairs; he was a member of F. &A.M. No. 66 Lodge. Fredrick W. Bertch passed away at his home on October 30, 1922.[56]

532 S. Grand, Lansing, MI

Mrs. Louise Bertch was born in Lucerne, Switzerland. In 1850 at the age of two she came with her parents to the United States and the family settled in Akron, New York. In 1876 Louise married Fredrick Bertch and moved to Lansing where her husband established a butcher shop. The couple had no children. Louise Bertch died at her home at 532 S. Grand Avenue on Tuesday October 7, 1924 and was survived by a niece Mrs. Sadie Magoon of Eire, Pennsylvania.[57]

The house at 532 S. Grand was torn down in 1968 and the double house at 526-528 S. Grand was torn down about the same time. From the Gould inventory of Darius Moon Buildings, listed as "2 Houses for Mrs. Fred Bertok, No Date".

---

56   *LSJ* 10/31/1922 and *Lansing Capital News* 10/30/1922, in the latter paper he is listed as Frederick W. Burch.
57   See *LSJ* 10/8/1924 and *Lansing Capital News* 10/8/1924.

MRS. SARAH ELIZABETH VAN DER VOORT EMERY APARTMENTS

320-328 W. Ottawa, Lansing, MI

The Gould list states that Moon designed apartments for Mrs. Emery in 1890. There has been much speculation that Moon designed the apartments at 320-328 W. Ottawa. If he did design these apartments Moon would have featured these buildings in his 1904 City Directory advertisement. Unfortunately these apartments were built in 1887 by Archibald M. Emery, Mrs. S.E.V. Emery's stepson.[58] It is assumed that the Mrs. Emery referred to in the Gould list was Mrs. Sarah Elizabeth Van Der Voort Emery, a nationally known Lansing resident who published in 1888 the controversial book Seven Financial Conspiracies. Mrs. S.E.V. Emery was very active in Lansing real estate in the 1870s and 1880s. In 1891 she acquired the property of Mrs. Newman R. Potter on the north east corner of Capital Avenue and Ottawa Street. The Potter property was a boarding house operated by Mrs. Potter. It is possible that Moon was commissioned to draw up plans for a new set of apartments or remodel the existing structure. However, Mrs. S.E.V. Emery donated the lot to the Universalist Church for the construction of the First Universalist Church.

---

58   *SR* 7/21/1887. I would be remiss if I did not mention that 320-322 W. Ottawa was built in 1888 while the structures at 326-328 W Ottawa were built in 1887. If you examine the structures closely you can notice subtle differences between the two buildings.

200-212 W. Ionia, Lansing, MI

After Mrs. S.E.V. Emery's death in 1895 her husband sold Lot 6 Block 84, 200-212 W. Ionia Street to Thompson T. Iddings of Manchester, Michigan in 1900. This property had six townhomes in one block. These townhomes were designed by the architect James Appleyard in 1882. The article refers to three French Flats being designed by Architect Appleyard for Emery. They were two stories in height and the entire building was 73 feet by 35 feet.[59] Is it possible that in 1890 Sarah Emery commissioned Moon to design three more apartments as an addition to the existing structure?

There is one final structure owned by Sarah Emery which Moon could have designed. It was a group of apartments that were located at 409 E Grand River, Lot 13 Block 5, property that she owned and which was left to her husband upon her death in 1895. The building is described in the 1930s as being an old barn and apartments. There is no image of this structure.

The best possibility for the apartments designed by Moon for Mrs. Emery is the three unit addition of French Flats located at 206-212 W. Ionia Street. If Moon would have designed the townhomes on West Ottawa street they would have been mentioned in his 1904 Advertisement in the City Directory. The commission for an addition to the flats on West Ionia would not have been noteworthy; he was essentially copying another architects design, and that James Appleyard probably would not have objected to this. Accounts of his personality point to a man that was willing to assist other architects in their careers. For example, as a young architect Fred Thoman was beginning his career in Lansing and James Appleyard served as his mentor. Architecturally speaking, there is little to say about these buildings. If these are a Moon designed project it is the only time Moon employed a Mansard roof, but remember the original design was Appleyard; Moon was only mimicking his original design.

---

59   *LRW* 6/25/1882.

Miss Sarah E. Van Der Voort, she was a prominent member of several reform movements and the author of Seven Financial Conspiracies. Sarah Elizabeth Van Der Voort was born on May 12, 1838 in Phelps, New York. After attending the local public schools she would seek a teaching degree at the Clinton Liberal Institute in Fort Plain, New York, one of the leading education colleges in New York. In 1870 she married Wesley Emery in Phelps, New York and then moved to Lansing. In the realm of politics she found her calling. She spoke at a variety of political meetings and had she not died so early, Sarah would have undoubtedly played a greater role in the women's suffrage movement. Sales of her work Seven Financial Conspiracies reached the then unheard-of total of 360,000 copies, and her second book, Imperialism in America sold 40,000 copies. Both works are both still in print today. Mrs. Sarah Elizabeth Van Der Voort, Emery passed away on October 10, 1895 after planning her own funeral. Her ashes were returned to Phelps, New York to be buried beside her parents.[60]

Sarah's husband was a remarkable man in his own right; Wesley Emery was born in Livingston County, New York and attended Lima Seminary and Genesee College. In 1851 Wesley would marry Miss Adelia Gibson in Barry Center, New York. Adelia died in 1852. Wesley would then marry Adelia's sister, Miss Laura Gibson, two years after the death of Adelia; the couple would have one child, Archibald M. Emery. Laura passed away on May 22, 1864. Early in Wesley's career he taught at the Union school in Okemos, Michigan alongside his new wife Sarah. They must have made an interesting combination. Sarah would become the Superintendent of the Midland school district while Wesley worked as the representative of an east coast publishing firm and traveled the state attending teacher's meetings and visiting schools. For several years he was the secretary for the Lansing Industrial Aid Society and helped to form the Central Michigan Agricultural Society. In 1873 he would establish the first bookstore in the city of Lansing, described by many as the finest in the state. Wesley would pass away at his son's home on March 19, 1916.[61]

Archibald Martelle Emery was one of the leading businessmen in Lansing and he inherited one of the best bookstores in Michigan. Archibald was born in Lansing on December 24, 1861. After the death of his mother in 1864 and his father remarrying in 1870, his childhood must have been quite interesting. His father and stepmother worked outside of Lansing and traveled extensively. In 1883 he graduated from the Michigan Agricultural College and began working at his father's bookstore. On August 4, 1886 Archibald M. Emery married Miss Orah Glaister, the sister of Joseph C. Glaister, who Moon designed a business block for in 1891. The couple would have one child Helen E. Emery. After the marriage of his daughter, Archibald would take his new son-in-law Hubert C. Pratt as his partner in the bookstore. Archibald Martelle Emery died on Wednesday evening November 12, 1941 at St. Lawrence Hospital.[62] From the Gould inventory of Darius Moon Buildings listed as "Mrs. Emery apts. 1890".

---

60   *SR* 10/10/1895 and *LJW* 10/18/1895.
61   *LSJ* 3/20/1916.
62   *LSJ* 11/13/1941. For Orah L.G. Emery see *LSJ* 3/19/1942.

MICHIGAN MILLERS' INSURANCE BUILDING

120 W. Ottawa, Lansing, MI

Michigan Miller's Block
Construction will begin at Once, and it will be completed in June.

"The Michigan Millers' fire insurance company is about to begin the erection of their new office building on the old Methodist church property, opposite the postoffice, for which purpose the property was purchased last January. The plans are already in the hands of Architect Bowd and work will begin April 1st. The building will be of red pressed brick, two stories high, 24x58 feet, and will cost $3,500. The main or first floor will be devoted exclusively to the company's offices and the upper floor will be used for offices or halls. The Michigan Millers' is one of the oldest of the fire companies and has gradually grown until larger headquarters are necessary. Secretary A.T. Davis expects to be installed in his new apartments by June" (*SR* 3/11/1890).

MICHIGAN MILLERS' BLOCK.

Construction Will Begin at Once, and it Will be Completed in June.

The Michigan Millers' fire insurance company is about to begin the erection of their new office building on the old Methodist church property, opposite the postoffice, for which purpose the property was purchased last January. The plans are already in the hands of Architect Bowd and work will begin April 1st. The building will be of red pressed brick, two stories high, 24x58 feet, and will cost $3,500. The main or first floor will be devoted exclusively to the company's office, and the upper floor will be used for offices or halls. The Michigan Millers' is one of the oldest of fire companies, and has gradually grown until larger headquarters are necessary. Secretary A. T. Davis expects to be installed in his new apartments by June.

State Republican March 11, 1890

The image above is provided for clarity. The article states the "The plans are already in the hands of Architect Bowd…" a curious statement given that Moon worked independently. Was Edwyn A. Bowd reviewing Moon's plans? Did Bowd work as the supervising architect of the project? Both scenarios present problems given the respective personalities of Moon and Bowd. Moon was a fiercely independent architect who only worked with one other person, Raymond Spice, and given his experience with the Fifth Ward School would never let anyone supervise his work. In contrast, Bowd had several architects as partners but he never acted as a superintendent of construction for another architect's work during this time period. It may be a case of the Michigan Millers' feeling that Bowd, who was an established architect, would be a conservative superintending architect. It is possible that both Bowd and Moon submitted plans for the building and Bowd's were accepted. There in no mention in any of Moon's written works of him designing the Michigan Millers' Building nor is it listed in Moon's 1904 City Directory advertisement. The design of the Michigan Millers' building would have been an impressive commission for Moon and being so would have been a building he would have wanted to mention in his advertisements.

Early image of Ottawa Street and Capitol Avenue

Moon's justification for moving to Chicago was that "…business was poor (that was 1891) and he had very little work as an architect, he closed his office, bid his wife, and four children goodbye, and went to Chicago, the month of February 1891."[63] This was an odd statement. Was he angry that his design was not accepted or that his plans were given to another architect? Moon had completed several important commissions by 1890; it is almost as if he left for Chicago in a fit of pique. It is important to remember that the Michigan Miller's building was not completed until late 1891; in January of 1891 the Michigan Millers' statewide meeting was held at the Lansing City Hall.

---

63 *Michigan in the Fifties*, Number One page 18.

120 W. Ottawa, Lansing, MI

There are aspects of this building that resemble those in the Moon designed building at 204 E Grand River and the Olds Mansion; notice the bartizan tower with the vertical indentations in the brick work. This is a visually striking building that combines both Romanesque and Italianate features into the structure. Observe how the tower on the right of the photograph, has a dramatic affect before the third floor was added to the Lansing Woman's Club Building. Ironically Bowd was responsible for the third floor addition to the Lansing Woman's Club. Bowd was a solid but workman-like architect. The Michigan Millers' Building would have been unlike any other structure he designed up to this time. Based upon the written record it seems safe to attribute the design of the building to Edwyn Bowd, however there are too many aspects of the building that point to Moon as being the architect. It seems possible Moon designed the building but the Board of the Michigan Millers' Insurance Company may have engaged Bowd's services to oversee construction and to modify the plans. It would explain why Moon left for Chicago after placing a full page advertisement in the 1891 Lansing City Directory. Using the architectural elements of a building to determine who was the architect is the designer of the structure is fraught with difficulties. Architects then as today, copy elements from other peoples work; an example of this is the Woodbury house in East Lansing. Moon seems to have copied several elements from Mead's design of the Woodbury home in Lansing in Woodbury's new home in East Lansing. Correspondences by the author with the Michigan Millers Insurance Company confirmed that Board minutes prior to 1898 are not extant so there is no historical record as to who designed the building. From the Gould inventory of Darius Moon Buildings, listed as "Millers Ins. Co. Building 1890".

ALROY A. WILBUR STORE

204 E. Franklin (Grand River), Lansing, MI circa 1935

"A.A. Wilbur has purchased the property at 204 Franklin street, three doors east of the bridge, and at once will commence the erection of a three-story brick store there. The three floors and basement will all be devoted to Mr. Wilbur's furniture and undertaking business. S.G. Scofield, who owns the two stores west of this property, will also erect new brick buildings on the lots this season" (*LJ* 4/4/1890).

Alroy A. Wilbur 1846-1912

Alroy A. Wilbur was a member of the Lansing City Council, the county coroner and a Mayor of Lansing who served in 1894. During his administration a new iron bridge was built on Michigan Avenue to span the Grand River. Alroy was born in 1846 in Genesee County, New York, to Noah and Rhonda Wilbur. He came with his mother to Lansing in 1861 where he found employment as a cabinet maker. In 1869 he married Miss Elizabeth Yeiter, they had one daughter Etta. Alroy was extensively involved in the Lansing furniture trade. After apprenticing with J.W. Barker he founded his own furniture and undertaking business in 1878. An odd combination of businesses in today's world but it made perfect sense in the 1800s when a cabinet maker and undertaker could build the casket you were to be buried in as well as attend to your physical remains.

State Republican Editorial Cartoon of Wilbur's Mayoral Victory in 1894

Wilbur incurred heavy financial losses due to the failure of the People's Bank of Lansing and the Ingham County Bank, and as such suffered a nervous breakdown in 1905 compelling his retirement. Alroy was described as an astute businessman who was fair and equitable. The undertaking business was located on the third floor of his furniture store and Alroy had a reputation as the best funeral director in the county, both for the quality of his work and his sincerity. Alroy A. Wilbur passed away at his home on July 12, 1912 never fully recovering from his illness.[64]

---

64   *LSJ* 7/13/1912 and (Cowles 270).

204 E. Franklin (Grand River), Lansing, MI circa 1940

The building at 204 E. Grand River is a striking example of Romanesque commercial architecture which is still standing in Lansing in 2015. Interesting details include the arched window with the keystone on the third floor and the interesting cornice, which seems lost without supporting detail on the columns. The columns seem to be missing a cap. Notice the similarities between the architectural features on this building and the Michigan Millers Insurance building which was designed by Edwyn Bowd. From the Gould inventory of Darius Moon Buildings, listed as "Wilburs Store North 1890".

EDWARD W. SPARROW BUILDING

Edward Sparrow 1846-1913

E. Michigan, Lansing, MI

" Another cause for locating the site of the new public building on the Pinckney block, on the corner of Grand street and Michigan avenue, besides that of the erection of O.M. Barnes' promised five story hotel on the opposite corner, is that the long wanted new Michigan avenue bridge, full width of the street, will be certain of the erection, and E.W. Sparrow once agreed to erect a block of six stores on the east side of the river upon the erection of the bridge" (*SR* 2/27/1890).

"Architect Moon has completed for E.W. Sparrow the drawings for a handsome brick building, three stories in height exclusive of the basement to be located at the east end of the Michigan avenue bridge where the Willard livery barn now stands. The building will be 40 by 80 feet in size, equipped with elevator and all modern conveniences, and according to the nearly completed arrangements is to be occupied exclusively by the Marple, French, McGrath Company, confectionery manufactures" (*LJ* 4/11/1890).

Ought To Be Done
E.W. SPARROW WILL BUILD A FINE BUSINESS BLOCK
East of the Michigan Avenue Bridge if the City will Establish a Permanent Grade.

"There is a prospect that that portion of the city on the south side of Michigan avenue east of the bridge, so long an eye sore to all citizens, will be improved, made to blossom like the rose, so to speak. E.W. Sparrow is the owner of the property and has long contemplated the erection of a fine business block thereon, but there has up to the present time been a serious difficulty in the way that has prevented the carrying out of contemplated plans, and that is the matter of street grade. It is well known that a new bridge on the avenue will soon be a necessity. Its needs are felt every day, and when the new one is built it will no doubt be the full width of the street, as it should be. It is also a well-known fact that the present bridge sets too low down, and when a new one takes its place it will be raised to the proper level. From Washington avenue to the bridge there is a fall of two feet and from the viaduct on the other side four feet. A resolution was introduced at the meeting of the common council last night to raise the grade on this side of the bridge twelve and on the other side eighteen inches, this to remain permanent that parties desiring to build would not suffer in the future from this score. The resolution was referred to the committee on streets and bridges and will without a doubt receive a favorable report next Monday night. Mr. Sparrow informed the Republican this morning it was his intention to build a handsome and modern block on the property at once if the grade was permanently fixed. He will no doubt be followed by others and that part of the city now so ragged and unsightly to strangers will be filled up with business houses" (*SR* 8/30/1892).

Unfortunately the large business block was never built on the south side of East Michigan Avenue at the bridge; the site would be occupied for many years by the Rikerd Lumber Company. It would be under the administration of Mayor Alroy A. Wilbur that the old wooden Michigan Avenue Bridge was replaced with a new iron bridge in 1899. It would seem from the newspaper accounts that the city failed to address the basic infrastructure problems of Michigan Avenue at the bridge over the Grand River, as a result Sparrow simply moved on. It is possible that Moon's plan for the business block was reused by Sparrow in one of his other developments; Sparrow was not a man to waste money.

1891

LEVI COTTINGTON HOUSE

126 E. St Josephs, Lansing, MI

"Levi Cottington has purchased the Westcott place, corner of St Joseph and Grand streets, and will build in the near future" (*SR* 7/7/1890). "Levi Cottington's new House is being wired for incandescent lights" (*SR* 2/2/1891). "Levi Cottington's new house is furnished with an automatic burglar and fire alarms, the latter system being connected directly with the fire department's alarm at engine house No. 1" (*SR* 2/19/1891).

The home was a mixture of Carpenter Gothic and Queen Anne styles. Interesting features include the wraparound porch, the ornate colonnettes and the delicate work on the frieze at the top between the two colonnettes; it is a four leaf clover motif, fitting for a man in Cottington's line of work. The brackets under the eaves add an Italianate flavor while the flat roof invokes a Victorian elegance to the home. In this house we see Moon again mixing elements of several design styles. The home was later owned by James J. Baird, owner of Baird's Opera House and later by Clarence C. Carlton vice president of Motor Wheel. The structure was torn down in May of 1966 to facilitate the construction of I-496.

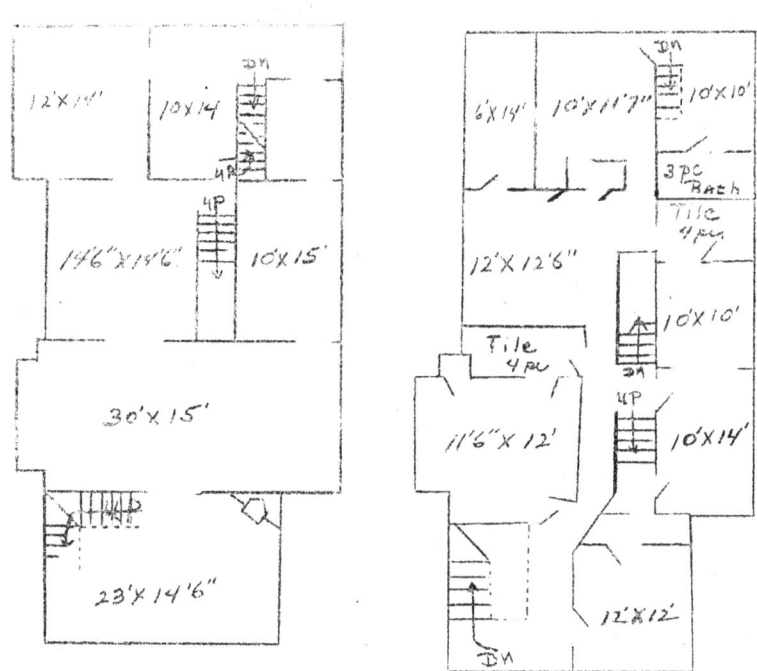

126 E. St Josephs, Lansing, MI, First & Second Floor Plan

Levi G. Cottington was a fascinating figure from Lansing's early days. He managed the Senate Restaurant and seems to have been, in today's terms, a sports bookie. Born in Elgin County Ontario in 1858 to George and Eleanor Cottington, Levi would be educated in the local public schools. In July 16, 1879 Levi, then 21 and a school teacher, married 16 year old Ida E. Wells in Aylmer, Ontario. After moving to Lansing he had several run-ins with the law, including being charged with selling liquor without a license and firing a revolver in a Windsor Township saloon.[65] The Cottington's left Lansing in 1896 and settled in Bowling Green, Ohio where Levi managed the Hotel Brown. Levi Cottington resurfaced in Detroit as the owner of a saloon on Griswold Street which was patronized by the staff of the Detroit News. A story in, Made in Detroit relates how Levi lost the business of the newspaper reporters due to his penny pinching to a rival establishment, Richter's, owned by Otto Hunrath. The story makes for interesting reading (Beasley 261). Cottington later appeared in the New York Times in 1916 as the "Detroit betting commissioner", placing odds on the upcoming presidential election.[66] Prior to Prohibition, Cottington operated the Marquette Café at Griswold and Fort Streets in Detroit, site of the present day Dime building. The Café was a gathering place for mayors, governors and the city's best and brightest. The establishment was noted for its fine cuisine and a superior selection of beers and wines. With the demise of the Marquette Café, he purchased Draper's at Griswold Street and Grand River Avenue in Detroit which he managed until his retirement. All in all Cottington was a fascinating character, he was described as Detroit's best known boniface, slang for landlord of a tavern or inn. Levi G. Cottington died in Detroit on November 26, 1931, survived by his wife Ida E., and son Lynn.[67]

From the Gould inventory of Darius Moon Buildings, listed as "Hse for Levi Cottington, 1891".

---

65 SR 2/15/1892 and SR 3/7/1895.
66 New York Times May 31, 1916 page 2.
67 The Detroit Times, 11/27/1931, the Detroit News, 11/27/1931 and the Detroit Free Press, 11/27/1931.

JOSEPH GLAISTER APARTMENTS

501-505 S. Washington, Lansing, MI

"J.C. Glaister will build a row of flats in the spring on Washington avenue south opposite the house of E.W. Sparrow. Architect Moon is now preparing the plans" (*SR* 2/10/1891).

"An estimated loss of $1,000, and possibly more, was the fire which broke out at in the Glaister flats at the corner of Washington avenue and Lenawee street yesterday afternoon" (*LJ* 11/5/1903).

In 1891 Moon designed this building for Joseph Glaister on S. Washington across from the Sparrow home; one wonders what Mr. Sparrow made of this. It has long been believed that Moon remodeled the Glaister house at 402 S. Walnut which still stands today. In all likelihood the Glaister home at 402 S. Walnut was designed by James Appleyard who was Glaister's friend. Rather, Moon designed the plans for these storefronts and apartments. The building is a plain but functional design. You can see the entrance to the center store and apartments located just to the left of the automobile. The business block has a side entrance which is unique and the capstones on the blocks columns add a bit of flair. There are three business blocks in this image. The one on the right is set off by the different style. The other two in the center and on the left, are part of the Glaister business blocks. The difference in the style of the blocks, 501-503 W. Washington and 505 S. Washington was a result of the 1903 fire after which 501-503 were remodeled. The structure at 505 S. Washington was the building that reflected Moon's design. The simple definition is that blocks were separate storefronts. Notice how the different blocks are set off by the columns. This is not always the case; one store could occupy several blocks. In this example it explains the separate entrances.

501-505 S. Washington, Lansing, MI, after 1988 fire.

Joseph C. Glaister was the only surviving son of Richard and Deborah (née Bough) Glaister and was one of the contractors employed on the building of the present Michigan State Capitol. Joseph was hired by his father and worked as a stonecutter on the Capitol. Joseph liked the business potential of the growing city and settled in Lansing. Born in England in 1856, Joseph immigrated to the United States in the 1870s. On July 11, 1898 Joseph married Miss Augusta Stansel in Mason, Michigan. The couple had eleven children reach adulthood, six sons: Cecil, Leo, Robert, Stanley, Russell, and Joseph Jr., and five daughters: Oma, Lucille, Alberta, Brough and Noma. Joseph C. Galister worked as a stone mason for several years then started a sand and gravel business on the east side of Lansing. Later in life Joseph purchased a farm north of Lansing in Clinton County where he resided until his death on November 12, 1937.[68]

From the Gould inventory of Darius Moon Buildings, listed as "Joe Glaistac apts, 1891." The buildings burned in 1988.

---

68   *LSJ* 11/16/1937.

ALONZO M. HENRY HOUSE

615 (609) S. Washington, Lansing, MI

"Klocksiem & Bailey have sold the residence of A.M. Henry on Washington avenue south to R.A. Montgomery for $5,500" (*SR* 5/26/1892).

This simple Queen Anne style home was built in 1891 for Alonzo Miles Henry, co-owner of Lansing Artificial Stone and a major stock holder in the Queen Bee Stove Company of Cleveland Ohio. In Tecumseh, Michigan on December 14, 1880 he married Miss Ella Gertrude Tilden. The couple would have five children: Alice L., Grace J., Helen R., Ralph A., and Burr A. Henry. In 1892 the family would leave Lansing and move to Ohio where Alonzo would work as a salesman for the stove company. Tragically in August of 1893 their young son Burr died at the age of one; his body would be returned to Lansing. Five years later tragedy would strike again when Alonzo's wife passed away in Toledo of unknown causes. Her body was returned to Lansing for interment at Mt. Hope Cemetery. The Henry's had many friends in Lansing and at Ella's funeral the pall bearers consisted of several well know Lansing residents. They were Ford J. North, Fred Keith, Frank G. Clark, L.C. Blood, Hart Farrand and E.V. Tooker. Alonzo would remain in Toledo, Ohio where he owned a grocery store which he operated with the help of his children. Alonzo M. Henry died in Toledo, Ohio on December 14, 1932 and his body was brought back to Lansing for burial at Mt. Hope Cemetery next to his wife and young child.[69]

---

[69] For Alonzo Miles Henry see the *Toledo Blade* 12/14/1932 and the *LSJ* 12/16/1932. For Ella G. Henry see the *SR* 12/3/1898 and for the death of their son Burr Henry see the *SR* 8/18/1893.

615 S. Washington, Lansing, MI

This is a Queen Anne style home with the usual variations in the roof line, multiple chimneys, and if you look closely, you can see some wonderful features over the windows. The pediment over the porch displays a sunburst motif while over the front of the second floor window is another sunburst motif in the triangle above the window. In the image below you can also see a pyramid style pattern on the front gable of the home.

Front Gable

The porte-cochère and the attached garage are later additions to the structure. The home is no longer standing and is now the site of a parking lot. The home was modified by architect R. Arthur Bailey, for the homes owner Richard A. Montgomery, who purchased the home from Henry in 1892 and remodeled the home in 1895.[70] From the Gould inventory of Darius Moon buildings "Lon Henry Hse" 1891.

---

70   *SR* 5/26/1892 and *SR* 6/3/1895.

HERBERT M. ROGERS HOUSE

528 N. Capitol, Lansing, MI

On April 19, 1892 Herbert M. Rogers purchased the North half of Lot 11 Block 69 from Julia Lang. Later he purchased from Hector Urquhart the East 10 feet Lot 12 Block 69 in 1894. What this means is that the Rogers' home was built 1894 and not in 1891 as has been believed.

"B.P. Corr yesterday secured the contract from H.M. Rogers to finish the stone from the Corr quarry for partially building and trimming Mr. Rogers' new house on Capitol avenue north" (*SR* 6/22/1894).

Built in 1894 this beautiful house is still standing on the campus of Lansing Community College where it is known as the Rogers-Carrier House. It is a wonderful example of the Queen Anne style and the restoration is one that should be commended. Notice the wonderful colonnettes incorporated into the second floor porch, the sweeping roofline which connects the third floor gable roof with the porch roof as well as the beautiful motifs on the front gables. What is interesting is the stick work on the third floor side gable and the spindles over the first and second floor porches. The architectural element on the gable end and the third floor dormer seem to be a hybrid of the palmette and sunburst motifs. Moon was extremely proud of his work on the Rogers' home and he used the home in an advertisement and on his business letterhead.

528 N. Capitol, Lansing, MI
(Image courtesy of Audrey Gould A.G.)

Herbert M. Rogers' life presented quite a mystery. Herbert was born in New York about 1850 to Harris D. and Charlotte E. Rogers and came to Michigan with his parents who settled in Williamston and worked as a commercial traveler. On September 15, 1874, Herbert's sister Carrie married Quincy A. Smith in Locke, Michigan. The lives of these three people would be intertwined for many years. Upon moving to Lansing, Herbert resides with his brother-in-law and sister. In Lansing Herbert was in the real estate business and had extensive property holdings throughout the region. When Herbert purchased the property at 528 [520] N. Capitol in 1892 from Julia Lang he then commissioned Moon to design a home. The first residents of the home were his brother-in-law Quincy and his sister Carrie, as well as Herbert. In fact, in the 1900 Census, Quincy Smith is listed as the head of the household while Herbert is recorded as being a boarder. After Herbert sold the home to Doctor Thomas Winters in 1901, the trio moved to 226 W. Washtenaw. When Judge Quincy Smith died while visiting Ann Arbor in 1907, Herbert remained with his sister and his niece Helen Rogers Smith at the home on Washtenaw. In 1919 Helen married Monroe E. Wright, an attorney, and the family left Lansing for Wichita, Kansas. Herbert M. Rogers passed away at his home, 423 N. Market Street in Wichita, Kansas on September 15, 1920.[71]

---

71   *Wichita Eagle* 9/17/1920.

RESIDENCE OF DR. WINTERS D. B. Moon, Architect

528 N. Capitol, Lansing, MI

Dr. Thomas Michael Winters was born on September 2, 1866 to Patrick and Mary (née Farrell) Winters on a farm eight miles south of Dansville, Michigan, in Bunker Hill Township. Thomas attended the University of Michigan to study medicine, and graduated in the class of 1887. After graduation Dr. Winters moved to Dansville to practice his profession.

Dr. Thomas M. Winters 1866-1904

In August of 1893 he was charged with assault by a local Dansville resident, Miss May Benjamin. On a late night visit to the Doctor's office accompanied by a friend, Mrs. Cady, it was stated that Dr. Winters employed a ruse to get Mrs. Cady to leave while Dr. Winters seduced the young Miss Benjamin; she claimed he pulled her to the floor and began his assault. The case fell on the fact that there were two other people in the office, a Stephen O'Brien and James Dakin, who both testified that the women were only there for five minutes and no one left the room. The charges were dismissed after the testimony of Andre Beers who was in the room next to the alleged assault and swore he heard nothing out of the ordinary that night. Several years later, in May 1900 Dr. Winters married Miss Agnes Loughlin of Fowlerville. The couple had one child, Thomas P. Winters. Dr Thomas M. Winters would pass away of neuritis on April 5, 1904 and his body was removed to Fowlerville for burial. His widow Agnes would sell the home to Ralph Carrier in April 1905; hence the name the Rogers Carrier house. Dr. Winters is all but forgotten.[72]

528 N. Capitol, Lansing, MI

In the 1903 advertising guide for Lansing there is a picture of Dr. Winters' home, listing D.B. Moon as architect (Illustrated 8). "A.R Hardy, executor of the estate of the late Dr. T.M Winters will sell on the premises at 520 Capitol ave. n., on Thursday, April 6 at 2 o'clock p.m. the fine brick residence now occupied by Mrs. Winters. This is undoubtedly one of the most substantial and modern houses that has ever been offered at public sale in Lansing. Those that are interested in securing a model House come in time to inspect it before the sale opens. Terms of sale fully stated at that time" (*SR* 4/3/1905). "M.R. Carrier has purchased the House of the late Dr. Thomas M Winters at 520 Capitol avenues north, paying $6,450 for it" (*LJ* 4/8/1905).

In Moon's 1904 City Directory advertisement H.M. Rogers is listed as one of the gentlemen that he had designed home for and from the Gould inventory of Darius Moon buildings, "H.M. Rodgers 1891".

---

72   For the death of Dr. Winters see the *SR* 4/6/1904. For the trial of the Doctor see *SR* 8/21/1893, *SR* 8/23/1893 and *SR* 8/25/1893.

THE JOHN WILSON HOME 1891

One of the difficulties in working with the Gould list is at times it is somewhat vague. In 1891 the inventory has Moon designing a home for John Wilson. But for just which John Wilson did Moon design a home? There are several options for the John Wilson house in Ingham and Eaton Counties which are outlined below.

There was a John W. Wilson who owned Sec 9, Twp 3, 2 W in Lansing Township. No other information has been found about this home.

There was also a John Wilson who died at his home on Mt. Hope Avenue in 1898 at the age of 86. No other information has been located about this property. But it seems doubtful that he would have had a new home built for himself at the age of 79.[73]

Another possibility is John T. Wilson of Charlotte, Michigan, one of that city's leading businessmen. He passed away on October 7, 1896. Unfortunately John T. Wilson's home at 319 E. Lawrence was built in 1880.

Finally there is John S. Wilson, who was later owner of the Wilson Sugar Bowl and several other businesses in Lansing. John S. Wilson came to Lansing in 1889 to work for Marple-French-McGrath Company Confectioners which went bankrupt in 1893. In 1891 Wilson was living at 150 S. Cedar, Lansing; however the Sanborn Maps show no structure at this address nor is that address listed in the 1894 City Directory. In 1894 John S. Wilson was living and teaching at the Boys Industrial School. It is possible that the 1891 home for John Wilson could have been in Ionia or Grand Ledge. John S. Wilson lived briefly in these cities before he moved to Lansing.

There is a variation of the spelling of the last name which is Willson.

The old John M. Willson's at home at 220 N. Capitol which was built prior to 1885 and torn down in 1907. John M. Willson died in 1891.

Any definitive information on just what home Moon designed for John Wilson in 1891 has yet to be discovered. It is quite possible that Moon drew up plans for a home for John Wilson and they were never executed. A search of the newspapers and property records from this time period seem to bear this out. From the Gould inventory of Darius Moon buildings, "Hse for John Wilson 1891".

---

[73] The *SR* 1/26/1898.

Darius Moon's 1891 Lansing City Directory Advertisement

THE CHICAGO INTERLUDE
1891-1893

In February 1891 Darius Moon relocated to Chicago for two reasons, a decline in architectural commissions in Lansing and to improve his design skills by taking advantage of the building boom that was occurring in Chicago as a result of the World's Columbian Exposition. It is also possible that Moon left because he was unhappy with Bowd's being awarded the contract for the Michigan Millers' Building. It seems odd that Moon would advertise in the 1891 City Directory only to leave while the advertisement was still running. In many ways his choice to work in Chicago for more then two years seems like a last minute decision rather then a carefully thought out plan. Darius returns only once to Lansing in 1892 to visit his family and to vote in the Presidential election. In 1892 Moon's young son Dell was sent on a visit to his father in Rogers Park. From all accounts, Dell was a pretty head strong young man. At the age of 11, he traveled alone to visit his father in Chicago and although he was told to wait in the railway car until his father arrived to collect him, Dell decided to set out for downtown Chicago. It was a fluke that Darius encountered his son at the station. After a few days with his father, Dell disappeared from the lodgings only to be found by his frantic father bathing in Lake Michigan.

Moon was employed by a building firm in Rogers Park, Illinois although there is no indication in his account, *Michigan in the Fifties*, which firm he was employed by, nor is Moon listed in the local city directories. The Gould inventory lists that he built two stores in Rogers Park, some type of building for John Rice in Rogers Park, the Smith Apartments in Ravenswood and some type of structure for Emmet Thomas in Lake Bluff, Illinois. These municipalities are all now suburbs of Chicago or incorporated into the city but at that time they were small towns that surround Chicago on the north side. The Chicago Public Library and the relevant historical societies have been consulted in regards to Moon and the names mentioned in the Gould list. They have no record of Moon or information on the construction of these buildings. Emmet Thomas was a prominent resident of the Chicago area and had business interests in Rogers Park, but may have lived in Lake Bluff, Illinois and had a home built around this time period. Given the increase of the population in the area as a result of the World's Columbian Exposition, it is difficult to obtain an accurate picture of the construction that was taking place. At this point in time given the limited information there is little to pursue here. Moon's account of his time in Chicago makes for interesting and colorful reading.[74]

1894

SYLVESTER SCOFIELD STORE

200-202 E. Franklin (Grand River), Lansing, MI

"A.A. Wilbur has purchased the property at 204 Franklin street... S.G. Scofield, who owns the two stores west of this property, will also erect new brick buildings on the lots this season" (*LJ* 4/4/1890).

---

[74] See Moon Part I p.18 and Part II p 35-38. For an idea of what was occurring in the Chicago area at this time see, Larson, *The Devil in the White City*.

"S.G. Scofield will erect two stone stores at the corner of Franklin street and Washington avenue in early spring" (*SR* 3/11/1891).

"Two of the largest plate glass windows in the city are being placed in the front of the S.G. Scofield's handsome red stone business block on Franklin street east today. Each pane will be 93x160 inches in size" (*LJ* 8/21/1891).

"The handsome double store which is just being completed by S.G. Scofield on Franklin street will be fitted up for D.C. Hurd, who will remove his stock of dry good thereto about Oct. 1" (*LJ* 9/5/1891). This building is often referred to as the Rork Block (Christensen 2).

Horton & Scofield Trade Card

Sylvester Green Scofield was born on January 1, 1822 in Elba New York; he came to Michigan with his parents in 1855 who settled on a farm three miles south of Lansing. In January 1864 he married Miss Mary Parmalee Bernard, in Lansing, Michigan. The couple would have six children, Edson, Frank K., Clara, Amorette, Ceila and Roberta. The couple would move to Lansing after their wedding. Sylvester owned and operated a lumber yard and sawmill on the east bank of the Grand River. He acted as Lansing Township clerk for several terms, was the first Fire Captain of the Lansing Volunteer Fire Company and served Lansing First Ward as an alderman. A member of the Methodist Episcopal Church, Sylvester held administrative positions with both the First and Central Methodist Episcopal churches; in both instances he was instrumental in the construction of the first structures for both institutions. Sylvester G. Scofield a stalwart of the Methodist Church passed away at his home at 418 N. Cedar Street on August 12, 1905.[75]

---

75   *LJ* 8/14/1905 and the *SR* 8/12/1905.

200-202 E. Franklin (Grand River), Lansing, MI

This is a wonderful building. It is a Romanesque style structure with the roughhewn stones, the arced windows on the second level over the east and west blocks and the pediment over the center block, whose second floor window has no arch, due to the large center arch which forms the pediment all of these features make this one of the architectural gems of North Lansing. What is especially attractive is the inverted sunrise motif on the center pediment. The half moon window, when combined with the stonework of the arch, creates a second sunburst motif. The four brackets on the upper stories along with the corbels along the cornice lends to the visual appeal of the building. The structure was designed by Moon in 1891, not 1894 as the newspaper accounts confirm. From the Gould inventory of Darius Moon buildings "Scofields Stores North 1894".

DARIUS MOON HOMES

116 (112) S. Logan (MLK), Lansing, MI
(Image courtesy of A.G.)

This beautiful home, built and designed by Darius Moon as his residence was constructed beginning in 1890 and was completed upon Moon's return from Chicago in 1894. Originally located at 116 S. Logan Street, the home was later moved in 1978 to 216 Huron Street by a group of local preservationists. For many years Moon's office was located at his home, no doubt to demonstrate to his perspective clients his design skills and simply to impress them. It is also interesting to consider that Moon never designed a home that resembled his own home; in a sense only the Rogers-Carrier home came close.

108-110 (106-108) S. Logan (MLK), Lansing, MI

The home at 116 S. Logan was not the first house Moon built for his own residence in Lansing. Moon described in his work *Michigan in the Fifties* that in 1872 he purchased a lot in the city of Lansing for $40 down and $50 a year for two years, for a total of $140.[76] During the winters Moon cut down trees on his brother's farm and hauled the logs to a sawmill, where the timber was cut into the lengths he needed to build his home. When all material was assembled to build his home he hauled the material to his property in Lansing. It took the winters of 1874 and 1875 for Moon to build his home by himself, except for the masonry work. He completed the home in the spring of 1875 and rented out one side of the home for $6 a month. The home was located at 108-110 (106-108) S Logan, and was a double house.

---

76   The deed lists the purchase price as $125. See Ingham County Register of Deeds Liber 53 p. 122.

108-110 S. Logan, Lansing, MI

While Moon was building his home, he boarded with his sister Ellen, who was married to Elbridge Dryer. Their farm was located on the north side of West Saginaw near Waverly Road. Each day Moon would make the trip from his sister's farm to the building site, a distance of over 2 miles. The Lansing Republican on September 21st 1880 published an article concerning a theft at Moon's home; the location given for the home in the article was the corner of Michigan Avenue and Logan Street. What is curious is that in the 1883 Lansing City Directory the Moon family is listed as living at 104 S. Logan. The street numbering system in Lansing in the 1880s was a bit chaotic. Moon lived at 106 S. Logan which was the southern unit of the double house and 104 was occupied by James Murray, a laborer who rented the unit. The double house's number would change to 106-108 S. Logan after the construction of the Murray house at 104 S. Logan and again in 1906 to 108-110 S. Logan when the local Post Office switched to the Philadelphia house numbering system.[77] Moon's description of the home he built in 1874 outlines that the house only had five rooms. Each unit of the double house at 108-110 S. Logan had only five rooms. This was an ideal location for Moon to live; not only did the property provide a source of income but later when he purchased the site for his new home, he was right next door to supervise the construction. One interesting aspect of the home is the large arch windows for the basement and the separate entrances, one on the north side [not visible] and one on the south side. The units were a mirror image of each other.

---

77   The Philadelphia house numbering plan assigned a number every twenty two feet with divisions at intersection, i.e. 100 Block or 200 Block, odd or even based upon which side of the street.

116 S. Logan (MLK), Lansing, MI
(Image courtesy of A.G.)

Moon began construction of his home at 116 S. Logan in 1890. He outlines in his work *Michigan in the Fifties* "As the years went by and they were more able, he built a modern house for a home with all the modern improvements, but when he had the house partly built, business was poor (that was 1891) and he had very little work as an architect, he closed his office, bid his wife and four children goodbye, and went to Chicago, the month of February 1891, and worked there, he drew plans, and supervised a number of buildings, and stayed in Chicago until the close of the world's fair in 1893, he only came home to Lansing once while he was working in Chicago." What this means is that the foundation of the home was begun in late 1890, it would have been risky to lay a foundation in the winter before Moon left for Chicago in February of 1891.

116 S. Logan (MLK), Lansing, MI notice the carriage house

The Chicago World's Fair, or as it is better known, World's Columbian Exposition, closed on October 30, 1893 and Moon returned to Lansing shortly afterward. Significant work on Moon's home occurred once he retuned to Lansing, as it is unlikely that Moon would leave this work to another contractor. By 1894 Moon's masterpiece was completed; he used the best woods he could find for the interior finishes and employed skilled craftsmen to do the work, unless he personally did the work. Moon was no fool; he knew his profession and undoubtedly used workmen who he trusted and were expert craftsmen. The home can best be described as a Victorian style home with stick style architectural features. The structure was a framed house with a steeply pitched roof with roof cresting along the ridge. When you observe the home your eyes are drawn to two features, the tower and the porch. The double gable on the porch is a unique feature; the result is a very stylized porch. There is so much going on with the architectural style of the home that it is difficult to describe. Observe the eave off the tower, in the above image it seems out of place, but when the home is viewed from the street blends with the roofline of the porch.

Darius Moon House Sunburst feature on the tower

The tower has a sunburst feature on a false gable along with a finial at the peak of the tower. The above image on the left is off center so the reader can better view the sunburst feature. In many other houses designed in the time period the tower would be one story higher, however Moon kept the tower shorter because of the view of the home from the street. One more story would have made the tower loom over the structure and divert the eye away from the porch.

Carriage House at the Moon Residence
(Image courtesy of A.G.)

The Carriage House at Moon's home has a Gothic appearance although he mixed different architectural styles. The arched widow of the second floor gable and the verge boards (decorative gable trim) on the gable are features of a Gothic structure. It is the first floor windows and entrance door that are out of place for a Gothic building. If you look closely the windows resemble those used at Moon's first residence in Lansing at 108-110 S. Logan. The Carriage house door mimics the design except for the upturned ends. The Carriage House was torn down in 1975 after it was damaged by fire and judged unsafe.

Darius Moon House being moved in 1978

The planned widening of Logan Street would have resulted in the destruction of Moon's home.[78] In 1975 a group of concerned Lansing citizens formed the Committee to Save the Darius B. Moon House Inc. The group would later be known as Save the Moon House Inc. The organization, under the leadership of Betty Downs, Ann Kimball and Diane Reedy, worked tirelessly to find a site for the Moon home. After Lansing Community College rejected a proposal to move the structure to a site on the campus between the Rogers Carrier home and the Herrmann house the organization began their search anew. The home was sold by then owner Jonathan Watts to the Save the Moon House Inc., for $1which in turn resold the house to Stan and Karen Kasuda for $1 who paid to have the home moved in May of 1978 to 216 Huron Street where the home stands today, fully restored.

---

78   Logan Street was renamed in 1989 to Martin Luther King Jr. Boulevard. The name Logan Street is used throughout the study for clarity and that was the street name when these homes were built.

1895

JOHN A. BISSINGER HOUSE AND STORE

624 N. Capitol, Lansing, MI

John A Bissinger House and Store is listed as being designed and built by Moon in 1895, but the structure was actually built in 1899. "Architect D.B. Moon has made plans for a new dwelling for J.A. Bissinger" (*SR* 5/22/1899).

"J.A. Bissinger is building a handsome two-story residence and office building at Capitol ave. and Jefferson street" (*SR* 7/8/1899).

This was a massive cross gabled home which not only incorporated living space for the family but a store front facing Capitol Avenue. The store front in this image has the awnings. The rounded front porch on the located on the front of the second story is a unique and attractive feature.

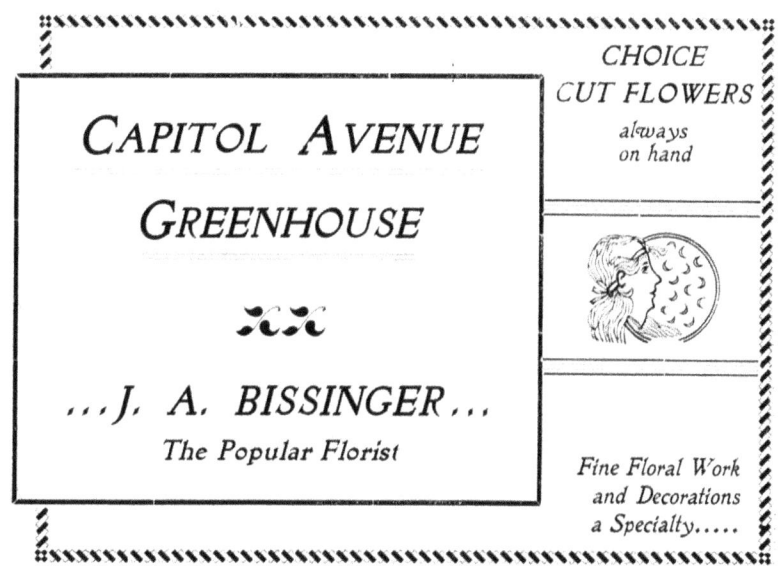

Capitol Avenue Greenhouse advertisement from the 1899 Oracle

John A. Bissinger, owner of Bissinger Floral Company was born in Württemberg, Germany, on April 27, 1863. He came to the United States in 1885 and worked as a gardener in Ionia and Charlotte, Michigan before finally settling in Lansing in 1888. On February 2, 1891 John married Emma Schultz; they had three children, Helen, Erena and John Frederick. In 1894 John and Emma opened the retail flower shop and greenhouse on the corner of Capitol Avenue and Saginaw Street. He was a prominent member of many Lansing Fraternal Organizations and associated with the First Church of Christ Scientists. John A. Bissinger passed away at his home, 624 N. Capitol on June 4th, 1928.[79]

---

79   *LSJ* 6/4/1928 and *Lansing Capital News* 6/4/1928.

624 N. Capitol, Lansing, MI
(Image courtesy of A.G.)

As with all Moon homes the striking feature is the porch. The spindles on the trim work of the first floor porch and fine turned balusters on the railing are delicate and lend lightness to the porch. The second floor porch has an entirely different design style. The posts are thin at the top then balloon at the bottom; they give the impression of vases. Over the store portion of the building you have a mansard roof that differentiates the public from the private parts of the building. Finally, Moon added a clipped gable and trim work to break up the plain façade of the side of the building. The structure was torn down in 1967. In Moon's 1904 City Directory advertisement Bissinger is listed as one of the gentlemen for whom he designed a home. From the Gould inventory of Darius Moon Buildings, listed as "John Bissinger Res, 1895".

JOHN A. BROOKS HOUSE

200 S. Sycamore, Lansing, MI
(Image courtesy of A.G.)

"John A. Brooks has purchased the lot on the southwest corner of Allegan and Sycamore streets and will at once erect a $2,500 residence" (*SR* 8/16/1895).

Moon had hit his stride as an architect with the design of the Brook's home. This is a massive house; the five side front dormer with the small gable front and the small eyebrow dormer are subtle architectural details. On one of the later photographs you can see that the eyebrow dormer is not repeated on the south side of the home, it was replaced with a small dormer. [80] Notice the side windows, especially the three sided bay window on the first floor with the sculpted detail on the underside and an oriel window on the third floor as well as the half arched window towards the back on the second floor. It is interesting to note the quarter moon window towards the back on the north side of the second floor and that this style window was repeated on the south side of the home only at the front. The basic design of home would be repeated by Moon in the Charles Whitman House, 124 E. Oak, Mason, Michigan. The eyebrow dormer would be replaced in the Whitman home with a traditional dormer. The automobile in the image is an Oldsmobile driven by R.E. Olds.

---

80   The large front dormer is seen in Moon's other designs, for example the Charles Whitman House at 124 E. Oak, Mason, Michigan. The dormer feature as well as the sloping gable end of the porch also appear in a home located at 2491 S. Okemos Road, Alaiedon Township, Michigan whose architect is unknown.

The Sun Burst detail at the end of the porch gable.

In the above image the gable at the end of the porch has been enlarged to show the sunburst motif, which was repeated in the smaller gable above the bay window. It is also important to observe the flaring under the porch gable which is repeated on the Whitman home. This home is best described as an Organic Home mixing several architectural features from other home styles.[81]

200 S. Sycamore, Lansing, MI
(Image courtesy of A.G.)

---

81   The accepted term is Organic Cottage, but in this study the term Organic Home is preferred. Basically an Organic Cottage refers to a home of local design that encompasses many features from different architectural styles. The reason the term Organic Home is preferred over Organic Cottage is that the definition of cottage has acquired a different meaning in the Twentieth and Twenty First Centuries.

Born on February 24, 1867 in Newaygo, Michigan to John and Delia (née Cassell) Brooks, John A. Brooks came to Lansing 1889 to complete his education to be a lawyer. He was admitted to the bar in 1889 and became a clerk in the office of the State Supreme Court. In 1896 John was appointed to the position of reporter for the Michigan Supreme Court, a position he would hold until 1906. In 1908 John opened the Brooks Abstract Company in partnership with his brother Hollis H. Brooks. In 1928 John would be elected President of the Ingham County Bar Association; he had reached the pinnacle of his professional career. On December 26, 1888 John married Miss Ada S. Sever in Newaygo, Michigan; the couple would have two children, Barbara and John A. Brooks. Ada Brooks would pass away on March 11, 1911 after a stroke. John married again on November 9, 1916 to Fern Weldan Wyman in Lansing, Michigan. The couple would have two children, Robert S. and James W. Brooks. By 1930 John and Fern were divorced and both children stayed with their father. John A. Brooks passed away on October 31, 1941 survived by his three sons, Colonel John A Brooks, Lieutenant Robert S. Brooks, James W. Brooks and one daughter Mrs. Barbara Willson.[82]

The south side of 200 S. Sycamore, notice the small dormer.

In Moon's 1904 City Directory advertisement Brooks is listed as one of the gentlemen for whom he designed a home. From the Gould inventory of Darius Moon Buildings, listed as "John Brooks Hse 1895".

---

[82]   *LSJ* 10/31/1941 and *LSJ* 11/1/1941. For Ada Brooks see *LSJ* 3/13/1911.

JACOB STAHL HOUSE AND BARN

211(209) S. Walnut, Lansing, MI
(Image courtesy of A.G.)

"Jacob Stahl was last evening granted permission to use part of Walnut street for building material. Mr. Stahl is making very extensive improvements to his property on this street and will have two very handsome residences when they are completed" (*SR* 5/12/1896).

"The work remodeling the residence of Jacob Stahl, which has been in progress the past three months, is complete and the building now ranks among our most beautiful and elegantly dwelling buildings. It will be occupied by the family next week" (*SR* 9/3/1896).

Detail of the dormer on the Jacob Stahl Home

Did Moon build one or two Houses for Stahl? It seems likely that Moon designed not only the Stahl house but also another home located at the back of his property at 211 S. Walnut. The home was incorporated in to the barn. It was not a carriage house, rather it was a home attached to the barn. The address given for this structure is 209 ½ S. Walnut and by 1913 the home at the back of Stahl's property was replaced with a large garage.[83] If you look carefully in the photograph of Moon's office you can see an image of Stahl's home hanging on the wall.

---

83   Jacob Stahl owned these properties on Walnut, Lot 10 Block 117 was his home and Lots 3-4-and north ½ of Lot 5 Block 118. There were no structures on any of the lots in Block 118. See also the *LSJ* 1/1/1932 which attributes the design of the Stahl home to Moon.

211 S. Walnut, with Barn
(Image courtesy of A.G.)

This is an impressive example of a Queen Anne style home. The house is a cross gabled structure with a crow's nest-like dormer on the third floor. Notice how it splits the second floor gable and the conical roof cover over the turreted second floor porch. The second floor porch resembles the one on the Bissinger home at 624 N. Capitol Avenue, except that the columns are straight and not flared at the base. The first floor porch is not as finely detailed as the one on the Bissinger home, but the use of triple columns on each corner provides a feeling of strength to this massive Queen Anne structure. Finally you can just make out the wonderful finial and cresting at the peak of the roof, which gives the impression of spines on the back of a dragon.[84]

The house was later moved to 332 Townsend, the Clara Davis corner, due to the construction of the new Post Office and Federal Building. Clara Davis was one of the few female doctors who practiced in Lansing. She is well known in France for her service to orphan children during World War One and the work she did in early childhood nutrition while working in Chicago. A native of Lansing, she is all but forgotten in her own place of birth.

---

84 The cresting is a decorative device that runs along the ridge of a roof and ends in a finial, an ending ornamentation.

Jacob Stahl 1845-1922

Born in Germany on August 23, 1845, Jacob Stahl immigrated to Cleveland, Ohio in 1867, where he served as an apprentice in metalworking; later he worked in a machine shop rising to the position of foreman. On January 21, 1868 Jacob married Miss Kate Hessert in Cuyahoga County, Ohio; the couple would have two sons, Frank and Louis. In 1871 Jacob started a hardware store in Amherst, Ohio; ten years later he relocated his business to Lansing where the hardware firm of Stahl & Son was established. Jacob served on the boards of the Boys Industrial School, the Lansing Electric Light and Water, was treasurer of the Lansing, St. Johns and St. Louis Railroad Company, and was a director of City National Bank. Jacob Stahl personally selected the stock for his store, much of which was purchased on his trips to Germany. His hardware business had one of the finest selections of toys in Michigan, which must have made his store the centerpiece for the dreams of all the children in Lansing. Although he looks stern, Jacob Stahl had a soft spot for children. He also had an interest in music and the arts; Jacob was one of the principal financial organizers for the Lansing Conservatory of Music. Jacob Stahl died on October 13, 1922 in Battle Creek, Michigan surrounded by his family. The pallbearers at his funeral included B.F. Davis and Frank L. Dodge; both respected Lansing citizens who along with Stahl placed civic duties in the forefront of their lives.[85]

Jacob Stahl House before its demolition, 332 Townsend, Lansing, MI

---

85   *LSJ* 10/13/1922, *Lansing Capital News* 10/13/1922 and 10/14/1922.

"There's virtually nothing about the remodeled Board of Realtors building at 332 Townsend street that resembles the old Jacob Stahl House. Lansingites can be forgiven if they fail to recognize the structure which once stood on the site of the post office. Most interior walls remain as they were when the Stahl's lived in the house, but the exterior has been completely altered. The third story, porches at the front and the rear, all dormers and "gingerbread" were removed. The new roof was erected at the second floor level. A square corner was built in place of the bay window at the front of the house. A second front entrance was inserted where the window had been. And the entire structure was covered with brick facing" (*LSJ* 4/18/1948).

In our everyday lives we never noticed Jacob Stahl's house because of the dramatic changes that were made to it in 1948. The surprising fact about this home is that it lasted as long as it did. The house was torn down in 2003-2004. The site is now the home of the new Michigan Beer and Wine Wholesalers Association building.

Jacob Stahl's Barn and attached rental home

The above image of the Stahl Barn demonstrates that the structure was used not only as a barn but as a residence. It is unfortunate that a full photograph of the structure did not survive. The clipped dormer above the windows on the second floor as well as the shed awning over the first floor windows points toward a structure that was much more than just a barn. There was a home attached to the barn undoubtedly built as a rental property to provide a source on income. The barn structure disappeared between 1906 and 1913.

In Moon's 1904 City Directory advertisement Stahl is listed as one of the gentlemen for whom he designed a home for. From the Gould inventory of Darius Moon Buildings, listed as "Jacob Stahls Res 1895 and Jacob Stahls Barn 1895".

JACOB STAHL STORE

213-215 N. Washington, Lansing, MI

The Gould list states that Moon designed Jake Stables office & Store in 1895. Could this be Jacob Stahl's office and store? There was no Jake Stables in Lansing or Michigan at that time so it is quite likely this was a misprint. Stahl's store was at 213-215 North Washington The building was standing in 1892, so this may have been an extensive remodel when the G.A.R. moved to the second floor or when the I.O.O.F. moved to the third floor with the façade also being redone. The structural elements on the façade of the building are in keeping with the styles Moon employed in other buildings. The elongated arch to the left of the photograph implies a tower element which is not unlike the structural features on the Wilbur Block. In January of 1881 Jacob Stahl moved from North Amherst, Ohio to Lansing and purchased from George M. Dayton the inventory of the George Betts Hardware store which Dayton had recently acquired. Through the years Stahl grew the business into one of the largest hardware stores in the state.

213-215 N. Washington, Lansing, MI

The other option is that Moon submitted plans to remodel the Stahl block at 401-405 N. Washington for the Grand River Boat Club. The contract for the remodeling went to Edwyn A. Bowd.[86]
From the Gould inventory of Darius Moon Buildings, listed as "Jake Stables office & Store, 1895".

EDWARD SPARROW HOUSE

506 S. Washington, Lansing, MI

---

86   See *SR* 8/10/1895.

The Edward Sparrow house which once graced Washington Avenue and stood just north of the B.F. Davis House was one of Lansing's grand houses.

"E.W. Sparrow has plans drawn for altering his residence on Washington avenue south to the extent of some thousands of dollars" (*SR* 4/14/1890).

"E.W. Sparrow is making some extensive alterations and additions to his residence on Washington avenue south" (*SR* 9/11/1894).

"A load of cherry red sandstone from the Excelsior quarry in Houghton county has arrived for E.W. Sparrow's residence, and may be seen at the Lake Shore derrick near Piatt's works. The new quarry is owned by S.L. Smith of Detroit, Judge Swan of Detroit, Judge Brown of the United States supreme court, C.H. Sager of Hancock, Otis Johnson of Racine, S.S. Olds and E.W. Sparrow of this city. James Segar, son of the late Schuler Segar, is superintendent and manager of the quarry. The stone is of excellent quality and withal beautiful" (*SR* 10/25/1894).

"The contract for the interior woodwork of E.W. Sparrow's residence was awarded this morning to Capital lumber company. It is expected that the woodwork will be the finest of any residence in the city" (*SR* 1/7/1895).

The Sparrow home was extensively modified between 1894 and 1895. From the above newspaper accounts it seems the remodeling included the interior as well as the exterior. The work that was done in 1890 may also have been executed by Moon; in 1890 Moon had designed a business block on East Michigan Avenue for Sparrow. What is certain is that Moon was responsible for the structure you see above but not the original structure which was built much earlier. The following is a description of the Sparrow House before it was torn down in 1931.

ONCE STATELY MANSION, BUFFETED BY YEARS, NOW PREY OF WRECKERS

"Once the show of Lansing and stately home of one of its most prominent citizens, the old mansion at the southwest corner of Lenawee street and Washington avenue is now passing into history. Thursday morning crews of the Capital City Wrecking company started their task of razing the old structure. The pounding of hammers and the screeching of nails being torn loose from boards they have held together for many decades, sounded throughout the vicinity of the old dwelling. This once beautiful residence was the home of the late Edward E. Sparrow, pioneer citizen, who participated in the establishment of several of the city's major industries including the Olds Motor Works and the Lansing Company, and was one of the founders of the City National Bank.

HAS "PLANS" FOR SITE

The property is now owned by William I. Bowerman, local real estate man who declared Thursday that he had "plans but nothing to announce at the present time," when asked what he was going to build on the site. The original building on the property was a square veneer house built in 1872 by Henry Walker, a pioneer settler. It was purchased by Mr. Sparrow in 1876, according to Frank Church, local realty dealer who was secretary to Mr. Sparrow.[87] The Sparrow family first lived in the old dwelling and about 1886 made several alterations in it. In 1890 expenditures totaling several thousand dollars were made in remodeling the building to its present form. Nothing was overlooked in making it the finest home possible at that time.

---

87   E.W. Sparrow purchased the home from William Betts for $6,000 in 1876 about $117,000 in today's money using the GDP deflator index. See the *LRW* 2/15/1876.

INCLUDES BALLROOM

The old house has many rooms and fireplaces of marble, tile, wood and brick of various colors in most of them. It includes a ballroom on the third floor, servants' quarters, guest rooms of all colors, numerous bathrooms, and a kitchen and pantry that is a suite of rooms in itself. Woodwork in part of house was hand carved and hand hewn and the outside walls contain some of the finest stonework that has ever been placed in a home in Lansing. The house stands on three-quarters of an acre, a third of which was acquired by Mr. Sparrow in 1891. The city had no water works when the house was built and the owner provided his own supply with a windmill for pump and large storage tanks at the top of the house and in the barn. Several of the oak trees on the property today are part of the original forest, while others were planted by Mr. Sparrow and Mr. Church. Many of the most beautiful trees were destroyed when Washington avenue was widened a few years ago, Mr. Church said. Mr. Bowerman purchased the property from the Sparrow estate in 1917 and since that time the home has been used as a rooming house and the yard as a used car lot. A fruit stand has recently been in operation on the site.

MUCH HAND WORK IN HOUSE

Dorr Gunnell and William Hoffman, operators of the Capital City Wrecking company, Thursday pointed out the many interesting features in the old house. The front door contains beveled leaded glass, which must have required considerable time to make years ago. The main stairway contains hundreds of hand carved and hand lathed pieces of wood, which represented an investment of hundreds of dollars. In many places the wreckers found radiators concealed under window seats, and in part of the kitchen they found a radiator with doors and shelves in which food could be placed and kept warm. One of the modern features in the kitchen is a built in refrigerator with an outside icer. The cupboard doors are hand carved and a dumbwaiter once served to carry drinks from the kitchen to the second and third floors.

FIXTURES REMOVED, BATTERED

In its present condition, however, the once stately mansion is only a ghost of its former self. The wall coverings have been marred through carelessness, mirrors above the fireplaces have been broken, and others have been removed, while plumbing and electrical fixtures have been torn from their places and carried away by prowlers who have visited the house during the months it has been unoccupied. Roomers, who lacked appreciation of the hand carved woodwork, have driven nails and hooks through some of the finest pieces of material in the building. On the third floor the wreckers found an antique cabinet in the ballroom, which contains plate glass doors and ornamental corners.

FIND UNIQUE TUB

Some of the inside partitions have even been covered with sheeting. The rooms on the second floor are numerous with metal numerals which have been nailed through the solid oak doors. In one of the bathrooms the workmen found a tub with the inlet and overflow both in the side, the second of this type ever discovered in a house being razed here. A remarkable feature in the construction is the 12-inch center of studding and joists placed in the walls. Builders now use 16 and 24-inch centers. The old dwelling has many additional features almost too numerous to mention, but they will all soon be forgotten and the site of the stately mansion of yesterday will enter a new era of usefulness in an age far different that the one in which Edward W. Sparrow helped to build the foundation of the present city of Lansing" *LSJ* (10/15/1931).

I think even Edward W. Sparrow would be surprised to learn that the "new era of usefulness" would mean that his mansion would become the site of a gas station and parking lot.

Edward W. Sparrow 1846-1913

The home is a mixture of many styles, mainly Queen Anne and Romanesque. What is conspicuous was the use of the roughhewn stone work, a trait used to draw a viewer's eye toward different aspects of the building. The stone work around the first floor window, the checkerboard use of stone to form the side porch and the square stone blocks that frame the window on the third floor of the tower are a unique mixture of architectural elements. The stone was cherry red sandstone from the Excelsior Quarry in Houghton County owned by Sparrow and the addition of the stone work seems forced. You can see that the home was originally a brick house and Moon used these embellishments to update the style of the house. The Porte-cochère on the side of the home is an interesting feature.[88] The pyramidal covering of the tower with an ornate weather vane at its peak was a strong addition to the home. There may have been a second tower at the rear of the house but due to the limitations of the image it is difficult to ascertain if this is true. The bowed window feature on the second floor is a wonderful addition which softens the overall appearance of the structure. This is an over the top house, which screams "I have made it". Moon was expanding his architectural range and giving his patrons what they wanted. There are some features of this home that were included in Moon's home at 106 S. Logan.

What is interesting is that three of Edward's five sisters' were married to men who engaged Moon's services to design either homes or commercial buildings. Sparrow's sister Alicia Lansing lived in a home designed by Darius Moon. While Isabella E. Ranney, Sparrow's sister, was married to Dr. Ranney who employed Moon to design two commercial buildings. Finally Delia Olivia (Eva D.) Davis, who was married to Benjamin F. Davis, engaged Moon to plan the couple's home on South Washington Avenue. Edward Sparrow's other sisters were Sarah Georgiana Oyer and Mary H. Sparrow who would become the Countess Mary Orloff, a fascinating story that is beyond the scope of this work.

---

88   The Porte-cochère was essentially carriage porch which covered an entrance to protect visitors from the elements as they entered the home.

E.W. Sparrow from *Our Michigan Friends*

Sparrow is a name that is familiar to Lansing residents principally through the association with Sparrow Hospital, which was a gift to the people of Lansing by Edward Wheeler Sparrow. Unfortunately few know the story of Edward W. Sparrow. He was born in Killibeg (Kilberg) House in the county of Wexford, Ireland on December 14, 1846, the son of Bartholomew and Sarah (née Lee) Sparrow. Young Edward must have had an interesting childhood; his father was a landed proprietor, which meant his income was derived from the estate and its rental properties. Sarah Sparrow and the children left Ireland in 1858 to settle in Lansing, while her husband Bartholomew remained in Ireland to salvage something from the 'wreck of his affairs'. In 1859 Bartholomew inherited £4,000 from his uncle Adam Rogers of Waterford Ireland.[89] Bartholomew intended to join his family in Lansing but fell ill in 1860 and died before his voyage to the United States. The bequest made by Adam Rogers explains how the Sparrow's live in a style unlike other Irish immigrant families in the United States. After arriving in Lansing, Edward worked as a page in the Michigan State Legislature and as a clerk in a dry goods store owned by Harley Ingersoll. Surprisingly Edward entered into a partnership with John J. Bush and Charles W. Butler to purchase land within the Lansing city limits for the purpose of plating and reselling the properties. Their first investment was the Bush, Butler & Sparrow subdivision, which encompassed a plat of land bound by Sycamore Street to the east, S. Logan (MLK) Street to the west, Michigan Avenue to the north, and St. Joseph Street to the south. Quite an outlay for a young man working as a clerk in Ingersoll's dry goods store; there must have been family money invested in this venture. The real estate speculation of the partners was a success which they soon parlayed into ownership of sixteen business blocks in downtown Lansing.

---

89 £4,000 in 1860 represents about $400,000 in today's currency.

506 S. Washington, Lansing, MI
(Image from MSU Archives)

In the late 1870s, with his financial success assured with his Lansing real estate investments, Edward partnered with John M. Longyear and the two purchased extensive holdings in mineral and timberlands resources in Michigan's Upper Peninsula. With another partner, William Kroll, Edward built a series of saw mills and had widespread lumber operations in Houghton County, Michigan. In 1887, Edward, along with other investors, would purchase the Mesabi Iron Range in Minnesota, a property rich in high grade iron ores; he later would become director of the Mesabi Iron Company. Sparrow was engaged in a variety of business enterprises throughout the world, too many to be detailed in a short biography. One of the most important for Lansing was his investment in 1897 in the young upstart Olds Motor Vehicle Company started by Ransom E. Olds. Sparrow was also President of Lansing Wheelbarrow and was one of the organizers of the City National Bank. In 1911 he established the Edward W. Sparrow Hospital to serve the needs of the residents of Mid-Michigan. On September 16, 1897, Edward married Miss Helen Therese Grant in Lansing, Michigan. Helen was the daughter of Chief Justice Claudius B. and Caroline (née Felch) Grant. Helen was born in Ann Arbor, Michigan, January 6, 1872 and received her early education at Kemper Hall in Kenosha, Wisconsin. She attended Vassar College where she completed her degree in 1893. Helen died tragically on June 16, 1899 soon after the birth of the couple's first child Edward Grant Sparrow as a result of uremic poisoning and other complications due to childbirth. Just what effect this had on Edward W. Sparrow is unknown. It may have been a major factor in his decision to build a modern hospital in Lansing. In June of 1903, Edward married Miss Margaret B. Beattie; the couple would have one child, a daughter Margaret Alicia Sparrow. The Sparrow family moved to New York City in 1907 and took up residence at 41 East 68th Street. Sparrow never forgot the city that helped to establish his fortune. At the time of his death he was working with his Lansing representative Frank E. Church to complete several buildings on South

Washington Avenue and construction of an infectious diseases wing for Sparrow Hospital. Edward Wheeler Sparrow died in New York City on February 21, 1913, his body was returned for burial in his adoptive city at Mt. Hope Cemetery.[90]

In Moon's 1904 City Directory advertisement Sparrow is listed as one of the gentlemen for whom he designed a home. From the Gould inventory of Darius Moon Buildings, listed as "E.W. Sparrow Res. 1895".

LEVI COTTINGTON RENTAL HOMES

300 N. Pine, and 528 W. Ionia, Lansing, MI

The Gould list has Moon doing some type of work for Cottington in 1895. Since it is doubtful that Moon remodeled a home he designed just four years previous, it is likely that this was new construction. In December of 1891 Levi Cottington purchased from Blance Mason the West 2 ½ rods of Lots 7 & 8 Block 87.[91] There were no homes on this property prior to 1895; the homes that were built were 528 W Ionia, 300 N. Pine as well as 310 N. Pine. The home at 528 W. Ionia and 300 N. Pine were a double residence fronting their respective street.

---

90 For Edward W. Sparrow see *LSJ* 2/22/1913, (Livingstone 2: 364) and (*National* 49: 298). For Helen Grant Sparrow see the *SR* 6/17/1899 and *LJ* 6/17/1899. For Margaret Beattie Sparrow see *LSJ* 7/23/1958.
91 *SR* 12/4/1891.

310 N. Pine, Lansing, MI

The home at 310 N. Pine was a single residence. This is a fantastic little home. Both of these homes display Moon's range as an architect. The homes at 300 N. Pine and 528 W. Ionia streets have some interesting architectural features. Imaging the home without a second floor porch and the first floor porch would have been radically different. By the time of this image, circa 1950, the home was divided into three residences, originally it would only have been two residences, one with an entrance on North Pine Street and one on W. Ionia Street. You can see in the photograph a hint of what the front porch would have been like by examining the side porch. Notice the narrow columns which are fluted at the time into the fine scrollwork of the frieze. The front porch would have had extensive detail instead of the square structure you see in the image. The stick-work front and side gable tell us there was more to the home then we are seeing in the photograph. The home at 310 N. Pine is an example of a well-designed small residence. Notice how the smaller porch gable blends with the front clipped gable to form a triangle. The pedestal supports for the front porch columns mimic the angles of the structure. Overall this is a pleasing and functional design for a home this size.

From the Gould inventory of Darius Moon Buildings, listed as "Levi Cottington Hse, 1895".

1896

DAVID N. SHULL HOME

David N. Shull residence, 507 S. Walnut, Lansing MI

At times it is difficult to determine just what structure Moon designed for a given person; the home for David N. Shull is one of these instances. The Gould list gives 1896 as the year Moon designed a home for David Shull. In 1896 David N. Shull, a retired grocer, was invested in the Lansing real estate market and had extensive property holdings in Lansing. His home at 507 S. Walnut was built before 1891 so is effectively eliminated from consideration. In all other instances the properties, except one, that Shull owned either had home built well after 1896 or much earlier then 1896. The only property Shull owned that fits the date criteria is 329 W. Allegan.

David N. Shull Property, 329 (319) W. Lenawee, Lansing, MI

Shull owned the West 54 feet of Lot 11, Block 147, 329 W. Lenawee. The home at 329 W. Lenawee was located just north of Shull's residence at 507 S Walnut. In fact you can see a small portion of his home just to the right in the above image. There is no home listed in the 1894 city directory located at 329 W. Lenawee, the last address listed is for F.L. Henderson's home at 323 (315) W. Lenawee. This was a massive Queen Anne home. Notice the three sided oriel windows, one is located on the below the gable and second quite large one is located on the side facing the street. There is also a two sided bay window located on the second floor just above the entrance porch. The fish scale pattern on the third floor façade and gable blends with the brickwork of the lower stories. As in many Moon designed homes the focus is on the porch. The porch on the Shull house is actually a veranda; it angles away from the busy street providing a quite space away from the traffic noise. Although it is difficult to see in the image below, the first floor structure of the house mimics the shape of the porch angling at the corner. The site of this home is now a parking lot.

329 W. Lenawee, Lansing, MI

Born in Union Town, Pennsylvania in 1835, David N. Shull came to Lansing after the Civil War. After arriving in Lansing he established the D.N. Shull & Company, Grocers and Dealers in Michigan Flour, located in the Lansing House Block on Washington Avenue. On September 9, 1856 Shull married Miss Candace Alton in DeKalb, Indiana. The couple would have three children: Eugina, Endora and Morton. On March 27, 1868 Candace tragically passed away in Lansing, Michigan. On August 12, 1869 Shull would marry again, to Miss Sarah Delamarter of Brighton, Michigan. The couple would have no children but Sarah would raise David's three children as her own. In 1902 David's daughter, Endora Shaw died of heart disease. Declining in health, David traveled to New Orleans for the winter in late 1914. On Wednesday February 17, 1915 he passed away in that city, his wife Sarah was at his side. He was survived by his son Morton Shull of Seattle and his daughter, Mrs. Eugina Park of Holt. Shull's body was returned to Lansing and buried next to his first wife, Candace at Mt. Hope Cemetery.[92]

From the Gould inventory of Darius Moon Buildings, listed as "D.N. Scull Hse." 1896.

---

92   *Lansing Evening News* 2/19/1915 and the *LSJ* 2/20/1915.

DR. GEORGE E RANNEY BUSINESS BLOCK

208 S. Washington, Lansing, MI

The Gould list records Darius Moon as designing the Ranney block in 1896, the Lansing newspapers however place the construction in 1890.

"Dr. Ranney will build a three-story store on the site of his present office. Work will begin in the near future" (*SR* 7/8/1890).

208 S. Washington, Lansing, MI

"The new Ranney block is nearly complete, and it will possess one unique quality as far as concerns Lansing at least. The entire front of three stories will consist of three magnificent panels of plate glass" (*SR* 11/17/1890).

208 S. Washington, circa 1923

The Dr. George E Ranney building is one of the best examples of a Romanesque style commercial block that survives in Michigan. The building's façade is Lake Superior cherry red sandstone. Notice the square blocks that begin at the side walk and proceed upward, forming the arch that frames the second and third story bowed windows.[93] The most distinctive feature of the block is the ornate parapet. It resembles that of a castle, with crenellations and imposing decorative caps on the tops of the battlements; notice the architectural decoration between the battlements. Quite simply, this is a remarkable building.

---

93   The sandstone probably came from the Excelsior quarry in Houghton County, Michigan which was owned by his brother-in-law Edward Sparrow.

Dr. George E. Ranney 1839-1915

Dr. George Emery Ranney, a respected Lansing resident, was born in Batavia, New York on June 13, 1839, to Joel and Elizabeth (née Champlain) Ranney. His family would later move to Sheridan Township, Calhoun County, Michigan. After attending the Stafford Academy and Rushford Academy, George enrolled at the University of Michigan to study medicine. When the Civil War began he enlisted in the Second Michigan Cavalry in September of 1861. Overwork forced his retirement from the service in 1863 and he returned to the University of Michigan to complete his studies in medicine. After graduation, Ranney returned to his old regiment as a surgeon. He was taken prisoner at the Battle of Chickamauga and was sent to Libby prison for 44 days. In 1901 he was awarded the Medal of Honor for, as the citation reads, "At great personal risk, went to the aid of a wounded soldier, Pvt. Charles W. Baker, lying under heavy fire between the lines, and with the aid of an orderly carried him to a place of safety."

He mustered out of the army in 1866 and settled in Lansing to practice medicine. Ranney was well known as a researcher; the first physician to discover the link between bad water and typhoid, diphtheria and other waterborne diseases. He worked tirelessly to make municipal water supplies safe, and had an international reputation for his work in this area. He was a member of the American Medical Association, the British Medical Association, a fellow of the British Gynecological Association and the Superintendent of Lansing City Hospital along with many other honors and awards. The citizens of Lansing are indebted to him for his work to have 11,000 trees planted in the city to improve its appearance. On September 15, 1869 Dr. Ranney married Isabella E. Sparrow; they had two children, Ralph S and Florence, both who predeceased their parents. Following the death of his wife Isabella on October 17, 1906, Dr. Ranney lived alone above the Ranney Block. After the death of his friend Dr. Julius A. Post on October 28, 1915, Dr. Ranney accompanied the body east to Bethany, New York. The strain of losing a lifelong friend and Civil War comrade overwhelmed Dr. Ranney; he died after suffering a stroke in his office on November 10, 1915. [94]

From the Gould inventory of Darius Moon Buildings, listed as "Store on Washington Ave for Dr. Ranny 1896".

---

94   *LSJ* 11/10/1915.

CHARLES PORTER STORE

118(108) W. Washtenaw, Lansing, MI

The Gould inventory of Darius Moon buildings lists that in 1896 he designed a "Store for Charles Porter". The likely candidate is 118 W. Washtenaw which was owned by Charles H. Porter in 1900. The building at 118 W. Washtenaw does not appear on the Sanborn Maps until 1898. In 1921 the area was cleared for construction of a gas station. Between 1896-1900 Charles is listed as living at 604 (401) River Street and was unemployed until 1900, when he is listed as a grocer. In the 1902 City Directory his occupation is owner of a Flour and Feed store at 118 W. Washtenaw. In 1902 Charles Porter owned W 40 feet of East 4 Rods of Lot 7 Block 115, or 118 W. Washtenaw. In the above image 118 W. Washtenaw is the one story building to the left of the Bishop building this is the only available image of the building. By 1908 the Flour and Feed Store has been replaced by the Gatley Instatement Goods Store and Charles H. Porter with his wife Mary, moved to Delhi Township. In the 1920 Census Charles H. Porter and wife Mary would be listed as farming in Williamstown Township, Michigan. On November 8, 1875 Charles married Miss Mary A. Kellogg in Allegan, Michigan; the couple would have two children: Phoebe and Henry E. Porter. Charles Porter died in Webberville on April 6, 1929, his wife Mary died shortly after; the couple is buried at the Delta Center Cemetery in Eaton County Michigan.[95]

The Porter block located at 303 S. Washington is not a candidate. Although the building shows many of the architectural traits of a Moon building the structure was designed by F.W. Hollister of Saginaw, architect of the Hollister Building.[96]

From the Gould inventory of Darius Moon Buildings, listed as "Store for Charles Porter, 1896".

---

95 *LSJ* 4/8/1929, *Lansing Capital News* 4/8/1929 and the *Ingham County News* 4/11/1929.
96 See *SR* 8/26/1892. The Porter Block was owned by James and Eunice Porter.

1897

The Gould inventory of Darius Moon buildings has no listings for 1897. This may be as a result of the Panic of 1896 due to the failure of the National Bank of Illinois in Chicago, a survey of the structures built in Lansing in 1897 show only six buildings designed by named architects as being constructed.

1898

GEORGE T. GORDON HOUSE

612 N. Pennsylvania, Lansing, MI

"George T. Gordon also has plans for a $2,500 residence which will probably be built on Pennsylvania avenue north" (*LJ* 3/5/1898).

The Gordon home is best described as an organic house, a structure that contains architectural elements from other styles incorporated in to it. In the above image, the bay widow on the first floor and a three sided rectangular oriel window on the second floor with a triangle window at its peak are quite unique. The dormer in the front, is curious because there is no window in the center; it may have been enclosed or it was as the architect intended. What is odd are the triple hung windows, something that is unusual for a Moon designed home. The porch is one of the great features of the home, Moon repeats the triple column corner design which was used in the Stahl house, but in this instance the columns are square.

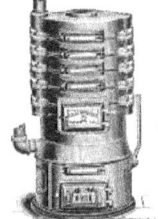

GEO. T. GORDON.   ROBERT J. BLACK

GORDON & BLACK

Sanitary Plumbing

Gas, Steam and hot Water Piping a Specialty.

Dealers in Bath Tubs, Pipes, Hydrants, Hose, Etc. All Work Warranted. Estimates Cheerfully given. First Class Work Guaranteed.

Sole Agents for the Ideal Boiler,—the only Boiler up to date.

114 MICHIGAN AVE. EAST.   LANSING, MICHIGAN.

S-G-O

George T. Gordon's advertisement from the 1895 Oracle

George T. Gordon was born in Brockport, New York on August 27, 1854. Gordon moved to Detroit and worked as steam fitter before moving to Lansing. Earlier in his life Gordon worked for the firm of F.C. Bennett & Company, which specialized in plumbing, steam and gas fittings. George left in 1891 and established Gordon Plumbing and Heating in the basement of Baird's Opera House. He was a member of the First Church of Christ Science and active in local business affairs. More importantly Gordon was a Master Plumber and served on various professional committees which means he would have been familiar with Moon's work. George T. Gordon died at his home on August 8, 1934 and was survived by his wife, Louise A. (née Barnes), and one son William B. Gordon of Lansing Michigan. [97] There is a short article concerning George T. Gordon which appeared in the *State Republican* on September 12, 1890 which gives some insight into George's personality. "Geo. T. Gordon, a practical gas and steam fitter who has the erection of the park fountain in hand, is considerably aroused from his usual quiet demeanor over the work and the talk of the citizens. He asked the morning the Republican, "What do you take me for, are you trying to hoodoo me? And then in a rather sarcastic voice he said: "yes I really think that the fountain ought to be fitted with steam, because we have some mighty cold weather here in Lansing, and steam could be very easily procured from some of the neighboring buildings." He says he cannot go on with his work any faster than he is, on account of lack of help. But now Ald. [Alderman] Bennett has given him orders to take a force of men from the streets to aid in the lifting and Lansing's fountain will soon be a thing of the present." What is interesting about the quote is that Aldermen Frank C. Bennett bought the plumbing business of Charles Herrick in 1895, and took as his partner, George T. Gordon. The house is still standing today and it is well worth viewing.

From the Gould inventory of Darius Moon Buildings, listed as "Hse for George Garden, No Date".

---

97   *LSJ* 8/21/1934.

GEORGE KEITH HOMES

317 W. Allegan, Lansing, MI

"Among the handsomest residences which may be built this season is that which George Keith contemplates erecting at the corner of Allegan and Walnut streets and which will be a very costly one." (*LJ* 3/5/1898).

During this time George Keith owned several properties in Lansing. He owned the West 4½ Rods of Lots 11-12 Block 117 or the entire NW corner of Allegan and Walnut Streets, or 315 W. Allegan, 317 W. Allegan and 207 S. Walnut. There were no homes standing on these lots in 1894, so it is reasonable to assume that they were built between 1894 and 1900. "George Keith was granted permission by the council last night to use a portion of Allegan and Walnut streets while erecting a new home on that corner" (*LJ* 5/15/1900).

The above image of 317 W. Allegan was taken after it was relocated to 211 S. Chestnut in 1932.[98] Notice the similarities with 315 W. Allegan and the home Moon designed for William Kirk of Fairgrove, Michigan. In this Queen Anne home your eyes are immediately drawn to the second floor porch with the ornate roof that has an Eastern European flair. Notice how Moon carries the theme forward on the second floor porch by using the columns that have a vase shaped base. The first floor porch is a veranda that wraps around the home; it is plain but functional. The stone porch was not original to the home at 317 W. Allegan, it must have been added after the home was moved to 211 S. Chestnut. The home was torn down during the building of the Lansing Civic Center in 1954.

---

98   The *City of Lansing Records for Moved Buildings*, see 1/7/1932, 317 W. Allegan to 211 S. Chestnut Permit 333 Lansing Building and Safety. See also *LSJ* 1/26/1932.

315 W. Allegan, Lansing, MI
(Image courtesy of A.G.)

The Gould lists says that Moon designed three houses for George Keith in 1898 plus another two whose date of construction is unknown. The home at 315 W. Allegan was a rental property owned by Keith. Some of the renters included, Louis Toles, a physician who occupied the home in 1904 with Hilda Cummings, his clerk and Jefferson Fulton, President of Lansing Gas Light Company. In 1908 Reverend William C. Hicks, Rector at St. Paul's Episcopal Church lived at 315 W. Allegan along with Liolen C. Difford, his assistant and Mary Simmons a domestic worker.

George Keith's Rental House, 830 S. Walnut, after the 1932 move

George Keith's rental property is best described as a Queen Anne home with an elaborate second floor porch and an Eastern European style tower that complements the porch. The second floor porch has a delicate balustrade that has a three quarter moon opening on the side which is a style of ornamentation that Moon only used once in his career. In the first image of 215 W. Allegan you can see that the roof had an ironwork cresting and an ornate finial on the end. There is also a weathervane at the peak of the tower. The first floor porch follows the pattern of previous porches in homes that Moon designed with three columns at the corner and a pair toward the center. The home also has fish scale siding on the third floor front gable. This is a remarkable home when you consider that it was used by Keith as a rental property. Keith probably intended to rent the home to members of the state house and senate. With the construction of the new Federal Building and Post office in 1932, Keith's home was moved to S. Walnut and William, see (*LSJ* 1/26/1932).[99] Unfortunately even moving the home to 830 S. Walnut would not preserve the structure. The home, was lost to the expansion of GM's Grand River Plant.[100]

---

99 The *City of Lansing Records for Moved Buildings* has 315 W. Allegan being moved to Walnut and Willow, which was not the case, see 1/18/1932, 315 W Allegan to Walnut and Willow Permit 335 Lansing Building and Safety.
100 The *City of Lansing Records for Moved Buildings*, see 1/7/1932, 207 S. Walnut to 215 S. Butler Permit 334 Lansing Building and Safety. See also *LSJ* 1/26/1932.

207 S. Walnut, Lansing, MI

The final home that George Keith owned was on the corner Allegan street and Walnut street, specifically at 207 S. Walnut. It was moved in 1932 to 215 S. Butler. Unfortunately the home was lost due to the building of the State of Michigan complex. The above image is after the home was moved to 215 S. Butler.[101] The home at 207 S. Walnut was a simple cross gable home. In the above image the enclosed porch was added at a later date, the original porch was open and may have wrapped around the side. On the second floor front gable you can just make out the vertical siding that extends halfway down the front.

George A. Keith died in Dearborn, Michigan on May 14, 1919 after a long illness and his body was returned to Lansing for burial.[102] He was born in Mansfield, Ohio in May 1843 and served with the 88th Indiana Infantry Regiment, Company D throughout the Civil War. After mustering out of the army George married Miss Mary J. Pratt on December 14, 1865 in Allen, Indiana. Mary was related to Walter Pratt, another Lansing resident whose home was designed by Moon. The couple would have two children, Wilber J. and Charles S. Keith. What is also interesting is that George's brother Frank and his wife Addella live with George and Mary from 1900 until George's death. It may be that the home at 315 W. Allegan was meant to be Frank's home but the brothers realized that both homes were far larger than either couple needed. George and his brother Frank were successful Lansing businessman, both as contractors and later in real estate. The *State Republican* relates an interesting story about George Keith that speaks to his personality.
"No one in Lansing who knows George Keith ever doubted his hunting or fishing stories, but during a recent visit here he told such remarkable tales about the immense potatoes he raised in the upper peninsula that some people actually felt that George was stretching the truth, to say the least. This was too much for George, so on his arrival home he shipped a barrel of his tubers to a friend. It took just 164 of the potatoes to fill the barrel, and George writes his large ones are all gone, those he sent being a few small ones he had saved for seed."[103] In Moon's 1904 City Directory advertisement listed Geo. Keith as one of the gentlemen for whom he designed a home.

From the Gould inventory of Darius Moon Buildings, listed as "3 Hses for George Keith, 1898."

---

101   Of all the homes in the 300 block of West Allegan the only one that survives is 311 W. Allegan which was moved to 616 W. Genesee. Although not a Darius Moon designed home it is a wonderful structure. See *SJ* 1/26/1932 and *LSJ* 10/16/1949.
102   *LSJ* 5/16/1919.
103   *SR* 6/2/1894.

CHRISTIAN E. STABLER HOUSE

115 (109) N. Chestnut, Lansing, MI

The *Lansing Journal* states that "Christian E. Stabler intends to remodel the residence on Chestnut street north which he recently purchased from L.A. Baker" (*LJ* 3/5/1898). The home at 115 N. Chestnut, was owned by Lafayette A. Baker and built prior to 1891. Unfortunately we do not know what the home looked like prior to its remodeling, therefore we do not know the extent of Moon's work. This is a wonderful home and is best described as an organic house with Victorian and Queen Anne architectural elements. On the side clipped gable is a finial cap in the style of one that would crown a tower, in this case in completes the end of the roofline. The second floor porch has three columns at the corner, but they seem crowded, and the projecting brackets on the second floor porch as well as the third floor clipped gable seem out of place. It would be different if the brackets were carried around the second floor trim as dentils would be, but the placement of the brackets is irregular. Keep is mind all comments are based upon the quality of the photographs that survive and in this case, it is a poor quality image. As a side note, it seems in the above image that the house has Sherriff Goslin style shingle; you can clearly make them out in the image of the Porte-cochère.

Porte-cochère at 115 N. Chestnut, Lansing, MI

Christian E. Stabler died at his home 412 W. Ottawa Street on January 26, 1955 at the age of 95. He had been a resident of Lansing for 89 years, coming as a young boy from near Ann Arbor. Christian was born on December 20, 1859 to Jon Jacob and Carolina (née Cook) Stabler on a farm twelve miles outside of Ann Arbor, Michigan. In 1866 the family relocated to a farm seven miles north-west of Lansing. Christian as a young man moved to Minnesota where he worked in a flour mill until 1882. Returning to Lansing he was employed at the Jordan brick yard. After carefully husbanding his funds Christian purchased 405 acres of timber south of Waverly Park where Christian would cut timber and sell it to the growing market in Lansing. After he had increased his personal wealth, Christian entered into the wood and coal retail business, partnered with Robert B. Woodard and established their business on the site of the old Oakland building. Woodard would leave the company and Christian would partner with his brother Charles F. Stabler. The rapid growth of the business forced the brothers to move the company to 636-638 E. Michigan Avenue. With the retirement of both brothers, management of C.E. Stabler & Company would be assumed by Christian's son-in-law, Clarence E. Dale. After retirement Christian was treasurer of the Capital Realty Company, owned the Stabler & Young Company and was a trustee of the Central Methodist Episcopal Church. On November 23, 1887 Christian married Miss Kate S. Epley in Muskingum, Ohio. The couple would have two children, Milburn Epley and Irma. [104]

The construction of the Capitol Complex office buildings resulted in the home at 115 N. Chestnut being moved in 1953 to 2123 W. St Josephs. Unfortunately the home was later torn down and the site is now a parking lot. In 1916 Moon would design another home for Christian Stabler.

From the Gould inventory of Darius Moon Buildings, listed as "C.E. Stabbins Hse, 1898".

---

104   *LSJ* 1/27/1955 and (Turner 666).

ETTA GLICMAN STORE

117-119 N. Washington, Lansing, MI

"The work of placing a new front in the store of I. Glicman, Washington avenue north, was begun this morning" (*SR* 9/24/1897). The Glicman family for many years would run a large and successful dry goods store in Lansing at 117-119 N Washington Avenue. ISRael Glicman established the dry goods store in the early 1880s with Nymon E. Yesner and later ISRael became the sole owner. The only image of the Glicman store that survives has been pulled out of a much larger image. Glicman's store is the white colored building in the above photograph. There is little that can be said about the remodel because of the limitations of the image. Later photographs of 119 N. Washington show a much later designed building which has the name Kedzie chiseled into a stone on the façade. Later 119 N. Washington was torn down and replaced with the W. T. Grant store which is now the downtown Y.M.C.A.

```
               OUR MOTTO
                 ❧ IS ❧
           SELL GOOD GOODS AT
               LOW PRICES
           Don't Buy Cheap Goods
         They are the Dearest in the End
```

OUR GOODS
ARE NEW   AND
             UP-TO-DATE

And Our Prices are the Lowest

E. GLICMAN   119 Washington Ave. North

Glicman Dry Goods advertisement 1898 Oracle

The management of the business fell to ISRael's wife Etta after ISRael had been injured in a street car accident in Lansing that damaged his spine as well as leading to crippling "nervous troubles". About the same time of his accident ISRael suffered a series of business and real estate losses brought on by a nationwide recession. ISRael's decline accelerated, both physically and mentally. In March of 1903 the building and its inventory was sold to William J Dancer, William Brogan, Harmon S Holmes and the Holmes, Dancer & Brogan Company was established.[105]

The Glicman family would move to Detroit where they eventually settled at 1056 Cass Avenue. On that fateful day, October 26, 1909 Etta left the home to have treatment on an injured knee while ISRael was left in the care of a maid. It was at this time that a despondent ISRael Glicman committed suicide by drinking a bottle of carbolic acid. ISRael was survived by his wife Etta, two sons, Morey and Henry and a daughter Mrs. Emma Mendelson of Brooklyn, N.Y.[106] From the Gould inventory of Darius Moon Buildings, listed as "Glickman Store remodeled, No Date".

---

105   *LJ* 3/26/1903.
106   For ISRael Glicman see *LJ* 10/27/1909, *Detroit Free Press* 10/27/1909 and the *Detroit News* 10/27/1909. For Etta see the *Detroit Free Press* 3/9/1926 and the *Detroit News* 3/9/1926.

GOVERNOR'S GUARD ARMORY

115-117 E. Ottawa, Lansing, MI

Built in 1898 a full description of the inside of the armory is presented because it is only one of a few extensive narratives of the interior of Moon's work that survives. The Grand Dedicatory Reception for the Governor's Guard Armory was attended by Governor Haze S. Pingree, his military staff and a who's who of Lansing society. The dedication/dance was considered the most brilliant social event ever to occur in the capitol city."

"The present armory is easy of access the rooms occupied by the Guards being reached by a stairway five feet wide from the entrance on Ottawa street, which is at the east side of the building. At the top of the stairs are two hallways, one running north and south and leading to the drill hall on the third floor, the other running east and west and leading to the parlors, banquet hall and officer quarters. The hallway running east and west is 11 feet wide and is handsomely completes. The first room to the left as you go down this hallway is a ticket office, to be used by the Guards when occasion demands. The parlor is the next room on the left is 16x24 feet. It is handsomely carpeted and furnished and in the center of the room is a circular seat, which makes an attractive lounging place for the boys. The side walls are handsomely decorated in terra cotta, while the ceiling is beautifully tinted. Off the parlor, on the east is the library, a room 14x18 feet, which is carpeted and furnished to correspond with the parlor, with which it is connected by an archway. A large bookcase, well filled, stands against the north wall, and the walls are finished in terra cotta, the same as the parlor. On the west of the parlor are the card and billiard rooms which are connected by archways and are entered from the parlors through folding doors. The card room is 14x24 feet and the billiard room is 22x24 feet, large enough to contain two billiard tables recently purchased by the Guards. On the west wall of the billiard room hangs a picture of the company which is 5x7 feet, and was recently made by R. Ellison. The walls of these rooms are decorated a dark green, while the ceiling is tinted in a light smoke color. On the right of this large hall is a ladies' cloak and toilet room, nicely papered and lighted. Further along is the banquet hall which is 22x60 feet, and is well lighted. The walls are handsomely decorated in blue, and the ceiling being of a lighter tint. The room is also to be used for a meeting room and gymnasium. West of the banquet hall and at the rear of the building is a kitchen, 16x21 feet, which is being fitted up with a sink, supplied with both hot and cold water and contains a large cupboard for the storage of viands[Viands Provisions; victuals] of various kinds. Walls are of a light terra cotta and ceiling of a light grey. The end of the large hall running east and west has been cut off by a railing and coat racks placed on the wall, making a very handy cloak room for the benefit of the social members of the company. The Lansing Telephone Company has placed a telephone near the cloak room for the convenience of both social and active members. On the west side of the building is another building is another hallway running north and leading to the quarters of the commissioned and non-commissioned officers and the bath room. The commissioned officers' quarters is a room 15x15 feet. It contains a wardrobe for uniforms and a secretary for writing and filling papers. The room is neatly carpeted and furnished. The walls are of terra cotta, while the ceiling is a light drab. The room for the non-commissioned officers is of the same size as that of the commissioned officers and also contains lockers and is carpeted and furnished throughout in good taste. The walls are a light blue, while the ceiling is covered with a light flowered design. Next comes the bathroom, which is wainscoted with Southern pine and contains one bath tub, besides a shower bath, wash stand and closet. The tub and shower baths are for the use of both social and active members. This completes the description of the rooms in this part of the building and one is compelled to go back to the entrance to reach the hallway running north and south. In this hallway, before reaching the stairway which leads to the drill hall, are rooms of the privates and quartermaster of the company. The private's room is 14x30 feet and contains lockers for uniforms and equipment. To the rear of this room is the quartermaster's department, where is stored the property belonging to the company. It is 14x30 feet, and gives ample space for its handy arrangement of the company's effects. The drill hall is a beauty. You climb the stairs to the third floor of the building and enter a room the dimensions of which are 64x98 feet, making it the largest and finest hall in the city, if not the State. A gallery 8 feet wide for the use of spectators has been placed on three sides of the room—the east, west and north. It in no way interferes with the drilling of the company, as it has been placed high enough to avoid coming in contact with the guns of the Guards. A wainscoting of Southern pine has been placed around the entire room, while the gallery has been finished in the same material. The floor is made of quartered sawed Georgia pine and is one of the finest in the city for dancing purposes. An elegant stairway, built entirely of Southern pine and handsomely embellished with scroll work, is situated in the north east corner of the room and leads to the gallery, while in the north west corner of the room is a nicely fitted up ladies' dressing and toilet room. Large trusses support the roof and gallery running east and west across the room. They have been neatly painted to contrast with the walls and ceiling and impress one with the idea at once that the building is substantially constructed. Five arc lights brilliantly illuminate this large room, and taken altogether it makes one of the handsomest drill hall in the state. The carpets and house furnishings used in the armory were supplied by Burcham & Company, while the furniture was purchased of M.J. & B.N. Buck" (*LJ* 1/27/1898 see also the *SR* 1/27/1898 for a shorter description).

"In its write up of the Governor's Guard Armory by the JOURNAL last night the name of the architect, D.B. Moon was unintentionally omitted" (*LJ* 1/28/1898).

115-117 E. Ottawa in the later 1950s

IS PERFECTLY SAFE
Architect Moon says the New Armory Building is All Right

"Architect D.B. Moon, who supervised the construction of the new armory, says there seems to be a great many people badly disappointed because the building did not fall down and kill someone, the night of the reception. In a communication to the REPUBLICAN, Mr. Moon says the building was under his supervision from start to finish and that nothing was left undone to make a complete job. That the building is perfectly safe and that people who are croaking about its being unsafe don't know what they're talking about" (*SR* 2/1/1898).

It is interesting that Moon felt the need to publically defend his architectural competence. The first instance was the Fifth Ward School, then the Governor's Guard Armory. This was not unique to Moon, Bowd was criticized for his design of the Michigan Building at the St. Louis World's Fair. It is always easier to criticize than to create. Moon understood this but there was something in his personality that would not brook any disparagement of his work.

The Governor's Guard, Company E was organized in Detroit on March 1, 1876 in the Senate chamber of Michigan's first Capitol. Several days later, on March 17 the company was mustered in with 57 men, by General Trowbridge of Detroit on the evening of March 17, 1874. After 1874 the company was commonly referred to as the Lansing Light Guard. The company was employed to provide order during the strike in Jackson, Michigan in 1877. In 1898 the Governor's Guard was became part of the First Regiment of the Michigan National Guard, Company E.

From the Gould inventory of Darius Moon Buildings, listed as "Armory for State Troops-Lansing, No Date".

MICHAEL BAUERMAN HOUSE

1174 Grand River, Meridian Township, MI

"Architect D.B. Moon of this city has completed plans for a $4,000 country residence for M.H. Bowerman of Williamston, who is well known in Lansing. It is to be built on a farm two miles east of Okemos and the barns and surrounding will be in perfect harmony with the residence. Contractor T.G. Beebee was here this morning and closed the contract with H.W. Rikerd for the interior finish for the residence" (*SR* 9/24/1898). The date on the article is interesting.[107]

"B.A. Liverance has leased M.H. Bowerman's residence and will occupy it as soon as vacated. Mr. Bowerman expects in April to move on his farm five miles west of here, where he has erected a fine $6,000 residence" (*SR* 4/1/1899).

---

[107] See also "M. H. Bowerman's house is progressing nicely" *Ingham County Democrat* 9/22/1898.

Michael Bauerman residence detail

This extensive county house was built in 1898 for Michael Bowerman (Bauerman) a Quaker who purchased the land in 1877, plus the surrounding 175 acres for $1000. This must have been a magnificent house to view in its prime; it had over 8000 square feet of living space as stated by the Towne Courier in 1988. These are the only images that has been located on this massive home, it is doubtful if it was 8000 square feet of living space, but it is possible, at one time the home served as an inn on the Detroit to Lansing plank road. Unique features include the rough hew foundation and the two story canted bay window with the conical tower. Look closely, it is in the center of the image. This is a wonderful example of an organic Queen Anne style home. It is unfortunate that a photograph of the opposite side of the home. was unable to be located.

1174 Grand River, Meridian Twp, MI

At the time of his death, Michael H. Bowerman was considered one of the wealthiest men in Ingham County. Little is known about his early life; Michael was born in New York to Silias and Lydia Bowerman on October 1, 1831. It is unknown when Michael moved to Ingham County or his profession. In the 1880 Federal Census he gives his occupation as a furniture dealer. On March 30, 1875, Michael married Mrs. Sophronia M. Revenaugh Sackrider, the widow of Edward B. Sackrider in Williamston, Michigan. The couple had four children: two daughters, Birdie and Permelie [Tie], and two sons, Jay S. and Willard I., the only child to live to a ripe old age. Michael Hoag Bowerman passed away at his country residence on June 21st, 1900. Sophronia would live the next 24 years as a widow. In 1903 Sophronia and her surviving children moved to Lansing where Willard attended high school. Sophronia was heavily involved in the Women's Christian Temperance Union; she organized the Ingham County Branch, the Y.W.C.A. and the Baptist Church. Mrs. Sophronia M. Bowerman passed away at her home on Monday February 18, 1924. Of the four Bowerman children, two died at a young age and a third took her own life. Jay S. Bowerman died after contracting pneumonia at the age of seven in 1883 and his sister Birdie died at birth in 1894. Permelie better known as Tie, would marry Sarles F. Edwards in January 1906 and the couple would have three children. In 1920 Tie would suffer a complete breakdown and four years later take her own life at the couple's home on Ionia Street.[108]

Michael Bauerman House, notice the finial on the tower.

The house had been used as a hippie pad in the 1960s and in the early 1970s and then sat unoccupied. There were several attempts at preserving the home, but all failed; the cost of moving the home was prohibitive. The point was moot when the home was destroyed by fire on April 1, 1988.[109]

From the Gould inventory of Darius Moon Buildings, listed as "Bauerman Residence (Country), 1892".

---
108   For Michael Bowerman see *Ingham County Democrat* 6/28/1900, his wife, Sophronia see the *LSJ* 2/19/1924 and for Tie see the *LSJ* 8/19/1924.
109   See the *Towne Courier* 4/23/1986, the *LSJ* 4/2/1988 and the *Towne Courier* 4/6/1988.

1899

WILLIAM COTTRELL HOUSE, RILEY TOWNSHIP, CLINTON COUNTY, MI

"Architect D.B. Moon of this city is making plans for a residence for William Cottrell, Riley" (*SR* 9/25/1899).

This may be William Cottrell of Macomb County, Michigan. On October 2, 1866 William married Miss Georgia Macomber in Macomb, Michigan. Georgia Macomber Cottrell received large sums of money from her father George Macomber which William Cottrell managed as his own. Later in 1877 George Macomber gave his daughter between $75,000 and $100,000 which was again administered by her husband William. When Georgia died on August 29, 1900 the money that Georgia Macomber Cottrell had according to William Cottrell was valued by him as amounting to $137. William had carefully moved all of Georgia's money under his control and the value of Georgia's estate should have been about $300,000 plus. William remarried on November 7, 1901 to Miss Mary L. Snook in Harrison Township, Michigan. William Cottrell passed away on August 11, 1907, at Grace Hospital in Detroit after an operation to remove a tumor.[110] After his death his estate was valued at $800,000 plus. Joseph Wolford, of Lansing, controlled William's personal accounting ledger and withheld it from the Macomber family. In the court case of Macomber v. Cottrell, the Supreme Court of Michigan does shed some light on William Cottrell's land holdings. There were no properties listed in Clinton County. But the 1900 tax assessment rolls for Riley Township, shows that Joseph Wolford agent, paid the taxes on the East ½ Southeast ¼ Section 34 Township 6N 3W and West 2/5 South ¾ Southwest ¼ Section 35 Township 6N 3W, the NE and NW corners of W. Howe Road and Lowell Road. Was Joseph helping William Cottrell to hide assets from the Macomber family?

"Mr. Cottrell made a will a few days before he went to hospital. The document has not been published, but it is known that he makes an old friend at Lansing executer" (Mt. Clemens Monitor 8/16/1907).

It seems quite possible that Wolford was paying the taxes on these properties to hide the assets of William Cottrell. There are no residential structures on either property today, but there was once was a home on the eastern section. Moon would later design a home for Joseph Wolford in 1908.

---

110   *Detroit News* 8/12/1907 and *Detroit Free Press* 8/12/1907. For the saga of Mrs. Cottrell estate see the *Detroit Free Press* April 21, 1901 and (*Northwestern* 127: 402).

JOHN VOISELLE STORE

John Voiselle Store the one story building with the 'painters' sign, 121 E. Michigan, Lansing, MI

A record has yet to be found of Moon doing any design for Mr. Voiselle. In fact in 1897 Architect Edwyn Bowd drew up plans for a new building for Voiselle on Michigan Avenue, who lived above his store. The Gould list says that Moon designed something for John Voiselle in 1899. Could this be a case of Moon preparing plans that were not accepted?

John B. Voiselle was born in Quebec on May 27, 1844 the son of John Voiselle and Sophin (née Bedaur). He came to Lansing in 1877 after leading an eventful life. At one point Voiselle served in the Ninth Battalion of the Quebec Volunteers at the time of the Fenian Raid into Canada in 1866. John came to Lansing in 1877 and worked painting and doing fresco work and the new Capitol. Later he partnered with Joseph Larose and formed the company Voiselle & Larose, a firm that specializes in fine interior finishes and painting. In early 1901 John Voiselle left Lansing for Everett, Washington. Just why he did this is unknown because he had a thriving business in Lansing. Voiselle died in Everett Washington on April 24 1907 of heart trouble; his body was taken by his nephew, Eugene Drolet to Quebec for burial.[111] The Portrait and Biographical Album: of Ingham and Livingston Counties, states that John Voiselle owned five residences on Allegan and Pine Streets in 1891 and devoted time to his real estate investments. He also owned property in Detroit and Petoskey. It is quite possible that Moon designed a home for John Voiselle outside of Lansing. From the Gould inventory of Darius Moon Buildings, listed as "John Vaisell Hse, 1899".

---

111   *Everett Daily Herald* 4/24/1907.

1900

OLDS MOTOR WORKS, LANSING, MI

Olds Motor Works, Lansing, MI

The Gould Inventory of Darius Moon Builds indicates that Moon designed "Most of the buildings Olds Motor wks., 1900" the construction of these building will be covered in the 1903 section. In 1899 the Lansing papers recorded that Fred Thoman a young Lansing architect designed the building for the Olds Factory in Detroit, so the dates on the Gould list are incorrect or Moon submitted designs that were not accepted.[112]

---

112   SR 6/10/1899.

JOHN WILSON

210 S. Logan (MLK), Lansing, MI

After reviewing all the data regarding which John Wilson Moon designed a home for in 1900, there is only one candidate, John S. Wilson. Although John S. Wilson lived at a number of different homes between 1898 and 1904 the only property he owned in 1900-1901 was Lot 1 Block 2 and the South ½ of Lot 2 Block 2 in the Kempf's Addition or 210 S. Logan. John lived at [113]

The home seems to be a simple cross gable home but it is not. Notice the roof line. There is a large structure that extended from the north side of the home forming an extensive structure on that side, which has a pyramid roof. Unfortunately the house has been torn down and this is the only surviving image of the structure. If you look closely you can see a bay window at the back of the porch. There is also shingle siding on the gable ends at the top while the remainder of the home is sided. In a sense the home is a plain stick style residence, one of the few Moon designed. The other intriguing aspect was that it was built in the area with the highest concentration of Moon designed homes in the Lansing area.

John S. Wilson was born December 13, 1871 in Ashland, Nebraska, the son of Seth and Pricilla (née Munsell) Wilson. After the death of her husband in 1874, Pricilla moved with John to Courtland, Illinois, two years later they relocated to Charlotte, Michigan. In 1889 John moved to Lansing to work for Marple-French-McGrath Company, a wholesale confectioner company.[114] After the failure of the candy company John would work briefly for the Capital Wagon Works as a receiving clerk and moved with the company when it relocated to Ionia.

---

113   *SR* 12/26/1900, *LJ* 12/26/1900 and *SR* 5/18/1901.
114   The Marple-French-McGrath Company went bankrupt in 1892 see *LJ* 3/22/1893.

On February 23, 1893 John married Miss Flora F. Flitton of Grand Ledge. Flora was born in Ross County, Ohio, the daughter of John F. and Elizabeth (née Leeher) Flitton. Soon after the marriage John and Flora returned to Lansing where they supervised cottage number four at the Boys' Industrial School, John worked as a carpenter and Flora as a teacher. In 1898 John purchased Cyril Blatt's confectionery store at 201 S. Washington, which he renamed the 'Sugar Bowl', later in 1903 he moved the store to 106 S. Washington. John S. Wilson later sold the business to Alex Andros in 1910. That same year John built the Wilson Block at 201 S. Washington. Between 1903-1910 John also managed Waverly Park in association with the street railway company and was involved in a variety of other businesses; a skating rink, designed by Moon, on East Ottawa Street with his partner Sigel David Kopf, the Colonial Theater with Charles Davis, the True Blue Gum Company and many others. Three years after the death of his wife Flora, John married Miss Mary French of Flushing, Michigan and they had one son George who passed away in 1922. John S. Wilson was active in civic affairs, he served on the police and fire commissions and was a member of the Lansing Lodge of Elks and twice served as exalted ruler of the lodge. John died at his home on Saturday, August 16, 1941.[115]

From the Gould Inventory of Darius Moon Builds list that Moon designed "John Wilson Hse., 1900."

FRANK MOORE'S HOUSE

Frank I. Moore House, 929 N. Washington, Lansing, MI

The whole saga regarding just which Frank Moore Moon designed a home for has been quite a challenge. Just like the residence Moon designed for the Frank Moore house in 1887 there are two options, Frank

---

115 See *SR* 1/26/1898, *LSJ* 8/16/1941 and Turner 721.

I. Moore and Frank W. Moore. Between the years 1887 and 1900 Frank W. Moore moved to 102 W. Willow; however this home was built well before 1900. In 1900 Frank I. Moore was still residing at 929 N. Washington Avenue. It seems likely that Moon renovated Frank I. Moore's home at 929 N. Washington. In the 1901 tax assessment rolls Frank W. Moore is listed as owning just one property, 102 W. Willow, while Frank I. Moore owned Lot 13, Block 42 or 1034 N Washington, where quite an intriguing house was later built in 1903. Most of the property held by Frank I. Moore's family was in his wife's name, Sarah J. Moore. It may be that her husband, in his role as city assessor did not want any hint of impropriety, or perhaps Sarah was a wealthy woman in her own right.

Detail of the porch at 929 N. Washington

Frank I. Moore's residence was an elegant Italianate style house. The ornate porch was the focal point of the exterior of the house. The intricate turnings on the porch frieze and bracket carvings blend well with the other aspects of the porch. Moon, instead of using the traditional bracketing throughout the Italianate design incorporated dentils into the porch and the eaves of the roof. In fact the design integrated two different size brackets. As can be seen in the image of the home, this makes for a pleasing appearance when viewed from the street. This is accentuated by the half circle window above the double second floor windows; notice the detailed stonework above the windows. When viewing photographs of the residence there are several architectural elements that stand out: the two story bay window on the south side of the home and on the north side a two story canted bay window that balances the home. Finally an undated description of the home tells us that the residence had fourteen rooms and a winding staircase. Frank I. Moore's house at 929 N Washington was torn down to create a parking lot.

Frank Iredell Moore 1831-1912

Frank I. Moore was a resident of Lansing for more than forty years and he was known throughout the city, having served as city assessor and as a successful businessman. He was born in Lyman, New Hampshire on January 26, 1831. As a young man he worked for the Pennsylvania Railroad, and then moved west working in Ohio and finally settling in Michigan in 1870 where he worked for the Detroit, Lansing & Northern

Railway. After he left the railroad, Moore became partners with Dr. J. H. Wellings and they opened a drug store in North Lansing. Later Hiram C. Hedges joined the partnership and the business flourished. Frank would marry Miss Sarah J. Koons in 1869; they had three children, Benjamin F., Roy S., and Inez J. Moore. In 1880 he was elected Lansing City Assessor, a position that he held for seven consecutive years. Later in life he would be elected assessor nine more times. In 1888 he opened a lumber yard in North Lansing which several years later he sold to the Capital Lumber Company. It was in turn acquired by Rikerd Lumber Company. Frank would again open a drug store and a dry goods store in North Lansing. After his retirement from business Moore spent his time reading and playing his old Jacoby Steiner [Jacobus Stainer] violin. On Friday, May 17 1912, Frank I. Moore passed away at his home preceded in death by his wife Sarah.[116]

From the Gould inventory of Darius Moon Buildings, listed as "Frank Moore Hse, 1900".

HARRIS TURNER HOUSE

313 W. Allegan, Lansing, MI (A.G.)

Harry (Harris) B. Turner house was built according to the Gould list in 1900. "Harry B. Turner will remodel quite extensively his residence on Allegan street west" (*LJ* 3/5/1898). Could this extensive remodeling have resulted in an entire reconstruction of the house? The home has the same footprint in the 1898 Sanborn map as it does in the 1906 Sanborn. This factor in itself is not conclusive and the home could have been totally reconstructed by Moon in 1900. Turner was listed as living at this address as early as 1894. In 1932 the Turner house, at that time the parsonage for First Presbyterian Church, was torn down due to the construction of the new post office.

---

116   Frank I. Moore see *LSJ* 5/17/1912, for Sarah J. Moores' death see *LSJ* 10/19/1911.

The home is a simple gable home with an added tower and an extended porch. There seems to be much more to the home but there is not. The porch with the three column corners extends on the east side to the base of the tower. The tower seems added, almost as if it was an addition, and seems out of place as it does not blend with the rest of the structure. The clipped gable and the third floor oriel window bring together the gable end structure. Overall this was not, to a 21st Century eye, a successful remodel on the exterior; the interior may be a different story.

Harris B. Turner was born in Attica, New York on April 7, 1841 the son of Charles B. and Caroline (née Duson?) Turner. He moved with his parents to Coldwater, Michigan and worked with his brother, Colonel George H. Turner in their drug store. Later, Harris was appointed to the State Land Office where he remained for eight years. After leaving the Land Office, he briefly partnered with Frank Wells in a drug store. Harris returned to state employment working for the State Board of Health, where he remained for twenty-six years. On July 29, 1879 he married Emma Louise Peck. Harris B. Turner died at his home on November 30, 1905; he was survived by his wife and daughter Mabelle, his brother Colonel George H Turner, commander of the Soldier's Home in Grand Rapids and his brother John F. Turner of Newaygo.[117]

From the Gould inventory of Darius Moon Buildings, listed as "Harry Turner House, 1900".

COLGROVE'S OPERA HOUSE

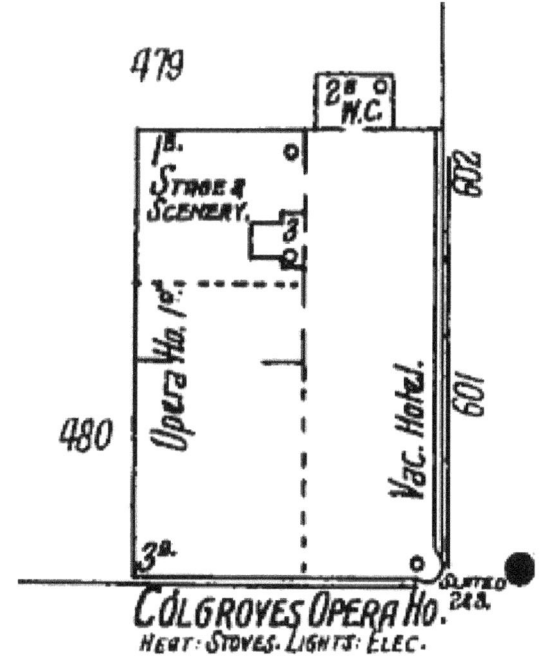

101-105 N. Michigan (Creek), Opera House and Armory, Hastings, MI

"Architect D.B. Moon of Lansing, has made plans for a brick and stone opera house and armory to be built at Hastings" (*DFP* 3/11/1900).

---

117   SR 11/30/1905.

101-105 N. Michigan (Creek), Barry Hotel, Hastings, MI

On the N.E. Corner of E. State and N. Michigan (Creek) stood the Colgrove's Opera House in October of 1900 according to the Sanborn Map of Hastings, Michigan, now the site of Hastings' City Hall. By 1908 it was the Hotel Mudge and in 1909 the site was occupied by the Barry Hotel. Notice the architectural elements with this building and compare them from Moon's other buildings, the fluting on the brickwork on the columns and the arched window on the first floor. This was in all likelihood a remodeling of the structure that was there in 1898. The tower with its striking dome was an addition that was not present on the 1898 Sanborn footprint for the building. It is interesting to observe that the caps on the facing columns mimic the dome on the main tower. It is unfortunate that the structure no longer stands. The Gould list gives the date of construction as 1906 which presents a problem, this may be a typo or that Moon was also hired by Colgrove to remodel the building into a hotel in 1906.

From the Gould inventory of Darius Moon Buildings, listed as "Casgrove Theater, 1906".

Philip Taylor Colgrove, 1857-1930

Philip Taylor Colgrove was born in Winchester, Indiana on April 17, 1857 to Charles H. and Catherine (née Van Zile) Colgrove. As a young man Philip attended Olivet College where he excelled in literary studies while at the same time, studied law under the guidance of H.P. Pennington of Charlotte. At the age of 21 Philip was admitted to the state, in 1879 Philip moved to Hastings and formed a partnership with Clement Smith. In 1893 Smith was appointed to a judgeship and the partnership was dissolved and Philip partnered with William M. Potter and the firm of Colgrove & Potter, was established. In 1892 Philip was elected prosecuting attorney for Barry County, a position he held until his election the state senate in 1888, in 1890 he refused to be renominated. Colgrove had extensive business interests in Barry County; he was President of the Hastings Iron Company, and the Hastings Table Company, as well as Director of the Hastings Shoe Company and the Hastings City Bank. On March 6, 1879 in Hasting Philip married Miss Rose Evangeline and the couple would have two children, Mabel and Lawrence Colgrove. In 1897 Philip and Rose divorced and Philip married Miss Carrie M. Goodyear on April 28, 1897. In Michigan, Philip is remembered as President of the Michigan Good Roads Association which sought to provide safe highways for Michigan residents. On February 10, 1930 after working in his office in the morning, Philip attended the Rotary Club meeting at noon during which he fell from his chair. Doctors McIntyre and Woodburne rushed to his aid but it was quickly determined that Philip T. Coldgrove had died instantly from a heart attack. [118]

---

118   *The American Bar*, J.C. Fifield Company, 1918, page 314, *Men of Progress: Biographical Sketches of Representative Michigan Men*. Evening News Association, Detroit, 1900, page 295 and the *Hastings Banner* 2/12/1930.

FREDERICK P. SCHROEDER HOME

303 N. Court, Howell, MI

"Architect D.B. Moon of Lansing,... Also made plans for a frame residence for Frederick P. Schroeder of Howell" (*DFP* 3/11/1900). This is a text book style Queen Anne home. Notice how the windows are stacked symmetrically, even on the bay window and the bump out on the north side. The window on the front gable which is surround by fish scale siding is interesting; it is best described as a Georgian style window. The porch is very light and does not overwhelm the home, it also gracefully wraps around the home. The home was meant to impress and it does.

Frederick P. Schroeder was born in Berlin, Ontario, Canada on January 20, 1855 to Henry and Johannah (née Weybrauch) Schroeder. When Frederick was one his parents moved to Detroit, Michigan where Frederick spent his childhood and his father plied his trade as a tinsmith. Frederick attended the German Lutheran School in Detroit and at the age of twelve he began delivering packages for the crockery store of R. W. King. In 1867 Frederick started his apprenticeship to the tinner's trade; in 1870 he became a journeyman tinner in Detroit. In about 1874 Frederick took a job with Cook & Laughlin of Fowlerville, Michigan. The firm dissolved after 6 months and Frederick managed the business for Laughlin for six years. Leaving the employ of Laughlin, Frederick worked for S. L. Bignall & Company, of Chicago selling hardware throughout the Midwest. After a year on the road Frederick returned to Fowlerville and purchased a half interest in Hugh Laughlin's business and the firm of Laughlin & Schroeder was established. After four years Frederick sold out his interest in this business and moved to Howell and established a hardware store at the corner of Walnut and Grand River. On July 18, 1882 Frederick married Miss Jennie E. Naylor a school teacher in Howell. It is said that Frederick remained in Howell at the request of his wife. Jennie passed away on January

12, 1903. Frederick remarried on September 14, 1904 to Mrs. Defolia Krause who passed away on May 21, 1910. In 1912 Frederick formed a partnership with J.J. Rutka of Grand Rapids who took over the operational management of the business. Frederick was active in the business until July of 1918 when he suffered a stroke, which paralyzed one side of his body and left him unable to speak. In September of 1918 Frederick was thrown from a buggy he was riding in and sustained a compound fracture of his arm. Eight days after the accident Frederick P. Schroeder passed away on September 23, 1918.[119]

1901

EDWARD N. REITZ HOUSE

809 W. Ionia, Lansing, MI

Built in 1901 for Lansing industrialist Edward N. Reitz, President of Beilfuss Motor Company and Queen Bee Cigar Company, Moon would later design a new building for the Beilfuss Motor Company on East Saginaw Street. It is a testament to Moon's professionalism that many of his patrons or their families used his services several times.

"…W.N. Reitz will build a residence on Ionia st." (*SR* 3/18/1901). "Architect D.B. Moon has just completed a handsome residence on Ionia st w. for E.N. Reitz. The building is of red brick, and is finished throughout in golden oak" (*SR* 11/14/01).

---

[119] *Livingston Republican* 9/25/1918 and the *Portrait and Biographical Album Ingham & Livingston Counties Michigan* p 762.

809 W. Ionia detail

At first glance the residence has many of the characteristics of a Queen Anne home, however it really isn't, it is an example of an Organic House. What sets it apart from the definition of a Queen Anne style home is that the structure is brick. While it's true there are some Queen Anne's that are brick, it's usually only on the first floor. The other aspect is the rough stone columns that support the porch. There are two bay windows, an appealing two-sided oriel window and the brackets that support the window blend well with the structure. In the above photograph, the second floor porch, you can see the vase style columns and the sunburst detail that frames the upper window. The above image was taken just prior to the destruction of the home; you can see that one of the brackets has been removed from under the soffit. Finally it is worth observing in the lower photograph the detail of the front porch. The use of the flat stones to create a rail with an open balustrade is quite ingenious.

Edward N. Reitz 1867-1946

Edward N. Reitz was born in Indiana in 1867. His parents Frank A. and Mary L. (née Zelt) Reitz moved with their growing family to Lansing in late 1867. Frank A. Reitz partnered with his brother-in-law Fredrick Thoman and established the Oriental Milling Company in Lansing. After 18 months in partnership, Fredrick Thoman sold his interest in the business to Frank. Unfortunately Frank died six months later on December 20, 1870. After Frank's death Fredrick Thoman repurchased the mill from Mary Reitz and the foundation for the Thoman Milling Company was established.

809 W. Ionia, just after completion (A.G.)

In 1872 Mary L. Reitz married John C. Schneider (Snyder) who adopted Mary's five children; she would bear John six children of his own, one of whom, Frieda Schneider would become the first woman elected to a governmental office in Lansing, becoming the city Treasurer in 1920. Edward N Reitz would marry Celia A Northup Bill in Lansing on May 16, 1899. The couple would adopt a young boy who they named Merle V. Reitz. Through hard work and business savvy, Edward established the Queen Bee Cigar Company and then became the manager of the Beilfuss Motor Company. Later in life Edward would retire from business and become a dairy farmer in Eaton County with his brother William Reitz. In 1938 William Reitz's wife died and less then a year later Edward's wife Celia passed away. In 1946 both brothers, who had always been close would die in a devastating trailer fire on February 1, 1946.[120]

The home at 809 W Ionia was torn down in 1978. From the Gould inventory of Darius Moon Buildings, listed as "Ed Rectz home-Lansing, 1901".

---

120   *LSJ* 2/1/1946 and *LSJ* 2/2/1946.

HORACE B. ANGELL HOUSE

335 E. Grand River, East Lansing, MI

BIGGER COLLEGEVILLE H.B. ANGELL WILL PLAT LAND NEAR THE COLLEGE
"H.B. Angell of Alma has recently purchased the 90-acre farm directly north and east of the agricultural college and will use part of it for platting purposes. J.A. Hamilton has just erected for him a barn on one of the lots facing the college and Mr. Angell's family will reside there while a handsome residence to cost $9,000 is being erected. D.B. Moon has just completed the plans" (*LJ* 7/29/1901).

Horace B. Angell and Charles B. Chase were business partners who developed the College Grove area of East Lansing; both had extensive property holdings in East Lansing. Angell owned one lot facing the agricultural college, Lot 21 Block 590, or 335 E. Grand River and for many years the structure was the home of the Alpha Gamma Rho fraternity. It is unclear if the new home designed by Moon for Horace B. Angell was ever built, or is the structure that was at 335 E. Grand River the home that Moon was contracted to design? Given the size of the structure and subsequent use it must have been a designed home, not just something that was quickly built. This was a massive intersecting New England style cross Gambrel house. In most homes of this style the pent roof is located between the first and second floor, but because of the size of this home - three floors plus an attic, Moon positioned the pent roof between the second and third floor to separate it from the porch and to balance the front façade. Observe the small Palladian style window on the attic level. This would have been an expensive detail to add on a home where the area was not intended to be used as living space.

Horace B. Angell was born in Lyon Township, Wayne County, Michigan on August 21, 1853 to Albert and Anna Angell. His parents moved to Clinton County, Michigan where Horace attended school in Maple

Rapids and after graduation taught in the Clinton County schools. At the age of 18, Horace moved to St. Louis, Michigan where he worked as a farm laborer. Three years later Horace purchased a farm in Pine River Township, near Forest Hills. On April 10, 1879 he married Miss Clara Travis (Traverse), the daughter of John Travis (Traverse) of Forest Hills. The couple would have three children, Anna, Ira, and Harriet. The family would move in 1886 to a farm in Elwell, Michigan and eleven years later, in 1897, the family moved to Alma, Michigan. In 1901 Horace approached his boyhood friend Charles Chase, then editor of the Ithaca newspaper to see if he was interested in forming a joint venture to purchase the Parmalee farm and plat property located near the Michigan Agricultural College. On July 1, 1901 the partnership was finalized and the development of the College Grove subdivision began. Horace and Charles would later fall out over a 15 acre lot, titled Lot 80. Horace and his son Ira would stay in Collegeville (East Lansing) for a few years to sell real estate. Horace would later return to Alma, and Ira would oversee his investments in College Grove. Horace served as chairman of the Farmer's Club of Seville Township and promoted the growth of sugar beets in Gratiot County. On August 26, 1941 Horace B. Angell, one of the forgotten founders of East Lansing would pass away at the state hospital in Traverse City. His wife Clara preceded him in death passing away in June of 1922.[121]

GEORGE KNEAL HOMES

210 S. Pine, Lansing, MI

Between 1902-1904 Moon designed five Houses for the contractor George Kneal; they were located at 207(205), 208(206), 210(208), 211(207) and 214(210) S. Pine.

---

121   *Alma Record* 8/28/1941. For the court case between Angell and Chase see Howard 108: 1105.

"New residences will be erected by George Neal and J.W. Hill. The houses being built by Neal are at 208 and 210 Pine street south" (*LJ* 8/2/1902).

"Architect D.B. Moon has made plans for a residence…. Also for a $2,500 residence for George Kneal" (*LJ* 8/11/1902).

The home at 210 S. Pine is a modest Queen Anne style home which is understandable given that it was built as a rental property. Both gables that are visible have fish scale siding and this design is continued on the front dormer. There are several small brackets along the soffits which seem to follow no pattern. The porch lends a sense of structure to the home while the columns and the brackets are inexpensive additions that help to soften the structure.

208 S. Pine, Lansing, MI

"Architect Moon has completed plans for a new house on Pine st for George Kneal. An old house of Mr. Kneal's is to be remodeled, and it is probable that two more houses for rent will be built for him besides these two" (*SR* 8/22/1902).

If you can get past the horrible faux brick siding that was added at a later date, the home at 208 S. Pine is quite appealing. Consider this, Kneal built these homes as rental properties and what is curious is that except for 207-211 S. Pine the homes are not similar. You would expect that Kneal would have commissioned Moon to design four homes that would be the same in appearance. The large dormer with the unique window design is something not seen in any previous home Moon designed. The porch is workmanlike but not exceptional. What is odd is the stacking of the windows. Usually windows would be stacked in a pattern, one on the first floor and two on the second or the reverse. Here you can see two over one and one over one on the façade. Why Moon did not follow the standard pattern is anyone's guess. What is also interesting is the oriel window on the side of the structure and the placement of the two small windows underneath. What was their purpose? They seem to crowd the upper window.

207-211 S. Pine, Lansing, MI

"George H. Kneal this morning awarded the contract to Croope & Hanson for the construction of a house on the corner of Pine and Allegan sts. D.B. Moon is the architect and the house will cost $3,500" (*SR* 4/5/1904).

"A new residence, built by George H Kneal on Pine st has been completed and rented by J.L. Fulton. D.B. Moon was the architect" (*SR* 8/29/1904).

Of the homes that Moon designed for Kneal these two are the most appealing. They are simple Queen Anne style structures. The porches on both homes have double columns along the front which is a different from Moon's usual design of three corner columns; notice that the porches are exactly the same. The two-sided bay windows on the second floor are an expensive detail that is odd to find in rental properties. It is interesting is that Kneal had Moon design three different style homes for him. From an investment standpoint it would have been cheaper to have the same style home built. It may have been the case that two of the homes were remodels. No image survives of Kneal's home at 513 W. Allegan. [122]

---

122   In 1906 George Kneal owned in Lot 11, Block 119, which was 207-211 S. Pine, the corner Lot 12 was a gas station. Kneal also owned in 1904 West ½ of Lot 1-2, Block 119, 513 W Allegan and the East ½ of Lots 1-3, Block 120, 208, 210 and 214 S. Pine.

George H. Kneal 1857-1922

In December of 1908 George H. Kneal and his wife Elizabeth made plans to relocate to Los Angles, California. Their home at 513 W. Allegan was to be rented to J.O. Maxey the state representative from Baraga County. However the move did not take place until 1919 when George, Elizabeth and George's brother John moved to 1414 S. Wilton Place, Los Angles, California. George was a well-known contractor in the state of Michigan whose company handled many of the road paving contracts in southern Michigan and northern Ohio. For example his firm paved many of the streets in Ypsilanti and Ann Arbor Michigan. His company also worked for several railroad companies in Lansing and they developed the Pere Marquette Railroad freight yards. Outside of his contracting company George had extensive real estate holdings and along with E.S. Porter established the Lansing Spoke Company. George H. Kneal died at his home in Los Angles on August 29, 1922.[123]

Two of the homes 207 S. Pine and 210 S. Pine, were moved when the Lansing Civic Center was built; unfortunately where these two homes were moved to is unknown. The other homes are no longer standing. In Moon's 1904 City Directory advertisement listed Geo. H. Kneal as one of the gentlemen for whom he designed a home. From the Gould inventory of Darius Moon Buildings, listed as "George Kneal 5 Houses, 1902-1904".

---

123   *LSJ* 8/29/1922 and *Lansing Capital News* 8/29/1922. Based on extensive research George may have married Miss Eliza S Cummings in Ashtabula, Ohio on April 11, 1883, there would be no children from the marriage.

1902

RALPH W. CREGO STORE

1024-1028 W. Allegan, Lansing, MI

A search of the property records for Lansing, the city directories and the 1900 and 1910 US Census reveals that there was no C.W. Crego, or for that matter any Crego's in Lansing until 1917. The date on the Gould list may be a mistake, and the actual date may be in the late 1910s or early 1920s. If this was a mistake the best candidate is Ralph W. Crego, who would later become Lansing's longest serving Mayor from 1943 to 1961. In 1917 Ralph acquired a small grocery store at 1028 W. Allegan which he purchased from Frank Freshour. The building was expanded in the 1920s to be several business blocks, 1024-1028 W. Allegan with apartments above. The addition to the building was the two story structure attached to it to the west of the storefront, 1024 W. Allegan. It is interesting that the building was located right across the street from Moon's home. From the Gould inventory of Darius Moon Buildings, listed as "C.W. Crego Flats, 1902".

JOHN B. NICKLE HOME

2463 Saginaw Highway, Roxand Township, Eaton County, MI

"D.B. Moon is making the plans for a fine farm residence, to be erected by J.B. Nichol [Nickle] of Mulliken" (*SR* 1/3/1902).

"Architect Moon today let to Grand Ledge parties the contract for the construction of a large brick house owned by J.B. Nickle of Hoytville" (*LJ* 8/30/1902).

This is a fine organic style home. It has hints of being a Queen Anne style residence but it is constructed entirely of brick. Notice the gable ends and how they are centered on the lower porches. Another interesting aspect is the small dormer and how it merges with the roof edge. Normally the dormer would be moved in from the edge, in this case if that would have been done it would have crowded the gable end. The columns on the porch are Tuscan style and it is interesting to see brackets along the soffits even though they are only at the corners.

John B. Nickle was born in Roxand Township, Eaton County, Michigan on November 7, 1840, to Andrew and Diadema (née Barton) Nickle who were early settlers in Roxand Township. John grew up on his father's farm and at the age of 21 married Miss Lucy Ann HieSRodt on December 4, 1861. The couple would have eight children, Dora and Martin, who died in early childhood, Samuel, Andrew J, John E., Frank, Addie and Mary. In August of 1903 he completed a spacious home, described as being "… one of the finest in the township, being modern in architectural design and all its equipment." John B. Nickle was a successful farmer who helped to develop Eaton County; he served as township treasurer and for many years was the township's drain commissioner. A pioneer of Eaton County John B. Nickle died at his home near Hoytville on October 23, 1916.[124]

From the Gould inventory of Darius Moon Buildings, listed as "J.B. Nickle Hse at Sunfield, 1902".

---

124   See the *LSJ* 10/24/1916, *Past* 457 and *Portrait and Biographical Album of Barry* 758.

RANSOM E. OLDS HOUSE

720 S. Washington, Lansing, MI (A.G.)

Designed by Moon in 1902 and constructed in 1903 this residence placed Darius B. Moon as the foremost architect in Lansing. The Olds' home would become the structure that made Moon's career and one that would be associated with his name for prosperity.

"R.E. Olds is having plans prepared for a new residence to be built on Main st w. Mr. Olds owns the property between the Barnes estate and the residence of E.F. Cooley. Upon this he proposes to build one of the finest houses in Lansing. The structure is to be of brick and stone and will be thoroughly modern and beautiful house. D.B. Moon is preparing plans, which are to be ready for the builders by July 1" (*SR* 4/28/1902).

"Architect D.B. Moon has made plans for a residence of cut stone and pressed brick for R.E. Olds to cost $12,000. Also for a $2,500 residence for George Kneal" (*LJ* 8/11/1902).

Olds House under construction (A.G.)

EVERETT HOUSE SITE SOLD TO R.E. OLDS

"It is understood that a trade has been consummated through the terms of which the old Everett house site at the corner of Washington ave and Main st has passed into the procession of Ransom E. Olds. Judge Edward Cahill was the former owner of the property and in exchange is said to have been made owner of a lot adjoining the Barnes property on Main st w. Architect Moon is preparing plans for a residence for Mr. Olds which will be one of the finest Houses in the city. It is to be of pressed brick and three stories high and will cost approximately $20,000.

It is understood that this structure will be erected on the Everett House site, the work to be begun about April 15" (*SR* 2/28/1903).

"Masons commenced work on the new residence of R.E. Olds this morning. Pressed brick will be used in the construction, and when completed the building will probably be one of the handsomest residences in the city" (*LJ* 5/27/1903).

"The cut stone work on the new residence of R.E. Olds is being greatly admired. The work is exceptionally fine, and is being done by William Butters" (*LJ* 7/2/1903).

WAITING FOR BRICK
Work on the R.E. Olds' New Residence Delayed by Non-arrival

"Progress on the residence R.E. Olds is erecting at Washington ave and Main st is delayed by the non-arrival of brick from Saginaw. Two carloads are here, but as the brick are of a special color, Mr. Olds will not have them laid until assured that he will not have to use any other kind to finish the work. The brick are light bluff colored. Much of the elaborate stone work is completed" (*SR* 7/25/1903).

"The new and palatial residence of R.E. Olds on Washington avenue south is nearly completed, and the owner expects to occupy it within a few weeks" (*LJ* 12/18/1903).

720 S. Washington, Lansing, MI

The Olds Mansion must have been a remarkable home to view in person. The residence was constructed of buff colored brick with some rusticated stonework on the first floor and built upon a fieldstone foundation. The stone trim was of red sandstone from a quarry in northern Michigan while the roof was green slate with an iron cresting with finials at each gable end. The tower has a false closed gable on the front and side and a Hexagonal roof over the turret. The home was a mixture of several architectural styles. There are elements from of Romanesque Revival, Queen Anne and Châteauesque style building incorporated in the design. Overall this is a wonderful home and when the color scheme is considered, a home that would not be missed by anyone who passed by.

720 S. Washington details

Observe in the above image the turban style caps on the projecting pier supports and the half moon window of the smaller tower with a sunburst of clam shell motif. What is interesting are the smaller attached mock bartizan towers attached to the smaller tower which mimics those on the Alroy A. Wilbur Store at 204 E Grand River and the Michigan Millers Insurance at 120 W. Ottawa. Was Moon trying to make a statement? The third floor of the home was a ballroom and in the time before air conditioning the third floor balcony allowed visitors to cool off between dances. The second floor which was the private area of the residence has two ornate oval windows flanking the porch. Next to the oval windows are what may be stained glass windows. The images are not clear enough to determine if they were stained glass, but the architectural plans held by the State of Michigan Archives bear out that in the original plan these windows were to be stained glass. Another feature on the second floor is that the porch extended to either side of the porch's covered area; they are set off by an oval balustrade. The first floor porch is what attracts the viewer's attention. Moon again repeats the three column pattern which he had used on previous homes. Notice how the capitals of the columns mimic the turban detail on the caps of the gable support on the third floor. The second floor porch columns are Ionic style, quite a departure from those on the first floor porch. Just six years later Olds would modify the structure and add a music room, a feature not present in the original design. "R.E. Olds will enlarge the automobile room at his residence, Washington ave s. and make it two stories instead of one, the second floor to be used as a music room. The addition will begin about the first of June and at that time some portions of the residence will be redecorated." (*SR* 4/9/1908)

720 S. Washington after the remodel in 1952

In 1952 Mrs. Gladys Olds Anderson spent $50,000 to update the exterior of the residence. The large front porch was removed and replaced with a landscaped terrace. The entire third floor structure as well as the turret and tower were also removed. The above image of the Olds residence is from the Library of Congress; for more images of the Olds Mansion after the remodel visit www.loc.gov.

Ransom E. Olds 1864-1950

No person is more synonymous with Lansing history than Ransom E. Olds. Born in Geneva, Ashtabula County, Ohio on June 3, 1864, to Pliny Fisk and Sarah (née Whipple) Olds, Ransom was 16 years old when the family moved to Lansing, Michigan, a city whose destiny he helped to establish and the development of which would be intertwined with his for many years. After completing his studies at Lansing High School and the Lansing Business College, he went to work for his father, Pliny and brother, Wallace S. Olds at P.F. Olds & Son. When his father retired Ransom acquired the entire business. P.F. Olds & Son was an experienced manufacturer of steam engines and pumps. It was Ransom's interest in the gasoline engine that changed the direction of his life. Working late nights and early mornings, so as to cloak his work from the view of the public, Ransom developed his first functioning vehicle, a three wheeled horseless carriage. With the assistance of Frank Clark, Ransom designed the prototype of the curved dash automobile that would later become the foundation of the Olds Motor Vehicle Company. In 1896 with the support of Lansing investors six horseless carriages would be produced in 1897. By 1899 other investors would take notice and in 1899 Olds Motor Works would be founded with capital stock of $350,000, with the understanding that the production facilities of the new company would be moved to Detroit. It may be prudent at this time to take a step back, Detroit at this time, much like Silicon Valley today, was a hotbed for new ideas and innovation, and it was only natural that the Olds Motor Works would be located there. While in Detroit Ransom became acquainted with Henry Ford, who had just founded the Detroit Automobile Company, which later failed in 1901. Ransom and Henry became lifelong friends. There are accounts of both men meeting to exchange ideas. Just who was the father of the modern assembly line is still in question. Olds used a moving production line where vehicles were moved from assembly station to assembly station on carts. Ford would later perfect the idea of the movable assembly line; it seems that neither Olds nor Ford cared who received credit; it was more about learning and the free exchange of ideas. In today's equivalent it would be the idea of open source software programming. The majority shareholder in the Olds Motor Works was Samuel L. Smith, a lumber and copper baron. Just why Ransom allowed control of the company to fall out of his hands is unknown. It may have been a case that he was too focused on the goal and overlooked his long term security, a mistake that he would not repeat. Samuel's son Frederic L. Smith, Ransom's cousin entered the business and after repeated clashes between the cousins, Ransom decided to leave the company he created. In 1905 Ransom disposed of his stock in the Olds Motor Works Company and formed the R.E. Olds Motor Car Company. The name was changed to the REO Motor Car Company after Smith threatened a lawsuit.

Ransom E. Olds from *Our Michigan Friends*

Ransom would serve as president and general manager of the REO Motor Car Company from 1905-1924, afterward he served as chairman of the board from 1924-1936. The REO Motor Car Company, under the guidance of Olds, produced innovative automobiles, the Reo Flying Cloud and Reo Royale, both the Cloud and the Royale need to be seen to be appreciated, and simply, they are stunning. The Great Depression would take a toll on the company; in 1936 the business ceased the production of automobiles. Under the direction of Olds' protégé Richard H. Scott the company focused on the production of trucks. Automobiles were not Ransom's only interests; he seemed like a driven man, producing new items for the consumer market. In 1914 he developed one of the first commercial power driven lawn mowers and founded the Ideal Lawn Mower Company. He was instrumental in the building of the Olds Hotel in Lansing, Michigan, now known as the Romney State Office building and the Olds Tower Building a 25 story office building located in the heart of Lansing. After a devastating fire in 1916 at the Engineering Building at Michigan State College, now Michigan State University he donated the monies for the construction of the R. E. Olds Hall of Engineering. He would also donate $130,000 to Kalamazoo College for the construction Olds Science Hall. Ransom, much like Henry Ford, would seek to create the perfect community and with that ideal in place Oldsmar, Florida was founded in 1913. It would become one of Ransom's failures in social redevelopment; a success was the REO Clubhouse in Lansing. Those are but a few examples of R.E. Olds charitable work, the names of organizations that he helped are too numerous to list in this short biography. Ransom also had extensive business interests outside automobile manufacturing. Banking, life insurance and the hospitality industry are all areas in which Ransom was active. On June 5, 1889 Ransom married Miss Metta U. Woodward in Lansing, Michigan. They would have four children, two of which died in infancy, Mildred Lucille in 1899 and a son Ralph Olds who died in 1902 of Ransom's two surviving daughters, Gladys would marry Bruce Anderson on October 17, 1914 while her sister Bernice would wed Clarence S. Roe on December 19, 1917. On Saturday August 26, 1950, Ransom E. Olds died peacefully at his home.[125]

Metta Ursula Woodward was born on June 6, 1864 in Pinckney, Michigan. She moved to Fowlerville then came to Lansing in 1888 to work as a clerk in Usa Forester's gift shop. While working at the store she met Ransom Olds for the first time. After a brief courtship they married on June 6, 1889 at the home of Metta's aunt and uncle. Metta Olds was active in the YWCA, donating the family's summer house at Lake Lansing to the organization which named it Camp Matta Miga. She was also on the Women's Board at Storer College and was an active member First Baptist Church of Lansing. After attending her husband's funeral, Metta Olds suffered a fall and broke her left hip. Complications set in and she died at the family home on September 2, 1950.[126]

There has been much speculation as to why the Olds Mansion was not preserved. Stories have circulated that Metta Olds did not want anyone else to live in the home that brought her and the Olds family so much happiness. It has also been suggested that the Scott family fought the relocation of the Olds residence to the Scott property which was located near the Old Mansion. Maurice M. Scott voiced his disapproval of moving the home to a site that was meant as a memorial to his father. Rather the answer is more mundane than that. The Historical Society of Michigan could not raise the $30,000 in matching funds to assure the completion of the proposed move. The Historical Society of Michigan did seek the help of the U.S. Department of the Interior, Historic Buildings Survey team, which sent a team of architects and historians who photographed the interior and exterior of the home.[127] What is interesting is that the original site for the Olds' home was to be on Lot 19 Block 177, between the Barnes Mansion and the Cooley home, which would have probably

---

125   *LSJ* 8/27/1950 and Fuller 9.
126   *LSJ* 9/2/1950
127   See the August 25, 1966 letter from William K. Alderfer, Historical Society of Michigan to Honorable Max Murninghan and City Council, regarding moving the mansion, see the Lansing City Council Minutes 9/6/1966 on file at the Lansing City Clerk's Office. For Maurice M. Scotts letter to Honorable Max Murninghan and City Council on June 29, 1966 see Lansing City Council Minutes 7/5/1966, on file at the Lansing City Clerk's Office and *LSJ* 7/7/1966.

resulted in the home's preservation. But it would have been a much smaller structure and not as impressive as the one that was built at 720 S. Washington. In 1902 the original plans Moon created for Olds was a smaller home, the cost of the structure was to be $12,000. Later, after Olds acquired the lot that the Everett House occupied, a much larger home was designed by Moon with a cost of over $20,000. Olds would sell his property, Lot 19 Block 177 to E.F. Cooley who would later engaged Edwyn Bowd to design a home for his son on the lot. The Olds Mansion was torn down with the construction of I-496.

In Moon's advertisement in the 1904 City Directory states that he designed "plans for fine residences and refer you to the following gentlemen as a few of the many for whom I have designed homes" R.E. Olds is listed as one of those gentlemen.

From the Gould inventory of Darius Moon Buildings, listed as "Residence for R.E. Olds, 1902".

HENRY SLEMMER HOUSE

232 S. Walnut, Lansing, MI

"Contractor James A. Hamilton has secured the contract to erect a $3,500 residence on the corner of Washtenaw and Walnut streets for Henry Slemmer. D.B. Moon prepared the plans" (*LJ* 5/9/1901).

The above photograph shows the Slemmer house in the 1940s. The back portion with the first and second floor porch was a later addition; the original began at the corner of the porches and extended toward Walnut. The multiple front gables are clad in fish scale siding as seen in the lower photograph; the gables are well positioned and give the home a balanced view when observed from the street. There is a bowed window on the second floor as well as a bay window located on the side of the first floor. The porch is interesting with plain square columns that have no ornamentation. The columns are repeated on the rear addition as well as the style of the balustrade, so they may be original. Observe how the first floor porch extends outward under the eave of the second floor porch, an architectural feature not seen in other Moon designed homes. Finally notice the stacking of the windows, one above the other, even the first floor bay window with the three panes has three windows above it. The house was later moved to 315 N. Walnut, where the house was converted into apartments. Unfortunately the residence was torn down due to the construction of the Ferris Park Towers. (*LSJ* 1/1/1932).

232 S. Walnut Detail

Locating information on Henry Slemmer was a challenge. He is listed in the 1900 census as living at 517 W. Hillsdale and was married to Elizabeth, with one child, a son, Dewitt [Dewey]. Henry worked for the Lansing School District as a janitor at Bingham Street School and the Townsend Street School. In the fall of 1908, Henry and Elizabeth Slemmer moved to Los Angles, California to be near their son Dewitt, who was a traveling salesman based in southern California. On February 3, 1909 Henry suffered a heart attack in his sleep and died at his new home located at 514 North New Hampshire Avenue, Los Angles. Elizabeth would stay in the Los Angeles area until her death in April of 1924.[128]

---

128   For Henry Slemmer's death see *SR* 2/9/1909 and *LJ* 2/9/1909. Henry wife Elizabeth died on April 4, 1936.

BATES & EDMONDS COMPANY

238 Mill Street Lansing MI

After a fire swept through this area in 1902, the Bates & Edmonds Company acquired a parcel of land from the Alexander Furnace Company just south of the Lansing Veneer Door Company. The parcel that the Bates & Edmonds Company purchased was further south on Mill Street. It would seem from news accounts that the Alexander Furnace Company was selling assets in order to rebuild the factory but that effort was not successful. The parcel of land the Bates & Edmonds Company purchased had 200 feet of frontage on Mill Street and extended 225 feet to the river. On this site they built a one story building with 50 feet facing Mill Street and extending 200 feet toward the river, the building was surfaced on the exterior in cement.[129]

PLANS FOR BUILDING
Oldsmobile Company to Build a Big Paint Shop.

RIKERD PLANT NEARLY DONE
Machinery Has Been Shipped-Bates & Edmonds Getting Ready to Build New Factory.

Architect Moon at noon today completed plans for the new paint shop to be erected at once at the plant of the Oldsmobile company. The foundry is now practically finished, it being expected to start work in it next Monday.
The new paint shop will be a two-story brick building, 55 feet by 200 feet in dimensions, having a capacity which will enable the workmen to finish thirty automobiles a day. Connecting the new paint shop with the main building is a brick addition 32 by 110 feet. Work will be commenced on the construction of the shop very soon.
Architect Moon also has prepared plans for a two-story brick warehouse to be erected by Frederick Thoman on Ionia street in the rear of the Robert Smith Printing Company's structure. It will be used by the state printers as a storehouse for paper.
The new plant of the Rikerd Lumber Company is now ready to receive the machinery, which has arrived and will all soon be installed. Work on the completion of the roof has been slightly delayed but is again in progress.
The plans for the building to be erected by Bates & Edmonds, near the factory of the Lansing Veneered Door Company, have been completed and it is said the contract will be awarded today.
A.M. Robson has commenced the erection of a new residence on St. Joseph street east, and the house being built by Mrs. Crosby at the corner of Capitol avenue and Lenawee street is going up rapidly (*LJ* 8/14/1902).

---

129   *SR* 6/24/1902, *SR* 7/12/1902 and *SR* 7/15/1902.

The article outlines the new construction that was taking place in the Lansing area. Some of the projects specifically mention Moon as being the architect, others do not. Given that Moon was injured in the construction of the Rikerd Plant and not listed as the architect in the article it reasonable to assume that Moon was the designer of all the structures that are listed in the above article.[130]

"The contracts for the Bates & Edmonds new machine shops were awarded yesterday. Edward Wright secures the contract for wood work and M.E. Fitzpatrick for the mason work. The new building is to be 50 by 200 feet in size and will be built of brick instead of cement, as originally intended" (*SR* 8/15/1902). This may be Edwin B. Wight not Edward Wright; Edwin was a contractor, Edward worked for the State of Michigan. Edwin would later work with Moon as the contractor for the Olds Motor Works Paint Shop.

The building Moon designed for the Bates & Edmonds Company was in the style typical of industrial buildings in the early Twentieth Century. A structure with large arched windows to allow as much natural light to enter the building, low shed roofs to facilitate the placements of skylights to again allow light to enter and an open floor plan to facilitate the movement of materials throughout the plant. It is unknown why Moon decided to enter the field of designing factories; in a short period of time he designed several, then he stopped. It may have been because of the amount of time this type of work entailed or he lost out to architects who specialized in this type architecture. What is a testament to his work is that a part of the Bates & Edmonds Company building is still in use today as part of the R. E. Olds Transportation Museum. The contract for the construction of the building was awarded to Martin E. Fitzpatrick with the understanding that the building would be completed by October 15, 1902. Fitzpatrick was good as his word and on October 20, 1902 the Bates & Edmonds Motor Company moved from its factory at the Lapham & Longyear plant on E. Michigan Avenue to its new facilities on Mill Street.[131]

James P. Edmonds 1866-1950

James Pelton Edmonds was one of those unique characters that only the state of Michigan could produce. Born January 13, 1866 in Lansing the son of John W. and Marilla J. (née Pelton) Edmonds, James would attend local public schools and take his first job at an early age as an adjuster for the American Fire Insurance Company of Philadelphia. With the boom of the automobile industry in the late 1890s, Edmonds realized the potential of the automobile and with M.F. Bates formed the Bates & Edmonds Motor Company, which specialized in the production of gasoline engines. Later the duo of Bates & Edmonds would briefly enter the business of automobile manufacturing with the formation of the Bates Automobile Company in which Edmonds served as secretary. Unable to compete with the mass production of the major automobile companies the Bates Automobile Company quickly folded.

---

130   *SR* 7/23/1902
131   *SR* 9/2/1902 and *LJ* 11/20/1902.

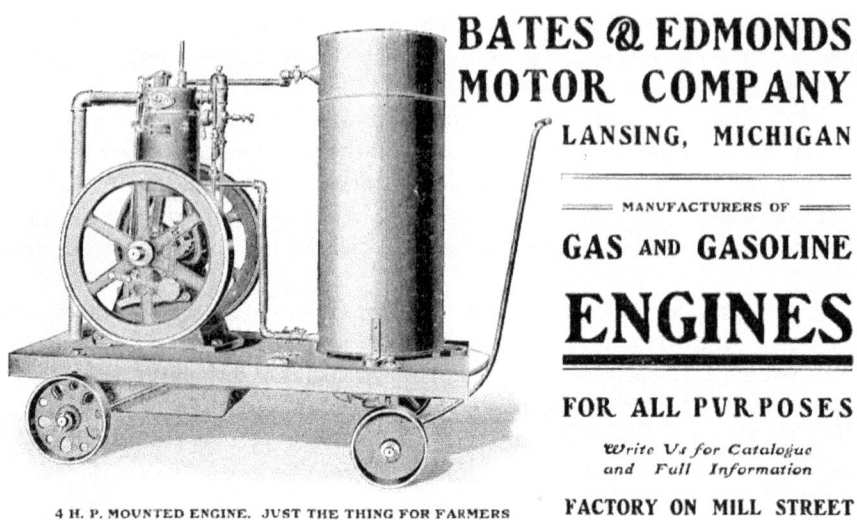

Bates & Edmonds Engine advertisement from 1902

On November 28, 1894 James P. Edmonds married Miss Neenah E. Jones the daughter of Nelson B. Jones, who interestingly enough was a special agent for the American Fire Insurance Company of Philadelphia. After the wedding the couple moved into their new home at 531 S. Capitol Avenue. John W. Edmonds, James father was one of the early settlers of Lansing. John was one of the organizers of the Lansing volunteer Fire Department and his son James preserved many of these artifacts which serves as the basis for the local history collection at the Forest Parke Library and Archives. James became the unofficial historian for the city of Lansing and wrote the *Development of the Automobile and Gasoline Engine in Michigan* and later the book *Early Lansing History*. James P. Edmonds died at his home on Wednesday evening July 26, 1950.[132]

---

[132] *LSJ* 7/27/1950 and Cowles 447.

CHESTER D. WOODBURY COTTAGE

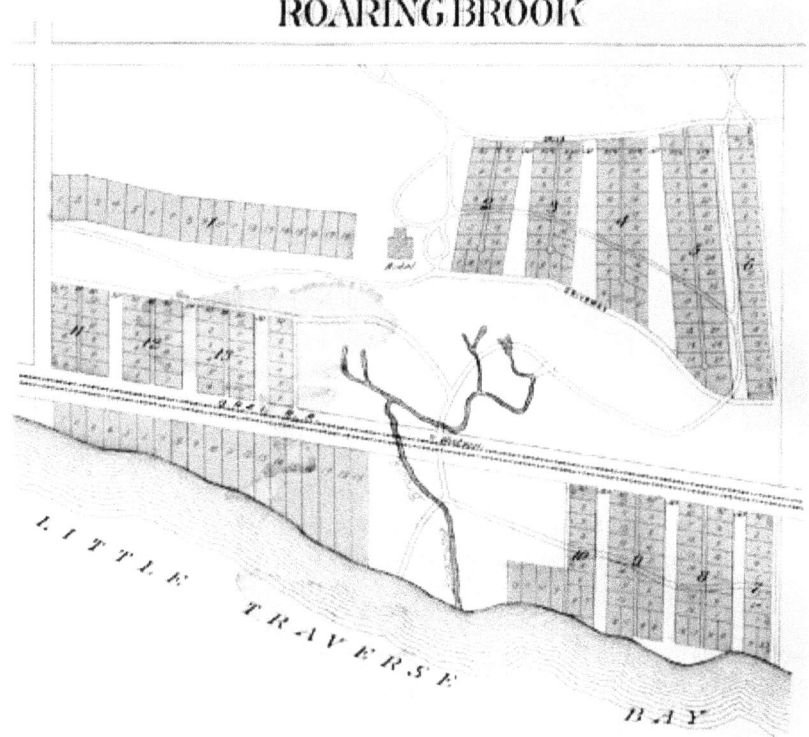

Roaring Brook Michigan

In March of 1893 a group of Lansing businessmen purchased 138 acres on Little Traverse Bay, adjoining the Wequetonsing resort and opposite Harbor Point. The founders were Judge Edward Cahill, Leroy C. Blood, Robert Smith, Chester D. Woodbury, Henry R. Pattengill and A. Beamer of Harbor Springs. The resort took its name from the picturesque Roaring Brook which ran through the property. The site was ideal, with over a half mile of shoreline and fresh water springs which fed the Roaring Brook, providing cold pure water for the residents. The bluffs behind the beach provided spectacular views of Little Traverse Bay, making the area a perfect location for a summer resort. In the summer of 1894 the association opened the Roaring Brook Inn, a three story building with spacious room and a dining room capable of serving over 200 guests. The lower porch of the hotel was 104 feet long by 20 feet wide, with a balcony that was 20 by 40 feet. The Inn was designed by Lansing architect Earl Mead. The list of residents of the Inn in 1895 reads like a who's who of Lansing notables. The association also recruited employees from the Lansing area, Floyd Evans the head bell boy from the Downey Hotel was persuaded to work at the hotel as well as Mrs. Peterson who would run the kitchen. The cost of purchasing a lot at the resort on the shoreline in 1898 property values, was $35 dollars a square foot. Thomas H. West of St. Louis, Missouri purchased three lots facing the water, all 60 feet in width for $4500, or close to three million dollars in today's money. [133]

---

[133] See the *LJ* 3/18/1893, *LJ* 3/24/1893, *LJ* 4/8/1893, *SR* 1/16/1894, *SR* 7/23/1894, *LJW* 8/30/1895, *SR* 5/21/1897, *SR* 5/22/1897, *SR* 6/28/1898 and *SR* 8/29/1900. The value of a dollar calculation is based upon the economic power value of the dollar, see http://www.measuringworth.com/index.php.

Chester Woodbury first erected a cottage at the northern resort of Roaring Brook in 1894. The *State Republican* on July 27, 1894 noted that the contractor W.E. Moore had just returned from Roaring Brook where he had been building a cottage for C.D. Woodbury. Just who designed the cottage is unknown, but it was probably not the extensive structure which would be built later.

"D.B. Moon is preparing plans for two cottages to be built for C.D. Woodbury on his land at Roaring Brook next spring. Mr. Woodbury is one of the original shareholders in the property at Roaring Brook. One of the cottages is for his own use and the other for rent" (*SR* 11/13/1901).

"Architect Moon has nearly completed plans for two handsome cottages, to be erected at Roaring Brook, for C.D. Woodbury, and one at the same resort for Arthur C. Stebbins "(*SR* 1/21/1902).

The *Polk Petoskey City Directory 1905-1906* lists that "Woodbury C.D. Lots $200 Little Traverse, Roaring Brook", so it is entirely possible that Moon designed two cottages for Chester Woodbury at Roaring Brook.

Architect D.B. Moon has made plans for summer residences at Roaring Brook for Arthur C. Stebbins and C.D. Woodbury" (*LJ* 2/10/1902).

"D.D. [B.] Moon has prepared plans for two new cottages to be built at Roaring Brook for C.D Woodbury. A.C Stebbins is to build at Roaring Brook also. Mr. Moon has designed a house for Mayor Whitman, of Mason, and is preparing to remodel the F.L. Dodge residence. The later will be especially attractive in the colonial style" (*SR* 4/3/1902).

A search of the tax records for Little Traverse Township in 1905 reveals that Chester Woodbury owned Lot 16 Block 8 in Roaring Brook. In 1908 he is listed as owning Lot 1 Block 1 and Lot 16 Block 8. No image of the cottage has been located and the structure has long since vanished.

Moon's advertisement in the 1904 *City Directory* states that he designed "plans for fine residences and refer you to the following gentlemen as a few of the many for whom I have designed homes" C.D. Woodbury is listed as one of those gentlemen. The 1904 advertisement is in all probability referring to the work that Moon did for Chester Woodbury at Roaring Brook. It is also entirely possible that the Gould listing for "3 Hse's for C.D. Woodbury, 1901-1907" may refer to two cottages at Roaring Brook and Woodbury's home in East Lansing. From the Gould inventory of Darius Moon Buildings, listed as "C.D. Woodbury, Cottage at Roaring Brook, Mich, 1902"

ARTHUR C. STEBBINS HOME

216 N. Sycamore, Lansing, MI

The history of just what two homes Darius Moon designed for A.C. Stebbins is a puzzle. A.C. Stebbins home in 1902 was originally 616 W. Ottawa, Stebbins owned the west ½ of Lots 7-8, Block 91 in 1901, the north east corner of Ottawa and Sycamore streets. Later in 1903 he would purchase Lot 9, Block 91, 216 N. Sycamore. In 1903 when Stebbins commissioned Moon to design a new home, the original Stebbins home was moved from its location on the West ½ of Lots 7-8, to Lot 9 of Block 91; the home would become 216 N. Sycamore. It would seem that the home Moon designed to occupy the site of the moved house on West Ottawa was never built, in fact no home would be built on this site until 1913. The Stebbins family would live at 216 N. Sycamore until 1907, until their new home at 109 S. Walnut was completed.[134]

In 1931 Charles J. Opdyke recounted a story of R.E. Olds driving his first automobile to the home of A.C. Stebbins.
"One of the first horseless carriages to be seen on Lansing streets was the one manufactured by Ransom E. Olds. One Sunday afternoon Mr. Olds drove his machine on the sidewalk on W. Ottawa st to the residence of Arthur C. Stebbins on the corner of Sycamore and Ottawa sts, and I well remember the crowd of curious men and boys who gathered to look at the contraption known then as a horseless carriage."[135]

"Architect Moon has plans under way for a new brick and stone residence for Arthur C. Stebbins on the corner of Sycamore and Ottawa streets, where Mr. Stebbin's present home stands. The old place which is of brick is to be moved to a lot a joining the one on which it is now located" (*SR* 3/16/1903).

---

134   The Stebbins' family, a well-known Lansing family generously shared many of the images that were used in this book.
135   *Lansing Capital News* March 31, 1931.

The Stebbins' residence at 216 N. Sycamore is an example of cross gable home, but there is much more here. The front porch was enclosed at a later date. Notice the columns incorporated into the structure of the porch; it is the enclosed area on the second floor which is of interest. Was this originally a porch? If it was, it is the only one this writer has ever seen in this architectural style. Or was it designed as a sleeping porch, where families slept during the warm summer months? The design elements of the first floor porch are repeated on the sleeping porch which points to the second floor sleeping porch originally being an open porch. Regrettably the home was torn down and the site is now a parking lot.

109 N. Walnut, Lansing, MI

"A.C. Stebbins has purchased the lot on Walnut street, just north of Justice F.A. Hooker's residence, and will erect a fine residence thereon. The place is being staked out. The site faces the capitol and the fine home, which it is understood Mr. Stebbins will build will greatly improve the looks of the street from the back capital entrance" (*LJ* 4/15/1907).

"A.C. Stebbins is getting along well with his new house on Walnut street north, west of the capitol" (*LJ* 5/17/1907). Later in 1907 a *Lansing Journal* article lists A.C. Stebbins home as well as Frank Hayes home on Lenawee as "handsome and costly homes" (*LJ* 11/2/1907). The Frank Hayes house was designed by Darius Moon; is this conclusive proof? It would explain why the Gould list has Moon designing two homes for A.C. Stebbins. The other alternative is that Moon handled the relocation and redesign of the home to 216 N. Sycamore and the plans for the home to be built on the West Ottawa lot were used for the home on Walnut Street.

109 N. Walnut Lansing MI

Whether or not Moon designed the Stebbins' residence at 109 N. Walnut, the home is still a remarkable structure. The home is a mixture of Tudor and Arts & Craft architectural details. The front of the home looms over the street, the second floor extends over the first floor while the third floor cantilevers over the second extending the home toward the street. The Arts & Craft elements are on the porch; remember that the building of the home was delayed for several years, more than enough time to incorporate new architectural details. Notice how the porch extends beyond the second floor overhang. There is also the curved first floor window. The columns used on the Stebbins home are similar to those on the Slemmer home. Finally observe the carriage house in the back of the lot; it is a striking structure in its own right.

Arthur C. Stebbins 1860-1946

The Stebbins family is a well-known name throughout Lansing's history. Arthur C. Stebbins is remembered in automotive history as secretary and early stock holder in the Olds Motor Vehicle Company, who put forward the motion that R.E. Olds "be authorized to build one carriage in as nearly perfect manner as possible, and complete it at the earliest possible moment," contributing to the founding of the United States automotive industry. However there was much more that Arthur Stebbins would contribute to Lansing throughout his life time. The son of Cortland B. and Eliza (née Smith) Stebbins, Arthur was born in the family home located at 227 N. Capitol on July 16, 1860. He was a graduate of the old Lansing high school, attended the MAC for two years, most of the time traveling between school and home by foot and completed his studies at the University of Michigan. After graduation Arthur began his career with Lansing Wheelbarrow Company, he started with the company in 1882 and worked in the shipping room; four years later he was manager of the Lansing plant and was instrumental in the establishment of a satellite plant in Parkin, Arkansas. Arthur would become president and general manager of the Lansing Wheelbarrow Company, later known as the Lansing Company. He also served as vice president of W.K. Prudden Company, president of New Way Motor Company, secretary of Olds Motor Vehicle Company, vice president of Capital National Bank, treasurer of Edward Sparrow Hospital and vice president of the Capital Savings and Loan Company. On November 18, 1885 Arthur married Miss Rena Stowell in New York City, the couple would have two children, Stowell C. and Cortland B., and tragically Rena Stebbins would pass away on June 16, 1890.[136] Arthur would remarry on September 22, 1892 to Miss Anna Burgoyne in Bridgeport, Michigan. They would have three sons, Francis B., Rowland C. and George A. Stebbins. Arthur was also one of the founding members of the Roaring Brook resort in northern Michigan and had property in the Lake Okeechobee region of Florida. He traveled widely across the world visiting every continent. Arthur C. Stebbins died at his home on Thursday morning, October 17, 1946.[137]

Moon's advertisement in the 1904 City Directory states that he designed "plans for fine residences and refer you to the following gentlemen as a few of the many for whom I have designed homes" A.C. Stebbins is listed as one of those gentlemen. The advertisement referred to the cottage which Moon designed for Stebbins at Roaring Brook.

From the Gould inventory of Darius Moon Buildings, listed as "Arthur Stebbins- 2 houses-Lansing, 1902." The home was torn down in 1961.

---

136 *LJ* 6/16/1890. Rena Stowell was the daughter of James Henry and Sarah B. (née Wood) Stowell.
137 *LSJ* 10/17/1946 and Cowles 404.

ARTHUR STEBBINS COTTAGE

Roaring Brook, MI

The Stebbins cottage is the only example of a summer house designed by Darius Moon that is accessible and still stands today. The cottage was a cross gambrel structure that sits on the shoreline of Little Traverse Bay. The home was designed with the views of the lake as its main focus. Notice the number of windows that face the lake, there are twelve windows on the home that have views of the bay and the doors are all glass allowing for even more vista of the lake. Moon stacked the windows in such a way as to focus the home toward the water. The porches are wide and provide room for chairs and outdoor dining. It is interesting that Moon used different style columns in his design of the first and second floor porches. The first floor porch has plain Tuscan style columns while the second floor has elongate urn style columns with a narrow base at the center of the porch while the corner columns are boxy pier columns. The second floor porch is the strongest aspect of the cottage.

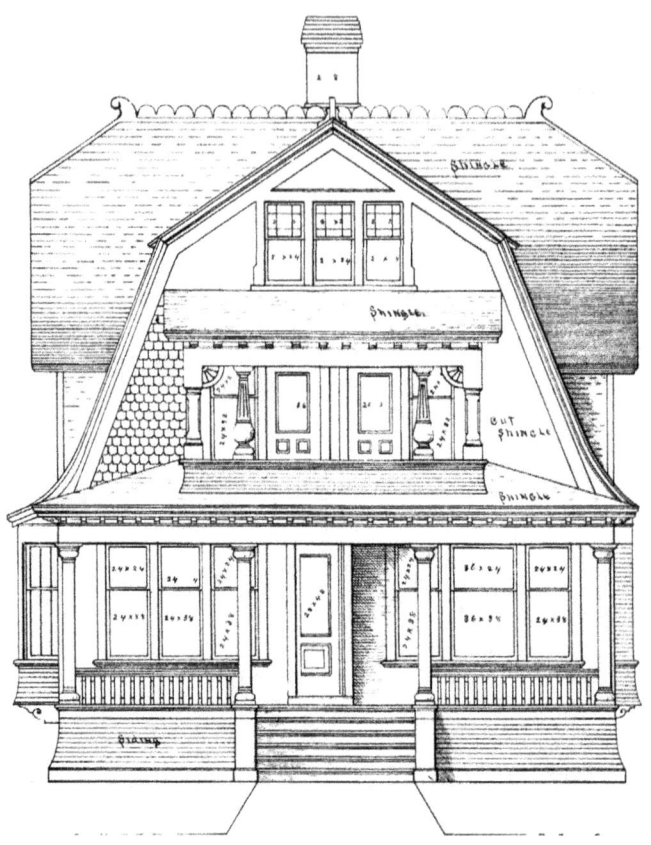

Moon's architectural drawing of the Stebbins Cottage at Roaring Brook, MI

"Architect Moon has nearly completed plans for two handsome cottages, to be erected at Roaring Brook, for C.D. Woodbury, and one at the same resort for Arthur C. Stebbins" (*SR* 1/21/1902).

SUMMER HOUSES
Will be built at Roaring Brook by Lansing Citizens.

"Architect D.B. Moon has made plans for summer residences at Roaring Brook for Arthur C. Stebbins and C.D. Woodbury". (*LJ* 2/10/1902)

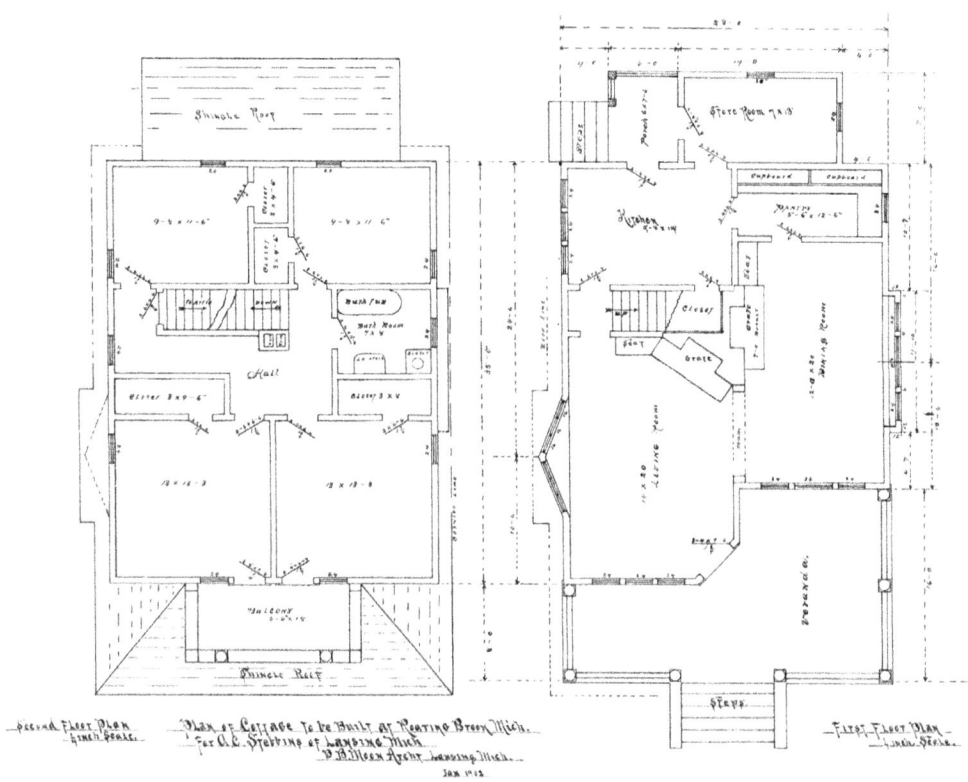

Moon's floor plan for the Stebbins Cottage

"D.D.[B] Moon has prepared plans for two new cottages to be built at Roaring Brook for C.D Woodbury. A.C Stebbins is to build at Roaring Brook also. Mr. Moon has designed a house for Mayor Whitman, of Mason, and is preparing to remodel the F.L. Dodge residence. The later will be especially attractive in the colonial style" (SR 4/3/1902).

Arthur C. Stebbins is listed in the 1903-1908 Little Traverse Township tax rolls an owning Lot 8 Block 9 Roaring Brook Michigan. The property is still held by the family.

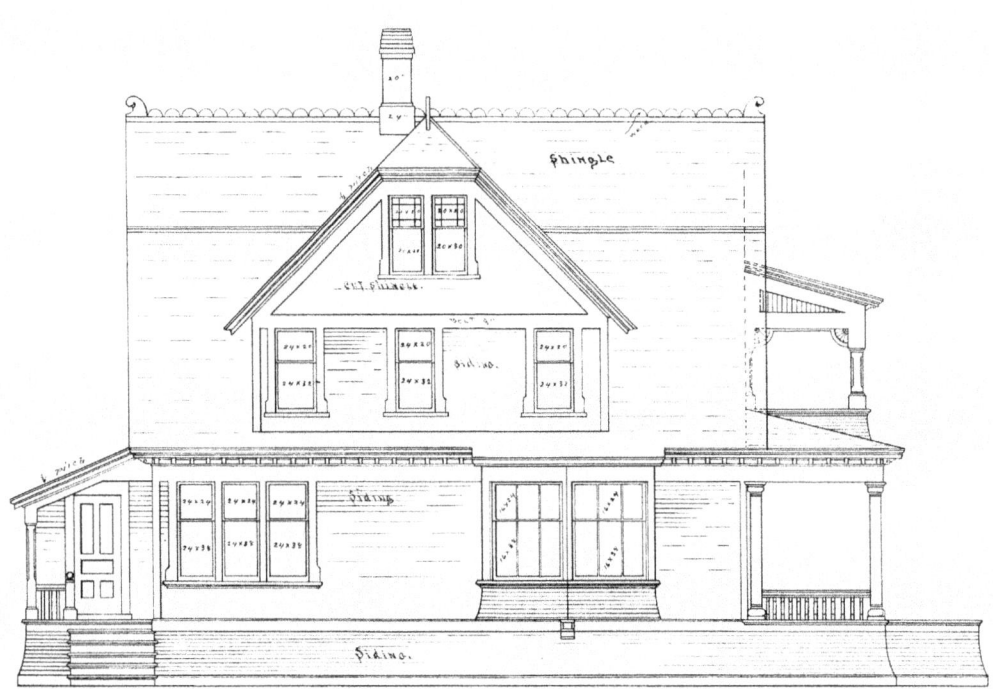

West elevation of the Stebbins Cottage

Born in Woodhull Township, Shiawassee County, Anna B. Burgoyne at the age of three, would move with her parents to a farm near Bridgeport, Michigan. Both her parents John and Julia A (née Foote) Burgoyne encouraged their daughter to attend college. She obtained a scholarship to Hillsdale College where she graduated in 1887. While at Hillsdale College she was a charter member of the Michigan Pi Beta Phi. In 1888 Anna came to Lansing to teach seventh grade at Walnut Street School. She left teaching four years later to marry Arthur C. Stebbins, at the time the manager of Lansing Wheelbarrow. In marked contrast to her husband Arthur, who was an early stock holder of the Olds Motor Vehicle Company, Mrs. Stebbins believed that the horseless carriage had no future. Bedridden the last seven years of her life, the result of two broken hips, Anna B. Stebbins died peacefully at her home on December 24, 1956.[138]

From the Gould inventory of Darius Moon Buildings, listed as "Arthur Stebbins, Cottage at Roaring Brook, Mich, 1902"

---

138   *LSJ* 12/26/1956.

CHARLES W. WHITMAN HOUSE

124 E. Oak, Mason, MI

"D.D. [B.] Moon has prepared plans for two new cottages to be built at Roaring Brook for C.D Woodbury. A.C Stebbins is to build at Roaring Brook also. Mr. Moon has designed a house for Mayor Whitman, of Mason, and is preparing to remodel the F.L. Dodge residence. The later will be especially attractive in the colonial style" (*SR* 4/3/1902). The Whitman residence is a perfect example of an Organic home. Moon repeats the triple column design on each corner of the porch, with double columns on the front of the porch; the resulted is that only the double columns are visible from the street. The massive five sided dormer, an architectural feature that Moon would repeat in several other homes notably the Saier home in Lansing, seems to overwhelm the façade of the house. Notice the flaring of the roof of the dormer. The placement of the smaller dormer, a traditional dormer, helps to soften the view of the house from the street. The photograph below shows the flaring at the base of the pediment of the porch. Also notice the shingles on the side gable.

124 E. Oak, Mason, MI

Charles W. Whitman was born in Elmira, New York on September 22, 1859 and as a young boy his parents settled in Ingham County. Later in 1881, Whitman joined the firm of Webb & Mead, upon the death of Mr. Mead, in 1891, Charles would purchase Mead's share of the business and the company was renamed Webb & Whitman, which grew to become one of the largest clothing stores in Ingham County. At the height of the buffalo clothing craze the firm sold thousands of buffalo robes and coats. In February of 1921 Webb & Whitman sold their business to Donald Densmore and Joy O. Davis. While in the clothing business Whitman began to invest in local real estate and after selling his retail business he began to manage his extensive real estate holdings. For many years Charles Whitman participated in local politics, serving as a Mason alderman in 1887 and 1898 and later as Mayor in 1901 and 1902. For many years he was active in the local Knights of Pythias lodge, which he joined in 1899. On October 9, 1881 he married Miss Mary Flynn in Okemos, Michigan; they had one child a daughter, Faye. Charles W. Whitman died suddenly at his home on February 13, 1936; he was survived by his wife, Mary and daughter Mrs. Faye Reed of Akron, Ohio.[139]

---

139   *LSJ* 2/14/1936 and *Ingham County News* 2/13/1936.

Orville True Home, 2491 S. Okemos Road, Alaiedon Township, MI

The Orville True residence seems to be a modification of the design of the John A. Brooks home at 200 S. Sycamore, Lansing, Michigan and Charles Whitman House, 124 E. Oak, Mason, Michigan both of which Moon designed. The home for Orville True was built around 1902. It was known that Moon sold plans for homes that he had designed and allowed for a home to be built at a discount. It is possible that the Orville True home was an example of Moon's work as an entrepreneur selling a duplicate of slightly modified plans to clients. From Moon's 1904 City Directory Advertisement, "I keep duplicate prints of all plans sent out from my office, and can furnish them complete at a very low price. Come and look them over and you may find just what you want; you will certainly get some new ideas about modern buildings that will make you happy. I have a great variety of modern house plans, and will be pleased to show them at any time; it will cost you nothing to see them, Estimate given and all work guaranteed to be satisfactory in every respect." Local architect Edwyn Bowd sold duplicate sets of plans for as low as $15.

THOMAS J. SHIELDS HOUSE

610 N. Pennsylvania, Lansing, MI

Thomas J. Shields was born in Fall River Massachusetts on April 14, 1867, the son of Patrick and Mary Shields, both of whom had emigrated from Ireland. At the age of 14 Thomas was apprenticed as a plumber and learned his trade working in a variety of New England States. In 1887 Thomas married Miss Annie Sadler and the couple had one child, Percy W., who died in 1917 at the age of 26 from a diabetic coma. Thomas J. Shields was a well-known Lansing business man who arrived in Lansing in 1889 to work at the F.C. Bement Plumbing Company. Later he formed a partnership with F.G. Leadley in 1899 and Shields & Leadley Plumbing was established. Shields would serve in 1909 as head of the state Board of Examiners of Plumbers, charged with the establishing standards in the industry. Shields along with Lawrence Price sought to eliminate the substandard plumbing work that was being installed at that time by developers building large tracts of homes for the working class.

An advertisement for the Shields & Leadley Plumbing Company from the 1906 Oracle

In April of 1913 the partnership with Frank J. Leadley was dissolved and Thomas Shields formed a plumbing business under his own name at 311 E. Michigan Avenue. Shields served as the director of the Michigan State Master Plumbers Association, was active in civil affairs, serving as an alderman from the Seventh Ward and was past Grand Master of the I.O.O.F and a past Exalted Ruler of the Elks Lodge. Thomas J. Shields passed away at his home on Thursday October 8, 1925 survived by his wife Annie.[140]

610 N. Pennsylvania, Lansing. MI

The puzzle with the Thomas Shields home is that the Lansing City Assessor places its date of construction as taking place in 1892. In the Lansing City Directories 1896-1900 Thomas Shields is listed as living at 318 N. Pennsylvania, from 1902 to 1904 at 516 N. Pennsylvania, finally from 1906 on at 610 N. Pennsylvania. The address changes are a result of the renumbering of the city streets during this period. A search of the 1901 and 1902 City Property tax records show that Shield only owned 610 N. Pennsylvania. It is entirely possible the Gould list has an incorrect date, that the date should be 1892 not 1902. The elegant front porch is the focal point of the home. Notice the triple columns on the corner as well as those framing the front entryway to the home and the palmette on the pediment of the porch. The false gable on the second floor with the sunburst detail, maintains the straight line of the roof when viewed from the street. The front gable with the two pent roofs and the two sided oriel window frame the front of the home and mimic the gable on the front porch. The rectangular tower structure which is similar to the one on the small tower on the Olds residence has a false gable as well as an ornate finial at its peak. The home is still standing in 2015.

From the Gould inventory of Darius Moon Buildings, listed as "Tom Shields hse., 1902".

---

140   *LSJ* 10/8/1925 and *Lansing Capital News* 10/8/1925. Annie Shields would pass away on April 22, 1945 in Williamston Michigan, *LSJ* 4/24/1945.

CHARLES SAIER HOUSE

610-612 W. Hillsdale, Lansing, MI

If the reader can look past the faux flagstone siding there is much to see in this design. First this was not a single family home; it was actually designed as a double house. There were separate entrances on both the left and right side of the structure with porches that wrapped around both sides but not across the front, the center entrance was a latter addition. This may explain the odd flagstone siding and the windows on the front of the home on the first and second floor. Notice how they differ from those on the remainder of the home. You can see how the color of the brick work changes above the flagstone siding on the left; the front of the home has been heavily modified. The two small windows on the left side have also been added and the brick work around those windows is different. The five sided dormer was used by Moon in other homes he designed, most notably the Charles Whitman house at 124 E. Oak, Mason, Michigan. The above image was taken in the early 1970s and by that time the home had been divided into at least four apartments; it is unfortunate that an earlier image of the home has not survived. What is significant is that both Thomas Shields and Charles Saier were in the building trades and employed Moon to design their homes, a testament to the respect that those in the building trades had for Moon's professionalism.

Charles Saier was a carpenter and contractor and was well respected for the professional standard of his work. Upon the death of his mother, Elnora, the Saier family became involved in a dispute over the terms of Elnora's will. The case was taken to the Michigan Supreme Court and makes for interesting reading.[141] On October 25, 1877 Charles married Mary (Lena) McClina Kern in Lansing, Michigan. They had four sons, Albert, Thomas R., Victor Sylvester and William Stewart both of Lansing, Michigan. Charles died at St. Joseph's Hospital in Detroit on September 14, 1927.[142] On a side note, Charles and Lena's son, Victor S. Saier played for the Chicago Cubs from 1911-1917 compiling a .265 batting average with the team and replaced Frank Chance, of Tinkers-to-Evers-to-Chance fame at first base. The home was torn down in the 1970s.

From the Gould inventory of Darius Moon Buildings, listed as "Charles Saier Hse., 1902".

---

141   *LJ* 5/16/1900.
142   *LSJ* 9/14/1927 and *Lansing Capital News* 9/14/1927. Lena Saier passed away on February 11, 1933, in Charles' obituary her name is given as Mary M. Saier.

MRS. CROSBY HOUSE

501 S. Capitol, Lansing, MI

PLANS FOR BUILDING
Oldsmobile Company to Build a Big Paint Shop.

RIKERD PLANT NEARLY DONE
Machinery Has Been Shipped-Bates & Edmonds Getting Ready to Build New Factory.

"Architect Moon at noon today completed plans for the new paint shop to be erected at once at the plant of the Oldsmobile company. The foundry is now practically finished, it being expected to start work in it next Monday.
The new paint shop will be a two-story brick building, 55 feet by 200 feet in dimensions, having a capacity which will enable the workmen to finish thirty automobiles a day. Connecting the new paint shop with the main building will brick addition 32 by 110 feet. Work will be commenced on the construction of the shop very soon.

Architect Moon also has prepared plans for a two-story brick warehouse to be erected by Frederick Thoman on Ionia street in the rear of the Robert Smith Printing Company's structure. It will be used by the state printers as a storehouse for paper. The new plant of the Rikerd Lumber Company is now ready to receive the machinery, which has arrived and will all soon be installed. Work on the completion of the roof has been slightly delayed but is again in progress.

The plans for the building to be erected by Bates & Edmonds, near the factory of the Lansing Veneered Door Company, have been completed and it is said the contract will be awarded today. A.M. Robson has commenced the erection of a new residence on St. Joseph street east, and the house being built by Mrs. Crosby at the corner of Capitol avenue and Lenawee street is going up rapidly (*LJ* 8/14/1902).

The *Lansing Journal* article from August 14, 1902 outlines all the work being completed in the Lansing area by Darius Moon. The Oldsmobile Company paint shop, the Thoman warehouse, the new plant for the Rikerd Lumber Company and the Bates & Edmonds building are all known structures designed by Darius Moon. The last two, the Robson house and the Crosby house, were previously unknown homes that were designed by Moon. According to the 1902 Lansing Property tax records Mrs. Louise Crosby owned West 110 feet of Lots 11 and 12 Block 149, translation 501, 505, 507 and 509 S. Capitol Avenue. All these address are present on the 1898 Sanborn maps except 501 S. Capitol which means the home at 501 S. Capitol was built after 1899. What is intriguing is that Mrs. Crosby was the mother-in-law of Samuel Kilbourne who Moon had designed a home for.

The home for Mrs. Crosby has some interesting features. The left side of the home has what can best be described as a canted bay window. The home also has a pent roof between the second floor and the third floor gables. The half circle window on the front dormer is a bit underwhelming; the window is too small which results in it being lost on the façade of the home. The home has a bay dormer which is an unusual architectural element not found on many homes.

Mrs. Louise H. Crosby was born in the state of New York as Louise Woodworth in July of 1839. In 1890 she relocated from Canastota, New York to Lansing to be near her daughter Mrs. Carrie M. Crosby Hyatt who on December 19, 1900 married Samuel Kilbourne. Mrs. Louise H. Crosby died at her daughters home 112 E. Main Street on February 18, 1905.[143] The home was torn down in the 1960s.

---

143   *SR* 2/20/1905 and *LJ* 2/20/1905.

ALBERT M. ROBSON HOUSE

121 E. St. Joseph, Lansing, MI

"A.M. Robson has commenced the erection of a new residence on St. Joseph street east" (*LJ* 8/14/1902). The construction of the Robson home is in the 1902 article detailing Moon's other work in that year. The style of this home is interesting; it resembles the Oscar McKinley house on Butler Street that was built by William Britten. There are some odd architectural elements of the home, the double second story gables, the center third floor gable, the first floor Palladian style window toward the rear, and the wrap around porch. The gables create an unbalanced appearance from the street and create a valley that is problematic for the front porch. The Palladian window was an expensive feature that is hidden from view by being located near the back of the home. Finally the porch seems too small and crowded into the corner. It might have been better if the porch extended across the front of the home with a central pediment.

Albert M. Robson was a lifelong resident of Lansing, born in 1862 to John and Julia S. Robson; he attended the MAC from 1877-1880. For a time Albert worked as the bookkeeper for his father and uncles, Charles and Robert, in the Robson Brothers Wholesale Grocers located on North Washington Avenue. He worked as a commercial traveler and as the manager of Bijou Theater. However he was best known as the owner/operator of the Peninsular Cafeteria which was located in the basement of the American State Savings Bank Building (100 S. Washington Avenue). On October 10, 1883 Albert married Miss Anna Appleyard in Lansing. Anna was the daughter of Lansing architect James Appleyard. The couple had one child, Albert Morell Robson. Albert M. Robson would pass away at his sister's home on April 9, 1938 outliving his wife, Anna who died on September 21, 1924, their son passed away on February 7, 1920. He was survived by three sisters, Mrs. Gordon Smith of Lansing, Miss Helen Robson of Pullman, Washington and Miss Mary Robson of Carlsbad, New Mexico; and two brothers, Frank E. Robson of Detroit and Theodore Robson of Seattle, Washington.[144] The home was torn down in the 1960s.

---

144 For Albert M. Robson see, *LSJ* 4/10/1938, for his wife, Anna E. Robson *LSJ* 9/22/1924 and Albert M. Robson Jr. *LSJ* 2/7/1920.

ROBERT SMITH PRINTING COMPANY

230 N. Washington, Lansing, MI, image circa 1898

"Architect Moon also prepared plans for a two story brick warehouse to be erected by Frederick Thoman on Ionia street in the rear of Robert Smith Printing Company's structure. It will be used by the state printers as a store house for paper" (*LJ* 8/14/1902).

It is unknown if this structure in the above article was ever built or if it was delayed. The above image from 1898 is of the Robert Smith Print Company just after completion; you can see quite clearly that there is no extension over the alley. The 1898 and 1906 Sanborn maps show that the only structures behind the Robert Smith Printing Company's building was a coal bin and alley and a shed for scrap paper, a one story wooden affair; beyond that point there was a series of row houses.

Fredrick Thoman's addition to the Robert Smith Printing Company, image circa 1938

By 1908 Thoman or his architect came up with an ingenious way to solve the problem of a lot that was separated from the main structure by an alley, when the city fathers refused to close an alley. Another one of Frederick Thoman's buildings located at 119-121 E. Ottawa was separated from another section of a Thoman owned property by an alleyway that the city would not close. The simple solution was to build an archway over the alley and build over it to connect the main building to the extension built on the other side of the alley.[145] Just who thought of this innovation is unknown; it may have been Moon or Frederick's son Frederick J. Thoman who studied as an architect under James and William Appleyard. However, Frederick J Thoman left Lansing in 1900 to settle in Jackson, Michigan and had stopped designing buildings after the fire at the Detroit Olds Motor Work Plant in 1901.[146] The addition to the rear of the Robert Smith Printing Company was an interesting piece of design; the addition fits seamlessly into the older structure.

---

145 *LJ* 6/19/1908 and the 1913 Lansing Sanborn Map.
146 Frederick J. Thoman designed several buildings in Lansing; his best known work was the Wentworth Hotel. He also drew up plans for several buildings at the Oldsmobile Plant in Detroit, Michigan.

The rear addition to the Robert Smith Printing Company

The addition was a three story, business block facing Ionia Street which spanned the alleyway allowing the movement of material to the back loading dock.[147] The fourth floor was a later addition.

Frederick Thoman was one of the leaders in Lansing manufacturing and real estate. Born in Fort Hamilton, New York on May 5, 1843 he would spend his childhood in Crestline, Ohio. During the Civil War he was a locomotive fireman with the Army Transportation line. After the war he was an engineer on the Pittsburgh, Fort Wayne & Chicago Railroad. In the 1860s he would marry Miss Elizabeth Reitz of Brooklyn, New York. Fredrick and his wife moved to Lansing in 1868 where he established with his brother-in-law, Frank A Reitz, the Thoman Milling Company. Frederick served as the Lansing alderman from the second ward and in his early days in Lansing was the engineer for the 'Silsby Steamer' fire engine. He held a variety of positions with Lansing companies; he was President of the Michigan Knitting Company; President of the Lansing Wagon Works; Vice President of Lansing State Savings Band and Vice President of the Lansing Capital Savings and Loan Association. Frederick Thoman died at his home on Tuesday December 28, 1915.[148]

The building was torn down in the redevelopment of North Washington Avenue in the 1960s. Moon may have designed other structures for Frederick Thoman after 1910 and are recorded on the Gould list as buildings for Fred Thoman.

---

147   *SR* 5/11/1909 and *LJ* 5/11/1909.
148   *LSJ* 12/28/1915.

RIKERD LUMBER COMPANY

130 Mill Street, Lansing, MI, image circa 1904

On May 27, 1902 at about 2:30 am a fire broke out at the Rikerd Lumber Company's plant on Mill Street. Despite the fire departments best efforts the fire spread to the Alexander Furnace Company and the Lansing Veneer Door Company. The fire department fought the blaze for over five hours; the majority of the buildings at Rikerd plant were destroyed. The fire began at the extreme western portion of the plant and spread eastward. The building owned by the Alexander Furnace Company was leveled as well. The Lansing Veneer Door plant suffered damage to the upper story and all the stock was lost. The sheds housing the wood for the Rikerd Lumber Company and the drying kilns were undamaged. The brick building which housed the company's offices were also severely damaged. The night watchman Frank Purdy was unable to explain how the blaze began, "Shortly after 2 o'clock, "said Mr. Purdy, "I was in the boiler room and threw a little fuel on the fire. Then I went out of the shop. I was gone not over five minutes. When I returned, the interior of the boiler room was ablaze. I shut the door leading into the workshop so as to keep the fire out and ran around to another door and tried to shut that, but a cart with some lumber on it that stood near the door was already on fire. I tried to push that back into the room where the fire was, but some of the burning lumber fell off and stuck in the doorway so that I could not close the door. Then the fire came through and I ran to the corner of Michigan avenue and Cedar street and turned in the alarm from box 55. When I got back the fire had swept to the northern end of the workshop and was running toward the lumber. I got to the boiler room and tied down the valve of the whistle."[149] Both the Lansing Veneer Door Company and the Rikerd Lumber Company would be rebuilt. The Alexander Furnace Company never recovered from this devastating fire. The total losses from the fire were estimated at $60,000. [150]

"The deal between Jacob Stahl and A.A. Piatt on one side and the Rikerd Lumber Co. of the other, which provides that MesSRs. Stahl and Piatt erect a new building for the Rikerd Lumber Co. on the company's former site, was closed this afternoon. The Rikerd company agrees to lease the building for 10 years. Work on the structure, which is to be two stories high, of brick, and somewhat larger than the old building of the Rikerd company, will be commenced at once and hurried to completion. The lease was drawn up by E.C. Chapin and was signed this afternoon" (*SR* 6/6/1902).

"Plans are now being prepared. Architect Moon is preparing plans for a new factory building to be erected by A.A. Piatt and Jacob Stahl on the ground formerly occupied by the factory of the Rikerd Lumber Company recently destroyed by fire" (*LJ* 6/9/1902).

---

149   *LJ* 5/28/1902. By 1904 Purdy had lost his job as a night watchman and was working as a roofer, later he would work as an inspector at the REO Motor Car Company.
150   *SR* 5/27/1902.

130 Mill Street, Lansing, MI

ARCHITECT MOON INJURED BY A FALL

"Architect D.B Moon was painfully hurt this morning at the Rikerd Lumber company's plant, which is in the process of reconstruction. He was walking on the floor to the second story building when he stepped on a loose plank and was precipitated to the ground, striking on his right shoulder and hip. His right arm was badly injured and he was otherwise bruised. He regained consciousness on being taken to his home" (*SR* 7/23/1902).

"The new plant of the Rikerd Lumber Company is now ready to receive the machinery, which has arrived and will all soon be installed. Work on the completion of the roof has been slightly delayed but is again in progress" (*LJ* 8/14/1902).

The Rikerd Lumber Company now the Impression 5 Science Center

It is interesting that Moon was supervising the work at the Rikerd plant at the same time he was drawing plans for the new Oldsmobile Plant. The Rikerd Lumber Company would cease millwork in 1955 and between 1959 and 1960 it would close its doors permanently. The building Moon designed still stands, if you want to spend an entertaining day visit the Impressions 5 Science Museum in Lansing and if you look carefully you can see the interior of the structure Moon designed for Rikerd. Spend some time on the second floor of the building where you can best see the work of Darius Moon; the arched windows and some of the interior work are still visible. Walk to the south end of the second floor, you are now in the old Lansing Veneer Plant. If you look up, you will be able to make out the charring from the 1902 fire. The exterior of the old Rikerd plant is covered by later additions to the plant, but in the area that functions as a loading dock, which faces Museum Drive, the old Mill Street, you will be able to see some of the original exterior. The above image shows a portion of the Rikerd Plant designed by Moon.

Hiram W Rikerd 1961-1937

The son of Daniel W. and Harriet E. (née Case) Rikerd, Hiram W. Rikerd was born in Birmingham, Michigan on February 15, 1861. His parents moved to Ingham County in 1864 where his father purchased 500 acres of land in Lansing Township. They lived there for two years before moving to the city of Lansing. Hiram attended Lansing schools until the age of seventeen, when he began a job working at Broas Clothing Store. In 1885 Rikerd became the Deputy Revenue Collector for the Sixth Division of the First District, which covered Jackson, Calhoun, Ingham, Genesee, Clinton, Shiawassee and Gratiot Counties. In 1889 he left government service to become treasurer of the Capitol Lumber Company and stayed until the company dissolved in 1895. Later that year Hiram formed the Rikerd Lumber Company which he ran as President until his retirement. The Rikerd Lumber Company was known for its fine millwork, an example of which may be seen today inside the Ingham County Courthouse in Mason, Michigan. Although he never married, Hiram had an adopted son, Arthur Randall Rikerd, who served as secretary and treasurer of the Rikerd Lumber Company after his father's retirement. Hiram was active in local fraternal organization and served on the Board of Public Works and the Police and Fire Board. Hiram W. Rikerd died on Friday, March 12, 1937 in his apartment at the Porter.[151]

From the Gould inventory of Darius Moon Buildings, listed as "Stable & Piatt Rickerd Mill, 1903".

---

151   *LSJ* 3/12/1937, Cowles 520, Turner 630, and *Portrait and Biographical Album of Ingham* 418.

1903

LANSING WHEELBARROW COMPANY

Lansing Wheelbarrow Company, Parkin, Arkansas

In 1902 the Lansing Wheelbarrow Company, later to be known as the Lansing Company, purchased a ten acre site in Parkin, Arkansas to establish a plant, and 12,600 acres of forest land in Earle, Arkansas to supply their southern operation. The plant at Parkin was situated on two railroads, the Illinois Central Line and the Iron Mountain Line; the latter rail line ran directly to their timber lands in Arkansas.[152]

Lansing Wheelbarrow Company advertisement from 1909 Lansing High School Oracle

---

152 *LJ* 5/24/1902.

DETAILS OF THE MEMPHIS PLANT
To Be Erected by the Lansing Company

"Plans for the large plant which the Lansing Wheelbarrow Company intends to erect at Memphis, Tenn., are now being drawn by Architect Moon. The entire plant, which the architect thinks will cost in the neighborhood of $100,000, will in the beginning consist of four buildings, although later another may be added. The plant is situated on the 'Frisco' railway and close to the Mississippi river. About thirty miles distant is the enormous tract of wooded land which the company recently purchased. The site it is said is an ideal one for a plant of its kind. The largest building will be the woodshop, 75 to 200 feet in dimension. In another building, 50 by 200 feet, will be the blacksmith shop and boiler and engine rooms. A third building of the same size as the second will contain the paint shop and bench room, each occupying a space 50 by 100 feet. The fourth building will be a warehouse, a large structure standing near the railroad tracks. Later it is expected to erect a drying kiln. The plant at Memphis will be operated in connection with the one in this city, and under the same name" (*LJ* 10/2/1902). There was never a plant built in Memphis for the Lansing Wheelbarrow Company, the mistake in the newspaper article cannot be explained.

"Architect D.B. Moon has completed plans for three new buildings for the Lansing Wheelbarrow works, two at the plant in this city and one to be erected on the company's plat of land in Arkansas. The two new additions in this city will be 36 x 120 feet and 80 x 120 feet respectively. The smaller of the two will be used for a bending room and the larger for a store room and dry kilns. ...The new structure to be erected in the south for the manufacture of wheelbarrows will be much larger building, being 48 x 250 feet" (*LJ* 10/16/1903).

"Large Plant in Arkansas, Lansing Wheelbarrow will erect it. D.B. Moon has completed plans for the new buildings to be erected by the Lansing Wheelbarrow company on its lands in Arkansas, which are located across the Mississippi river from Memphis. The main building will be 251 feet long and forty-eight feet wide, and will be made of brick and wood. There will be several smaller buildings. This will be a completely equipped plant, and is intended to supply the southern trade" (*LJ* 11/16/1903).

Parkin, Arkansas was 30 miles from Memphis and was not located on the Mississippi River. One of the most interesting aspects about Parkin, Arkansas, besides the fact that many streets were named after Lansing residents, Stebbins, Davis and Sparrow, was that the Parkin Plant was at one point managed by Mrs. Agnes Hamill Park, one of the first female plant mangers. Mrs. Park came from Lansing in 1912 to manage the Lansing Wheelbarrow Company's office. The daughter of Henry and Mary (née O'Neil) Hamill, Agnes was born in Michigan in 1862. Later she would marry Elijah C. Parks on August 28, 1902 and they would have one child, Neil H. Park. When Agnes arrived in Parkin with her husband, the Lansing Wheelbarrow Company employed 300 men and had a semi-monthly payroll of $5,000 to $6,000 excluding timber cutting and logging operations. At that time, Donald S. Watrous was the manager of the southern division of the company.

From the Gould inventory of Darius Moon Buildings, listed as "3 Blgs for Lansing Co., 1902".

LANSING WHEELBARROW COMPANY

603 N. Cedar, Lansing, MI

In the fall of 1902 the officers of the Lansing Wheelbarrow Company voted to enlarge the plant in Lansing. It was decided to build a steel pressing plant to allow the company to produce a line of steel scrapers. Judge Claudius B. Grant emphasized the point every day that the decision to build the steel pressing plant was costing the company money and it was in the best interest of the shareholders to act immediately. It was agreed that the new steel pressing plant be located south of the present company's buildings, the cost of the buildings would be $40,000 to $50,000 and the shop would be fireproof. The plant would be used mainly to manufacture steel scrapers. In the new plant sheets of steel will be pressed into shape. The board also approved the building of a plant to service the southern markets. The new machine shops were to be 232 feet long and 60 feet wide and two stories in height. The shipping rooms would also be 200 feet in length and 60 feet wide. [153]

"Architect Moon is preparing plans for the new steel scraper factory to be built by Lansing Wheelbarrow Works" (*LJ* 9/16/1902).

---

153   *LJ* 9/10/1902 and *LJ* 9/11/1902.

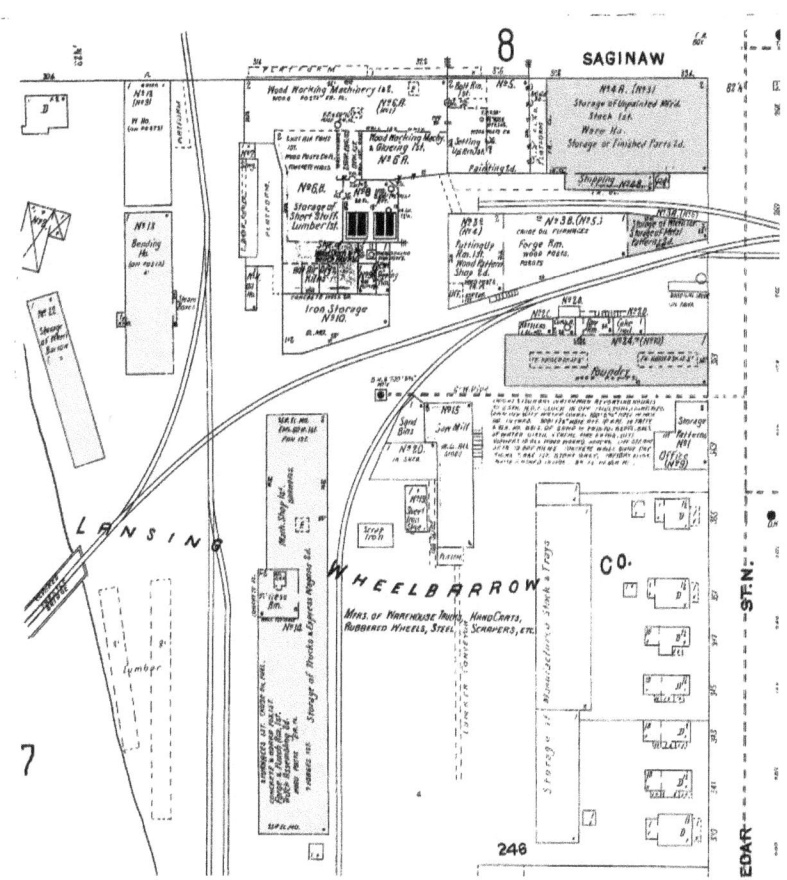

Lansing Wheelbarrow Company, Lansing plant
The buildings Moon designed are in light gray; buildings he may have designed are in dark gray.

Less than ten days after the purchase of an adjoining lot it was decided by the board to add a second building, placed on a right angle from the new machine shop. The contract for the masonry work for the new machine shop was awarded to Fitzpatrick & Early, who estimated that over 375,000 bricks would be needed in the building. The Rikerd Lumber Company was awarded the contract for the lumber while Frank Stolte was engaged as contractor. The work on the building was to be completed by December 1, 1902. It is amazing to see at what pace these buildings were constructed.[154]

---

154   *SR* 9/26/1902 and *SR* 10/2/1902.

A postcard of the Lansing Wheelbarrow Company

THREE NEW BUILDINGS
Capacity of Wheelbarrow Plant to Be Increased

CONTRACTS HAVE BEEN LET
For the Construction of Two New Building[s] in Lansing and One in Arkansas

"Architect D.B. Moon has completed plans for three new buildings for the Lansing Wheelbarrow Works, two at the plant in this city and one to be erected on the companied plat of land in Arkansas. The two new additions in this city will be 36x120 feet and 80x120 feet respectively. The smaller of the two will be used for a bending room and the larger as a store room and drying kilns. Charles Slocum and Andrew Harton have been awarded the contract for driving piles, but the contract for the brick and carpenter work has not been awarded. Work on the new structures will be commenced at once and the company hopes to occupy them by the first of the year. The new structure to be erected in the south for the manufacture of wheelbarrows will be a much larger building, being 48x250 feet. The company this morning bought a new 250 horse power Corliss engine to be used in the plant here" (*LJ* 10/16/1903).

Lansing Company buildings along Saginaw Street

The buildings Moon designed for the Lansing Wheelbarrow Company fit the standard for industrial building at that time. The numerous windows allowed for natural light to enter the building supplemented by the skylights. The buildings were built of brick to decrease the risk of fire. Oddly no buildings from this once sprawling complex survived. Lansing Company ceased production in 1967 with the company's Lansing plant being torn down in 1974.

From the Gould inventory of Darius Moon Buildings, listed as "3 Blgs for Lansing Co., 1902".

MISS SUSAN E. STEBBINS HOME

227 N. Capitol, Lansing, MI

"Miss Susan E. Stebbins will have remodeled the residence which she occupies, located just south of the First Baptist church, Capitol ave n." (*SR* 3/16/1903). This remodeling is noted in an article that describes all of Moon's work at the beginning of 1903.

"Changes are being made as well in Miss Susan Stebbins' house, also on Capitol avenue north" (*LJ* 10/5/1903).

Susan E. Stebbins Starks 1863-1937

Surprisingly this lovely home is still standing. The home was acquired by the First Baptist Church in 1945 and was eventually incorporated into the Church' offices at 235 N. Capitol. The home is often overlooked because Capitol Avenue is one-way from north to south. But if you walk northward along Capitol Avenue you will see the home. Just who the original architect of the home at 235 N. Capitol Avenue was is unknown, the two architects practicing in Lansing at that time of construction were ISRael Gillett and James Appleyard. The two-story bay windows, the paired front doors and the scrollwork over the clipped gable make this home an example of a gabled ell Italianate home. Just what remodeling work Moon did on the home is unknown, but in all likelihood it was on the interior of the structure not the exterior. The house is similar in appearance to the James B. Seager home at 533 S. Grand which still stands today.

Mrs. Susan Stebbins Stark was a lifelong resident of Lansing and was born August 7, 1863 to Cortland B. and Susan E. (née Burley) Stebbins at the family home 221 N. Capitol Avenue, where she resided her entire life. Her father, Cortland B. Stebbins was at one time the editor of the State Republican Newspaper and on July 1, 1858, he entered the State Office of Public Instruction, becoming the Deputy Superintendent of Public Instruction, a position he held for twenty years under five different superintendents. On June 27, 1908, Susan married Byron Wade Stark Jr. in Lansing, Michigan. Susan E. Stebbins Stark was a lifelong antique collector and after her death many items from her collection were donated to the Henry Ford Museum in Dearborn, Michigan. Susan E. Stebbins died at the home of her brother, A.C. Stebbins on Saturday, March 13, 1937.[155]

From the Gould inventory of Darius Moon Buildings, listed as "Susie Stebbins, No Date".

---

155 *LSJ* 3/14/1937, her husband Byron W. Stark Jr., died on October 4, 1935.

OLDS MOTOR WORKS

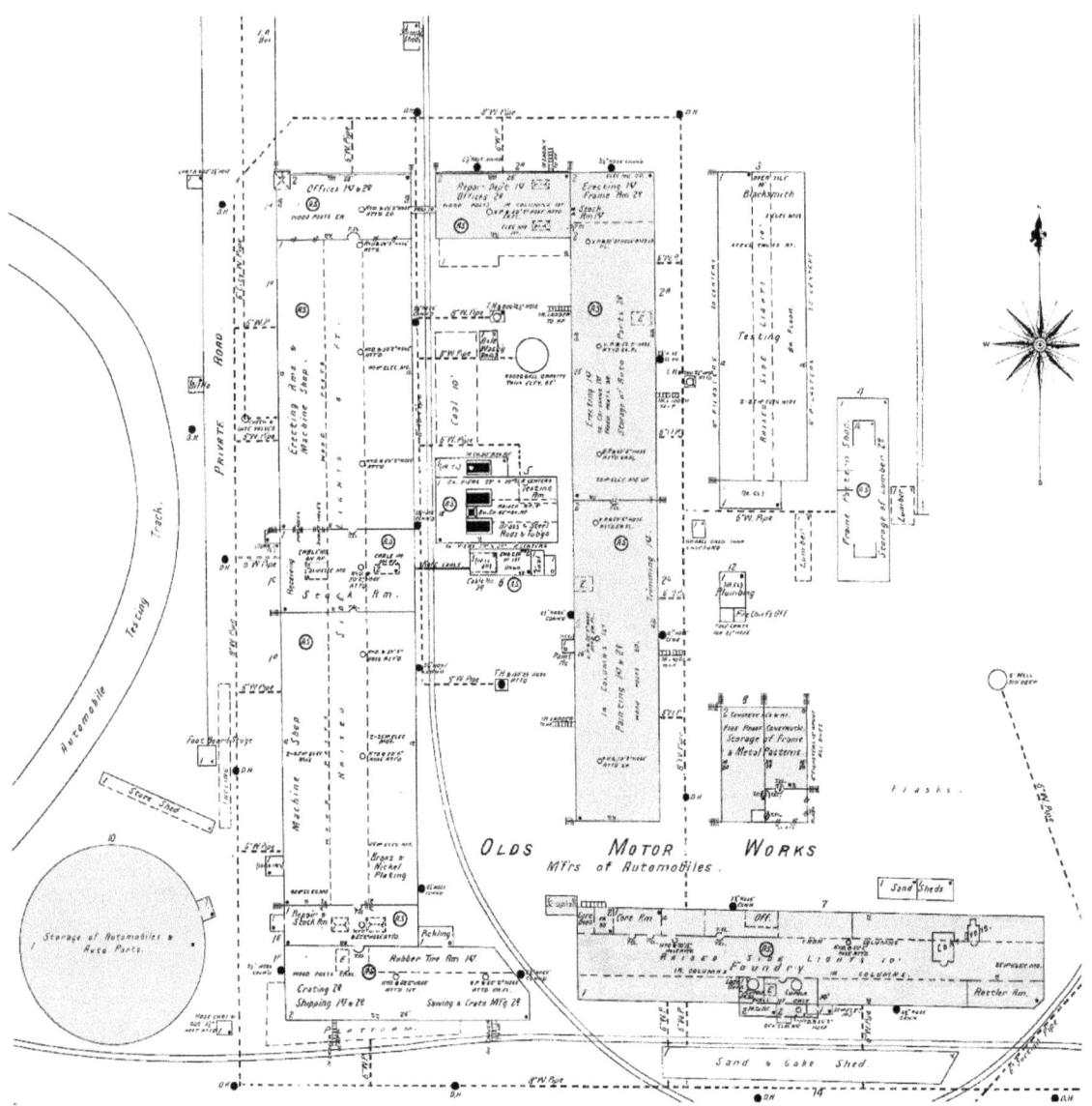

Olds Motor Works Lansing, MI
The buildings shaded in grey were designed by Darius Moon at the Olds Motor Works.

"SPRING BUILDING— Two new buildings are in the process of erection at the Olds Motor works. A brick one-story building 60 by 80, is being built on the west side of the plant. Part of it will be used for testing purposes and the balance as a paint shop. On the south side a pattern vault, 17 by 46 is being erected" (*SR* 4/27/1901).

NEW BUILDINGS AT THE OLDS WORKS. BIG FOUNDRY NEARLY COMPLETED
AND PAINT SHOP PLANNED

"A brick foundry one story high and 70x160 feet in dimension, is now being constructed near the main building. Mr. Olds said this morning that the building would be completed in a week or two. The construction of a paint shop 60x200 feet in dimensions is about to commence and the building will be completed this summer, it is expected" (*SR* 7/7/1902).

"Architect Moon at noon today completed plans for the new paint shop to be erected at once at the plant of the Oldsmobile company. The foundry is now practically finished, it is expected to start work in it next Monday. The new paint shop will be a two story brick building, 55 feet by 200 feet in dimensions, having the capacity which will enable the workmen to finish thirty automobiles a day. Connecting the new paint shop will the main building will be a brick addition 32 by 110 feet. Work will commence on construction very soon" (*LJ* 8/14/1902).

"E.B. Wight has been awarded the contract for the erection of the new paint shop to be built by the Olds Motor works. The dimensions of the new building are 55 by 200, and will be built of brick" (*SR* 8/30/1902).

OLDS MOTOR WORKS TO ADD TWO LARGE BUILDINGS TO ITS PRESENT EXTENSIVE PLANT
One Will be Machine Shop 500 by 150 Feet and the Other a Foundry 200 by 70 Feet—To be Erected at Once Additions Will Furnish Room for the Employment of 300 More Men, Who may be Needed This Season

Large extensions to the automobile plant of Olds Motor works are being planned, and it is expected work will be commenced within ten days.
One building, 500 feet long and 150 feet wide, will extend north and south paralleling the present main building. It will occupy a position on the extreme east of the old fair grounds. This will be a machine shop. The foundry will be added to by an extension to the east 70 by 200 feet in dimension. The foundry was only recently built to do all the foundry work required by both the automobile and gasoline engine factories in this city, but it has been necessary to practically double its capacity.
The foundry extends east and west, lying at the south end of the grounds, and, leaving out of consideration the space occupied by a spur track, the foundry is connected with the main building. The main building is 700 feet long, and with the foundry and its addition the "L" shaped structure will be 1300 feet, or a quarter mile in length.
The location of the new machine shop will be such as to form a court, in which are situated many of the old frame buildings which were on the grounds when the property came into the possession of the Olds company.
"The new additions will furnish room for 300 more men, said R.E. Olds this afternoon. 'We are now working on plans and want to let the contracts within ten days, so that the additional capacity can be used in production for this season's orders'" (*SR* 4/10/1903).

"Ground was broken today for the addition to the foundry at the Olds Motor works. Frank A. Stolte is the contractor for the building, the dimensions of which will be seventy by 150 feet. The plans are not complete for the other and larger building, which will be built this summer. R.E. Olds was not able to say last evening just how many machines will be shipped to Germany on the order of E. Weingartner and R. Loube, who came here to buy automobiles yesterday. It is a question of how many the company can supply and not how many the Germans want. The two dealers came with a plentiful supply of cash" (*SR* 4/17/1903).

"Ground was broken this morning for the new foundry to be built at the Olds factory on Division street. The foundry will be 161 feet long by 72 feet wide" (*LJ* 4/21/1903).

An early image of the Olds Plant

CONTRACT WILL BE LET TOMORROW
Olds Motor Works To Duplicate Main Building at Division Street Plant

"Tomorrow the Olds Motor works expects to let the contract for its second large building, a counterpart of the long structure which constituted the original factory building on the fair grounds. The building will require about 1,000,000 brick and 500,000 feet of lumber.
Architect D.B. Moon has almost completed plans for the circular building, which will furnish an enclosed test track on an inclined plane" (*SR* 6/25/1903).

WORK COMMENCED ON TESTING BUILDING
Olds Motor Works Erecting One of Unique Design — Entrance Underground

"Work has been commenced by Olds Motor Works on its new testing building, which is of a unique design. The building is circular and speeding tracks are inclined at a considerable angle. Entrance is gained through an underground tunnel, which brings the automobile in the center. In diameter the structure is 150 feet. Its foundations have been laid west of the first main building of the automobile works, where the wind mills use to be at the fairs.
The work on the large machine shop is still delayed owing to the non-arrival of brick" (*SR* 8/26/1903).

Oldsmobile Plant circa 1906

NEW BUILDING NEARLY DONE
Large addition to Old's Motor Works' Plant to be Ready Soon

TESTING HOUSE FINISHED
Power Capacity Increase by Installation of New Engine

"The large addition to the Olds Motor Works, the building at the east of the grounds which is practically a counterpart of the first main building is now almost under cover and within two weeks will be completed. This can also be said of the "round house," which is west of the main factory, and which will be used for testing the autos when the half-mile track cannot be used. The machines will run the required number of miles on an inclined plane, and the entrance is to be in the center through an underground passage" (*SR* 11/11/1903).

HANDSOME BUILDINGS
Oldsmobile Company is Moving Into Them

"The Oldsmobile Company is moving into the two new machine shops which it has lately erected as an addition to the present plant. The buildings are of brick, are two stories high and one is 50 by 130 feet and the other is 75 by 500 feet. Both shops are heated by steam and are completely equipped for the uses for which they are intended. The new testing house will also be finished this week. This is a circular building 150 feet in diameter with two tracks for testing autos. The outside track is an incline, the inner is level. Both are planked. The roof is supported by forty columns and lighted by a skylight. The entrance in through a tunnel that goes under the track. When this building is completed it will likely end the company's building until next spring" (*LJ* 12/14/1903). [156]

The majority of the buildings that Moon designed for the Olds Motor Works were of the accepted industrial design for the period, but what was exceptional was the enclosed test track that he designed. Although it was a magnificent failure the test track with its innovated design bears recognition as an attempt by Moon to provide year round testing of automobiles for the company.

From the Gould inventory of Darius Moon Buildings, listed as "Most of the buildings Olds Motor wks. 1900".

---

[156] The circular building was Building 10, built June 1903, razed in 1912. It was 150 feet in diameter and was called a winter test building. This information was provided by Dave Pfaff.

HOMER D. LUCE HOUSE

711 S. Capitol, Lansing, MI

"Architect D.B. Moon is preparing plans for a handsome frame residence to be constructed for Homer D. Luce on the lot adjoining that occupied by the residence of Hugh Lyons; Capitol ave s. Mr. Luce has sold his present residence at 806 Ottawa st w to Chas. Herrmann" (*SR* 3/2/1903).

"Homer L. Luce has broken ground for a new residence adjoining that of Hugh Lyons, corner of Capitol avenue and Main street" (*LJ* 4/18/1903).

711 S. Capitol, Lansing, MI

An eclectic mix of several architectural styles, the Luce residence can best be described as a Queen Anne style home with some Victorian features. Beginning with the front porch which has Ionic columns, notice how the roof of the porch extends almost to the start of the steps, something not seen before in other Moon designed homes. The porch extends across the front of the home and gracefully curves toward the side, ending near the half circle bay window, which must have been wonderful to view from the interior. The second floor as seen in the above image has a side porch toward the back that blends seamlessly with the exterior of the home. The first image of the Luce home clearly shows the sunburst detail on the pediment of the porch. There also is a bay window on the second floor stacked above a boxed bay window on the first floor. Towards the back of the home is an odd clipped open gable which can be seen in the first image. In the history of Lansing there were three homes which needed to be preserved, the Olds Mansion, the Barnes Mansion and the Luce home, Lansing is poorer for their loss.

Homer D. Luce 1862-1940

Homer D. Luce was born in Coldwater, Michigan on December 14, 1862 the son of Cyrus Gray and Julia A. (née Dickinson) Luce. Homer's father Cyrus served two terms as Michigan Governor from 1887-1891. In 1884 Homer graduated from Michigan State College and three years later married Miss Grace Burnham on June 22, 1887. The couple would have two daughters; Julia B. and Mary E. Luce. After he graduated from the MAC, Homer opened the Luce Drug Store which he managed for several years during which time he was a respected member of the Michigan Pharmaceutical Association.

Homer D. Luce

In 1893 Luce entered into a partnership with Hugh Lyons and Elgin Mifflin to form the Hugh Lyons Company, which manufactured store fixtures and later in 1930 he established the Luce Manufacturing Company which built truck bodies. He was president of the Country Club of Lansing, actively participated in the National Grange, served on the Lansing police and fire boards; in 1917 he was a member of the local draft board. At the time of his death in October of 1940 Luce was vice president of the Citizens Loan and Investment Company.[157]

In Moon's 1904 City Directory advertisement listed Homer Luce as one of the gentlemen for whom he had designed a home. The residence was torn down 1966 as a result of the construction of I-496.

From the Gould inventory of Darius Moon Buildings, listed as "Homer Luce Res. 1903".

---

157   *LSJ* 10/15/1940.

TURNER DODGE MANSION

Turner Home, 100 E. North, Lansing, MI, circa 1859

"Architect Moon is making plans for the remodeling of the residences of J.H. Wellings and Col. Fred Schneider, and the old Turner home on North street" (*LJ* 3/21/1902).

West end of the Turner Dodge Home (A.G.)

"D.D.[B] Moon has prepared plans for two new cottages to be built at Roaring Brook for C.D Woodbury. A.C Stebbins is to build at Roaring Brook also. Mr. Moon has designed a house for Mayor Whitman, of Mason, and is preparing to remodel the F.L. Dodge residence. The later will be especially attractive in the colonial style" (*SR* 4/3/1902).

100 E. North, Lansing, MI (A.G.)

It is not clear when James Turner built his home at 100 E. North Street. An image of the residence appeared on the 1859 Topographical Map of Ingham County so it is safe to place its construction after 1855. The home was originally a Greek Revival structure with a two story core and one story wings on either side. The decorative frieze around the flat roof as well as the side porches would have made this one of the most stylish home in Lansing when it was constructed. After Frank Dodge acquired the home he engaged Moon to do a complete reconstruction. The result was the Colonial Revival mansion that exists today. The focal point of the residence was the massive porch. This was a porch that was meant to make an impression on the visitor and inspire the passerby. The large Ionic columns that support the porch, especially the third floor porch would become a trademark of a Moon designed porch; he would repeat it in the Smith home in Eaton Rapids, Michigan and the Nice apartment house at 1025 N. Washington, Lansing, Michigan. It is interesting that the gables on the mansion are open gables while the dormers that frame the gables are closed. Notice that the dormers are not identical, one is a double window dormer while the other is a single window dormer. The dormers are the only disproportionate aspect of the residence. It is intriguing that the original entryway to the home was kept which resulted in the entrance being off center on the home, while the exit to second floor porch is stacked above the main entryway which places it off the centerline of the residence and mimics the placement of the first floor entryway. The door from the ballroom on the third floor is centered, which you would believe would lead to the residence having an unsymmetrical view from the street, but it does not. Moon's successful stacking of the windows creates a balanced view when the residence is observed from the street. One last architectural aspect that bears mention is the use of the large dentils used along the soffits, they are almost Italianate in appearance, and along with the roof cresting they add an almost fierce appearance to the home. If you are ever in Lansing it is well worth your time to view this remarkable structure.

Frank L. Dodge

Frank L. Dodge was born in Oberlin, Ohio on October 22, 1853 to Hervey and Angeline (née Stevens) Dodge. His early education was in Oberlin schools and later Frank would live with his brother John S. Dodge in Cleveland, Ohio to continue his schoolwork. At the age of seventeen Frank found employment as a locomotive fireman and began his studies in law by reading James Kent's *Commentaries on American Law*. After quitting the railroad, Frank moved to Eaton Rapids and worked with his brother William in the hotel business.+3.

Later, Frank was able to save enough money to take up the study of law in the office of the Honorable Isaac M. Crane in Eaton Rapids, Michigan. In 1877, he was admitted to the Michigan bar before Justice F.A. Hooker. Isaac Crane then took the young lawyer as a partner in his law firm, a relationship that continued until 1884 when Isaac retired. In 1879 Frank moved from Eaton Rapids to Lansing to open a law office. In 1885 Frank was appointed United State Commissioner for the Eastern District of Michigan a post that he held for ten years. Frank was active in local politics serving on the Lansing City Council for twelve years, served on the police and Fire Board, the Lansing School Board and was appointed by Governor Ferris to serve as chairman of the State Board of Arbitration and Conciliation. In 1882 and 1884 Frank L. Dodge was elected to the Michigan State House, introducing a bill that established a Circuit Court in Lansing. True to the ideal of public service, he supported the building of a new courthouse in Mason, Michigan, even though he fought to establish a Circuit Court in Lansing just 20 years earlier. Often overlooked is the legislation he introduced requiring fire escapes in hotels, theaters and other public establishments. In 1926 Frank was the Democratic nominee for the United States Congress against Grant M. Hudson; Dodge captured only 32% of the vote.

100 E. North, Lansing, MI

Dodge had extensive business holdings and was Secretary of the Lansing and Suburban Traction Company; he also partnered with his brother-in-law, James M. Turner and established the firm Turner & Dodge at Springdale Farm which was involved in livestock. Frank L. Dodge was a member of several Masonic organizations, the Knights of Pythias, I.O.O.F. and the K.O.T.M.

In November of 1888 Frank Dodge married Abigail Turner daughter of James Turner; the union resulted in five children, Sophie Dane, Franklin L. Jr., Wyllis Osborne, Josephine Nicholson and Marion Elizabeth. Frank Dodge would later purchase the Turner home from his mother-in-law, Marion Turner in 1896. Frank L. Dodge died at St Lawrence Hospital on December 24, 1929.[158] Abigail Turner Dodge, or as she liked to be known Abby, was a tremendous influence of her husband's life. The daughter of James and Marion Turner she would become a fixture in Lansing society. A patron of the Lansing Matinee Musical Society and a member of the Daughters of the American Revolution she helped to establish Lansing as a center for culture in the state. Abby died at her home on Sunday afternoon, February 23, 1947 the last of the ten children of Frank and Marion Turner to survive.[159]

In Moon's 1904 City Directory advertisement listed F.L. Dodge as one of the gentlemen for whom he had designed a home. From the Gould inventory of Darius Moon Buildings, listed twice "F.L. Dodge Residence 1903" and "Frank Dodge Res. 1903".

---

158   *LSJ* 12/24/1929 and *Lansing Capital News* 12/24/1929 and 12/26/1929. For Frank L. Dodge's professional life see Frazier 105.
159   *LSJ* 2/24/1947.

LIEDERKRANZ HALL

Liederkranz Hall before fire, 536 N. Grand, Lansing, MI

On the evening of February 23, 1903 at 6:30 pm, the Lansing Fire Department responded to an alarm from Box 43 regarding the blaze at the Liederkranz Hall. Because of a short in the alarm system, which read Box 43 as Box 53, there was some delay before the fire department arrived. The fire originated in the kitchen; due to the nature of the structure the firemen had some difficulty reaching the conflagration which by this time had spread to the attic. Only after the firefighters chopped a hole through the roof and maintained a steady stream of water were the flames brought under control. Unfortunately about one hour after the fire department had left the scene, the fire reignited and the fire department returned. The flames were quickly extinguished. The only injuries were sustained by Chief Sedina whose cutter struck a post throwing him over the dashboard and to the ground. The building was fully insured and it was at the time the organization decided to remodel the structure.[160]

---

[160] *SR* 2/24/1903.

Liederkranz Hall after renovation, 536 N. Grand, Lansing, MI

"Sealed proposals will be received up to Monday, July 6, 1903, noon for remodeling the Liederkanz Hall. Plans and specifications can be seen at the office of D.B. Moon, Architect. A certified check for two hundred dollars to accompany cash bid as a pledge of good faith to enter the contract. The right is reserved to reject any and all bids. Address Leiderkranz Building Committee, Box 88 Lansing Michigan" (SR 6/20/1903).

"Liederkranz Hall to be remodeled. Plans have been drawn for remodeling the Liederkranz hall in this city. The roof of the building will be lifted and another story with a twelve-foot ceiling constructed. This room is intended for a dance hall. Two commodious verandas will be added to the east side of the hall, fronting on the garden, and the interior repaired and refitted. Bids are being open this afternoon for the contract to do the work" (LJ 7/24/1903)

After the fire Moon's services were engaged to remodel the building. Essentially what Moon did was to design a new first floor for the Liederkranz Hall, and raise the old structure to become the second floor. By closely examining the photographs and you can see that many of the original architectural elements from the old building are still in place: the gables still have the same form, the triple sash windows are no longer on the lower level and are now on the second floor, and what was the entrance was enclosed. All in all, a creative reuse of the old Liederkranz Hall structure into the construction of the new building.

On February 1, 1905 the new hall would be dedicated. Over 500 people attended the ceremony including Mayor Lyons, C.E. Bement and Judge Q.A. Smith. Afterward the Liederkranz and Arbeiter societies preformed a series of musical numbers followed by a dance.[161]

---

161   LJ 2/17/1905.

The Lansing Liederkranz Club was formed in 1868 as a singing organization for German speaking vocalists. The founding officers read like a who's who of early Lansing pioneers. The president was Frederick Schneider, vice president was Rudolph Kern, secretary, Christian Ziegler and treasurer was Louis Bertch, all familiar names to people with an interest in Lansing history. The Liederkranz Hall was built in 1872 on North Grand Avenue, after a fire in 1883 a new hall was designed by James Appleyard. Another fire would occur in 1903 and Moon would be employed to remodel the hall. The Liederkranz Hall property was acquired by the city of Lansing during the First World War and later torn down. The Liederkranz Club still exists today and is located on south Pennsylvania Avenue.

From the Gould inventory of Darius Moon Buildings, listed as "Ledercranze Clubhouse-Lansing 1903".

WILLIAM KIRK HOUSE

2106 Main, Fairgrove, MI

"Architect D.B. Moon is just completing plans for a handsome new residence to be erected by Rep. Wm. Kirk, Fairgrove, Tuscola county" (*LJ* 8/1/1903).

The home that Moon designed for William Kirk was an exact duplicate of the house that Moon designed for George Keith in 1898. Keith's residence was located directly south of the state Capitol building. Kirk who was elected to the State House in 1900 would have seen Keith's residence on a daily basis. The highlight of the home is the second floor porch with the Turkish style roof. Although the second floor porch columns are damaged, you can observe that the same urn style columns were used here as well as the Keith home. Over the first floor porch is a two side bay window, but notice on both the first and second floor porch how the brackets are identical to those used on the Keith residence. The only difference between the two homes was the stone porch on Keith's house and that is not entirely certain because the only surviving image of Keith's house was from after it was moved to 211 S. Chestnut.

The upper porch on the Kirk home

Born in Glenwherry, Antrim County, Ireland in 1844, William Kirk moved to Michigan in 1861 from Canada. He went west in 1867 for the laying of the last rail of the Union Pacific Railroad. After his return from the west, William purchased swamp land near his father's farm and developed the property in to one of the finest farms in the area. In 1872 he married Elizabeth Drysdale in Kippen, Ontario, Canada and they had nine children, six of whom survived infancy, Anne, Sadie, Susie, Robert, James and Veva. In 1900 he was elected to the State House where he served two terms. In 1903 William sold his farm to his son-in-law and moved to Fairgrove to occupy his new home. William remained active in area affairs; he was president of the Tuscola County Fair Association for 17 years and a County Supervisor for 7 years. In 1920 William and Elizabeth moved to Caro, Michigan where William would pass away on May 31, 1927; he was buried in the Brookside Cemetery in Fairgrove Michigan.[162] The home still stands today.

---

162   *Tuscola County Advertiser* 6/3/1927.

HILDRETH MOTOR & PUMP COMPANY

A advertisement for the Hildreth Motor & Pump Company, 1131 Race, Lansing, MI

"The Hildreth Motor & Pump company has begun work on a new three story building, to be added to the plant on Race street, North Lansing. The building will be three stories in height, 72 by 40 feet in dimensions and will be built of brick. The new building will be used for a molding room, pattern shop and offices. D.B. Moon made the plans" (*LJ* 10/29/1903).

Unfortunately no image survives of the Hildreth plant. An aerial image of North Lansing from the 1930s shows only a corner of the plant, but not enough to allow a detailed description.

William W. Hildreth established a foundry and machine shop in Lansing just after the end of the Civil War. For a time the plant was located at the corner of Washtenaw Street and Capitol Avenue and was the only foundry and machine shop in central Michigan. At a later date William would bring his brother in to the business which was renamed W. W. Hildreth & Brother. The business grew as the firm established standardized products, molded metal pillars for store fronts and supports. With the support of local businessmen the firm was recapitalized, a new plant was built on East Shiawassee Street and the firm's name was changed to Lansing Iron Works. The financial panic of 1873 forced the business to close. The old plant would operate as the Lansing Boiler and Engine Works although no longer under the control of the Hildreth family. William Hildreth along with his son Ned entered into a partnership with the Glassbrook Foundry and Machine Shop. In May 1893 Curtis T. Cady, William W. Hildreth and Ned E. Hildreth formed the Cady & Hildreth firm. With the financial panic of July 1893, the firm was hard hit and suffered through two bank failures but managed to survive and later grow. The shop produced the first marine gas engine to be built in Lansing. Marine engines produced by the company were used in boats that won races in Natal, South Africa and New Orleans. The Hildreth's acquired the business and renamed it the Hildreth Motor & Pump Company. The plant produced a variety of products; the foundry even produced some of the early castings for REO Motor Car Company. The name would later change to the Hildreth Manufacturing Company in 1908. [163] The plant later became the home of the Standard Casting Company. The property was cleared in the 1950s and is today a parking lot.

---

[163] *LJ* 9/30/1908, *SR* 9/30/1908 and *LSJ* 7/14/1924.

Ned E. Hildreth 1866-1958

The son of William W. Hildreth, Ned Elmer Hildreth had a lifelong connection to engineering. Involved in his father's business from an early age, Ned served as the superintendent of the Hildreth Motor & Pump Works and later treasurer and superintendent of the Hildreth Manufacturing Company. Ned Hildreth sold his family's interests in Hildreth Manufacturing in 1908 to R.H. Scott and E.F. Peer. A year later Ned would leave Lansing to work as an engineer with the Cushman Motor Works in Lincoln, Nebraska where his considerable engineering skills were employed by the company. In 1911 the Hildreth Manufacturing Company was renamed by C.E. Bement and became the Novo Engine Company. In 1920 Ned would resign as the superintendent of the Cushman Motor Works and accepted the position of manager at Witte Engine Works in Kansas City, Missouri. After 1930 Ned Hildreth dropped from view only to resurface in St. Petersburg, Florida in 1945 working as a mechanical engineer. Ned Elmer Hildreth died in Pinellas County, Florida in March of 1958 and was followed two years later by his wife Estelle Louise Hildreth who died in January of 1960.[164]

BEILFUSS MOTOR COMPANY

701 E. Saginaw, Lansing, MI

LAND PURCHASED FOR NEW FACTORY
Beilfuss Motor Co. Will Erect plant on Saginaw Street East

"The Beilfuss Motor Co. have purchased of (from) George Lathrop a piece of land on Saginaw st e, running alongside of the M.C. and P.M. railroads, for a site for their proposed engine works. Architect D.B. Moon has completed the plans for their building, which is to be brick, and 30x100 feet in size, fronting on Saginaw

---

164   Cowles 457-458, Turner 351 and *American Machinist* 47: 407. The *SR* 2/15/1896 reported that Ned Hildreth was to marry Miss Elizabeth Cowdery in Cleveland, Ohio, it cannot determine if this wedding ever took place.

St. It is expected that the contract for the building will be let this week, and work will be begun at once. The company has contracted for new machinery to be delivered April 1, by which time their new building is expected to be ready for occupancy" (*SR* 2/11/1903).

Big Increase of Business
Makes the erection of a New Factory Necessary

"An extraordinary increase in business has resulted in the Beilfuss Motor Company's determination to erect a new plant at the corner of Saginaw street and the Michigan Central railway. The structure will be built this spring as soon as weather permits. Plans for the building, which will include the machine shop, store rooms, office and engine room, are now being drawn by Architect Moon. They will be completed and submitted to the company by Thursday, if not sooner" (*LJ* 2/11/1903).

The Beilfuss Motor factory was a typical example of early Twentieth Century Industrial design, large arched windows and skylights to allow in as much natural light as possible. What is appealing about the Beilfuss Motor Building is the façade. The cornice of the building resembles that of a castle with battlements with caps and brick corbels on the face of the façade. The building was later purchased by Prudden Company and used for storage; later the structure was torn down with the expansion of the Motor Wheel Company.

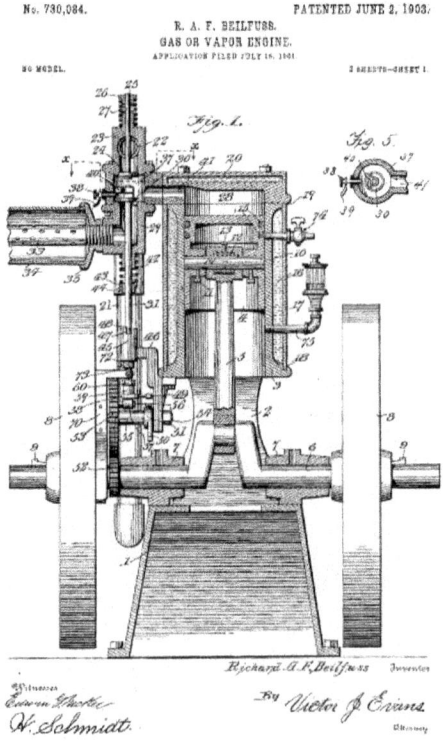

The Beilfuss Gas or Vapor Engine

The Beilfuss Motor Company was owned by Edward M, Reitz, President, Louis Ehinger, Vice President and Richard A.F. Beilfuss, Superintendent. The company was founded in Lansing in June of 1902 and began producing engines in the old Presbyterian Church located on the corner of Washington Avenue and

Genesee Street. The gasoline engines they produced were based upon four patents held by Richard Beilfuss, Edward N. Reitz and John F. Betz and they were used in automobiles and as a stationary power source. With increasing demand the company expanded in 1903. George Kohler was contracted to build the new plant with the understanding that the plant was to be completed by March 25, 1903 so that production would not be interrupted. Construction of the plant was finished on time under the supervision of Martin E. Fitzpatrick and machinery was moved to the plant the following week. In about 1909 demand for the Beilfuss engine began to decline and the company ceased production in 1912.[165]

Richard A.F. Beilfuss was born on June 24, 1874 in Albion, Michigan to Ferdinand and Sophia (née Stemdus) Beilfuss. Nothing is known about Richard's childhood. On September 8, 1897 Richard married Miss Ida Boumann in Lansing; there were six children by the marriage, Irene, Eileen, Helen, Alfred, Vern and Lucile. Richard's wife Ida Matilda Beilfuss an active member of Christ English Lutheran Church and died at the family home on Tuesday December 21, 1943.[166] Richard A.F. Beilfuss passed away on October 10, 1946 in Kalamazoo, Michigan and his body was returned to Lansing for burial at Mt. Hope Cemetery.[167] No other information has been located on Richard A.F. Beilfuss other than he was issued a patent for a Speed-Regulator for Explosive-Engines in 1902 and another in 1903 for a Gas or Vapor Engine. By 1915 he was working as a machinist at W.K. Prudden Company.

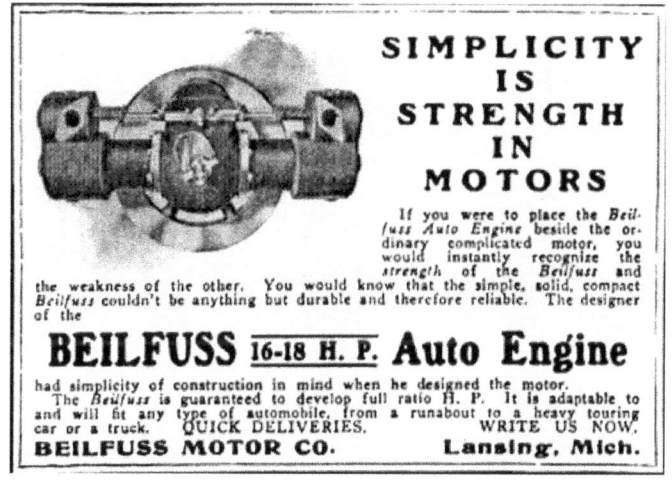

Beilfuss Advertisement Motor Magazine August 1906

"The Beilfuss Motor Co., of Lansing, Mich., are marketing a two cylinder horizontal opposed water-cooled motor with the mechanically operated values and all other working parts on the top and side. The motor is claimed to be able to develop from 16 to 18 H.P. and has a bore and stroke 5x5 inches. It is 34 inches long, 14 inches in width, and weighs complete with balance wheel, 300 pounds. The manufactures point out that it is most simple and compact and is adaptable for any type of motor car, from runabout up to a heavy car."[168]

From the Gould inventory of Darius Moon Buildings, listed as "Rietz Y Betts Factory 1903."

165	See *SR* 1/17/1903, *SR* 2/14/1903, *SR* 2/26/1903, *LJ* 3/25/1903 and *SR* 3/25/1903.
166	*LSJ* 12/21/1943. Ida was the daughter of E. Baumann and Sophia (née Stemdus) Baumann.
167	*LSJ* 10/11/1946.
168	*Motor* 114.

MRS. SARAH C. WILSON DOUBLE HOUSE

716-718 N. Washington, Lansing, MI (A.G.)

"Architect D.B. Moon has prepared plans for a three story double residence, 35x37 feet, for Mrs. S.C. Wilson. It will be built of wood and will cost $5,000" (*SR* 9/14/1903).

"Mr. Moon has also made plans for a new three story double house to be built on Washington avenue north for Mrs. S.C. Wilson. The contract has not been let for this house, but the building is to be ready for occupation March, 1 1904" (*LJ* 10/29/1903).

A view of the upper stories of the Wilson home

Mrs. Sarah C. Wilson the widow of Lucius D. Wilson was a respected Lansing resident. She was a member of the Women's Relief corps and of the First Presbyterian church. Born in Ohio, Miss Sarah C. Sheflet (Shiflett) married Lucius D. Wilson in 1869 and move to Chicago. Lucius began his business of manufacturing sewing machine stands. Unfortunately in the great Chicago fire of 1871 Lucius' business was destroyed and he suffered a serious financial loss. The family would move to Lansing in 1873 where the couple raised their four children, Rena, George, Harry and Dot. Lucius died in Lansing on February 11, 1901 of dropsy.[169] Sarah lived as a widow for 25 years supporting herself and her children by running a rooming house. Sarah C. Wilson died at her home on November 19, 1926.[170]

---

169   *LJ* 2/11/1901 and *SR* 2/11/1901.
170   *LSJ* 11/20/1926.

The Wilson house prior to demolition

This was a three story cross gable double home with a variety of architectural features. On the first level notice the separate porches and entrances. The porch to the right originally had a rounded front extension which can be seen in the first photograph, while the smaller porch on the left wrapped around the home. The second floor has a two sided bay window on the left followed by a more ornate three-sided bay window with at tent style roof finished with a ornate finial, notice in the first photograph the two-toned shingles on the tent-style roof. The massive dormers finish off the structure, the front gable is a closed dormer with a pent roof at its base while the side dormers are open; in a sense they could be described as gables. This was a structure whose style told prospective tenants that this was one of the finest residences in Lansing. Sarah Wilson lived at 716 N. Washington, the ornate unit on the right in the photographs. Interestingly Sarah Wilson's daughter Rena M.B. Wilson sold a piece of property in Section 17 to Moon in 1904. From the Gould inventory of Darius Moon Buildings, listed as "Sarah Wilson apts-Lansing, 1903". The home was torn down 1979.

EDWIN PORTER HOME

300 Townsend, Lansing, MI

In 1903 the Gould list has Moon designing a home for Ed Porter. There were two Ed Porters in Lansing at that time, Edgar and Edwin; Edgar lived at 215 N Capitol from 1898 to 1908, Edwin occupied 120 (114) S. Walnut in 1904, the home of his late father-in-law, Charles E. Nash whose home was remodeled by Moon in 1882. Edgar only owned one property in Lansing in 1903, 221 N. Capitol. Edwin and his wife owned several properties in Lansing in 1903. Therefore Edwin is the best option for the Porter, who Moon designed a home for in 1903. There are several possibilities, 300 Townsend, 114 S. Walnut, 326 W. Maple and 1100-1104 N. Walnut. In 1908 Edwin and his wife moved to 300 Townsend a newly built home. It is possible that Moon was the architect for this home, but the date is incorrect. This is an odd home for Moon to have designed for this period; it is a typical four square residence. In many ways it is not unlike George Wilson's home, plain but practical. Although the home was simple in appearance the interior may have been quite grand and the house originally had a porch that ran the full length of the front. The residence may have reflected the tastes of Edwin and Emily, practical and unadorned.

1104 N. Walnut, Lansing, MI

Emily, Edwin's wife owned Lot 4 Block 109, 114 S Walnut through her father, the couple later sold the property to the First Church of Christ Scientists in 1908, so it is doubtful that the Porters would have renovated a home that they were planning to sell. In 1903 Edwin briefly owned, the West 4 Rods of Lots 7-8 Block 36, 326 W Maple and 1100-1104 N Walnut. The home in 326 W Maple was built in 1870 according the Lansing City Assessor. While the structure at 1100-1104 N Walnut was listed in the Assessor's records as being constructed in 1906. It is possible that the Porter's hired Moon to design plans for renovating 114 S. Walnut or 410 W Allegan which was also located on Lot 4 Block 109, but this is doubtful. The most likely candidate for a Moon structure is 1100-1104 N. Walnut. There is one other scenario that needs to be considered. Edwin and Emily Porter owned the majority of the Handy Home Addition, Subdivision; it is possible that Moon was designing model homes for the subdivision, something that Moon would do later for the Potters.

Born in Marcellus, New York on December 16, 1822, the son of Reverend Seth J. Porter and Cynthia M. (née Haines) Porter, Edwin H. Porter came to Kalamazoo, Michigan with his parents in 1833. After her husband's death in 1834, Mrs. Porter married Homer Stimson and the family moved to a farm in Van Buren County, Michigan. After the death of his step-father Edwin apprenticed as a carriage maker to support the family and later began his own carriage business. Later Edwin would become Assistant Postmaster under his brother-in-law James A. Walker, who was Postmaster in Kalamazoo, Michigan. With the start of the Civil War, Edwin Porter enlisted in the Fourth Michigan Cavalry as the Commissary Officer and served throughout the war and was present when Lieutenant Colonel Benjamin D. Pritchard Regiment captured Confederate President Jefferson Davis.

E. H. PORTER. MRS. E. H. PORTER.

PORTER & PORTER,

...GENERAL FIRE AND CYCLONE INSURANCE AGENTS...

LANSING, MICHIGAN.

OFFICE IN REAR OF PEOPLES SAVINGS BANK,
NO. 109 MICH. AVE. W.

ATTENTION GIVEN TO THE RENTAL OF PROPERTY, PAYMENT OF TAXES AND CONVEYANCING.

Porter & Porter advertisement, note that Edwin is in business with his wife Emily

In October of 1866, Edwin came to Lansing to serve as a land commissioner under Benjamin D. Pritchard, Commissioner of the State Land Office, who was an old army acquaintance of Edwin's. After retiring from state service in 1871 Edwin entered the retail shoe business, in the same building that would later become the site of John S. Wilson's Sugar Bowl. Edwin changed careers and would become a leader in the local insurance business. On December 22, 1845 Edwin married Miss Adeline E. Walter and they had four children, Harvey W., Charles E., Alice A., and Nellie. Adeline E. Porter died on June 23, 1865. Edwin would later marry Miss Emily Nash of Lansing, the daughter of Charles E. Nash. What is fascinating is that in 1894 Emily would purchase the J.B. Porter's portion of the J.B. & E.H. Porter Insurance Agency and become a partner with her husband Edwin, becoming one of Lansing's early female business leaders. Edwin H. Porter died on Monday May 6, 1912 at his home in Lansing.[171] His wife Emily died in 1924 and was remembered in the words of the Lansing State Journal, "During the warm days of last spring and summer she [Emily] was often seen on her porch, where so many passed, and she has a customary greeting for many, The life flowing past from the state office building was a delight of her declining days." .[172]

From the Gould inventory of Darius Moon Buildings, listed as "Hse for Edd Porter, 1903".

---

171 See the *LSJ* 5/6/1912 and *Portrait and Biographical Album of Ingham* 401.
172 *LSJ* 3/22/1924.

GEORGE WILSON HOUSE

720(614) N. Washington, Lansing, MI

In 1903, George L. Wilson was a machinist at Hugh Lyons Company; his mother was Sarah Wilson who lived next door at 716-718 N. Washington, in a Moon designed home. On June 30, 1904 George married Miss Louise Grammel; there were no children by the marriage. George opened the Wilson Machine Works at 124 E. Madison Street which he founded in 1914. He died working in his shop on Saturday, October 6, 1934. He was survived by his wife Louise G, one brother, Harry Wilson of East Lansing and two sisters Mrs. Dot Fratcher and Miss Rena Wilson, both residents of Lansing.[173]

George Wilson's home which Moon remodeled in 1903 is a paradox. The home itself is an unassuming structure, a single gable home with little exterior ornamentation. It is possible that Moon's work on the George Wilson home consisted of an interior remodel and a new porch being added to the home. There are no images that survive of the exterior of the Wilson home before the remodel and interior images of homes from this period are limited, this may be unwarranted speculation.

In Moon's 1904 City Directory advertisement listed Geo. Wilson as one of the gentlemen for whom he had designed a home. From the Gould inventory of Darius Moon Buildings, listed as "George Wilson- Remodeled Hse, 1903".

The home was torn down in 1967.

---

[173]   *LSJ* 10/8/1934.

DR. JAMES H. WELLINGS HOME

915 (911) N. Washington, Lansing, MI

"Architect Moon is making plans for the remodeling of the residences of J.H. Wellings and Col. Fred Schneider, and the old Turner home on North street" (*LJ* 3/21/1902).

It is unknown just what type of remodeling work Moon performed on the Wellings' residence. It is possible that Moon remodeled the porch on the home as well as the interior. The porch has many of the characteristics of a Moon designed structure, especially the sunburst element on the pediment of the porch which can be seen in the photograph below. You can also observe at bay window on the south side of the home. In regards to the interior it is unknown what improvements Moon may have made.

915 N. Washington, Lansing, MI

Dr. James H. Wellings was a Lansing pioneer, a student in the early days of the Michigan State Agricultural College (MAC) and was active in Lansing's business community as well as the city's social life for many years. Wellings attended MAC from May 1860 to 1863 and in December of that year joined the 2nd Michigan Infantry, Company E, enlisting as a private and mustering out as a 2nd Lieutenant. After the war he attended Bellevue Hospital Medical College, New York City. Upon graduation in the spring of 1874 he returned to Lansing and in 1880 he received an honorary M.S. degree from the MAC. Wellings was the physician at the Michigan Industrial School for Boys and held a similar position at the MAC.

On May 1, 1869 James married Miss Josephine Myra Hammond. The couple had one child, Maude, who married G. Carl Bronson and settled in Tucson, Arizona. Maude would pass away in Arizona on December 17, 1905 of tuberculosis, James and Josephine would raise Maude's two daughters, Marion and Ruth Benson.[174] Upon his retirement in 1919 Dr. Wellings moved to Hollywood, California to reunite Maude's children with their father Carl. Dr. James H. Wellings died in California on July 19, 1920 and his wife Josephine would be killed several months later when the automobile she was a passenger in was struck by a train.[175] The house is still standing in 2015.

From the Gould inventory of Darius Moon Buildings, listed as "Dr. Wellings-Remodel Hse, No Date".

---

[174] *LJ* 12/19/1905 and *SR* 12/19/1905.
[175] See *LSJ* 7/20/1920 and *Journal* 73: 1144. For Josephine Myra Wellings death see the *LSJ* 9/7/1920.

CHESTER D. WOODBURY HOMES

110 W. Grand River, East Lansing, MI

Between 1901 and 1907 Moon designed three houses for Chester D. Woodbury. All indications are that these homes were built in East Lansing. In 1899 Chester Woodbury, Dr. J.W. Hagadorn, Judge Edward Cahill and A.C. Bird purchased a portion Dr. Miles farm just north of the MAC. The parcel they purchased was 95 acres of which 54 acres would become the Oakwood plat.[176] In October of 1899 the *Lansing Journal* stated that "Dr. J.W. Hagadorn is already engaged in building and Judge Edward Cahill and C.D. Woodbury will build such fine residences in the spring that they may decided to move into them" (*LJ* 10/14/1899).

This gets confusing since we are searching for three homes that Moon designed for Woodbury between 1901-1907, so all the properties that Woodbury held in East Lansing need to be reviewed. Woodbury owned in the Oakwood Subdivision, Lots 21, 22 and 23, and in College Grove Subdivision he owned Lot 2. The Oakwood lots would have been located on the north-west corner of Abbot Road and Grand River Avenue, 110 W. Grand River Avenue and 229 Abbot Road. The property in College Grove would have been located at south-east corner of Abbot Road and Albert Avenue; in 1913 it was 308-312 Abbott Road, later 218-226 Abbott Road and 315 Albert Avenue, later 104 Albert Avenue.

---

176   *LJ* 7/22/1899.

415 MAC Avenue, East Lansing, MI

It is not known exactly when the home at 110 W. Grand River was constructed. The home does appear on the 1906 Sanborn map for Collegeville. It may very well have been the home referred to in the 1899 article concerning the home Woodbury was building in Oakwood in 1900. The 1905 and 1906 City Directories have Woodbury living at 101 Short Street in Lansing and the 1908 City Directory lists him as living in East Lansing but no address is given, in the 1910 Census Woodbury is living on Abbott Road. By 1916 Woodbury is listed as living in his father's old home at 422 Townsend in Lansing. In 1911 house at 110 W. Grand River was sold in 1911 to the Hesperian Society (Beal 206). The home was moved in 1926, to 323 Ann Street then moved again in 1984 to 415 MAC Avenue where the home still stands today. The second home may have been located at 229 Abbott Road. There was no structure on this lot according to the 1906 Sanborn map, but there is a house present on the 1913 Sanborn map, no image survives of this home.

415 MAC Avenue, East Lansing, MI

The Woodbury home is one of the architectural ornaments of East Lansing. Notice the flaring of the siding between the first and second floor and on the third floor gable. Look closely at the first image of 110 W. Grand River and you can see that the flaring was also incorporated in to the side of the porch. In that photograph you can also observe a small railed landing in front of the porch, with a balustrade with two newel posts capped with ball ornaments. The third floor porch which is recessed into the gable is a striking attribute but what has been removed from the home is the second floor porch on the opposite side, it can just be seen when viewing the first photograph, it is located just to the right over the end of the first floor porch. When the home is viewed from the street the eye is attracted to the tower, or rather what seems to be a tower. The bowed windows on the second floor are capped, quite creatively with a bay dormer, which gives the illusion of a tower, especially since the dormer is covered by a false conical roof.

104 Albert, East Lansing, MI

"Busy year for Builders. …Dr. J.W. Hagadorn and C.D. Woodbury near the college" (*LJ* 12/9/1905). The previous article outlines the new homes being built in the Lansing area in 1905. The article may be a reference to the homes Woodbury was building on Abbott Road and Albert Street.

The 1913 Sanborn map shows three homes on the College Grove Lot 2, 308-312 Abbott Road, renumbered 218-226 Abbot Road and 315 Albert Avenue, which later became 104 Albert Avenue. By 1926 the homes at 308-312 Abbot Road had been torn down and replaced with the current apartment block. No photographs survive of these homes; however there is a 1940 image of the home at 104 Albert. It is likely that the other two homes Moon designed for Woodbury were two of these homes, either 229 Abbott Road, 308-312 Abbott Road or 104 Albert Avenue.

The home at 104 Albert Avenue is a gambrel residence with a large porch, little else can be observed except for the shed dormer on the side of the home. The home would have been inexpensive to build and is of no exceptional merit.

606 Townsend, Lansing, MI

The Woodbury home at 606 Townsend Street in Lansing has long been attributed to Darius Moon but all indications are the home was designed by Earl Mead. The home at 606 Townsend was built between the years 1892-1894; Moon spent the majority of this time period in Chicago.

"J.B. and E.H. Porter sold the residence of C.D. Woodbury, Hillsdale street west, to Rev. Leroy Warren of Olivet yesterday. Mr. Warren will take procession this fall. Mr. Woodbury will immediately have plans drawn for a $5,000 residence on the southwest corner of Townsend and Hillsdale streets" (*SR* 6/17/1892).

"C.D. Woodbury will erect another $5,000 residence at the corner of Townsend and Hillsdale streets the coming summer, plans for which are now being prepared by E.H. Mead," (*LJ* 4/8/1893).

All but forgotten in Lansing and East Lansing, Chester Downey Woodbury was instrumental in the development of both cities. Born in 1857 near Portland, Michigan, Chester D. Woodbury worked in the lumber business in Mississippi as a young man. He was well known in Lansing as the owner of C.D. Woodbury shoes and later the men's furnishings store Woodbury & Savage. Later in life he was associated with the Capital Savings & Loan and was President of the New Way Motor Company. Woodbury also was instrumental in the founding of the Roaring Brook Resort on Little Traverse Bay, along with Judge Edward Cahill, L.C. Blood, Robert Smith, H.R. Pattengill, A. Beamer and William Crosby; the group purchased

135 acres adjoining the famous Wequetonsing Resort. What is often overlooked was his involvement in the development of Collegeville (East Lansing). In 1899 Woodbury along with Judge Edward Cahill, A.C. Bird and Dr. Johnson W. Hagadorn developed the Oakwood subdivision just north of the Delta. Chester D. Woodbury died at his home at 422 Townsend on August 24, 1936 just three weeks after the passing of his wife May.[177] Born May Goodrich in Portland, Michigan in 1854, little is known about May's early life. On January 14, 1879 May married Chester D. Woodbury and the couple would have one child, Charles G. Woodbury who would become head of the Bureau of Raw Products Research of the National Canners Association and an expert on American Horticulture. May G. Woodbury passed away at her home on August 2, 1936.[178]

In Moon's 1904 *City Directory* advertisement listed C.D. Woodbury as one of the gentlemen for whom he had designed a home. From the Gould inventory of Darius Moon Buildings, listed as "3 Hse's for C.D. Woodbury, 1901-1907".

---

177   *LSJ* 8/24/1936. The home at 422 Townsend, where Chester Woodbury spent the remainder of his life, was also designed by Lansing Architect Earl Mead for Chester's father, John D. Woodbury in 1893.
178   *LSJ* 8/3/1936.

1904

JOHNSON W. HAGADORN HOUSE

215 Evergreen, East Lansing, MI

"Architect Moon is preparing plans for a brick residence to be built for Henry Kositchek on Capitol ave n. Plans are also being made for a handsome framed residence to be constructed for Dr. J. W. Hagadorn in Collegeville" (*SR* 3/4/1903).

NEW ONE FOR OAKWOOD
Dr. J.W. Hagadorn Gives Contract for Large House near M.A.C.

"Architect D.B. Moon has just let the contracts for a fine modern residence on Michigan ave e, at the entrance to the college grounds for Dr. J.W. Hagadorn. The building will be three stories in height and modern in every way. The contract has been let to Clarence Croope, who is to complete the building June 1, 1905" (*SR* 9/26/1904).

215 Evergreen, East Lansing, MI

HESPERIAN HOUSE
Society at M.A.C. has new House

"Agricultural College June 13. — The Hesperian society has rented for the coming year the new house completed for Dr. Hagadorn, just east of the residence of A.C. Bird. The old Hesperian society rooms were in the ill-fated Wells Hall and the majority of the members of the society had rooms in that building at the time it burned. The new rooms will be so divided as to give the society a new House and to provide rooms for the members. The first floor will be for the general society and the second and third floors will be used for the rooms for the members" (*LJ* 6/23/1905 see also *SR* 6/13/1905).

"Busy year for Builders. ...Dr. J.W. Hagadorn and C.D. Woodbury near the college" (*LJ* 12/9/1905). The previous article outlines the new homes being built in the Lansing area in 1905.[179]

---

179   Dr. Hagadorn owned three lots in 'Collegeville', in the Oakwood Subdivision, Lots 13, 14 and 15. The home at 215 Evergreen occupied Lots 13 and 14. Lot 15 was an odd shaped lot with a dwelling at 315 Evergreen.

215 Evergreen, East Lansing, MI

Johnson W. Hagadorn's home was an enormous house along Grand River Avenue and was built in 1904 on the west side of Evergreen. It was moved in 1916 to the back of the property, when it became 215 Evergreen. The Hesperian Society rented the Hagadorn home from 1905 to 1911 when in that year the society purchased the Woodbury house for their new home. The next occupant of the home was the Kappa Delta Sorority. The home at 215 Evergreen has often been described as a Queen Anne style home; it seems a better description would be that of an organic house. The home has elements of the Queen Anne style but has many other features that do not quite fit with the definition of a traditional Queen Anne home. First discount the porch in the above image, it was added later, although the rubble stone foundation is interesting. The first photograph in the section is probably the earliest image we have of the Hagadorn residence, notice that the foundation is different. You can also observe the oriel window on the second floor along with the back of the home which was quite extensive. The porch entrance also changes; in the first photograph it has a side stairway while in the second it is a centered stairway. In the second image you can also see the tower of the home at 148 W. Grand River in the background. Why is this important? It tells us that the first photograph is probably of the home before it was moved to 215 Evergreen and therefore it is how the home looked before any alterations were made because of the move. In the first image you can see a large front dormer with the diamond style leaded glass window in the center. Towards the back of the home on the third floor you can also observe a shed dormer similar to the one that was on the Woodbury home. The final photograph shows a bay window suspended over a basement doorway and the extensive rear of the home, which seems to be a home in its own right. Essentially the home was chopped up at this time to form typical off-campus housing.

Johnson W. Hagadorn 1839-1910

Johnson W. Hagadorn was born near South Lyon, Michigan on September 9, 1839. He attended the state normal school in Ypsilanti (Eastern Michigan University), later he entered medical school at the University of Michigan graduating in 1870. Hagadorn later studied at the Eye and Ear Infirmary and Rush Medical College in Chicago. After graduation he worked as a physician in Ovid, Michigan for two years, then relocated to Lansing in 1873 and opened a medical practice. In the fall of 1866 he married Miss Dora Raymond of Adrian, Michigan. While practicing in Lansing he served for many years as the physician at the Michigan School for the Blind and the Boys Industrial School. Dr. Johnson W. Hagadorn passed away at his home on April 17, 1910, survived by his wife Dora and two brothers, Dr. Alexander D. Hagadorn of Lansing and Albert Hagadorn of California.[180] The home was destroyed by fire in 1972.

From the Gould inventory of Darius Moon Buildings, listed as "J.W. Hagadorn Hse-E. Lansing, 1904".

---

180   *LJ* 4/18/1910, *SR* 4/18/1910 and Cowles 231.

HENRY KOSITCHEK HOUSE

514 N. Capitol, Lansing, MI (A.G)

"Architect Moon is preparing plans for a brick residence to be built for Henry Kositchek on Capitol ave n. Plans are also being made for a handsome framed residence to be constructed for Dr. J. W. Hagadorn in Collegeville" (*SR* 3/4/1903).

The Herrmann Home and the Kositchek Residence notice the size of the Kositchek House

The above image was added to give a sense of perspective as to the size of the Kositchek home; you can compare its size to that of the Herrmann house. The Kositchek residence was an organic home that incorporated many different architectural design elements. The first floor porch with the faced stone foundation and a balustrade, which was also of stone, blends with the Ionic columns that support the structure. There is an oriel window on the north side of the home, while on the second floor there is a small porch with a five-sided wooden balustrade and a shed dormer, supported by the less formal Tuscan style columns. What is intriguing is the window on the second floor on the far right. It seems to be a Chicago-style window, a three section window with a large fixed center pane flanked by two smaller double hung sash windows, however in this case the center pane is a double hung window. It raises the question of whether Moon learned about this style of window while he was working in Chicago? The third floor front gable also has an impressive Palladian style window and a small dormer with a small lunette window above the lower window. This style dormer was not previously used by Moon. There is also a large south facing dormer and to finish off the home a finial which can be seen in the above image.

514 N. Capitol, Lansing, MI

H. KOSITCHEK & BROS.

"The firm of H. Kositchek & Bros., of Lansing, has established a reputation for fair dealing which has brought the proprietors of the store a substantial trade. The members of the firm are friendly to the labor cause. H. Kositchek & Bros, sell clothing and dry goods, keeping in stock only the best. Their prices are right and the customer is always sure of getting his money's worth. Their clothing store is located at 113 Washington avenue north and the dry goods store at 210 Washington avenue south" (*Michigan Federation* 233).

Henry Kositchek 1852-1925

Henry Kositchek was born in 1852 in Bohemia when the Austro-Hungarian Empire ruled over the lands of the Czechoslovakia Republic. Henry came to the United States in 1868, with his sister Bertha and her husband Jacob and settled in Eaton Rapids, Michigan. His parents Solomon and Katte Kositchek along with a younger brother Max joined Henry in 1870. The family for many years operated a Kositchek Dry Goods store in Eaton Rapids; Henry would later open a separate clothing store in Eaton Rapids. Unique for that time period the Kositchek family guaranteed the items they sold and established a name for quality that still exists today. A pioneer clothing merchant in Mid-Michigan, Henry Kositchek moved his clothing business in 1889 from Eaton Rapids to Lansing and established H. Kositchek & Brothers at 113 N. Washington Avenue where the business still operates today. On September 30, 1883 Henry married Miss Bella Weil in Newark, New Jersey and the couple would have a daughter Edith, and two sons, Sol and Louis M. Kositchek. Henry was active in Lansing affairs and was a member of Lodge 68, F. &A.M. Henry Kositchek died at his home on July 9, 1925 and was buried at Mt. Hope Cemetery.[181]

The home was torn down in 1967. Moon's 1904 *City Directory* advertisement Kositchek is listed as one of the gentlemen for whom he had designed a home. From the Gould inventory of Darius Moon Buildings, listed as "Henry Kosichek Res. 1904".

JUDGE ROLLIN H. PERSON HOUSE

319 (311) W. Lenawee, Lansing, MI

"S.A. Dunphy, who recently came from St. Louis, MO., to assume the management of the Hammell Cracker Co., has rented the residence of Judge R.H. Person, Cedar st s, where he will establish his family in the course of a few weeks. Judge Person will move into the house at 311 Lenawee st w, which he has purchased and remodeled" (*SR* 3/26/1905).

---

181 *LSJ* 7/10/1925, *Lansing Capital News* 7/10/1925 and Munn 55. For Belle Kositchek death see *LSJ* 4/1/1943.

It is evident from the above article that Moon remodeled the home at 319 [311] W. Lenawee and that it was not new construction. The problem is we do not know the extent of the renovation. From the Sanborn maps we know that the footprint of the home changed between 1898 and 1906. The porch that originally wrapped around the home and extended to the rear was modified to just the front of the structure. Part of the area that used to be the porch was enclosed and became part of the residence. Finally a bay window was added to the home. The front porch in the above image was a later modification as was the addition on the left.

Judge Rollin H. Person 1850-1917

Rollin H. Person was born in Livingston County, Michigan on October 15, 1850, the son of Cornelius and Lucinda (née Stafford) Person. After working for two years as a school teacher in the Howell area, Person was appointed Deputy Register of Deeds in Howell. In 1872 Person began the study of law in the office of Dennis Shields and attended the University of Michigan Law School in 1872-1873 being admitted to the state bar in 1873. In July of that year he married Miss Ida M. Madden, daughter of James G. Madden of Illinois; they had four children, Harlow, Harry, J. Armond and May. After living for a period of time in Republican City, Nebraska where Rollin served as the temporary Register of Deeds for the city he returned to Lansing with his family. After his move to Lansing, Person held several public offices; he was the Circuit Judge for the Third Judicial Court and senior partner in the law firm Person, Shields & Silsbee. In 1916 he was appointed to the Michigan Supreme Court a position he held until early 1917. Besides being an active member of the State and National Bar Association, Person was a Mason, having taken all degrees to the Knights Templar and was also a member of the Lansing Elks Lodge. Supreme Court Justice, Rollin H. Person died at his home in Lansing, Michigan on June 4, 1917.[182] The site of Judge Rollin H. Person residence is now a parking lot.

From the Gould inventory of Darius Moon Buildings, listed as "Judge Person Hse, 1904".

---

182   LSJ 6/4/1917. On a side note, Person's son Harry J., served with the British Army in South Africa in the Kitchener's Fighting Scouts Regiment during the Boer War, he later would establish Deepdale Cemetery in Lansing. Another son, Harlow S. Person, was Dean of Dartmouth's Amos Tuck School of Administration.

DR GEORGE RANNEY BLOCK

500-504 E. Michigan, Lansing, MI

"Dr. George E. Ranney has plans prepared for the erection of three store buildings on Michigan ave. just west of Larch st. They will be constructed this coming summer" (*SR* 2/8/1905).

THREE BRICK STORES FOR THE EAST SIDE. DR. GEORGE H. RANNEY WILL ERECT FINE STORE BUILDINGS AT ONCE

"Michigan avenue east is to have some new store buildings, and the vacant lots between Cedar and Larch streets south are to be at least partially occupied. The new buildings are to be erected for Dr. George H. Ranney, and are to be placed on his property between the streets named. There are at present two small wooden buildings at the corner of Cedar street south and Michigan avenue. They are occupied at present by the Gilkey Awning factor, and the Rouser grocery. Preparations were begun yesterday to move these buildings father east and make room for the new ones. Three modern brick buildings are to be built on the Cedar street corner, the work to be commenced as soon as the old buildings are out of the way. These will be two stories high and will be in an up to date style, and will add greatly to the appearance of the street" (*LJ* 3/31/1905).

"The Ranney stores on Michigan avenue east are to be larger than was at first intended. According to the revised plans they will be three stories in height, and one of them at least, the building on the corner, will have the top floor arranged for an apartment house. The first story will be used as announced for stores, and in the basement there will be room for such establishments as barber shops" (*LJ* 4/11/1905).

In this full version of the article is also mentioned the German Lutheran Schoolhouse, the parsonage, the Ranney building and a house for John Kneal; all buildings constructed by Moon.

500-504 E. Michigan, Lansing, MI

TO OPEN FINE STORE
RANNEY BLOCK BEING PREPARED FOR DRYGOOGS STORE

"W.A. Fairweather, for many years one of the progressive business men of Cass City, recently sold out his store in that city, while on a visit to relatives in this city, was so pleased with Lansing and its business opportunities that he decided to locate here. As a result, he has leased the Ranney store, at the corner of Michigan avenue and Cedar street, and will shortly open a fine dry goods store there, with new fixtures and a complete new line" (*LJ* 7/26/1906).

The Ranney building on East Michigan Avenue was a four business block structure. The building has the windows stacked symmetrical one above the other. The corbelling on the façade just below the parapet is a typical architectural feature of a commercial building of this period; it is accomplished by stepping the brickwork backwards. The odd cap to the pediment seems to be too large for the structure; although decorative, the building many have been better without this addition. The Ranney Business block was torn down and the site is now the home of the Stadium District Apartments.

From the Gould inventory of Darius Moon Buildings, listed as "Business Black for Dr. Ranny, 1904".

EDWIN PORTER SHERMAN HOUSE

Edwin Porter Sherman House, Bancroft, MI

"In 1905 Mr. Sherman (Edwin) had erected a private residence which without a doubt is the finest House in Bancroft. Its cost was about twenty thousand dollars" (Moore 2036).

The house was later abandoned and became know as Bancroft's haunted house; it was destroyed in the 1960s and now is the site of the city park. This must have been a remarkable home in its day, a centerpiece for the community of Bancroft. The home had four bathrooms, music room, conservatory, butler's pantry, sewing room, six bedrooms on second floor, a ballroom on the third floor and a laundry drying room in basement. The double stone porches with the stone columns are an architectural feature not employed before by Moon. Notice the rounded canted bay window, the structure resembles the false tower on the Woodbury home. The roof of the canted bay window mimics an architectural element known as the witch's hat except it is not a hat but extends into the gable roof. The formal colonnade on the third floor front gable is an interesting feature; considering that it does not really fit with the overall design of the home, but it does work. Moon splits the gable into two sections with the pent roof over the colonnade; it creates the impression of a Roman temple. Finally there is also a Porte-cochère, present to the right in the image which has a sunburst motif on the facing of the pediment and adds an elegant finish to the residence.

Edwin Porter Sherman was born in Conoctah Township, Livingston County on February 13, 1870 to Roger and Emma F. (née Swarthout) Sherman. In about 1880 Roger Sherman moved his family to the village of Bancroft, Michigan and began farming on a large scale. Edwin's father was one of the organizers of the local Exchange Bank and established a large mercantile business; one store for hardware, a second for farm implements, and a third which sold dry goods. Edwin attended Detroit University and after graduating managed his father's businesses. In 1912, Edwin sold the hardware and dry good businesses and concentrated on farming his 600 acres and raising Holstein cows. He married Miss Myrtie B. Wilcox from Portland, Michigan on February 25, 1891 and the couple had one child, a daughter named Celeste. In 1905 Edwin erected a private residence which was the finest home in Bancroft. Its cost was about twenty thousand dollars and all the wood used in construction came from his land (Durling 33). In 1914 the family moved to Ann Arbor then later Detroit, Michigan. Edwin P. Sherman died at his home in Detroit, Michigan on December 3, 1926.[183]

From the Gould inventory of Darius Moon Buildings, listed as "Sherman Hse at Bancroft, 1904".

MRS. ELIZABETH HAMILTON BLOCK

1208-1212 Turner, Lansing, MI

"A building which is to contain stores on the lower floor and apartments above is to be built on Turner street this summer for Mrs. Elizabeth Hamilton. Architect D.B. Moon has nearly completed the plans for the structure, which is to be 63 by 180 feet; it will be built of wood and will be two stories" (*LJ* 7/6/1904).

"North Lansing is to have three new stores. The buildings will be erected by A.N. [Alvin N.] Hamilton on property just north of Vetter Bros' grocery store. The frame building which was formally occupied by George H. Gregory with a tin shop has been torn down and a brick structure for three 20-foot front stores will replace it. The old Gregory building was one of the old landmarks of the north end. The new building will extend back 70 feet" (*LJ* 8/25/1904).

---

183   *Owosso Argus* 12/3/1926, *Detroit Free Press* 12/4/1926 and *Durand Express* 12/9/1926.

"A.N. [Alvin N.] Hamilton has broken ground for three new stores on the east side of Turner st, north of Franklin ave." (*SR* 9/6/1904).

"Ground was broken this morning for three stores and apartment block on Turner st, North Lansing, by Mrs. I. E. [Isabella E.] Hamilton. They are to cost about $8,000. The architect D.B. Moon drew the plans" (*SR* 9/8/1904).

"A.W. [Alvin N.] Hamilton has let the contract for the erection of two stores on Turner street to Henry Schwalm and the lumber contract to the Hall Lumber company" (*LJ* 10/18/1904).

"A.L. [Alvin N.] Hamilton has completed the foundation for the erection of three brick stores on Turner st, directly north of Vedder Bros.' Grocery" (*SR* 4/10/1905). The 1904 CD lists Vetter Bros Grocery at 301 E Franklin.

FINE NORTH END STORE
HAMILTON BLOCK WILL BE FINISHED NEXT MONTH

"A new three-story brick building is being erected on Turner street next to the North Lansing postoffice, by A.N. [Alvin N] Hamilton, for his mother, Mrs. J.E. [Isabella E.] Hamilton.[184] The building is 73 1/2 feet long by 53 feet wide. The lower two stories will be used for mercantile purposes, while the upper floor will be utilized for living rooms, arranged for three families, with seven rooms and a closet for each household. The building will be steam heated and will be lighted by gas. The building has not yet been leased, although several outside parties have asked for leases. It will be completed and ready to occupy by October 1st" (*LJ* 9/1/1905).

The above article is mistaken. It was a three-block brick building of two stories as there were no three story buildings next to the North Lansing Post Office. In fact there was only one three story building in North Lansing on Turner Street at this time and that was owned by Paul Dunham. Hamilton only built the two story building consisting of three stores at 1208-1212 Turner Street. Just why did it take so long for this building to be completed? The *Lansing Journal* quotes Mr. Hamilton as having problems acquiring the building materials he needed to complete the structures, hence the delay.[185]

---

184   The North Lansing Post Office was at the corner of Franklin Avenue and Turner Street, it was known as "Station A". The clerk in charge of Station A was William B. Vetter of Vetter Brothers, grocers at 301 Franklin Avenue East, so the Post Office was located in his store.

185   *LJ* 9/8/1905.

Hamilton Block detail observe the corbelling

The business block is often overlooked by the passerby when they visit North Lansing. It lacks the ornamentation of many of the other structures in the area. But look again; the corbelling along the parapet continues along the façade in a solid manner instead sectional style which was typical at that time. Observe the six piers of the frame the structure; at their tops you see additional corbelling which creates the appearance of columns. It is notable that Moon splits the base of the corbels to add detail to the plain front of the building.

Isabella Elizabeth Hart was born in Lapeer, Michigan on July 24, 1836 the daughter of Judge Alvin N. and Charlotte F. (née Ball) Hart. On October 1, 1858 she married Robert Wilson Hamilton and came to Lansing in 1861 with her father and year old son, Alvin settling at 1303 Center Street with her father. The daughter of a prominent political figure in Lansing Mrs. Hamilton was witness to the building of the Amboy, Lansing & Traverse City Railroad as well Detroit & Bay City Railroad in which her father, Judge Hart was one of the principal investors. Isabella E. Hamilton died at her home at 1303 Center Street on March 9, 1915 and was buried at Mt Hope Cemetery in Lapeer Michigan.[186]

Alvin N. Hamilton was a long time resident of Lansing and the builder of the Hamilton Business Blocks on Turner Street in North Lansing. Born in the town of Lapeer, Michigan on October 14, 1859 to Robert Wilson and Isabelle Elizabeth Hamilton. Alvin N. Hamilton came to Lansing in 1861 with his mother and grandfather. He attended the First Ward School in Lansing, and then attended Notre Dame University in South Bend. Alvin engaged in railroad work for a brief period before he returned to Lansing and established himself in the real estate and restaurant business; he was the proprietor of the New Hamilton Restaurant at 120 Turner Street. On September 15, 1886 Alvin married Miss Rose Cook; they would have one child, a daughter, Isabelle Elizabeth Hamilton, who was for many years a teacher at the Walnut Street School. Alvin N. Hamilton died at the home where he lived his entire life, 1303 Center Street, on Thursday September 9, 1927.[187]

From the Gould inventory of Darius Moon Buildings, listed as "Mrs. Hamilton 2 Stores No Date".

---

186   *LSJ* 3/10/1915.
187   See *LSJ* 9/8/1927, *Lansing Capital News* 9/8/1927, *LSJ* 5/6/1965 also Turner 498 and 504.

ORA E. MURRAY HOUSE

104 S. Logan (MLK), Lansing, MI

There was a small bit of confusion over the name which is understandable when you read the following: The Gould list has Moon designing a home for Mr. Murray in 1904, in fact the home was built for a Mr. Murrey. In 1905 O.E. Murrey living at 104(106) S. Logan two doors from Moon' home, he was the owner of Murrey and Murrey Heating. In 1908 Edward O. Murrey is living at 110 S Logan, next door to Darius Moon, and is part owner in 'The Auto' a cigar and tobacco store. It must be stated that the house numbers on Logan Street from this period are unreliable. O.E. Murrey and Edward O. Murrey are the same person; it seems Murrey had a difficult time using one name consistently. His actual name was Ora Edward Murrey. Murrey moved around quite a bit and changed jobs frequently during his early years in Lansing. He is also listed in various years of the city directories and newspapers as Ora Edward Murray, Ora E. Murrey and Edward O. Murray. His death notice in both the *Lansing State Journal* and the *Lansing Capital News* give his name as Ora E. Murray, his probate record lists his last name as Murrey, while his tombstone lists his name as Edward O. Murrey. Ora E. Murrey was born in Michigan in 1860 and came to Lansing in 1894. He was married to a wealthy widow Mrs. Cora L. (née Ceiles) Chapman on October 24, 1896. Cora had two sons, Nathan and John from her marriage to Charles H. Chapman. Tragically Cora L. Murrey committed suicide, shooting herself four times in 1917. Her son John is quoted that since a fall down a flight of stairs and striking her head, his mother 'had been subjected to morbid attacks'. In the article Mrs. Murrey is described as owning a large amount of real estate in the city of Lansing; in fact the property at 104 S. Logan was in her name.[188] Later in life O.E. Murrey worked for the Olds Motor Company as a machinist for over 20 years, and was a member of the Capital Lodge F. & A.M. (Free and Accepted Masons).Ora Edward Murrey passed away at his home on Thanksgiving Day, November 26, 1931; neither of the stepsons attended the service.[189]

---

188   *LSJ* 3/27/1917. Oddly Mrs. Murrey is buried at Mt. Hope Cemetery, Lansing under her former husband's name, Chapman. Charles H. Chapman, Cora's first husband was a beloved Lansing citizen who died March 30, 1892.
189   *Lansing Capital News* 11/27/1931 and the *LSJ* 11/27/1931.

The home at 104 S. Logan is a side gable home with an offset open gable on the front of the structure. There is really not much left to see of the original structure; the image above is from the 1960s and the large front porch has been removed and some of the windows have been updated. The home was built in 1905 and according to the 1913 Sanborn map the home at 104 S. Logan originally had a porch that ran the entire front of the home.

From the Gould inventory of Darius Moon Buildings, listed as "Mr. Murray Hse & Veranda, 1904".

FREDERICK A. WOOD BUNGALOW

508 W. Franklin (Grand River), Lansing. MI

Frederick A. Wood was born in Lansing in 1876 the son of John J. and Clara (née Price) Wood. Frederick would grow up in Lansing and on February 15, 1898 married Miss Grace K. Lemon. In 1907 Frederick assumed the management of National Coil and reorganized the business. National Coil was located at 420 E. Michigan Avenue and was created by Ransom Olds as a subsidiary of the REO Motor Car Company to be a reliable parts supplier for REO. Under Wood's leadership National Coil Company would expand and move to 221-223 N. Cedar Street.

Frederick A. Wood 1874-1936

On January 1, 1913 Frederick Wood became President and General Manager of the National Coil Company, but by 1915 Frederick A. Wood had left Lansing to work for the Earle C. Anthony Company in Los Angeles with his wife and son Harold. Fredrick A. Wood would die in California on September 3, 1936; his wife Grace passed away on December 1, 1964.

508 W. Franklin (Grand River), Lansing. MI

The Fred Wood residence is an example of a hipped roof bungalow, a style that Moon rarely was commissioned to design and as a result less then two are still standing. The hipped roof bungalow is a classic design, the center dormer on the front of the home and two matching dormers on the east and west side of the home. There is a smaller, off-center, dormer on the back of the home. The shed roof of the porch is supported by four plain Tuscan columns and unlike many Moon designed porches, this one is rather understated. On the east side of the home there is a bay window which is balanced on the west side by another bay window. There is also a bay window on the front of the home, to the left in the photographs.

As of 2015 the home is still standing. From the Gould inventory of Darius Moon Buildings, listed as "Fred Wood Hse-Bungalow, 1904".

CAPITAL PEAT COMPANY

Old Maid Swamp, Windsor Township, Eaton County, MI

Finally there is this small notation in the *American Machinist* on April 28, 1904. "It is stated at Lansing Mich., that plans are being made by Architect D.B. Moon for the first of the buildings to be erected for the manufacture of peat at the Old Maid Swamp." The Old Maid Swamp was located in Eaton County, specifically the North West corner of Windsor Township and southern Delta Township. The only peat manufacture located in this area is in Section 6 of Windsor Township, the Capital Peat Company. The Capital Peat Company, sometimes listed as the Capitol Peat Company, was formed around 1904 with William B. Otto as the largest share holder. The initial capitalization of the company was $300,000, other shareholders included R.E. Olds.[190] Oddly enough Moon use to walk through Old Maid Swamp as a young man while working on a job in the village of Sevastopol [West Windsor]. No structures from this period survive on this site.

---

[190]   See the *SR* 4/14/1904 and *Past* 130.

1905

MISSES SWEAZY HOUSE

609 Cherry, Lansing, MI

Fine New Houses

"Contracts have been let for the Construction of Two. A contract was let today to Col. Gorham for a fine double house that is to be built at once on Washtenaw street west for M.F. Bates. The building will be a handsome one, frame, two stories high and modern in all respects. Another new house, which is to be finished this fall, is one on Cherry street which will be property of the Misses Sweazy. Both of these houses were designed by Architect D.B. Moon" (*LJ* 8/28/1905).

The residence at 609 Cherry Street is an attractive Queen Anne home with several noteworthy architectural features. There is a central hip roof with an irregular roofline. Notice how the front and side dormers are closed. If you compare the closed dormers with the open-style dormer on the Murray home, the closed dormer adds a certain style to the home. Toward the back of the home, on the left side in the above photograph, a sleeping porch can be seen. Notice the double windows on the second floor over the porch and how in the image below they have been replaced with a curious combination of windows that overwhelms the front of the home and crowds out the small second floor window directly over the pediment. The placement of this three window set also destroys the symmetry of the second and third floor windows. On the positive side there has been no change to the wraparound bay window on the first floor corner. The wrapping of the bay window around the corner of the home is something Moon had never used before employing it here. The porch with many Moon designed structures is the focal point of the home. The pediment over the entrance to the porch, the turned balustrade railing along with the dentils around the soffit makes this an attractive but simple porch. The only property that Miss Adelia Sweazy (Sweazey) owned in Lansing was Lot 8 Block 155, at the south east corner of Hillsdale and Cherry. The Sweazy's lived at 603 Cherry; the lot was divided and 609 Cherry was built. Splitting a lot was a common practice in the early 1900s, it allowed for the owners to capitalize on their initial investment which allowed Miss Sweazy to rent the home for a source of income. This is a wonderful, yet simple Queen Anne home, the porch is original (*Report* 19). The home is still standing today.

609 Cherry, Lansing, MI

Miss Adelia E. Sweazy was born in Dewitt, New York on June 21, 1846. Her family moved to Lansing in 1870. With her sister Isadore, Adelia work for the State Republican and later the W.S. George & Company as a gatherer and folder. She lived at 603 Cherry Street for more then 50 years and was active in the First Presbyterian Church. She passed away on April 2, 1920 while walking to church at the age of 73.[191] Isadore Sweazy came to Lansing at the age of 12 with her family. She never married and lived with her sister until her death on October 14, 1909. [192]

---

191   *LSJ* 4/3/1920. The Sweazy name appears in some records as Sweazey.
192   For Adelia see *LSJ* 4/3/1920 for Isadore see *LJ* 10/14/1909. The Sweazy name appears in some records as Sweazey.

EVANGELICAL LUTHERAN TRINITY SOCIETY PARSONAGE

623 N. Chestnut, Lansing, MI

German Evangelical Lutheran Trinity Church

"The German Lutheran congregation, whose church is on Saginaw street, expects as soon as the plans are finished to commence the erection of a new parsonage, and a school house. Both buildings will stand on land adjoining the church site. Both will be of brick and well arranged for the purposes for which they are intended. The schoolhouse will be two stories with school rooms below and a hall with stage and other conveniences on the second floor. In the basement there will be a kitchen for the use of the ladies of the church.

The parsonage will be a well built, modern house and will stand east of the church, on a site of a house that is being moved to make room for the parsonage" (*LJ* 4/11/1905).

Moon's letter to George Kohler regarding the Parsonage

NOTICE TO CONTRACTORS

"Sealed bids will be received until 5 o'clock p.m., Saturday, May 6, 1905, by the building committee for the construction of a parsonage at Lansing, Michigan for the Evangelical Lutheran Trinity society. Plans and specifications and details can be obtained at the office of D.B. Moon, architect, room 5 and 6, Dodge block. The committee reserves the right to reject any or all bids that may be submitted, J.C. Schneider, Chairman of the Building Committee" (*SR* 4/29/1905).

New Parsonage German Lutheran Church has let contract for one

"The contract to erect a fine new parsonage for the German Lutheran church has been let by the trustees to George J. Kohler, at $3,000. Plans for the residence were made by D.B. Moon and it is to be a modern house in every way, with brick veneer walls. The church has also accepted the plans made by Architect Moon for a new parish school house that will be erected on the site of the present school house on Saginaw street west and will probably cost about $7,500. The parsonage is to be erected at the corner of Chestnut and Saginaw streets" (*LJ* 5/17/1905).

The above photograph is the only image to survive of the Parsonage of the Evangelical Lutheran Trinity Church. The Parsonage was a simple front gable home with a smaller gable stepped in front of it, while on the side there is an open gable. Since this was the parsonage for the church, decorative elements were in all likelihood kept to a minimum, however for a house of this time period a bay window was a standard feature. The parsonage was torn down circa 1958.

From the Gould inventory of Darius Moon Buildings, listed as "Luthern Parsonage 1905."

JASON E. NICHOLS HOMES

619 S. Washington, Lansing, MI

JUDGE NICHOLS TO BUILD
Purchased Lot on Washington Ave at St. Joseph St.

"The consideration for the lot on Washington ave was $3,000, and Judge Nichols intends building a residence thereon" (*SR* 12/31/1903).

"Among the fine houses that will be erected this summer will be a handsome brick residence for Judge J.E. Nichols, which will stand at the corner of Washington avenue and Hillsdale street. The plans for this house are almost complete, and are for a beautiful and convenient modern house" (*LJ* 4/11/1905). The article also lists other houses and buildings designed by Moon. However the Nichols' house was not built of brick, rather it was a frame home and located on S. Washington and St. Joseph.

"Work has been commenced on the frame residence which Jason E. Nichols is to build at the corner of Washington ave and St. Joseph st. The contract calls for the completion of the work by Aug. 1" (*SR* 4/17/1906).

The Jason Nichols residence at 619 S. Washington was an interesting mixture of architectural styles. On the front we have a gambrel style front gable while the side open gables follow the more traditional type. There was a bay window on the south side of the home and two bay windows, each different on the north side.

One was a three-sided rectangular bay with five windows, while the other was a traditional three window bay. What is interesting is that the windows on the second floor are a Queen Anne style with small panels on the upper sash. On the front gambrel gable there is a Palladian window that was framed with a pointed window head, something you almost never see with a Palladian style window. The front porch in the above image has been enclosed, originally the porch was open. It is unknown how the original porch looked, however if some of the elements of the original porch were reused the columns would have been square with a recessed panel on the front. The home is no longer standing.

512 S. Pine, Lansing, MI

The Gould inventory of Darius Moon Buildings lists Moon as designing "Jason E. Nichols Res. (3 Bldgs) 1905". The problem is determining which buildings Moon designed for Nichols besides his residence. The abbreviation term 'Res' describes homes while 'Bldgs' describes commercial buildings. The problem is that Nichols owned no commercial buildings in 1905; it is possible that the rental properties were considered commercial buildings. The structure was a traditional open side gable home with a closed front gable and a pent roof on the front of the home. The home has a series of brackets spaced evenly along the soffit. The columns on the porch are a bit overwhelming and may not be original to the home. It is odd that there were no center column on the porch. The home is no longer standing.

516 S. Pine, Lansing, MI

Nichols owned several properties around Lansing. In the Third Ward he owned Lot 3 Block 144 on which two houses were built in late 1906, 512 S. Pine and 516 S. Pine. He also owned property in Fifth Ward, Lansing Improvement Company Addition, but there were no structures present in 1906 on any of the lots Nichol's owned. Were the homes at 512-516 S Pine built as rentals? This house is an odd little home; it has some features that you would not normally find in a rental property. The image of this home is distorted, but it seems that the windows were Queen Anne style with a series of small panels on the upper sash. Notice the three grouped windows on the first floor; there seems to be a flaring over these three windows, almost a shed dormer. The porch is also interesting; the square columns are a departure from Moon's traditional porch design, as well as the stick work balustrade on the second floor porch. The home is no longer standing.

Jason E. Nichols 1851-1946

Jason E. Nichols was born on January 13, 1851 in Watertown Township, Clinton County, Michigan to Jason and Abigail Nichols. Jason E. Nichols graduated from the University of Michigan in 1876 and was admitted to the bar the same year. On August 14, 1876 he married Fanny Jones a classmate from Lansing High School and they had one child, Fredrick J. Nichols. Jason E. Nichols was well-known in the community and active in civic affairs. He met Chief Okemos as a child and helped to survey the first line of the Ionia & Lansing Railroad. Later he was instrumental in the founding of the Ingham County Bar Association, was a member of the Lansing School Board and was chairman of the building committee for the Carnegie Library. From 1882-1886 Nichols served as Ingham County's prosecuting attorney, later he was elected Probate Judge and served from 1901-1905. He was a delegate to the national convention that nominated Theodore Roosevelt for president on the Progressive ticket. After the death of his wife Fanny, Nichols sold the home at 619 S. Washington and moved around the corner to 115 E. St. Joseph, where he lived the remainder of his life. Jason E. Nichols died at his home on February 7, 1946.[193]

From the Gould inventory of Darius Moon Buildings, listed as "Jason E. Nichols Res. (3 Bldgs) 1905."

---

193   *LSJ* 2/7/1946.

EVANGELICAL LUTHERAN TRINITY SOCIETY SCHOOL

423 W. Saginaw, Lansing, MI

GERMAN LUTHERAN SCHOOLHOUSE
"The schoolhouse will be two stories with school rooms below and a hall with stage and other conveniences on the second floor. In the basement there will be a kitchen for the use of the ladies of the church….Plans for this are also nearly ready in the office of Architect Moon" (*LJ* 4/11/1905).

WILL ERECT NEW SCHOOL
GERMAN LUTHERAN TRINTY CHURCH TO REPLACE FRAME STRUCTURE
NEW BUILDING TO BE OF BRICK, TWO STORIES IN HEIGHT
"The German Lutheran Trinity church society has advertised for bids for the construction of a brick school; building on the site of the present frame school on Saginaw st. between Chestnut and Walnut sts. Bids are to be open March 24. The building will be two stories and a basement. It will contain two school rooms on the first floor and a large assembly room on the second. The plans were drawn by Architect D.B. Moon. It is estimated the building will cost between $8,000 and $10,000" (*SR* 3/14/1906).

CONTRACT FOR SCHOOL HOUSE
GERMAN LUTHERAN TRINTY SOCIETY TO HAVE BUILDING OF BRICK AND STONE
"The contract for building the school house for the German Evangelical Lutheran Trinity society on the corner of Saginaw and Chestnut sts, has been awarded to Nichols & Mahoney of this city. The bid was $7,447.15. The building is to be of red brick trimmed with stone and will be two stories in height. The frame building on the site is being removed and excavating for the new building will start next week" (*SR* 4/11/1906).

"The school building of the Trinity church is one of the finest of its size in the city. It was built by MesSRs B. Nichols and Mahoney contractors, according to the plans and specifications furnished by D.B. Moon, architect. The congregation highly appreciates the work of these gentlemen as well as that of the building committee, MesSRs. Theo. Stoppel, W. Reitz, P. Bienert and George Koehler" (*LJ* 9/27/1906).

The façade of the Evangelical Lutheran Trinity Society School

It is unfortunate that more images of the Evangelical Lutheran Trinity School have not been discovered. Moon had designed two other schools prior to his work on the Evangelical Lutheran Trinity School. There seems to be several modifications in the design of the building from the architectural drawing. As you can see in the first image, the corbelling over the second floor windows on the tower was removed as well as the key stone of the arch over the front entrance. What is striking about the school house is the large tower it is rather squat and not as tall as other school towers which were built at this time, but overall it does work. Notice that the entrance now matches the level of the first floor windows in the above image, whereas in the original drawing it is one level below, which makes the entire façade symmetrical. One other interesting point is the lunette window on the side of the tower, an expensive addition to the structure; it is curious why it was included. The building was torn down circa 1970.

From the Gould inventory of Darius Moon Buildings, listed as "Luthern School Building 1905."

MRS. ALICIA LANSING HOUSE

713 S. Washington, Lansing, MI

Fine Residence to be erected on Washington Avenue for Mrs. A.J. Lansing
"Work will be commenced almost immediately on a handsome residence for Mrs. A.J. Lansing, which is to stand on Washington avenue south opposite the residence of R.E. Olds. The house will be a comparatively small one, but will be elegant in all its details. It will be of wood, two stories high. C.O. Crandall has the contract to build the residence" (*LJ* 5/26/1905).

The front porch was rather subdued with classical columns and a delicate balustrade, while the second floor porch, which was not a functional porch but repeated the balustrade element from the lower porch. At the back of the home, just visible to the left in the photograph was another porch. You can also observe an oriel window, which was probably located at the landing on the interior stairwell. On the front open style gable there is a Palladian window which was framed with a pointed window head, a detail that Moon also employed on the J.E. Nichols' residence. At the base of the gable on both sides was an ornate bracket, which is not repeated elsewhere on the home.

Mrs. A. J. Lansing was born Alicia J. Sparrow in County Wexford, Ireland on August 11, 1844. Alicia moved to Lansing with her mother and siblings in 1858. On December 11, 1864 Alicia married Garrett Y. Lansing; the couple would have two children, Edward and Wheeler, both of whom died in infancy. In 1875 the couple adopted William Stanfield from Linchfield, Michigan and renamed him William S. Lansing. In 1889 Garret and Alicia divorced. Garret was born in Fremont, Ohio on September 14, 1840 to Solomon and Adoliza (née Penhollow) Lansing. After moving to Lansing with his parents in 1855, he worked with his father in their blacksmith business. Garret would pass away on September 9, 1891 and his estate would contest in the case Lansing v. Haynes which would be decided by the Michigan Supreme Court in favor of Geraldine Haynes, Garret's sister.[194] Unfortunately in 1906 their adopted son William would die after his sixth surgery on his kidney, before his death he met one of his biological brothers.[195] Mrs. Alicia J. Lansing died at her home on May 17, 1923 after being bedridden for the three years.[196] From the Gould inventory of Darius Moon Buildings, listed as "Mrs. Lansing House, No Date".

MADISON F. BATES DOUBLE HOUSE

709-711 W. Washtenaw, Lansing, MI

Fine new houses Contracts have been let for the Construction of Two.

"A contract was let today to Col. Gorham for a fine double house that is to be built at once on Washtenaw street west for M.F. Bates. The building will be a handsome one, frame, two stories high and modern in all respects. Another new house, which is to be finished this fall, is one on Cherry street which will be property of the Misses Sweazy. Both of these houses were designed by Architect D.B. Moon" (*LJ* 8/28/1905).

---

194   For Garret Lansing's death see *LJ* 9/7/1891 and *SR* 9/7/1891. For the court case Lansing v. Haynes, which makes for fascinating reading, see Howard 54: 699.
195   *LJ* 8/8/1906 and *SR* 8/9/1906.
196   *LSJ* 5/18/1923.

The Bates Double House is 709-711 W. Washtenaw, Madison F. Bates owned Lots 1-2 Block 122 in the Bush, Butler & Sparrow Subdivision, or 709-711 W. Washtenaw.[197] This was a massive side gable structure with an open front gable. At the peak of the front gable was an ornate lunette window, a detail which is odd to be used in a rental property. The two sides of the structure mirror each other; the placement of the windows is symmetrical. The large porch with its narrow Tuscan columns wrap around the sides of the front structure. Because of the limitation of the image it can not be determined if Moon employed three columns at the corners of the porch. The home was torn down in 1974.

From the Gould inventory of Darius Moon Buildings, listed as "M.F Bates Double Hse. 1905".

DR GEORGE RANNEY DOUBLE HOUSE

613-615 W. Ottawa, Lansing, MI

From Gould list which states that Moon designed a double house for Dr. Ranney in 1905. Ranney owned Lot 1-2 Block 104 or 613-615 W. Ottawa.[198] This was a beautiful structure. The ornate porch is what first captures the viewer's eye. The porch had a spindle frieze which complemented the finely turned balustrade. The columns were wider at the top and narrowed at the base. What is interesting is Moon's use of the larger bracket at the top of the column. Notice the ornamentation on the pediment of the porch, frankly this was a very elaborate porch for a rental property. The structure of the home was a large hipped roof structure with a large front dormer and smaller dormers on each side. Notice how the entrances to the residences are separated, this may mean that the living spaces were an over under combination as opposed to side by side. Compare this structure to the Bates' double house; the Ranney double house is far more ornate.

From the Gould inventory of Darius Moon Buildings, listed as "Dr. Ranney - Double Hse 1905".

---

197   See the 1906 City of Lansing Tax Assessment Rolls.
198   See the 1906 City of Lansing Tax Assessment Rolls.

GEORGE MCKENZIE REMODELED HOUSE

712 W. Ottawa, Lansing, MI

In 1904 George McKenzie is recorded as living at 706 W. Ottawa, later in 1906 he is listed as living in 712 W. Ottawa. The renumbering of the homes which occurred in 1905-1906 did not affect this section of West Ottawa. The corner of Ottawa and Sycamore was known as "McKenzie's Corners" because George owned Lot 5-6 Block 90 Original Plat, which included the homes at 201 N. Sycamore, 209 N. Sycamore, 706 W. Ottawa and 712 W. Ottawa.

712 W. Ottawa, Lansing, MI

The remodeling of the George McKenzie home brings to mind a few questions. First just which McKenzie property did Moon remodel? There were four options to choose from and second if Moon remodeled the home that George McKenzie occupied at 712 W. Ottawa the majority of the work was probably done on the interior of the home. This is an assumption based upon the surviving photographs of 712 W. Ottawa; the home still displays the Gothic Revival style vergeboards, at the peak of the gables. It is doubtful that Moon would have remodeled the exterior of the home and left such a dated architectural element. The home had a mixture of architectural styles and cannot be classified as Gothic Revival. It was a cross gabled home and the porch was a later addition added sometime after 1952.

712 W. Ottawa porch detail

An image of the original porch is above; the porch had four sets of square double columns across the front. The balustrade has an interesting stick work pattern. It is possible that Moon designed the porch but the dated style of the porch precludes this.

201 N. Sycamore, Lansing, MI

George McKenzie was born in Woodstock, Ontario in 1839; he immigrated to the United States in 1860 and settled in Lansing, Michigan. He worked as a carpenter and did much of the interior finish work at the Michigan State Capitol.

209 N. Sycamore, Lansing, MI

For thirty years George McKenzie lived in a room at the Wentworth Hotel until he moved to West Ottawa. He never married but was cared for by his niece Jennie (Jane) Sutherland Murray who lived with him until his death on December 29, 1918.[199] In Jennie S. Murray's obituary she was listed as living at 712 ½ W. Ottawa.[200] Although not conclusive it may point to the fact that Moon remodeled 712 W. Ottawa.

---

199   *LSJ* 12/30/1918.
200   *LSJ* 12/30/1918. For Jennie's death see *LSJ* 7/16/1943.

706 W. Ottawa, Lansing, MI

The homes from "McKenzie's Corners" were torn down in this order, 706 W. Ottawa in 1975, 201 N. Sycamore in 1976 and 712 W. Ottawa in 1983. From the Gould inventory of Darius Moon Buildings, listed as "George McKenzie-Remodeled Hse. 1905".

JOHN KNEAL HOUSE

617 W. Allegan, Lansing, MI

"Another fine house is to be built for John Kneal, on Allegan street west. Plans for this are also nearly ready in the office of Architect Moon" (*LJ* 4/11/1905).

John Kneal had extensive property holdings in the Lansing area. The best candidate for the home mentioned in the 1905 article is 617 W. Allegan. Kneal owned Block 120 Lot 11-12 E ½ of lot 11-12, 617 and 621 W Allegan. In the 1904 City Directory 621(615) W Allegan is occupied by John Q. Adams and Ray Lohman. There is no listing in the 1904 City Directory for 617(613) W. Allegan. All other property that John Kneal owned in 1905 had structures on the lots. John Kneal's home a 617 W. Allegan was a hipped roof structure with an open gable dormer on the front and two closed gables on each side. You can also see in the above image a finial at the peak of the roof. The windows are stacked in a symmetrical order except for the windows to the left in the photographs. The single first floor window has two windows above it which is rather odd, because it is not balanced.

617 W. Allegan, Lansing, MI

Not much is know about John S. Kneal, the 1883 City Directory lists his occupation as teamster, then in later years as being involved in real estate. Even his date and location of his birth are a mystery; it is listed as 1858 or 1859 and the location is either Michigan or Canada. John never married and in the late 1910s he moved to Southern California with his brother, George H. and sister-in-law, Elizabeth M. Kneal. John Kneal passed away in Los Angeles on March 1, 1944.[201] From the Gould inventory of Moon buildings, "John Kneal Hse 1905."

---

201   See California, Death Index, 1940-1997, familysearch.org.

RAY POTTER HOME

117 W. St Joseph, Lansing, MI

The Gould inventory of Darius Moon Buildings listed Moon as designing plans for a "Hse for Ray Potter 1905" and a "Hse for Ray Potter 1907". Just what houses Moon designed for Potter is something of a mystery. The *State Republican* records that "M. Ray Potter has nearly completed a fine brick residence at 113 St. Joseph street west" (*SR* 9/22/1897). Could Moon have designed the home at 117(113) W. St. Joseph in 1897 and that the Gould list was mistaken in the years 1897 vs. 1907? Something that lends credence to this proposal is that Ray Potter was in Oregon between 1903 and 1906 managing the Potter family's business interests. The home at 117 W. St Joseph was quite a stylistic departure from Moon's previous work. The steeply pitched front gable and the three small arched windows which resemble those on the north side of the Herrmann house, may be an indication that the residence was designed by R. Arthur Bailey who was still working in Lansing in 1897.

Ray Potter property, 801 E. Main, Lansing, MI

It is entirely possible that Moon may have been employed by Potter to design track housing for the workers at Cove Manufacturing. James Potter, Ray's father, owned the entire subdivision Manufacturers Addition No. 1 where the homes were to be built and where Cove Manufacturing was located. The only homes in the area in 1908 were at 801 E. Main, 903-911 E Main 813(707) S. Hosmer and 817(711) S. Hosmer. The home at 801 E. Main Street resembled other structures that Moon had designed. While the home at 813 (707) S. Hosmer was a standard front gable home a typical working man's residences, the structure at 903 E. Main was a front gambrel style home with a dormer on both sides and a circle top window at the gable peak. No image survives of the other home, 817(711) S. Hosmer.

Ray Potter property, 903 E Main, Lansing, MI

Through the years Ray Potter was responsible for having numerous homes built and was involved in the development of several subdivisions, the following article for the *Lansing Journal* demonstrates that Moon may have designed several homes for Potter in 1907. "M.R. Potter has just broken ground for about a dozen homes at the corner of Hosmer and Main streets, and expects to have them ready for occupancy by the middle of December. The house will be occupied by families from Charlotte who will remove here as soon as the new factory of the Cove Manufacturing company[202] is ready to commence operations which will be in a few weeks. The houses being erected by Mr. Potter will be comfortable cottages for workingmen and of this class of houses there is a good demand in Lansing" (*LJ* 11/2/1907). The above *Lansing Journal* article from 1907 also mentions two other homes that were built by Moon, the A.C. Stebbins home on Walnut Street and the Frank Hayes house on Lenawee Street. Is this conclusive proof that Moon designed the homes at Main and Hosmer Streets? No, but it does lend some credence to the theory.

---

202   Cove manufacturing Company produce window sashes and doors. They were later known as the Cove Lumber & Finish Company.

Ray Potter property, 813(707) S. Hosmer, Lansing, MI

In 1907 both James and Ray Potter acquired an interest in the Cove Manufacturing Company. James Potter would serve as Vice President, while Ray Potter would serve as the Secretary and Treasurer of the company, the new plant would be built at 750 E. Main across from these homes.[203] It is not unreasonable to assume that Moon was designing tract homes for the Potters.

---

203   *SR* 4/25/1907 and the *LJ* 4/25/1907.

Ray Potter Home, 313 W. Hillsdale, Lansing, MI

The final option is the home Ray Potter acquired when he returned to Lansing from the west coast. The home at 313 W. Hillsdale was built in the early 1890s. Ray purchased the home when he returned to Lansing in 1907, so it is possible that Moon remodeled Ray Potter's house in 1907. Although altered much later then the dates given in the Gould list it is not unreasonable to include this home as one of the probable structures that Moon designed. "Ray Potter is planning to remodel his residence on Hillsdale st. The plans include a porte cochere on the side" (SR 6/3/1910).

Notice the triple columns on the corners of the porch. The facing of the porch moving left to right there were triple columns then a pair of columns, then a triple set because it was the end of the porch, then a Porte cochere and a triple column at the corner of the porte cochere. The dormer is an odd element; it really does not fit the definition of a dormer but on the other hand it is not a gable. It is a bay style dormer which intersected the roof ridge. The second floor corner with the two small windows on the front and the one small window on the side were added, you can see that in the awkward roofline which it creates. The eyebrow dormer is something not often seen in any of the Moon's other design accept for the John A. Brooks home.

Miles R. Potter, known throughout his life as Ray Potter, was an extraordinary man. He was born in Potterville, Michigan on November 15, 1872, in a community named after his grandfather Linus Potter. Ray learned the lumber business under the guidance of his father James W. Potter. Later Ray would put that knowledge of wood and woodworking to work when employed by A.E. Stebbins and the Lansing Wheelbarrow Company to survey their lumber tracts in Parkin, Arkansas. For a time Ray with his father as a partner, owned a lumber mill and several lumber tracts in Klamath, Oregon which Ray managed until they were sold to Weyerhaeuser in 1906. When he returned to Lansing his business savvy attracted the attention of R.E. Olds who approached him about forming a new company Michigan Screw. Ray Potter stayed with the company for the next 27 years until it became Lundberg Screw Company. Ray entered the banking profession with the old Capital National Bank and its successor Lansing National Bank where he served as that institution's president until retirement in 1940. He would serve on the boards of Motor Wheel and REO Motor Car Company and various others businesses in the Lansing area. More importantly Ray Potter and his wife Sarah Louise were instrumental in the development of Sparrow Hospital. On January 15, 1895 Miles R. Potter would marry Miss Sarah L. Porter of Grand Rapids, Michigan; there were no children. A devotedly religious man, Ray taught Sunday school at Plymouth Congregational Church and was a member of several fraternal organizations. Ray Potter died in April of 1961 at his home at 1348 Cambridge Drive, in a neighborhood he helped to develop in the 1920s; he was buried next to his wife Sarah at Mt. Hope Cemetery in Lansing.[204]

PAUL DUNHAM HOUSE

1250 Clark, DeWitt Township, MI

OWNED BY P.E. DUNHAM
Dwelling Burned at Gunnisonville, Entailing Loss of $800

"A house owned by P.E. Dunham of this city burned at Gunnisonville last night. The fire was discovered by neighbors, who turned out and fought the fire with a bucket brigade, numbering about 50 men. Their efforts were unavailing in saving the house, but they removed the furniture and kept the flames from the barns and sheds. The loss was about $800, with $400 insurance on the building" (*SR* 3/11/1905).

"Paul Dunham, while working on his new house just north of the city stepped off the scaffolding and fell striking on the side of his back on some timber that was piled near. He will be confined to his home for a few days" (*SR* 6/21/1905).

---
204   *LSJ* 4/18/1961.

"Paul Dunham hurt. Fell from scaffold and was badly bruised. While standing on a scaffold, superintending the construction of a house, just five miles north of the city on the Gunnisonville road, Monday night, Paul H. Dunham, of this city, was severely injured by the scaffolding falling to the ground. Mr. Dunham fell upon some boards and lumber, hurting his hip, one side and his back, but the injuries amount to little more than bruises, and it is expected he will be about in a day or two" (*LJ* 6/21/1905).

The Paul Dunham home in DeWitt Township was a large Queen Anne style home. Notice the irregular roof line, the closed gables and the finial on the hip roof. The gable ends undoubtedly had some type of decorative siding, the use of a lunette widow on the gable hints at a different type of siding. The recessed second floor porch which sits under the gable and on top of the main porch is an architectural element Moon had not previously employed. Take a look at the porch and the unique design on the capital of the columns.

Although no date is given on the Gould inventory of Darius Moon Buildings for when Paul Dunham's home was built, 1905 seems the most likely due to the fire at Dunham's home and its rebuilding. Moon had done quite a bit of work in North Lansing and in Clinton County; Dunham would have been well aware of Moon's qualifications. From the Gould inventory of Darius Moon Buildings, listed as "Paul Dunham Hse & Store, no date". The home was torn down between 2009 and 2011.

PAUL DUNHAM STORE

1216-1218 Turner, Lansing, MI

Paul Dunham, a leading Lansing businessman had several structures built in North Lansing; there are two candidates for the building Moon designed. The first is the two-story structure seen in the above image. The building has all the hallmarks of a Moon designed building. Notice the columns and arches on the building which resemble those at 204 E. Grand River. The heavy stone arches in the center of the building on the second floor with the incorporated columns and the interesting double gable on the façade make this one of the finest Romanesque business structures still extant in Lansing. [205] The building was constructed between 1895 and 1898.

1242-1246 Turner, Lansing, MI

The other option for a Moon building is 1242-1246 Turner, which was built in 1905. "Work has commenced yesterday on a new harness shop for the Dunham Hardware company. The building is to be of brick, two stories in height and located in the lot between the present buildings of the firm on Turner street" (*LJ* 8/25/1905).

There is really no way to determine just what store Moon designed for Paul Dunham. It seems likely that Moon designed the store at 1242-1246 N. Turner Street, the building of which would have occurred at the same time as the rebuilding of his home on Clark Road. The building at 1242-1246 N. Turner was a pretty conventional business block. There was a belt course that ran along the entire front of the building between the first and second floors and another subtle belt course below the corbelling on the parapet. The brick piers along the cornice have an interesting roll-shaped cap. The building was torn down in the 1970s. Paul Dunham was quite active building both homes and an addition to his hardware business. Without design dates for the Dunham properties it is difficult to know for sure if Moon designed them. From the Gould inventory of Darius Moon Buildings, listed as "Paul Dunham Hse & Store, no date".

---

205   The proper architectural term for this is voussoir, sweeping stone work to form an arch.

Paul Dunham 1862-1937

Paul Elmer Dunham was a fixture in North Lansing business and civic matters. Paul was born in 1862 in Clinton County, Michigan to William Lee Brayton and Margaret Rebecca (née Partridge) Dunham. At the age of fourteen he was apprenticed as a tinsmith and later established a small shop on his father's farm. Paul Dunham came to Lansing in 1882 and opened a tin shop which over the years he expanded into a hardware store. In 1889 Paul's father William, joined his son in the hardware business and thus was founded the Dunham Hardware Company. After the death of his father in 1900, the company was incorporated with Paul E. Dunham as President and Manager, M.D. Walker, Vice President and Alice A. Dunham as Secretary and Treasurer. The business would expand to four stores and carry a range of goods from hardware and farm implements to buggies and harnesses which where manufactured by the Dunham Hardware Company. On November 27, 1882 Paul married Miss Alice A. Gregory of Clinton County and they had one child, Elton Clare Dunham. Paul was elected to the school board for the Gunnisonville District. He was a member of several fraternal organizations, the Modern Woodmen, the Royal Arcanum Lodge of Lansing, the Masonic Blue Lodge of Dewitt and Protective Lodge, No. 321, I.O.O.F., North Lansing. He was also a member of the Horseshoe Club of Lake Worth, Florida, in which he took great pride. The North Lansing hardware merchant passed away at his home in Gunnisonville, Michigan at 9:25 am December 28, 1937 at the age of 75.[206]

---

206   *LSJ* 12/28/1937 and *Past* 302.

1906

MOORES PARK SCHOOL

Lansing, MI., after addition in 1910

Moon submitted plans for the new school to be located on Lots 15-19 Block 1 of the Park Place Addition The structure was to be a four room school house of two stories facing Sparrow Avenue. "Other architects who presented plans were, D.B. Moon, E.A. Bowd, White and Hussey and H.J. Holbrook & Son" (*SR* 5/22/1906). The plans of Judson N. Churchill were accepted. The intended name of the building was to be the Sparrow Avenue School; this was later changed to the Moores Park School.

STUART GANUNG HOUSE

426 (416) S. Washington, Lansing, MI

"Prof. and Dr. Ganung have bought the property at 416 Washington ave s., of H.S. Hilton" (*SR* 4/19/1905).

"Prof. Stuart F. and Dr. Cora P. Ganung are having plans made for a handsome brick residence to be erected on their lot, 416 [426] Washington ave s, the property formerly owned by L.S. Hudson. The frame house thereon will be removed to another lot. The plans are being made by Architect Moon" (*SR* 2/3/1906).

"The work of the house owned by Stuart F. Ganung, adjoining the J.J. Frost residence, was commenced this morning. Prof. Ganung will build on the lot during the coming season" (*LJ* 2/13/1906).

"Bids have been submitted for the construction of the residence of Prof. and Dr. Ganung on Washington ave s., and it will be likely the contract will be awarded tomorrow. The residence will be three stories in height and will be built of pressed brick. The estimated cost is about $10,000" (*SR* 3/14/1906).

Professor Ganung's large brick home on South Washington Avenue had a noteworthy porch that wrapped around the residence on the north side and a bowed addition at the front of the porch that extended away from the home. There was a two-story canted bay window on the south side that was matched by a smaller two story bay window on the north side of the home. There is a small second story porch in the indentation over the first floor porch, a column is just visible in this image. The porch has an element above the entrance which seems to be of a scallop shell motif. The stonework surround of the third floor window was an appealing architectural feature; notice the stone brackets beneath the window sill. The roofing was of concrete roof tiles.

An interior view of the Ganung House (A.G.)

Stuart Ganung was born in Montour Falls, New York on August 6, 1856. He was a graduate of the Cook Academy in Montour Falls, studied music in New York City and Berlin, Germany. Afterward Stuart moved to Michigan and became a Professor of Music at Albion College, a position he held for eight years. He moved to Lansing in 1890 and established himself as a well-known music teacher, a patron of the arts and a member of the Masonic Capital Lodge, No. 66. He had been the organist for eleven years at Plymouth Congregational Church, two years at St. Paul's Episcopal Church and one and a half years at the First Baptist Church. Stuart F. Ganung passed away at his home on November 16, 1914 with his wife by his side.[207] Cora Lou Pope was born in West Burlington, New York on May 4, 1862 to Chester D. and Elizabeth Pope. She attended local schools and later a women's preparatory school near Richfield, New York. Cora attended Albion College and studied medicine at the University of Michigan where she graduated in 1883. Dr. Cora Pope returned to Albion to practice medicine, where she met and married Professor Stuart Ganung. In 1890 the couple moved to Lansing where Dr. Ganung established her practice, serving on the staff of the city hospital, specializing in Obstetrics. Her mother was Dr. Elizabeth Pope Westcott, of Ellerson v. Westcott fame.[208] Cora's mother was one of the earliest practicing women physicians in New York; she graduated from the New York Medical College in 1865. Both of her daughters, Cora and Clara followed their mother into the medical profession.[209] Dr. Cora P. Ganung would pass away in her sleep on July 5, 1923.[210]

The home was torn down in September of 1950. From the Gould inventory of Darius Moon Buildings, listed as "Hse for Ganuny1906".

---

207   *LSJ* 11/16/1914 and the *Lansing Evening Press* 11/16/1914.
208   Dr. Elizabeth Pope Westcott was accused of killing here husband Monroe Westcott by giving him morphine, aconite and atropine. *NYT* 6/10/1897.
209   Dr. Elizabeth Pope Westcott would move to Lansing in 1907. She passed away at Cora's home on March 27, 1919 see *LSJ* 3/28/1919.
210   *Lansing Capital News* 7/5/1923 and *Lansing Capital News* 7/6/1923.

LUCIEN J. DRIGGS BUNGALOW

156 Benachi, Biloxi, MS

In 1916 Lucien J. Driggs of Lansing, Michigan purchase Lot numbers 145 and 147 on Benachi Avenue in Biloxi, Mississippi through the Roy Reality Agency. Construction of the garage was completed in 1916 with the home to be completed in 1917.[211] The Gould list records that the home in Biloxi was designed in 1906. Could this be a mistake and the home was actually designed in 1916? Or did Moon design the home in 1906 and the plans were held by Driggs until 1916? In 1913, Moon would design a 'Public Garage' (Gas Station) for Driggs and later in 1916 he would design store and apartments for Driggs, both structures were located in Lansing. Everything points to the home being designed in 1916 rather then 1906. Biloxi was a favorite winter vacation destination for many Lansing residents in the early 20th Century. The Driggs' residence in Biloxi is a classic bungalow design. The home has a low pitched gable over the core of the home and a matching pitched gable over the screened porch. Notice the stick work decoration on the porch gable as well as the interesting extension on the front entrance column. At one time there may have been a brick base for this column which matched those on the screen porch. Finally observe how the gable brackets extend just beyond the fascia of the roof, a subtle design element. As of 2015 the cottage is still standing and even survived Hurricane Katrina. An odd coincidence, Driggs' home at 205 Regent Street bears a strong resemblance to his home in Biloxi, Mississippi and was built in 1915.

---

211 *Gulfport/Biloxi Daily Herald* 2/14/1916.

Lucien J. Driggs 1849-1938

Born on February 14, 1849 in Bronson, Michigan, Lucien J. Driggs came to Lansing in 1882 to work for the Piatt Brothers Manufacturing Company. Later Driggs with E.S. Porter formed the Lansing Spoke Works Company located in North Lansing. Lansing Spoke Works not only manufactured wagon spokes but porch columns and other architectural features. When the first automobile was built in Lansing, Driggs realized that there would be a change in transportation and revamped the Spoke Works to produce spokes for automobile wheels. The company began the production of automotive wheels and was reorganized as the Auto Wheel Company, later to merge with Prudden Wheel to form the Motor Wheel Corporation. With E.S. Porter, Lawrence J. Price, Harry E. Bradner and Harris B. Thomas, Driggs also formed the Auto Body Company. In its heyday it was one of the largest automobile body manufactures in the world. Lucien was active in civic affairs, elected as alderman for the First Ward, he served two terms on the Lansing City Council and later he was appointed to the Police and Fire Board. On December 22, 1870 he married Miss Helen J. Clark of Branch County and they had two daughters, Bernice and Luella. Lucien and Helen spent the winters in Biloxi and in the spring they retuned to Lansing and traveled throughout the state of Michigan. Helen would pass away in 1926. On June 6, 1929 Lucien married Alice J. Walker in Lucas County, Ohio. Lucien J. Driggs died at his home, 205 Regent Street on April 26 1938. He was survived by his widow, Alice, daughter Luella and his grandson, Ivan H. Driggs a renowned airplane designer.[212] From the Gould inventory of Darius Moon Buildings, listed as "L.J. Driggs Bungalow (Biloxi, Miss.) 1906". Photograph courtesy of Jamie Ellis.[213]

---

212   *LSJ* 1/4/1926 for Helen Driggs' obituary and *LSJ* 4/27/1938 for Lucien J. Driggs.
213   Jamie Ellis worked as the Local History & Genealogy Librarian at the Murella H. Powell Local History & Genealogy Collection at Biloxi Public Library Harrison County Library System.

GEORGE E. RANNEY HOME

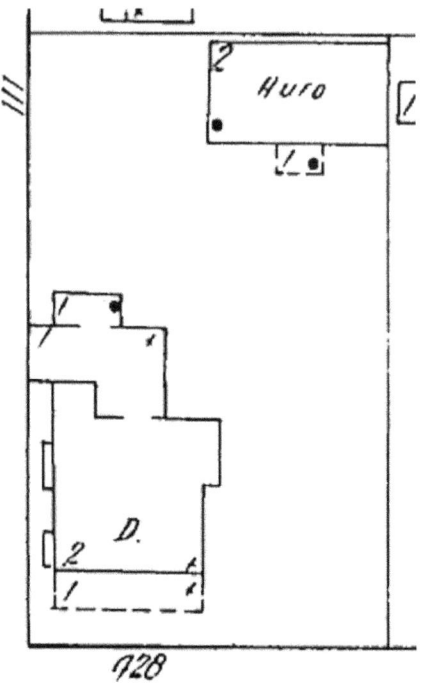

426 W. Allegan Lansing, MI

"Architect D.B. Moon has prepared plans for the proposed $3,000 field stone and frame residence to be erected at Lansing for George Ranney. The building will have natural wood interior finish, nickel plumbing, electric light, tile work, mantels, art glass and furnace heating" (*DFP* 10/7/1906). In 1906-1907 Dr. George Ranney owned the W ½ of Lots 5-6 Block 109 or 426 W. Allegan in Lansing, no image survives of the structure. There was a home on the lot in 1898; this may have been a total reconstruction much like Moon's work on the Stahl home.

1907

BEA DAVIS HOUSE AND COTTAGE

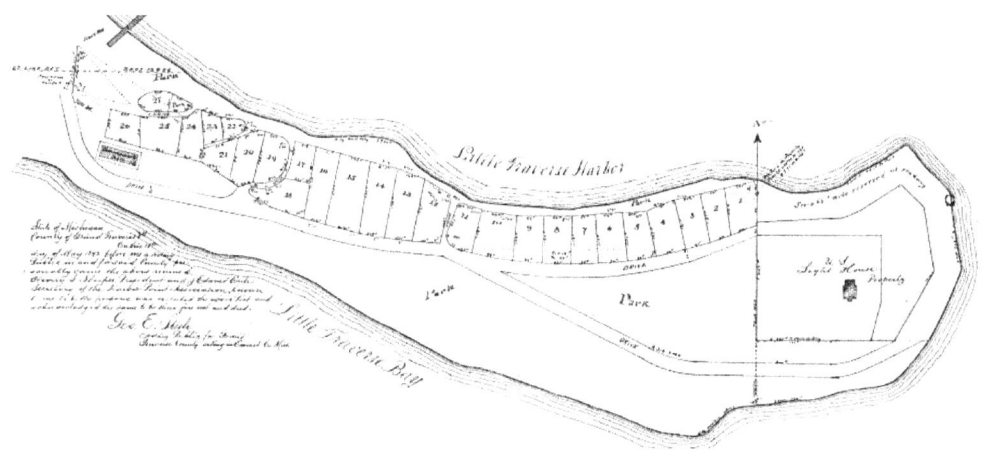

Harbor Point, MI

There are two listings on the Gould inventory of Moon Buildings for a Bea Davis in 1907. "Bea Davis Hse and Cottage" and "Bea Davis Cottage at Roaring Brook, Mich." The problem is the Davis cottage was at Harbor Point, Michigan. "Mr. [Benjamin Franklin] Davis acquired Cottage 57 in 1895 and it has remained in his family since, being held in 1977 by his grandson, James D. Reasoner" (Creecy 38). Mrs. Davis was fondly remembered by the other cottagers as the "reigning dowager" of Harbor Point. In fact the season began with her arrival when all the cottagers would call on her to exchange news at the tea parties she hosted (Creecy 14). Could Moon have been mistaken in regards to the location of this cottage? It would have been pretentious and expensive for B.F. Davis to have maintained a cottage at Roaring Brook and one at Harbor Point. A search of the property tax records for 1908 reveals that no Davis owned property at Roaring Brook. The cottage Moon designed must be the one at Harbor Point. However the *State Republican* on March 23, 1899 noted that Earl Mead had made plans to remodel the B.F Davis cottage at Harbor Point. It is possible that Davis built a new cottage at Harbor Point in 1908.

The name Bea also presents a problem. Bea is commonly uses as shortened version of Beatrice. Benjamin Davis' first wife, Eva died in 1890; he later married Miss Sara Day on April 3, 1902. It seems likely that the cottage was designed for one of Benjamin's daughters, either Edith Eva Davis or Bessie Davis; the cottage may have been a gift from Benjamin F. Davis to one of his daughters. Edith Eva Davis married Thaddeus Leon Hoffman on April 25, 1908; the couple would have one child Benjamin F. Hoffman, better known to Lansing residents as Benny Davis. At some point Thaddeus and Edith divorced and Edith returned to live in Lansing with her son Benny. Edith would revert to her maiden name and Benny's last name was changed to Davis. Tragically Benny would die on January 2, 1920. Benny must have been quite a boy; he was credited with developing a system of surviving in water called 'bobbing'. In January of 1951 Mrs. Edith Eva Davis donated funds for a pool at the downtown of the Y.M.C.A.; the pool was named the Benny F. Davis pool. Edith never remarried, she lived at the Davis home at 528 S. Washington until just before her death on June 7, 1967. Edith was connected to several civic organizations, the Red Cross, Y.M.C.A., and Sparrow Hospital which was named after her uncle. [214]

---

214   *LSJ* 6/8/1967, *LSJ* 1/8/1951 and *National* 28: 60.

On June 6, 1912 Bessie Davis married James M. Reasoner in Lansing, Michigan. James was the son of Nelson and Marion (née Turner) Reasoner; Marion was the daughter of James and Marion (née Monroe) Turner. James would serve as a clerk for the Michigan Supreme Count and as an attorney for the firm of Black, Reasoner & Hayden. James would also develop the Maple Park Subdivision where Reasoner Park is located today. After his marriage to Bessie Davis in 1912 the couple would have one child, James D. Reasoner. On November 24, 1922 after a long illness James passed away and was laid to rest at Mt. Hope Cemetery in Lansing, Michigan.[215] Bessie Reasoner lived for another forty four years as a widow. Bessie D. Reasoner was a graduate of the Liggett School of Grosse Pointe, Michigan, an active member of the Lansing Woman's Club and like her father a member of the Lansing Country Club. Bessie died at her home in Lansing on May 10, 1966.[216]

It seems likely that the cottage was designed for Edith Eva Davis. In Creecy's history of Harbor Point, the owner is always referred to a Mrs. Davis. Edith had reverted to her maiden name after her divorce, while Bessie kept her married name Mrs. Reasoner. Moving from the Davis cottage to just where the Bea Davis home was located is open to speculation. After reviewing the property owned by the Davis family in 1908 the most likely candidate is the north east corner of Hillsdale Street and Capital Avenue. Benjamin F. Davis owned this property in 1908, it was very close to the Davis home at 528 S. Washington and the home may have been intended as a gift for Thaddeus and Edith Hoffman after their marriage. No home was built on the lot in 1907-1908. All the other Davis properties in 1907-1908 had houses already on the lots. This may be a case of plans being drawn by Moon but the structure was never built.[217]

---

215   *LCN* 11/25/1922. There is a lot more to this story but you need to discover that on your own, it makes for interesting reading.
216   *LSJ* 5/11/1966.
217   There is another possibility. In researching the life Benny Davis there is a reference to a home at White Lake, Michigan. No supporting information has been discovered.

HUGH LYONS HOUSE

717 S. Capitol, Lansing, MI

"Hugh Lyons has his new residence at the corner of Capitol avenue and Main street nearly enclosed" (*LJ* 11/10/1902).

"The commodious new House which Hugh Lyons has been erecting during the winter at the corner of Main street and Capitol avenue is nearly complete. The house was designed by Charles H. Stroud. It has a handsome exterior appearance, while the interior is planned for a most convenient and acceptable House with an elegant finish of quarter-sawed oak. A feature of the house is the hall, with its effective window arrangement, paneled wainscoting of oak and hand-carved newel post" (*LJ* 3/16/1903).

717 S. Capitol, Lansing, MI

The front gable of the residence has some interesting architectural features. The gable is a closed style gable, usually this is accomplished by extending a pent roof across the base of the gable, and in this case Moon blends the shingles into the pent roof creating the flaring affect you see on both gables. The triangular section at the top of the gable is extended forward and combined with the recessed window on the third floor it provided an amount of shade for gable's western facing double window. The tower on the Lyons' home was a classic component of a Queen Anne style home with conical topped tower. On the third floor gable on the south side of the residence there was a palladium window, with a triple ribbon window on the second floor. On the north side of the home there was a double sided oriel window on the second floor and a bay window in the first; notice the flaring of the wall between the first and second floor. The wrap around porch with the delicate balustrade and the Tuscan columns with inlayed wooden pedestals are an appealing element. The shingling on the pediment on the porch it is rather plain when you would usually see some type of motif.

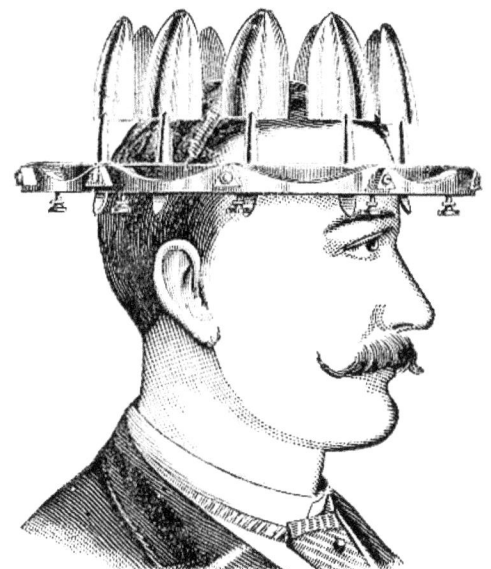

Hugh Lyons Hat Conformator

The Gould list records that Moon designed the Hugh Lyons residence in 1907, however the above article states that the home was designed by Charles Stroud and built between the years 1902-1903. Charles H. Stroud worked for Hugh Lyons in 1904 as the Superintendent of Hugh Lyons Company, and is listed in the 1910 Lansing City Directory as an architect. No other structures designed by Stroud have been indentified the Lansing area.[218] Lyons' home was standing in 1903; it is mentioned in an article which described the construction of Homer L. Luce's home on the adjacent lot next to Hugh Lyons home.[219] Could Moon have worked as a consulting architect to assist Stroud in the design of the home in 1903? Or did Moon remodel the home in 1907 to correct Stroud's work? Given Moon's workload in 1903 it is entirely possible that Stroud oversaw the construction of the home while Moon designed the house. Either way the home is a beautiful example of a Queen Anne home. The city of Lansing was deprived of much of its character and history, as well as many other homes as a result of the construction of I-496; but hindsight is always 20/20. The home was torn down in 1966.

From the Gould inventory of Darius Moon Buildings, listed as "Hugh Lyons Res. 1907".

---

218   Charles H. Stroud was born in Ingham County and was a long time resident of Lansing. His career was varied; in his obituary he is described as a successful builder, real estate developer and architect. See *LSJ* 9/26/1924, *Lansing Capital News* 9/26/1924 and the *Ingham County News* 10/2/1924.
219   *LJ* 4/19/1903.

Hugh Lyons 1847-1909

Hugh Lyons was a former Mayor of Lansing and prominent businessman. He was born in Sutton, Canada on March 17, 1847 the son of John Lyons and the youngest of the nine children. At the age of eighteen he enlisted in the 90th New York Infantry, Company I in Medina, New York on September 28, 1864 and transferred to Company E on November 28, 1864 and served in this company throughout the war as a private. The regiment took part in the engagements at Pleasant Hill, Franklin, Green Bayou and Cedar Creek. After mustering out of the army on June 3, 1865 Lyons traveled to Chicago and then on to Wisconsin eventually he came to Michigan and settled in Howell to work with a bridge crew in the construction of the rail line that ran between Howell and Lansing. In 1870 Hugh moved to Lansing and helped to build the Mineral Wells Hotel. While working as a clerk for Charles Broas he invented and patented the hat conformitor. From this invention grew the basis for Lyons' business in store fixtures and displays for merchandising. Later in 1890 the Hugh Lyons & Company was formed and became one of the leading retail supply stores with branches in New York and Chicago. In 1904 Lyons was elected Mayor of Lansing and reelected in 1906 as a Republican. On July 9, 1879 he married Miss Laura Brooks and they had one child, Arthur L. Lyons. Hugh Lyons died at his home on February 4, 1909 after a short illness.[220]

---

220   SR 2/5/1909, SR 4/2/1904 and Cowles 166.

CLUBHOUSE

Golf Course Clubhouse, Lansing, MI

OPENS UP DRIVE IN FEW MONTHS
J.H. MOORES WILL GRANT PUBLIC USEOF NEW ROADWAY ALONG GRAND RIVER
GOLF CLUB IS PROPOSED
MOON & SPICE HAVE PREPARED PLANS FOR ARTISTIC CLUB HOUSE

"Very early in the spring J.H. Moores will open his drive that extends along the east and south bank of the Grand river from a point near the Logan st bridge to Waverly park. The grading was practically finished in the fall and little remains to be done to put the drive in condition. It is one and three-fourths miles in length. The new roadway is reached over Cadwell st, just east and south of the Logan st bridge, but during the week days last year it could be gained from Washington through Moores park and a private drive on the property of E.W. Sparrow. The drive is along the top of the hills at varying distances from the river, but with the stream always in sight and affording a splendid view of the country on the other side. Mr. Moores will open the drive to the public but will ask that there be no heavy teaming upon it. During the coming season Mr. Moores intends erecting several summer cottages along the drive and will make some of them acceptable for permanent use. Plans are on foot for a golf club and links to be located on the drive, and Moon & Spice, architects, have prepared plans for a clubhouse of novel style and attractive design. The style is of old mission and Dutch colonial. The building as planned has a commodious club room, ladies parlor, dining room and kitchen on the first floor and a ball room and half-open balcony on the second. A Dutch fireplace occupies one end of the club. The interior finishing and woodwork will be old mission style, with beamed ceiling. Features of the exterior will be a fieldstone foundation, a first story of brick, and a wide veranda with brick columns for the support of the balcony. The location would be one affording shade and a fine view of the river and convenient to grounds to be used as links. The estimated cost of the building is $6,000" (*SR* 1/31/1907).

Accompanying the *State Republican* article from January 31, 1907, was an image of the clubhouse; the exact same image appeared in the 1907 Lansing High School yearbook, the *Oracle*, from where the above image is taken. A sketch of the clubhouse can be seen in the image of Moon's office, right behind Raymond Spice's head. The drawing of the clubhouse by Moon for J.H. Moores was an example of 20th Century idyllic fantasy of county life. The club house was to be in the style of a Dutch Colonial home; the interesting aspect of Moon's architectural rendering is the method he employed to incorporate a large second floor gambrel dormer with a porch into the structure. The large brick columns on the porch were a departure for Moon as well as the trellis in anchor by a brick column.

CLUBHOUSE TO BE OPENED NEXT WEEK
Structure Erected by J.H. Moores one of the finest in state

"The new club house which has been erected for the golf club by J.H. Moores will be opened for use the last of next week. The club house is built on the lines which are approximately the same as those affected in Florida bungalows. The exterior of the structure is stained a deep green with white trimmings, the siding being turned to present a rough surface. The main room of the building is 16x24 feet and adjoining this is a lean-to, 10x24 foot, containing toilet rooms, dressing rooms and a small kitchen. A roof veranda, 8 1/2 feet wide, extends around three sides. When open the club house will be one of the finest in this part of the state" (*SR* 6/18/1910). An image of this clubhouse, which was quite a departure from the one in the above drawing, appeared in the *State Republican* on June 30 1910.

The descriptions of the two club houses are very different in almost every respect. It is doubtful that the 1907 Clubhouse was ever built and it has not been determined if Moon designed the second clubhouse that was built for J.H. Moores. It seems unlikely.

From the Gould inventory of Darius Moon Buildings, listed as "Clubhouse 1907".

GUNNISONVILLE SCHOOL

Clark and Wood Roads, Gunnisonville, MI

"Presence of mind in Miss Effie Foster, teacher in the Gunnisonville school district, perhaps saved a bad panic among her pupils this morning when it was discovered that the schoolhouse was on fire. The school was dismissed and assistance summoned but in spite of the little that could be done with the means at hand, the building was totally destroyed" (*LJ* 2/15/1907).

"Bids will be received up to and including April 15, 1907, for the erection of a brick school house at Gunnisonville. Plans and specifications can be seen at Dunham's Hardware Store, North Lansing. The job will be let to the lowest bidder, but the board reserves the right to reject any and all bids. B.A. Kyes, H.P. Kraus, A.J. Rupp, building committee" (*SR* 4/4/1907).

Paul Dunham was familiar with Moon's work; previously Moon had designed a home for Dunham in Gunnisonville as well as a business block in North Lansing. The Gunnisonville School was located less then ¼ mile from Paul Dunham's home. The Gunnisonville schoolhouse was an interesting change of pace for Moon at this time in his career; he must have taken on the project as a favor to Paul Dunham. What is interesting in regards to the design of the schoolhouse is that Moon added a vestibule to the front of the building, probably to be used as a cloak room. Oddly enough this was not a standard practice in rural schoolhouse design; most one room school houses from this period had the students enter directly into the clasSRoom. The open gable over the entrance door which itself has a transom window above it was not a typical feature on a rural schoolhouse, especially when you consider the brackets at the base of the gable. The ornate bell tower also was not a standard element. These were expensive extras at a time when most rural school districts were strapped for money. The building with the shed roof was a latter addition.[221] From the Gould inventory of Darius Moon Buildings, listed as "School Hse at Gunnisonville 1907".

---

221   See the *Clinton Republican* 2/21/1907 for more information about the fire at the Gunnisonville School.

FARMER'S BANK

322 S. Jefferson, Mason, MI

TO REMODEL MASON BANK
PLANS PREPARED TO ENLARGE BUILDING BY FARMERS' BANK

"Plans have been prepared by Architect D.B. Moon of this city for remodeling the building occupied and owned by the Farmers' bank of Mason. The repairs are to be quite extensive and the entire appearance of the building will be changed. An entire new front will be put in and it will be so arranged that the steps which now extend into the street will begin at the lot line. The present building will be extended thirty-five feet in the rear, new vaults will be put in and the banking room will be equipped with new fixtures and a handsome tile floor. Work will start July 1" (*SR* 6/22/1906).

FARMERS' BANK HAS FINE OFFICE
REMODELING OF ITS BUILDING AT MASON ALMOST COMPLETED

Mason Jan. 16 — The Farmers' bank at Mason has almost completed the improvements of its building. The interior has been remodeled and the building extended thirty-five feet in the rear, making room for three fine suites of offices on the second floor. The first floor, originally some feet above the sidewalk, has been lowered. The desks, railing, and wood fixtures are all solid mahogany. The floor of the lobby is paved with tile. And the wainscoting is of white marble, the baseboards and ledges of the windows being of black marble. The walls and ceilings are finely frescoed. The rear part of the building contains a directors' room. The old vault has been entirely removed, a new larger one, with the latest electric burglar alarm having been installed. The building is heated by steam. The entire cost of the improvements will probably amount to $6,000 or $7,000" (*SR* 1/16/1907).

"The remodeling of the Farmers bank building of this city which has been going on for several months is rapidly nearing completion. There has been an entire change in the interior and the building extended 35 feet in the rear, making room for three fine suites of offices on the second floor. A new front wholly of glass has been put in making a very fine well lighted room. The first floor, originally some feet above the sidewalk, has been lowered. The desks, railings and wood fixtures are of solid mahogany. The floor of the lobby is paved with tile, and the wainscoting is of white marble, the baseboards and ledges of the windows being black marble. The walls and ceiling are finely frescoed. The rear part of the building contains a director's room. The old vault has been entirely removed, and a new and larger one, with the latest electric burglar alarm, having been installed. The building is heated with steam" (*ICD* 1/23/1907).

322 S. Jefferson, Mason, MI (Rodney Jewett)

The Farmer's Bank building on which Moon worked, from the first photograph, is a two story structure with the double doors under the sign that says Bank. The building was heavily modified over time and none of the original façade remains. The above image shows the building after remolding work performed by Moon. Observe that the front entrance steps have been set back from the sidewalk. The three arched windows on the second floor framed with ornate brickwork are complimented by the pilaster columns which were also of brick; notice the stone caps on the columns. The cornice with the Italianate bracket finishes the building. The interior of the structure is described in the newspaper accounts and needs no further explanation. The Farmers Bank is still in business and is known today as the Mason State Bank. From the Gould inventory of Darius Moon Buildings, listed as "Bldg. for Farmers Bank (Mason) 1907".

BROWN'S STORE

304 S. Jefferson, Mason, MI

Brown's Shoe Store was located at the southwest corner of Maple and Jefferson streets, the current home of Ware's Pharmacy. The Brown Brothers Shoe Store was established in 1896 by Henry L. Brown and his brother Frederick J. Brown. In August of 1900 Charles sold his portion of the business to Carl J. Loomis, and the business became known as Brown & Loomis Shoes. Four years later Loomis sold his half of the shoe store to Frederick, who would become sole owner of the business. Frederick J. Brown was born in Mecklenburg, Germany in 1850 to Charles and Mary Brown; the family immigrated to Michigan in 1857. Frederick married Miss Sallie L. Leonard in Jackson, Michigan on March 18, 1875. There were no children; Sallie passed away on January 18, 1907 from cancer. In 1910, Frederick sold the entire business back to his brother Henry and moved to Detroit with his new wife Anna, where he purchased a home at 136 Lincoln Avenue.[222] Later Frederick J. Brown would again work in the shoe industry as a representative of a large shoe manufacture. Taken ill in Chicago after retuning from a trip to Winnipeg, Frederick's condition deteriorated and he passed away in December of 1929.[223] It is difficult to establish just what work Moon did for Frederick Brown; he may have remodeled the façade of the building and it's interior. There is no reference to any work being done to Brown's Shoe Store between 1907 and 1909. The façade of Ware's Pharmacy is a reproduction of the original front of the building. The ornamentation which wraps around the structure just below the cornice is an architectural feature not seen on many structures. It was accomplished by a skilled brick mason who faced the brick; this was intricate and expensive work. The cornice is not original; at one time there was a series of brackets which descended from the parapet to pilasters and the large Vs. From the Gould inventory of Darius Moon Buildings, listed as "Brown Store in Mason 1907".

---

222 The information on Frederick J. Brown's life is derived from several sources. The death of Sally Brown see the *Ingham County News* 1/24/1907. For Henry L. Brown see *Ingham County News* 12/9/1943 and the *LSJ* 12/3/1943. For Charles P. Brown see the *Ingham County News* 10/27/1921.
223 *Ingham County News* 12/5/1929 and *Ingham County News* 1/2/1930.

FRANK H. HAYES HOME

110 W. Lenawee, Lansing, MI

"Architects Moon & Spice have prepared plans for a $9,000 house for Frank Hayes, to be erected on Lenawee st just west of the Frost terraces" (*SR* 3/19/1907).

The remarkable thing about the Frank Hayes residence is that it is still standing today. The home is located at the southern edge of the Lansing's downtown business district and has survived while its neighbors, the Sparrow and Davis residences, have been torn down. There are several interesting architectural elements incorporated into the home. On the front closed gable there is what appears to be a palladium window, but it is not. Moon recessed the brick work surrounding the windows, placed a stone sill at the base of the windows, and added brick work above the window to complete the illusion of a frame. There is also a bay dormer which is stacked above the second floor window that protrudes slightly from the building. This window is matched by the triple window on the second floor which also projects somewhat from the residence; notice how the sills of the windows complete the frame. The curved porch is interesting in that the placement of the columns frame the first floor windows. Notice how the windows on the left from the first to the third floor are stacked symmetrically. The entrance to the home is recessed and has a canted window to match the curve of the porch.

In the *Michigan Federation of Labor Year Book 1906-1907*, Frank Hayes is portrayed as a friend of the working man.

FRANK H. HAYES

"Somewhat of a philosopher is the subject of this sketch, Frank H. Hayes, dealer in wines, liquors and cigars at 109 Michigan avenue east, Lansing. On the back of his card is a short disquisition showing that, out of a bushel of corn, the distiller gets four gallons of whisky, worth $16, the government $3.30, the railroads $2 and the poor farmer but 20 cents. This is a strong argument in favor of organization of the farmers, who have recently joined in the labor movement.
Mr. Hayes is a hospitable host and it goes without saying that all who work for a living will be cordially received and fairly treated at his thirst parlors. He keeps only the best goods. His Bell telephone is No. 292."[224]

Frank Henry Hayes was a long time Lansing businessman; born in New York City on June 14, 1856 Fred was engaged in a variety of businesses before coming to Lansing. He arrived in Lansing in 1877 and worked as a foreman at Lansing Wagon Works. Later he served as a member of the Lansing Police Department. With the formation of the Lansing Brewing Company in 1898 Hayes became Vice President of the company and at the same time he owned the Arcade, a retail store of Fine Wines, Liquor and Cigars located at 109 E. Michigan. When the Lansing Brewing Company disbanded because of Prohibition he became the Lansing representative for Burghoff Products. On May 24, 1881 Frank married Miss Alvina Litzan. Frank Henry Hayes died at St. Lawrence Hospital on June 8, 1928 at the age of 72; he was survived by his wife Alvena, daughter Mildred and son Frank J. Hayes. [225]

From the Gould inventory of Darius Moon Buildings, listed as "Hse for Frank Hayes 1907".

---

224 See *Michigan Federation* 233.
225 *LSJ*, 6/8/1928, *LSJ* 6/9/1928 and the *Lansing Capital News* 6/8/1928. His wife Alvena R. Hayes would live until the age of 93, and passed away in May 17, 1954.

LOUIS BECK STORE

Beck Store before remodeling, 112 N. Washington, Lansing, MI

FOR A NEW FRONT
Louis Beck's store to be fixed up in the latest style.

"Moon & Spice are drawing plans for a fine new front for Louis Beck's clothing store on Washington avenue north. There will be a middle entrance with deep plate-glass windows on each side, of the most modern design. The floor will be marble and there will be hangers for the clothes on the inside of the store, in place of the shelves that are now used" (*LJ* 7/08/1907).

From the 1907 Oracle

"The store presents a pleasing appearance. It occupies the first floor and the basement. In that latter is the crockery and tinware department, neatly arranged, while the main floor is decorated with ferns and palms in profusion. The store is long and wide, finished in mission oak, with cases of the same wood. The walls are white, against which the displays and decorations are shown to great advantage. One feature of the store is the rest alcove, separated from the rest of the store by pillars of oak. The room is finished in green, with walls paneled in mission style. Chairs and a desk will be placed in it, and here the ladies of the city, when ever they are down town, may stop and rest, write or address post cards. Throughout the opening this afternoon, and evening as well music will be furnished by Miss Princess Moon" (*LJ* 9/30/1908).

Beck Store after remodeling, 112 N. Washington, Lansing, MI

The above photograph is from circa 1910 and it is from a parade image. One of the ways photographs are dated is by examining the businesses that are present and in this case the John A. Hicks store operated in this location beginning in 1910 and only for a short time. The work on the interior is described in the above article. The façade of the store had a traditional Italianate style cornice with brackets and dentils. The stone lintels over the second floor windows are either of cast stone or lime stone. If you compare the before and after photographs it seems that the majority of the work was carried out on the entrance of the store. The image below shows the structure before it was torn down. An additional window was added on the second floor at some point between the two blocks, to allow light to enter the stairwell.

112 N. Washington, in the 1960s

Louis Beck was born in New York City in 1860 and when he was just 6 years of age when his family moved to Lansing. His father Samuel opened a clothing store at 112 N Washington Avenue. Later, after Louis had finished high school, he worked in his father's business and later managed the store. In 1881 Louis married Sarah Wolfe of Fort Wayne, Indiana and the couple had one child, Samuel A Beck. Louis was active in many of the local fraternal organizations; he was a member of the Lansing Lodge No. 33, F. & A.M., Capital Lodge No. 4, I.O.O.F., the Elks, the Foresters, the Royal Arcanum and the Lansing Liederkranz Society. Beck also served on the Electric, Light and Water Works Board, the Public Works Board and at the time of his death was serving as a member of the Cemetery Board. Louis Beck died in 1910 on Christmas Night. The list of the pall bearers at Louis' funeral included Henry Kositchek, Henry Behrendt, Joseph Gerson, J.B. Simone, Leo Ehrlich and Adolph Kositchek plus honorary pall bearers H.H. Larned, J.E. Roe, Charles Hammond, J.E. Ziegler, Frank McKibben, Christian Herrmann and Jacob Stahl a who's who of prominent Lansing citizens, confirming the great esteem that Louis Beck was held in by his fellow citizens.[226]

From the Gould inventory of Darius Moon Buildings, listed as "Lew Becks-Remodeled Store 1907".

---

226   SR 12/27/1910 and the LJ 12/27/1910.

GEORGE H. KNEAL STORE

220 N. Washington, Lansing, MI

"The stone building at 220 Washington ave n. being remodeled by Geo. H. Kneal will be not only a novelty, but the front will be the only one of its kind in the city. Polished white marble, trimmed with polished brass, will constitute the base of the front, and a large plate glass window will afford a means of display" (*SR* 5/11/1907).

ONE OF THE CITY'S FINEST BLOCKS
STORE OF WASHINGTON AVE N. OWNED BY GEO. KNEAL, ENTIRELY REMODELED EVERYWAY UP-TO DATE
PROBABLY WILL BE OCCUPIED BY LADIES' OUTFITTING CONCERN

"The Kneal block, Washington ave n, has been remodeled from cellar to garret of its three stories and is now one of the finest business blocks in the city. George Kneal, the owner, following plans prepared by Moon & Spice, architects, lengthened the store to 100 feet and installed a new front which has been highly praised. It consists of marble copper corner pieces and a plate glass with and handsome tile display window floor and woodwork of mahogany finish. The upper front of the window contains tile prism glass, while the top rear windows of the store are of sheet prism glass, by means of which the light is carried to the center of the store, making it exceptionally well lighted throughout the interior. A new steel ceiling, oak woodwork and newly decorated walls complete the interior in exceptionally fine style. The two upper floors have also been refinished in oak with new wall paper and oak floors and woodwork. A feature of the remodeled building is a hall way with its tiled entrance, handsome door and hall telephone by which communication can be carried on from the upper floors with any one at the entrance below. The entire building is to be heated with steam. Mr. Kneal states that Chicago parties are negotiating with him for a lease of the building as a ladies' outfitting store, including millinery and tailoring" (*SR* 9/6/1907).

STORE ROOM IS A THING OF BEAUTY
GEORGE KNEAL HAS FINISHED ELEGANT JOB OF REMODELING

"A nifty and pleasant store is being completed next door to John Herrman & Sons Tailoring establishment, Washington avenue north. The building has been remodeled by George H. Kneal, the owner. Moon & Spice were the architects. Plenty of light is the feature of the place. The front was also remodeled and rebuilt that the tile prism glass above the one large window permits the light to flow over the rolling awning. Tile is used for the entrances as well as for the floor of the display window. The interior is finished off in oak with green paper and has a row of incandescent lamps around the ceiling. The improvements do not stop on the first floor, but continue throughout the three stories. The stairway street door is always to be locked. When the floor bell rings, through the speaking tube the lady of the house upstairs can first talk with the visitor. If she wishes to admit them then all that is necessary for her to do is to press the electrical button, releasing the lock. Old partitions in the second and third of the brick were torn out and new rooms built. The second floor is finished off in oak" (*LJ* 9/6/1907).

The façade of the Kneal building is striking. The detailed corbel brickwork below the cornice and the brick detail on the pilaster visible on the left in the photograph makes this building visually appealing from the street. The stone framed windows give the impression of a gothic window while the inlaid stones of the arches lend to this illusion. Notice the clever use of stone banding on the façade.

From the Gould inventory of Darius Moon Buildings, listed as "George Kneal store 1907".

DR. FRANK NICE HOUSE REMODEL

1025 N. Washington, Lansing, MI

"Dr. F.R Nice has purchased the Smith/Peck property [for $2,200], on Washington avenue north, between Kilborn and Maple streets, and will completely remodel the house, making a fine residence of it. The plans have not been drawn as yet, but the residence will be in colonial style, not differing greatly from the present exterior appearance of the structure. An architect will soon prepare plans for remodeling the building" (*LJ* 4/20/1906).

"The historic Smith or Peck house the old colonial style mansion on Washington avenue north, is being remodeled into an apartment house which will be one of the finest and the most beautiful in the city. The plans are at the office of Moon and Spice, and they show the building as it will look when completed to be a modern structure of three stories, with five apartments. There will be two apartments on the first floor, two on the second, and one on the third. Each apartment will contain five rooms and they are to be provided throughout with the most modern and metropolitan adjuncts. The building will be in the colonial style. With two great pillars in the front, balconies on the second and third floors and on the ground floor porch on each side of the entrance. It will be a framed building, the walls of the old Peck house are being used as far as possible in its construction. When finished it will be a fine ornament to one of the city's principal streets. It was designed for Dr. F.R. Nice" (*LJ* 4/22/1907).

It is not clear in the above articles if the work on the Smith/Peck house was a complete tear down with a completely new building or if it was renovated and greatly expanded. The only image of the Smith/Peck home prior to the rebuilding is from the 1866 Birdseye Map of Lansing and the home is unassuming. All indications are that the Nice home was an entirely new structure. As with many Moon structures the porch is the main feature of the home. The porch with its massive columns is a Colonial Revival style porch. The lower porch frames the paired doors that have side light windows and a triple window transom over the Door. Notice how this detail is repeated on the second floor individual doors each with at transom overhead. This was a porch that was meant to impress the visitor. The hipped roof has a large dormer on the front which is repeated on the north and south side. On the back is a shed roof dormer while on the front there are two eyebrow dormers on either side of the large dormer; they are larger than the traditional eyebrow dormer and have a lunette window. It is also interesting to note both sides of the building mimic each other in their design, with bay windows on both the north and south sides of the house.

1025 N. Washington, Lansing, MI

The Smith/Peck home was built in 1852 by Hiram H. Smith a prominent resident of Lansing. H.H. Smith was born in Malone, New York on December 9, 1809 and grew up in Brandon, Vermont. In 1836 he moved to Ingham County to take up farming. Smith was elected Ingham County Treasurer in 1836; in 1847 Smith relocates to Lansing where he built the first flour mill in the area. He continued in the milling and mercantile business and was instrumental along with James Turner in the building of the plank road that ran between Howell and Lansing. In 1859 Smith was elected as the first mayor of Lansing and served just one year. Afterward he became Vice President and managing director of the Jackson, Lansing & Saginaw Railroad. Smith moved to Jackson, Michigan in 1864 and was active in the building of the Jackson & Ft. Wayne Railroad, the Detroit, Lansing & Lake Michigan Railroad and the Detroit & Bay City Railroads. He retired from business in 1873 and devoted his time to his real estate investment. Hiram H. Smith was married four times; his first wife was Miss Frances Denison of Rutland, Vermont, and after her death he married the widow Mrs. Mary Jane Waldo of Williamston. After her death in 1859, Hiram married the widow of Judge Ephraim B. Danforth, Elizabeth P. Danforth of Ann Arbor; after her death he married the widow of Dr. George W. Gorham of Jackson, Harriet Gorman, in 1865; who passed away in 1893. Smith outlived his four wives and one son, Dwight R. Smith. He was survived by his son Henry H. Smith and daughter Mrs. Kate Newman. Hiram H. Smith died at his home in Jackson on May 15, 1898.[227]

---

227   SR 5/16/1898, *Ingham County News* 5/19/1898 and the *Ingham County Democrat* 5/19/1898.

George Washington Peck was born in New York City on June 4, 1818 to Walter and Catharine (née Dally) Peck. George attended Yale University and pursued a degree in Classical Studies and after graduation he studied law in New York City. He came to Lansing when the state Capitol was moved from Detroit and partnered with, MesSRs. Lee, Thomas and Bush who opened several businesses in Lansing. Peck would become Lansing's first postmaster and was Speaker of the State House of Representatives in 1847. He would serve as the Secretary of State for Michigan in 1848-1849 and was the owner of the *Lansing Journal* from 1852-1855. After he sold his interests in the newspaper, he was elected to the Thirty-fourth Congress of the United States as a Democrat. Defeated in 1856 he would leave Congress and later be elected mayor of Lansing in 1864. He was a member of the 1860 Democratic National Convention in Charleston that nominated Stephen A. Douglas for president. Peck married Miss Sophia (Sarah) Lee of Brighton on May 31, 1849; the couple had one child, Isabel. George Washington Peck, considered by many the finest orator produced by the state of Michigan, died in Saginaw on June 30, 1905.[228]

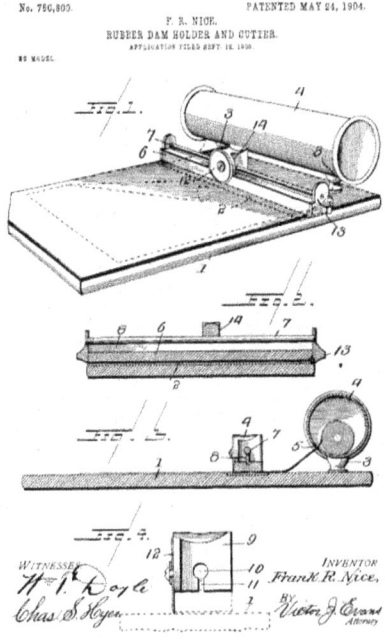

Dr. Frank R. Nice's Patent

Dr. Frank R. Nice born in 1864 and died in St Petersburg, Florida on October 13, 1949; his body was returned to Lansing for burial. Dr. Nice was a well-known Lansing dentist who practiced in the community for many years. He was married to Mary C. Rouse on May 9, 1886. Mary was born in Lansing on November 2, 1866 and passed away at their home in Lansing on Sunday December 13, 1925. She was survived by her husband, one brother, W.F. Rouse and two sisters Mrs. Emma Carey and Mrs. Catherine Brown, who all resided in Lansing.[229] Frank R. Nice held several patents, one for the Jar-Closure Tool and the Rubber Dam Holder and Cutter for dentists.

---

228   SR 7/1/1905, LJ 7/1/1905 and the *Saginaw Courier-Herald* 7/1/1905. There are several inconsistencies in Peck's background. He is listed in the *State Republican* as being born on May 18, 1818, while the Saginaw paper lists his birth as May 18, 1816. The *Lansing Journal* has him owning the *Lansing Democrat* in 1852.
229   See the *LSJ* 12/14/1925 and the *LSJ* 10/14/1949.

OLIVER W. HALSTEAD BLOCK

305-309 S. Washington, Lansing, MI

PLANS FOR BUILDINGS
Washington Avenue Stores are to be put up Soon

"Plans are completed for the new brick stores to be built opposite the Hotel Downey on Washington avenue south, and bids will be received this week by the architects Moon & Spice. On the south lot next to the American Laundry, Oliver W. Halstead, of Mason, will construct a fine brick building 44 by 90 feet and two stories in height. The front will be pressed brick. Swan & Fleming, who owns the south lot, will construct a building of the same size and shape at the same time" (*LJ* 8/21/1907).

"O.W. Halstead of Mason is just completing a new structure at 309 South Washington ave, two stories in height and made of brick" (*LSJ* 8/3/1911).

305-309 S. Washington, Lansing, MI

In 1907 Moon designed 305-307 S. Washington for Oliver Halstead; they are the first two buildings on the left in the photograph. It was not until 1911 that 309 S. Washington was built, the last business block in the photograph occupied by Kinney Shoes. Both business blocks 305-307 S. Washington were torn down in the late 1950s, but 309 S. Washington still stands and it is a mirror image of 305-307 S. Washington. You can see the slight difference between 309 S. Washington and the other two blocks along the roof line and in the slight setback along the cornice. It is unknown if Moon designed 309 S. Washington but the Gould inventory has Moon designing a store for a Holstead in 1912. The business blocks are typical commercial buildings from this time period. There is extensive corbelling and ornate brickwork along the upper façade of the building; observe how the corbelling imitates the dentils along the cornice. The brick pilasters frame each business block. There is one architectural element that is often overlooked, the recessed rectangular brick work over the second floor windows which is surrounded by brick lintels over the blocks of windows. This was an inexpensive detail when compared to adding limestone banding.

Oliver W. Halstead 1840-1913

As a leader in the business community and highly respect by his peers, Oliver W. Halstead was one of the most influential citizens of Mason. Born on September 5, 1840 near Adrian, Michigan he attended Adrian College. Halstead settled in Mason in 1864 and began working as a carpenter and taught school at Hubbard school in Vevay Township. Oliver later opened a drug store, a business he owned for over 30 years. In 1898 he became president of the First State & Savings Bank of Mason and had extensive holdings in commercial real estate throughout Ingham County. In 1866 Oliver married Elizabeth Seely of Mason and they had one child, Herbert A. Halstead. Oliver W. Halstead died on December 12, 1913 at his son's home in Lansing. From the Gould inventory of Darius Moon Buildings, listed as "House for Holstead, Hse & Store 1912". In regards to a home for Oliver Halstead, in 1912 Halstead owned the property at 227 N. Sycamore, Lot 2 Block 90. Whether Moon designed the home or remodeled the structure is unknown at this time.

JAMES W. POTTER HOUSE

700 S. Washington, Lansing, MI

The Gould list states that Moon designed a house for James Potter, "Hse for Ray Potter's father 1907". Ray Potter's father was well known industrialist James W. Potter. The house at 700 S. Washington was built in 1889 and torn down by R.E. Olds in 1926. The home was constructed out of native field stone, from Potterville, Michigan, as was the Larned House at 102 S. Walnut and the Thomas House at 114 S. Walnut. R.E. Olds, after he purchased the home, he tore down Potter's house and donated the stone to the First Baptist church where it was used to build the social hall. The home does not fit Moon's architectural style; it is more that of architect Edwyn Bowd, who designed the H.H. Larned residence in 1889. The fieldstone construction and the ornamental ridge cresting point toward a mixture of Romanesque and French Second Empire styles. The home has a certain heaviness about it which is unlike Moon's other designs. Could Moon have remodeled this home for James Potter in 1907? The only property James Potter owned in 1906, aside from the land to be donated to the city to create Potter Park, was Lot 1-2-3 of Block 171 upon which his home at 700 S. Washington stood. But in1913 on Lot 2-3 Block 171 a home appears on the Sanborn map, 111 W. St. Joseph which abutted the Potter home. The home was not present on the 1906 Sanborn map. This seems the only possibility for a new home designed by Darius Moon for James Potter in the year 1907. No images exist of this structure.

James W. Potter 1843-1926

James W. Potter, one of the early pioneers to the area is remembered today by Lansing residents as the man who donated the land for Potter Park, but there is much more to his story. He was born in Saline, Michigan on February 13, 1843, one of seven remarkable children born to Linus and Diana Potter. Two years later his parents settled in Eaton County, near what is now Potterville; the town was eventually named after Linus Potter. There the family established a homestead. Unfortunately two years after their arrival Linus Potter would die suddenly leaving Diana with seven children to raise, the oldest was seventeen and the youngest was age three. James decided to head west, possibly following in his brothers footsteps and settled in Minnesota. At the start of the Civil War, James enlisted in the 3rd Minnesota Infantry Regiment at the age of 18. His service during the war would be spent on America's western frontier. After the war James stayed in Minnesota where he married Celia G. Ray on August 26, 1866, they would have two children, Ray (Miles) and a daughter Gertrude, who would die tragically in a train wreck in 1890.

James W. Potter's Company Letterhead

While residing in Minnesota, James would become an expert lumberman and fine tuned his business skills by managing a local sawmill. James and his wife returned to Potterville, where James worked the family lumber tracts. In 1889 he moved to Lansing and established a furniture factory which eventually became part of the Hugh Lyons Company. Potter was active in Lansing business; he was heavily involved in the Lansing Savings Bank which he guided through the financial crash of the late 1890s. In 1901 after the sale of his furniture company, James was active in civic affairs, donating the land for Potter Park to the city in 1912. After the death of his first wife, Celia on August 2, 1877, James married Sarah J. Porter Rosserion on August 24, 1878. James W. Potter died at the home of his son Ray, 313 W. Hillsdale on July 29, 1926.[230] James' brother was Theodore E. Potter the well known historian.

1908

UNION BUILDING AND LOAN ASSOCIATION BUILDING

119 W. Allegan, Lansing, MI

In June of 1909 Frank McKibbin purchased the Gillam Block, 119-121 W. Allegan, from Daniel J. Gillam for the sum of $13,000. Mr. McKibbin signed a five year lease with the Union Building and Loan Association to occupy 119 W. Allegan. McKibbin was also the secretary of the Union Building and Loan Association and at that time the laws governing building and loan associations did not allow ownership of their office buildings. Prior to 1909 the Union Building and Loan Association occupied space in the Hollister Building. In regards to the sale, both Lansing papers commented on the renovations that were to take place, "The new

---

230   *LSJ* 7/29/1926 and *Lansing Capital News* 7/29/1926.

offices will be a great improvement over the ones which are now occupied by the association. Modern bank fixtures, a burglar proof safe and a well appointed director's room make the offices among the best in the city" (*LJ* 6/1/1909). "They [Union Building and Loan Association] are equipped with a commodious vault and a burglar proof safe" (*SR* 6/1/1909).

Moon's work on this building for all intents and purposes was a remodeling of the existing structure, not unlike the work he performed at the Farmer's Bank in Mason, Michigan. The building at 119 W. Allegan along with the structure at 117 W. Allegan underwent a major face lift in 1978, resulting in the building you see today. All indications are that the remodel was a complete tear down. The current structure is clad front and back with the same style brick work, something you would not do if you were renovating the building. It is unknown if Moon renovated the façade of the building besides the interior? Unfortunately no images exist of the building prior to the 1930s. In regards to the outside structure notice the diamond inlay along the parapet and a smaller rendering above the second floor windows. It is interesting to observe the brick columns that frame the block, on the top there is a limestone cap while at the base there is a limestone block to complete the column.

The Union Building and Loan Association was organized on June 2, 1886 as a limited corporation. It was reorganized in 1890 with some stockholders elected as directors, President, Alfred Wise; Vice President, D.M. Nottingham; Treasurer, Nelsen Bradley; and Secretary, H.D. Bartholomew. On October 15, 1956 Union Building and Loan Association merged with Lansing Savings and Loan Association, conveniently located next door at 117 W. Allegan. The new establishment became the Union Savings and Loan Association. Later in 1983 the institution became Union Federal Savings after it adopted a Federal charter. On December 27, 1991 the organization was acquired by Community First Bank, which on July 10, 1999 was purchased by Old Kent Bank. Later Old Kent Bank would become Fifth Third Bank.

From the Gould inventory of Darius Moon Buildings, listed as "Union Bldg & Loan Assoc., 1908".

JUDGE AARON V. MCALVAY HOUSE

620 S. Capitol, Lansing, MI

"W.D Sabin has sold his fine residence at the corner of Capitol avenue and St. Joseph street to Judge A.V. McAlvay of the supreme court" (*LJ* 8/19/1907).

"Judge A.V. McAlvay has purchased the residence of W.D. Sabin, 620 Capitol ave s." (*SR* 8/19/1907).

Although Moon did not design the residence, all indications are that this was a wide-ranging remodeling project. What we know from comparing the 1906 to the 1913 Sanborn maps is that there was extensive work to the front porch and the back of the house. Based upon the Sanborn maps the porch was extended and the tower was added. The tower matches the architectural Gothic Revival style of the residence. The dormer on the front of the tower is interesting and a detail that Moon never repeated. With the limitations of the photograph it is difficult to describe the porch. What can be extrapolated is that the columns formed the entrance, but the placement of the tree prevents any further description.

Aaron Vance McAlvay was born in Ann Arbor on July 19, 1847, to Patrick Hamilton and Sarah (née Drake) McAlvay. Patrick H. McAlvay was a farmer and Aaron spent his childhood on the farm. After Aaron graduated from the Ann Arbor Public Schools he entered the University of Michigan to study Literature. Following four years of study he entered the Law Department at the University of Michigan, graduating in 1869. He married Miss Barbara Bassler on December 9, 1872; they had six children, a daughter Margaretha died soon after birth. In 1878 Aaron was appointed judge of the nineteenth district, later he was appointed non-resident Lecture of Law at the University of Michigan in 1897, a post which he held until 1903. In 1910 the University of Michigan conferred on him the degree of LL.D. In 1904 he was elected to the Michigan State Supreme Court. Supreme Court Justice Aaron V. McAlvay died at his home on July 9, 1915, survived by his wife and five of his children, Harry S. of New York City, Carl E., of Lansing, Bard T., of Traverse City, Mrs. D.J. Gillam of Polson, Montana and Mrs. Frances M. Rosewater of Omaha, Nebraska.[231] The home was torn down in 1960. From the Gould inventory of Darius Moon Buildings, listed as "Judge McAlvery Remodeled Hse, 1908".

LACY & ABRAMS HOUSE

2230 Covert, Leslie, MI

"Mr. and Mrs. Philo Lacy and Alice Abrams of Lansing have begun the erection of a fine $4,000 home on their farm across from P.P. Backus' farm. Mrs. Lacy's mother, Mrs. L. Backus, "broke" ground for the new home, throwing out a few shovels full where the house is to stand. The house will be built of cement, and when completed will be one of the prettiest farm houses in the county. Mr. and Mrs. Lacy will make it their home when completed. B.J. Brown is doing the work" (*Leslie Local Republican* 5/27/1909).

"Mrs. Alice Abrams and Mr. and Mrs. P. Lacy of Lansing, are moving into their very handsome new House on the M.U.R. road two miles north of Leslie. Mr. Lacy and Mrs. Abrams will live on their farm and still continue their business in Lansing. It is quite a noticeable fact that many new houses are being built along this new road" (*SR* 3/19/1910).

---

231   *LSJ* 7/9/1915.

Helen and Alice's father Harry Backus (d1899) owned part of Section 9 Leslie Township, east of North Leslie. The home was built on the site of Harry's original log cabin. The Abrams and Lacey residence is an interesting home. The residence was constructed using cinder blocks and cement, a medium that Moon used extensively for the first time. On the porch; the balustrade and railing are made entirely of cast cement and so are the columns as well as the rusticated blocks that comprised the home's foundation, the base of the porch columns and the quoins, the decorative stone work at the corners of the home. On the west side of the home there is a bay window towards the back while on the east side there is a matching bay window.

Philo and Helen Lacy on the porch at their home

Helen A Backus was born in Leslie, Michigan on August 6, 1861 to Harry and Abigail A. (née Palmer) Backus; later in 1884 Helen moved to Lansing, Michigan after her marriage to Philo E. Lacy (Lacey) on January 13, 1884. Mrs. Lacy was an active member of the Pilgrim Congregational Church, the Unity Club and a life member of the White Shrine of Jerusalem. In 1910 the Lacy's built a home two miles north of Leslie at Backus Crossing. Later on July 15, 1924 Philo Lacy passed away at his home at Backus Crossing. Philo was an active businessman in Lansing and was engaged in the produce business with A.H. Whitehead. The location of the home at Backus crossing was ideally situated for access to the Michigan United Railways interurban line which ran to Lansing and Jackson, Michigan.[232] After moving back to the Leslie area Helen A. Lacy became an active member of the E.O.T.C. Club of Leslie and the Royal Daughters. Mrs. Lacy died at her niece's home in Lansing on April 12, 1941.[233]

---

232   *Leslie Local Republican* 7/17/1924 and *LSJ* 7/15/1924.
233   *LSJ* 4/13/1941 and *Leslie Local Republican* 4/17/1941.

The porch at 2230 Covert, Leslie, MI

Miss Alice A. Backus, sister of Helen was born in Leslie in 1864 several years later on September 30, 1891 she married David D. Abrams they divorced several years later. For many years Mrs. Alice A. Abrams was a respected milliner in both Lansing and Mason. She later shared the home on Covert Road with her sister and brother-in-law for a short period of time. Mrs. Abrams was well-known for her generosity; in June of 1914 she hosted a p*ICN*ic for the employees of the Mills Dry Goods Company at the home on Covert Road. Over 150 people attended, original songs were composed, and an athletic contest was held as well as an extensive p*ICN*ic (*LSJ* 6/27/1914). Mrs. Alice A. Abrams died at her home at Backus Crossing on May 11, 1915 after a short illness.[234]

From the Gould inventory of Darius Moon Buildings, listed as "Mrs. Lacy & Abrams Hse – Leslie, 1908".

---

234   *Leslie Local Republican* 5/13/1915, *LSJ* 5/11/1915, *Ingham County News* 5/13/1915 and the *Ingham County Democrat* 5/12/1915.

OSCAR S. CASE HOUSE

523 W. Grand River, Lansing, MI

"Oscar S. Case has moved from 807 Capitol avenue north into his new residence, 523 Franklin avenue west" (*LJ* 10/7/1908).

This is a traditional style organic home; it resembles the Lacey home at 2230 Covert in Leslie, Michigan except that this was a framed structure not cider block. Where the Lacey home has a shed roof over the porch the Case home has a roof with a conventional pediment over the entrance that frames the front door. The columns are a traditional Tuscan style as opposed to the lager banded columns of the Lacey residence. Both homes have a closed gable end on each side with a pent roof and a front gable which is also closed with two similar windows. The placement of the second floor windows differs between the two homes. This may have been a case of Moon reselling plans with slight modifications.

Oscar S. Case was born on December 10, 1864 to Orrin S. and Mary (née Teeter) Case. Little is known concerning Oscar's early life in Lansing. On October 18, 1899 he married Agnes George of Detroit; the couple would have two children, Theodore F. and Mary Margaret. The family would move to Philadelphia in 1900 where Oscar managed a local iron works factory. In 1906 his family moved back to Lansing and Oscar was employed as Secretary of the Eureka Machine Company, a manufacturer of construction equipment. After the demise of the Eureka Machine Company, Oscar relocated to Cleveland where he worked for the Red Cross as a traffic manager. Oscar S. Case died in Detroit on December 30, 1928.[235] The Case house was still standing as of 2015. From the Gould inventory of Darius Moon Buildings, listed as "O.S. Care Hse Lansing, 1908".

---

235   *LSJ* 12/31/1928 and the *Detroit Free Press* 12/31/1928.

COLUMBIA PARK SCHOOL

Foster Avenue School after its rebuilding in 1918

The story of the Columbia Park School is a fascinating tale. In July of 1908 Dr. Joseph Foster offered the residents of District 6 in Lansing Township four lots located north of East Michigan Avenue with the understanding that the property would be used as a site for a new school house, replacing the old wooden structure which was located on Saginaw Highway. The local district school board decided to ask the taxpayers for $1,500 to build and equip the new school house. The board hoped to erect a one story, red brick building, with a main room of 62 x 40 feet, a cloak room 10 x 20 feet and a vestibule. There would be a cellar running under the entire length of the building, as well as an artistic tower. "The building will probably be erected as designed by G.W. Ashby, Chicago's expert architect" (*LJ* 7/29/1908). It was later decided to increase the funding for construction to $1,800 after a very boisterous meeting where several residents threatened to secede from the district. What is interesting is the following notice that appeared in both Lansing papers.

NOTICE TO CONTRACTORS
"Your attention is being called to the fact that the District Board of School District No. 6, Lansing, will be receiving sealed proposals for the construction of a brick schoolhouse to be built on lots 287 and 288, Foster Farm addition, in accordance with the plans and specifications on file in the offices of Moon & Spice, Architects, Dodge Block, Lansing. Proposals to be received up to 12 pm., Saturday, August 22, 1908. Each proposal to be accompanied with a certified check of twenty-five dollars. The board reserves the right to reject any and all offers. F.E. Church Director Lansing, Aug. 15, 1908" (*LJ* 8/18/1908 and *SR* 8/19/1908). In this instance Moon & Spice may have been acting as the supervising architects of the project to protect the interests of the local school district.

The Columbia District School was described as being a brick veneer building of two stories with two rooms on each floor. On July 10, 1916 the Columbia Park School District merged with the Lansing School District. In 1917 the name of the school was changed to the Foster Avenue School and the building was remodeled. In 1918 the school was completely rebuilt and the students attended the Allen Street School while the construction was taking place.[236]

---

236 From the *History of the Foster Parent Teacher Association History 1918-1942*, [1942].

An Ashby design for a Schoolhouse

George William Ashby (1860-1933) was an architect in Chicago who was known for his work in the Craftsman and Prairie School style. Several of his structures appear on the National Register of Historic Places. He worked with the Radford Architectural Company of Chicago and is listed as the Vice President of the company in 1908. It is unclear if the School District purchased plans from Ashby or the Radford Architectural Company with Moon & Spice acting as supervising architects. The latter is quite possible as the district would have saved quite a bit of money by purchasing stock plans from the Radford Architectural Company and using a local firm to interpret and implement the drawings. It is also possible that Moon & Spice developed their own plans, which I find doubtful.[237]

In 1919 the Columbia Park School was described by J.W. Sexton. "In the place of a small five-room building, poorly heated and ventilated, with no water or toilet facilities, in the Columbia Park or Foster Avenue school, which was the case when this was annexed to the school district of the city of Lansing, we find today a modern ten-room building with an auditorium" (*LSJ* 1/1/1919). It is doubtful given Moon's experience that he would design a school house without toilet facilities. The school was completed in 1910 with a west facing tower entrance. The Columbia Park School was annexed into the Lansing School District 1916 and then was redesigned by local architect Judson N. Churchill. It is doubtful that any of the original building still survives in the current structure, the Foster Community Center.

---

237   No image survives of the Columbia District School. The image used is of an Ashby designed school that closely resembles the description of the school, Department Circular 28.

Dr. Joseph Foster 1868-1912

Just who was Dr. Joseph Foster, the man that donated the land for the construction of Columbia Park School? Born in Detroit on February 22, 1868 to John E and Margaret (née Vigil) Foster, Joseph graduated from the Michigan Agricultural College in 1890 as a Doctor of Science. Four years later he would receive his medical degree from the University of Michigan and work as an assistant to Dr. Fleming E. Carrow, a Professor of Ophthalmic, Aural Surgery and Clinical Ophthalmology at the University of Michigan. Foster then became a lecturer at the university specializing in topics concerned with the study of the eye, ear, nose and throat. In 1896 he went to Europe to further his studies and upon his return settled in Lansing. Foster would later return to Europe and study in Vienna, London and Berlin. Returning to Lansing he established a hospital at 128 W. Allegan Street. On July 7, 1903 he married Miss Norah Baird in Lansing; they would have three daughters, Josephine, Jane and Margaret. Dr. Joseph Foster was described as being "genial, good natured and his kindly acts for the unfortunate, always done in a modest self-deprecating way. Those closely associated with this say that his skill was given freely to the poor from whom he could expect no financial returns. He had been known to keep patients in his hospital for more than a year at a time, and when the suggestion was made that he had boarded and cared for one man long enough, he replied. 'Well, where can he go? I don't like to send him to the poorhouse.'" Dr. Joseph Foster died of pneumonia at Harper Hospital in Detroit on June 2, 1912 at the age of 44.[238]

From the Gould inventory of Darius Moon Buildings, listed as "School House (Columbia Park, E. Lansing), 1908".

---

238   *LSJ* 6/3/1912.

FRANK DODGE DOUBLE HOUSE

111-113 E. North, Lansing, MI

Frank Dodge had extensive land holdings in the Lansing area. The only double house located on property Dodge owned in 1908 was located directly across from the Turner Dodge Home at 111-113 E. North Street. The double house that Moon designed for Frank Dodge was not as ornate as the ones he planned for Madison Bates and Doctor Ranney. The double residence has a large hip roof with a front dormer facing south and one on each side facing east and west respectively. What is interesting is that the rear of the home has a gambrel gable attached that is essentially another home. The original porch extended across the entire front of the home, while there were two recessed back porches at the rear of the structure which are still intact. It may be of interest to examine the lives of the first residents of the respective units of the double house.

One of the residents, La Du Betts was born in Michigan in 1852. He married Miss Mary E Crandall on January 12, 1882 in Allegan, Michigan. They would have one son George L.D., and three daughters, Alice, Pearl R., and Itha. La Du worked for the Lake Shore and Michigan Southern Railway, and later the New York Central Railroad as an engineer. The family moved from one residence to another in Lansing which may have been due to La Du's job or for other unknown reasons. La Du Betts passed away in Chicago on May 11, 1925; his body was returned to Lansing for burial at Mt. Hope Cemetery.[239]

---

[239]   *LSJ* 5/12/1925.

Simon S. Kaltenbach was born in Pennsylvania in 1874; Simon came to Lansing about 1910 to work at the Owosso Sugar Company plant on North Seymour. He left Lansing in 1919 to become the assistant manager of a sugar plant in Macomb County, Michigan. By 1930 he worked as a butcher in Mt Clemens, Michigan. He married Miss Barbara Englert and the couple had six children, Leo, Joseph, Lawrence, Thomas, Charles and Rose Marie. Tragically, Rose Marie would die at the age of 6 of pneumonia on September 24, 1913 in Lansing. Simon would continue to live in the Mt Clemens area passing away on March 2, 1956. His wife Barbara passed away on June 21, 1950 in Mt Clemens, Michigan.

From the Gould inventory of Darius Moon Buildings, listed as "F.L. Dodge - Double Hse 1908".

CHARLES A. PARKHURST

229 E. Maple Street, Mason, MI

In July of 1899 County Clerk Fred D. Woodworth engaged the services of the architects Mead & White to prepare plans for $1500 residence in Mason, Michigan. A month later their plans were accepted and construction began; A.V. Peck of Lansing was hired as the contractor. In November of that year the home was completed and County Clerk Woodworth and family occupied the home in time to celebrate Thanksgiving.[240] "C.A. Parkhurst has purchased the Dr. F.D. Woodworth house on east Maple street" (*ICD* 12/11/1902). Woodworth's term as county clerk ended on November 29, 1902. Less than a year later, on April 7, 1903 the former County Clerk Woodworth was convicted of embezzling $732.34 of public funds while county clerk. He was sentenced to two years in Ionia Prison.

---

240   See the *LJ* 7/17/1899, *SR* 8/5/1899 and *SR* 11/10/1899.

"C. A. Parkhurst has commenced extensive improvements upon his residence on east Maple street. While the work is in progress the family will reside in the Kane house on Ash st" (*ICN* 5/7/1908).

"C.A. Parkhurst has been remodeling his residence on east Maple st and has expended several thousand dollars in making it one of the most spacious and convenient houses in the city. They have just moved into it having lived in a rented house while their own was unsettled" (*SR* 4/1/1909).

It is interesting that Moon was employed to remodel a home that was designed by Mead & White; Earl Mead at this time was practicing in Harbor Springs and too far away to be employed, while Thomas White was still working as an architect in Lansing. The structure is a Queen Anne style home which is a cross gable with a large gable at the rear and a small closed gable at the front. The framing of the windows on the front gable resembles a style used in the arts and craft movement. It is interesting to note how the second floor windows are centered above the porch and on the side have wooded pilasters that simulate columns. The image below shows the east side of the residence, the two story bay window with the large window on the stairway landing allowed for early morning light to enter the living room. The wrap around porch has a pediment over the entryway and a second pediment on the side of the porch; the half circle elements at the base of the porch lends lightness to the porch structure. At the rear of the home there was a second floor porch which has been removed. This is a remarkable house that is currently in desperate need of preservation.

229 Maple Street, Mason, MI

Charles Ashel Parkhurst was born in Jackson, Michigan on June 25, 1871 to Charles G. and Emma D. (née King) Parkhurst. As a small child his parents moved to Mason, Michigan, where his father worked as a druggist. In 1894 Charles took over the dry goods business that was established in Mason by his grandfather

Ashel Parkhurst. Charles or "Cap" as he was known to his friends ran the business successfully for 42 years until he retired in 1942. Besides his business Charles Parkhurst was active in local public affairs. He served two terms on the Mason Board of Education and later was eventually elected president of the board. On November 14, 1900, Charles married Miss Marie Teresa Burns of Mason; the couple had three children, Charles King, Mary Elizabeth and one child who died in infancy. Charles A. Parkhurst died in Mason on March 8, 1952; he was preceded in death by his wife Teresa who passed away in June of 1951.[241]

From the Gould inventory of Darius Moon Buildings, listed as "Hse for Parkhurst (Mason), 1908".

LOUIS DRISCOLL STORE

Driscoll Store before remodel, 107 E. Michigan, Lansing, MI

"One of the Finest Cigar stores in Michigan L.A. Driscoll to Remodel Building One Door East of Washington Ave. L.A. Driscoll, who is now located in the Ingersoll block at Washington and Michigan aves. announces that he has employed D.P.[B] Moon to prepare plans for remodeling his store one door east of the corner of Michigan ave and will fit it up for one of the finest cigar stores in the state. Recently Mr. Ingersoll, owner of the corner property, has endeavored to purchase Mr. Driscoll's store building in order to ultimately erect a fine block on the property at the corner, but the two have been unable to agree on terms. Mr. Driscoll says he has secured ideas as to perfect modern cigar stores in many different cities and proposes to fit up his store to compare with the best of them, with an open front, marble and tile floors and the finest fittings" (*SR* 10/30/1907).

---

241   *Ingham County News* 3/14/1952.

"Louis Driscoll and Raymond Spice of the firm of Moon & Spice, were in Saginaw yesterday looking over the cigar stores in that city to get ideas for Mr. Driscoll's new store on Michigan avenue east" *(LJ 1/11/1908).*

Driscoll Store after the remodel, 107 E. Michigan, Lansing, MI

NEW CIGAR STORE OPENS TOMOROW
Steel Ceiling and Floor in Egyptian Tile All Wall Cases of Mahogany
Sanitary Drinking Fountain in the Middle of Louis A. Driscoll's New Store

"Tomorrow evening the formal opening of Louis A. Driscoll's new cigar store at 107 Michigan avenue east, will be held. The place is one of the finest of its kind in the middle west. The entrance is about six feet from the walk and the glass doors, which extend across the entire front, are so arranged that in the summer they can de thrown back, making the place wide open. The ceiling is finished with steel, and the floor is tiling of an Egyptian pattern. Along the west side there is fifty feet of show cases and wall cases for storing the stock. Each contains a moistener for keeping the tobacco damp and in fresh condition. All the wall cases are of mahogany and the lower part of the show cases is finished in marble. The private office, paper stand, and the telephone booth are on the east side of the store. In the center of the floor is a sanitary drinking fountain. Mr. Driscoll has expended close to $12,000 on the building. The ticker will be moved from its present location under the City National bank, and returns from the baseball games will be received by innings. Architects Moon & Spice designed the building and the work was done by Lohman & McHenry" *(LJ 7/13/1908).*

107 E. Michigan in the late 1940s

The newspaper accounts describe the work Moon performed in the interior of Driscoll's store, but unfortunately there are no images of the interior. Based upon the accounts, the interior must have been quite luxurious. It is unknown if Moon renovated the exterior of the building.

Born in 1873 at the family home located across from the state Capitol, Louis was the son of Michael and Bertha (née Coffee) Driscoll. As a young man Louis attended Olivet College and afterward apprenticed as a printer, a trade he would never practice. Early in his life Louis owned and operated a cigar and candy store, Driscoll's, located a 107 E. Michigan. He would later assume control of the family Coal Business, L.A. Driscoll & Company which he managed until he retired in 1919. Louis was heavily invested in real estate and several business ventures, he helped to establish the Small's Men's Shop in Lansing. On November 26, 1903 Louis married Miss Mary Laughlin who passed away in 1943; the couple had no children. Several years later in 1947, Louis married Mrs. Rhea Smith a widow. Louis retired from business at the age of 46 and began to travel the world. He embarked on several world cruises and visited Europe many times. On November 27, 1951, Louis A. Driscoll died at his home at 624 W. Ottawa at the age of 78.[242]

From the Gould inventory of Darius Moon Buildings, listed as "Lew Driscoll Store-Lansing, 1908".

---

242   LSJ 11/28/1951.

SPARROW HOSPITAL

1215 E. Michigan, Lansing, MI

"Local Firm Will Make Plans for Hospital…Three Lansing Architects are in competition for the honor – Committee is giving plans much consideration. From present indications it seems probable that Lansing's new hospital will be built along the lines proposed by architects from this city and set forth in the three local sets of plans which the committee is now discussing" (*SR* 7/7/1910). Seven days later the Sparrow Hospital Building Committee selected the plans of Edwyn A. Bowd for the hospital.[243] The other two local architects who submit plans were, Moon & Spice and White & Butterworth.[244]

From the Gould inventory of Darius Moon Buildings, listed as "Sparrow Hospital, 1908".

---

243   *SR* 7/15/1910.
244   American Contractor 7/2/1910.

JOHN S WILSON AND S.D KOPF SKATING RINK

120 E. Ottawa, Lansing, MI

Plan Skating Rink on Ottawa Street. Will break ground tomorrow for $10,000 Building.
One of the Finest in State.
Can be used on Special Occasions as a Convention Hall as it will Seat 3,000 Persons

"Ground will be broken tomorrow on the vacant lot at 120 Ottawa street east for a $10,000 building to be used as a skating rink and convention hall, John S. Wilson and S.D. Kopf having secured a long-term lease of Mrs. Elizabeth Whitney, who owns the property. They intend to erect one of the finest skating rinks in the state. According to plans prepared by architects Moon & Spice, the building will have a frontage of 65 feet and will be 160 feet long. It will be one story in height, but above the auditorium will be a gallery extending around two thirds of the entire building giving the building the seating capacity of nearly three thousand persons. About 25 feet of the front will be devoted to office space, check and skate rooms, smoking compartment, and the toilet rooms. The front will be attractively designed, and it is planned to make the entire building as attractive and convenient as possible. The floor of the auditorium will be of two thicknesses of hard maple so constructed as to do away with the usual amount of noise. Both the front and the rear walls will be built of cement and all of the material will be as fire proof as possible. Not only will the new building be used as a skating rink, but on special occasions will be turned into a convention hall or banquet hall. It will, to a certain extent fill the long felt need of a convention hall, and it is expected that it will prove a financial success from the very start. S.D. Kopf, who is in partnership with Mr. Wilson on the proposition has managed the Waverly Park rink this summer and has considerable experience in that line of business. He formerly managed a large skating rink at Grand Rapids and will be in a position to give the patrons the best possible service" (*LJ* 8/26/1908).

"The floor is 136 feet long and 66 feet wide and can accommodate 350 skaters without crowding. A wide balcony extends around the entire inside of the building, which has a seating capacity of 500 persons" (*LJ* 11/2/1909).

Wilson & Kopf Skating Rink after its conversion into a garage

It is unfortunate that this building was lost to the urban redevelopment of North Washington Avenue. Later Moon would design the Wilson & Kopf Skating Rink at Broad Ripple Park, Indiana. The building in Lansing was constructed of cast stone, a medium that Moon used in the Lacey home. The building's façade had a stepped gable with a parapet reminiscent of a castle. By 1916 the structure would be converted into the automobile dealership Wolverine Auto Company which sold Studebakers and Maxwell automobiles.

Sigel David Kopf was born in Lowell, Michigan on December 28, 1862 the fifth of ten children born to John and Mary Jane (née Langs) Kopf. Sigel would marry Miss Lillian M. Harrington on November 24, 1887 who sadly died at the age of 33 on December 3, 1902. The young couple would have one child, a daughter Eveline Mary Kopf, who married Major General Gladeon Marcus Barnes.[245] S.D. Kopf had a wide-ranging

---

245   Major General Gladeon Marcus Barnes was head of Research and Development Service of the Office of the Chief of Ordnance during World War II, which was instrumental in the design of the Sherman Tank, the ENIAC computer and many other wartime advancements. After the war he supervised the development of the former German V 2 rocket program in the United States,

life. He was a partner in the Thornapple River Electric Company with Wesley Hyde and Charles Mercer; the company provided electrical power to the city of Hasting, Michigan. The business was later sold to Consumers Power. Kopf was also involved with John Wilson of Lansing in developing a series of indoor skating rinks in Lansing and Broad Ripple Park, Indiana. In the 1920s Kopf would move to George County, Mississippi and become a pecan farmer. Sigel D. Kopf would die in a New Orleans hospital on Wednesday, September 18, 1940, survived by his daughter Mrs. G. W. Barnes, a grand daughter Barbara, two sisters, Mrs. Myrtie Banks of Lowell, Michigan, Mrs. Alice Hurley of Grand Rapids Michigan, and a brother C.H. Kopf of Middleville, Michigan.[246]

TUSSING BUILDING

106 W. Ottawa, Lansing, MI

The tale of the construction of the Tussing Building began in 1906, when Daniel Tussing obtained a 99 year lease to the property from the owner Dr. Clara M. Davis. The property at the time was the site of the old Central M.E. Church, which then housed a harness store and a barber shop. It wasn't until 1909 that construction of the building began. Unfortunately the erection of the building was dogged by delays, some of which were financial and Tussing's own demand for a large building from what was originally planned. Tussing who acted as the contractor for the excavation of the site which was plagued by setbacks due to cave-ins; the crew later encountered a large vein of quicksand. Three months into the construction of the

---

New York Times 11/16/1961.
246   *Georgia County Times* 10/11/1940. I would like to thank Christine McCullough for her help with Sigel David Kopf background, or as she refers to him, 'Uncle Sigel'.

building, Tussing asked Moon to expand the building from the originally planned three-stories to five-stories to accommodate the demand for office space in the building. Moon accomplished this redesign in three weeks and the plans were described as being "… a very fine exhibition of architects' work" (*LJ* 7/31/1909).

An interview that Moon gave to the *Lansing Journal* in regards to the Tussing building is reproduced below, it is one of the few times that we have Moon speaking about a project.

"In an interview today, D.B. Moon of the firm Moon & Spice, architects for the proposed building at the corner of Ottawa street and Washington avenue, gave out the following information: A contract has been awarded to Early & Fitzpatrick for erecting the building, to the revised plans prepared by Moon & Spice, architects. Last spring a permit was granted by the common council for erecting a three-story building. The plans now are for a six floor, five-story structure. The basement floor of the proposed building is planned to be equally well adapted for business as the first floor. This will be an important department of the Dancer, Brogan Co., with lofty ceilings and a floor capacity equal to six ordinary floors, each eighty-two feet in depth. The basement story, first story, and half of the second story will be built of structural steel and iron. A perspective of the building in water color has been prepared by Mr. Spice of the firm of Moon & Spice, which may now be seen at the Dancer, Brogan Co.'s store window. The building will be thoroughly modern in every particular and the construction will make it a practically fire-proof building. The carpenter work and mason work were let to Early & Fitzpatrick. The basement, excavation and masonry, structural iron, prism lighting system for the basement, the elevator, heating plant, wiring, compressed air plant, and mercantile equipment are not let with this contract. The estimated cost of the entire plant when completed is $75,000, of which Early & Fitzpatrick's part is $37,500. The walls will be the same pressed brick used for the new high school, except at the corners no masonry will be shown below. Iron columns only will reach the sidewalk on the Ottawa and Washington avenue sides. All glass on these two sides will be plate glass."

Tussing Building under construction (A.G.)

Mr. Moon said: "People who know the facts are very well pleased with Mr. Tussing's plans, including the much talked of delays. Had it not been for these delays, this corner might have been built as weak and cheap as some other good corners have been, to the permanent injury of the city. Yet such work goes without criticism. One of the strongest proofs of the benefit of this improvement is in the long term lease for the Jennison stores at a very high rent, for a thoroughly modern double store, which Mr. Jennison has contracted to prepare for S.H. Knox Co. Not only was this made possible by Mr. Tussing's proposed building, but Mr. Tussing himself promoted the new Knox store without knowledge of Mr. Jennison himself, until after Mr. Tussing had written and submitted specifications for the store and had a written agreement with the Knox company to lease it and pay his services, if it could be procured. I was acquainted with the whole deal and saw Mr. Tussing get his commission. Mr. Tussing also had some Detroit parties in prospect for a second modern double store, including the Glickman store, now occupied by Mr. Brogan and the Kedzie store, occupied by Mr. Killian. Both Mr. Tussing and Dr. Wellings, interviewed me to consider the costs of improvements. I was informed by Dr. Wellings who represented the Glickman property that this deal would also have succeeded had not the facts about these other important deals been known. But an offer of higher rental for the Glickman store than for any store in the city of Lansing by another responsible Detroit party, intercepted the third large deal. Dr. Wellings informs me that his offer never would have been made if Mr. Tussing had built a cheap building instead of the fine block, which is to be occupied by the new enlarged business of our popular Dancer, Brogan Co.'s store. This is the kind of injury this corner proposition, with all its delays, is doing to every piece of business property above Ottawa street as well. Property in that vicinity, you will observe, is not vacant now. It promises to greatly improve over present conditions, too. The promotion of these two corner enterprises will establish a new business center for the city. Those who criticize are usually people who never did much for Lansing. Their silence would be better appreciated by citizens than their criticism, and would be in better taste." D.W. Tussing was also interviewed today. He said: "The delay in building has not been for the purpose of completing financial plans, as reported. The building was financed weeks ago, and awaiting other developments. Changes in the plans and negotiating a contract required some time. Then the purchase of more ground for the Commercial Insurance Co. and other matters connected with making a clear abstract of title for the land in the old alley way and for other property involved in the deal, each came in for consideration, which has taken time. The work will be rushed right along from this time" (*LJ* 9/29/1909).

A Modern Building
"The building is in many respects the most modern building in the city. It is six stories high, including the basement, and is constructed of pressed brick and steel. The basement extends out under the sidewalk, thereby adding about one-third more room. In the basement Dancer-Brogan company will have a carpet and drapery department as well as a rest room, and a large stock room in which the goods will be unpacked and stored. The building is finished in gray elm with the exceptions of the lobby which is in oak and a portion of the second floor which will be occupied by the dry goods company. This part of the store is finished in mahogany.

Office Accommodations
On the second, third, fourth and fifth floor are suites of offices which are modern in every respect. A portion of the offices are ready to be occupied and the others may be finished within a week Many of the offices open together in order that certain firms which are closely connected may be near each other. There is a balcony between the first and second floors in which the offices of the dry goods firm are to be located. Workmen are today completing the arrangement of the office and installing the cash delivery system.

The building was constructed under the supervision of Architects Moon & Spice by whom the plans were drawn" (*SR* 1/17/1910). The building opened in July 1910 and the first tenant to move in to the new Tussing building was Dr. P.A. Tyler who occupied his offices on July 20, 1910.

That however was not the end of the saga of the construction of the Tussing building. Because of the delays in the excavation of the foundations of the building, which was overseen by Tussing himself, a clause in the contract with Early & Fitzpatrick was invoked by Tussing.[247] The contact essentially stated that if the masonry work performed by Early & Fitzpatrick was delayed over the contracted time then the owner could demand the forfeiture of the agreement. The masonry work was completed three months after the agreed upon time, due to the delays in the excavation of the basement, work that was Tussing's responsibility. Tussing demanded the forfeiture of the contract and withheld the final payment to Early & Fitzpatrick. The dispute went to arbitration, which ruled in favor of Tussing. The case was appealed to the Michigan Supreme Court who reversed the decision of the arbitrators, finding that the owner of the building himself caused the delay in the contract and that no forfeiture could be collected. The court ruled, in 1914, that Tussing had to repay Early & Fitzpatrick $2000 plus four years interest.[248] The Tussing building was expanded in 1913-1914 to three times the size of the original building and at one time was home to the Plaza Theater. The design of the expanded building was supervised by another Lansing architect Samuel D. Butterworth. The building was a victim of the Model Cities Project and torn down in 1971.

From the Gould inventory of Darius Moon Buildings, listed as "Tussing Block, 1908".

FRED KEITH HOUSE

532 Townsend, Lansing, MI

---

247   Early & Fitzpatrick were well known Lansing building contractors. Thomas Early was born in County Roscommon, Ireland in 1856 and came to Lansing at the age of 24. He partnered with Martin Edward Fitzpatrick, a native of Oakland County, Michigan. Together they work on numerous structures in the Lansing area. Thomas Early died on April 17, 1918, many years later his partner Martin E. Fitzpatrick passed away on October 5, 1934 at the age of 80.
248   *Michigan Reports* 182: 314.

It has commonly been accepted that Moon designed the home at 532 Townsend for Fred Keith, but unfortunately the home currently at this address was built after 1920 and the home on the site prior to 1920 as built circa 1894. Fred Keith owned the East 7 Rods of Lot 6 Block 147 which also included the home at 310 W. Hillsdale. The rear of Keith's home at 532 Townsend was modified in about 1908 to accommodate the building of a residence at 310 W. Hillsdale. The house at 310 W. Hillsdale was built as a rental home which Keith originally leased to Andrew Jarvis Patten, a chemist at the MAC. The properties were separated at Fred Keith's death in 1926. The home strongly resembles the Wilcox home as well as the Murray residence. It seems to be a design that Moon favored and there are many other examples of this style home in the Lansing area.

310 W. Hillsdale, Lansing MI

Fred C. Keith was a druggist in Lansing for more than fifty years. He was born in Prescott, Massachusetts in September of 1855 to Oliver and Hattie (née Sears) Keith. The family moved to Lansing in 1866 where Oliver worked for the State Reform School. After graduation from Lansing's public schools Fred was employed at Homer Luce's Drug Store. On September 14, 1887 Fred married Miss Addella J. Fling of New York; they had one child Grove M. Keith. In 1890 Fred Keith resigned his position at Homer Luce's Drug Store to take a position as a traveling salesman with the wholesale drug company, Williams, Shelley & Brooks of Detroit. The *Lansing Journal* on February 2, 1890 describes Fred Keith's new career. "As to his success as a commercial man – well, there is no doubt on that point. The same genial qualities which have made Mr. Keith so deservedly popular during his nine years' drug store experience will assure him equal favor and warm friends on the road." Later, Fred would return to work as a retail druggist in Lansing where he remained until his retirement. On Saturday January 2, 1926, Fred C. Keith died at his home; he was survived by his son Grove M. Keith, a sister L.V. Moore and a nephew Earl V. Moore.[249] Earl V. Moore was the son of Frank W. Moore, who Moon designed a home for in 1887.

From the Gould inventory of Darius Moon Buildings, listed as "Fred Keith, 1908".

---

[249] *LSJ* 1/2/1926. Fred Keith is listed at times as Fred C. Keith and at others as Fred J. Keith. Just why the middle name changed is unknown.

NATHAN JUDSON HOME

602 N. Washington, Lansing, MI

In April of 1907 Nathan Judson's home was damaged by lightning which struck the tower of his home, broke the widows and damaged the electrical system (*LJ* 4/30/1907). After the lightning strike, the home at 602 N. Washington went through a major renovation. Nathan Judson had extensive property holdings in Lansing in 1908, but all of these properties had homes on the lots built prior to 1908, leaving only Judson's damaged home as the only option for which Moon designed a set of plans. Examination of the Sanborn maps for the years 1906 through 1913 shows that the structure at 602 N. Washington changed during the period. A Lansing City Assessor record placed the construction of 602 N. Washington in 1879, but the home in the above image is a style of home from a much later time period, unless of course the residence was completely rebuilt. In 1901 Nathan Judson was to have built a new home on the northwest corner of Capitol Avenue and Lapeer Street, the current location of the Bohnet and Newbrough homes. Nathan owned all three lots, and intended to build a home which would have cost over $15,000, required over 100 cords of stone and used over 78,000 bricks. The home was never built and it is possible that Moon designed this home for Nathan Judson.[250]

The home for Nathan Judson is an interesting design. Notice that on the front façade the windows are laid out in a symmetrical pattern. Ignore the window air conditioners; there were two windows over two and a single window on the second floor over the entrance. The porch wrapped around the home and ended at the entrance that was on the side of the home and may have been at the base of the tower which was destroyed by lightning. There was also a bay window just beyond the base of the tower. Notice the nondescript brick columns on the front porch. The rear of the home has two separate porches, one on the south west corner and one on the north-west corner.

---

250 *LJ* 3/2/1901. No other Lansing architect is recorded as designing and working for the Judson family.

James B. Judson's sons Lowell, Wilbur and Paul

Nathan Judson was born January 30, 1855 in Richland, Michigan and spent his early years near Paw Paw. After coming to Lansing in 1878, he partnered with his brother James B. Judson and developed a successful real estate business, Judson, Wiley & Judson, later known as the Judson Brothers Real Estate. On June 30, 1887, Nathan married Miss Ellen B. Burton, the sister of Clarence Monroe Burton, the well known historian. After the death of his brother James in 1902, Nathan oversaw the schooling of his three nephews Wilber, Lowell, and Paul Judson. Nathan was a member of the Lansing Commandery, No. 25, Knights Templar and active in civil affairs. Nathan Judson died at his home, 602 N. Washington on June 22, 1933 where he lived for 33 years.[251] The home was torn down in 1972. From the Gould inventory of Darius Moon Buildings, listed as "Judson Hse-Lansing, 1908".

HOTEL RANSIER

125-131 E. Washtenaw, Lansing, MI

---

251   *LSJ* 6/26/1933, for Ellen Burton Judson see *LSJ* 5/14/1919.

In June of 1909 a building project was announced for the northwest corner of Washtenaw Street and Grand Avenue, it was to be the new home for the Findley & Lewis American Laundry while the second floor was to contain three apartments. Julia Findley purchased the property on the corner of Washtenaw Street and Grand Avenue in 1908 from W.E. Crotty for $6,500 shortly after the building that she rented for her business at 309 S. Washington was sold to Oliver H. Halstead by Dr. Joseph Foster. The new structure was to be 63 x 65 feet and cost $12,000, Early & Fitzpatrick were hired as the contractors. Later in September of 1909 Miss Findley decided to add a third story and to lease 2/3 of the first floor and all of the second and third floors to Edward E. Ransier, owner of the Elite Café. By November the building had been dubbed the Hotel Ransier, a three story red brick building that was to be a modern European plan hotel with 42 rooms. The first floor was to operate as a restaurant with the basement housing the culinary department. Concerned about the use of wood in the construction of the supports for the balconies in the rear of the building, the architects Moon & Spice, stopped construction. Although the plans and changes made by the contractor had been approved and a building permit issued by the city council building committee and reviewed by Fire Chief Delfs, the architects thought this inclusion of wooden balconies too great of a risk. Because of the actions of architects Moon & Spice, Alderman Parker moved that an amendment be offered to change the city ordinance.[252] It is remarkable that the two architects would stop construction of a project, which no doubt cost them money, to point out flaws in the Lansing city building ordinances. Would this happen today? It speaks well of the integrity of the firm. By 1916 Edward E. Ransier left and the hotel was renamed the Hotel Fleming, managed by James Fleming.

Hotel Ransier window detail

The entrance to the Hotel Ransier was through the double doors just to the right of the automobile parked on Washtenaw. The door led to the lobby and the restaurant while on the left through the entrance was a snack bar and the hotel office. As with many commercial buildings in this era, the basement was used for business purposes. Just visible in the first image is the entrance to the lower level, it is surrounded by the railings and there were two other entrances to the basement along Washtenaw Street. The building is a typical commercial structure for this time period. On the façade are brick pilasters that separated the blocks;

---

252 See *SR* 6/21/1909, *LJ* 6/21/1909, *LJ* 9/18/1909, *LJ* 11/30/1909 and *LJ* 12/21/1909. The *State Republican* newspaper is lost from July 1, 1909 to December 31, 1909.

notice how one separated the hotel block from the last business block. Observe how Moon had the second and third sections of the façade set back slightly. The second and third floor windows are symmetrical while pairs of windows have a brick surround which can be seen in the above image. The cornice is very simple with dentils running the length of the soffit. The structure has a modern appearance much like the Tussing Building demonstrating Moon's ability to keep his work relevant by realizing that architectural styles were transforming in the early Twentieth Century. The building was torn down in 1939 and replaced with a new building for the Central Trust Company.

Miss Julia Findley must have been an interesting woman. The daughter of Charles V. and Susan Findley she was born in Illinois in 1873. Her widowed father moved to Lansing in the 1880s to work as a carpenter. Julia would form a business partnership with Edwin M. Lewis and form the Findley & Lewis Company, proprietors of American Laundry at 111-113 E. Washtenaw Street, Lansing, Michigan. By 1925 Edwin Lewis would buy out Julia's interests in the company and become the sole owner of American Laundry. On August 11, 1925 Julia age 51 married Fred R. Kalck in Detroit. She would become mother to Fred's three children. The couple moved to Philadelphia, Pennsylvania where Fred would work in the shoe business. Julia died on April 17, 1963 in Philadelphia.[253] From the Gould inventory of Darius Moon Buildings, listed as "Hatch Flemming, 1908".

ARMORY

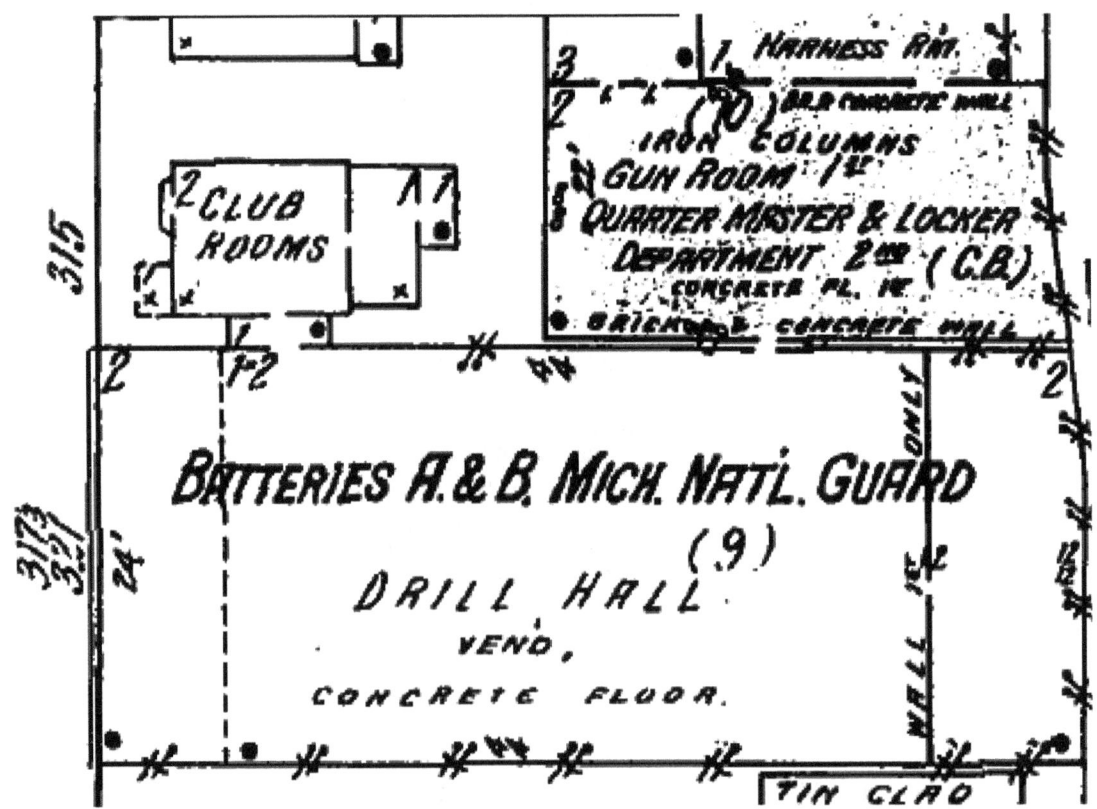

319 S. Capitol, Lansing, MI

---

[253] *Philadelphia Evening Bulletin* 4/19/1963.

>   Fine Artillery House of Battery A is to be enlarged and Improved
>
> "The contract will be let next week for expensive alterations and improvements to the armory of Battery A. A new lease has been entered into by the state and the owner, James P. Edmonds, for five years and a fine gun room two stories high is to be erected in the rear of the drill hall with a wash room for pieces and harness, a locker room, quartermasters office and shower baths will be placed in that building
> At the front end of the armory the rooms are to be remodeled, repaired and the drill hall placed in fine condition for the battery. The front is to be painted and a cement driveway laid from the entrance way to the pavement" (*SR* 5/22/1909).
>
> "W.T. Britton has been awarded the contract for building the gun room and making improvements to the Battery A. Armory" (*LJ* 6/8/1909).
>
>   For a New Gun Room-W.T. Britton Awarded the contract for Artillery Armory.
>
> "The contract for erecting a new gun room and making several changes and improvements at the artillery armory has been let to W.T. Britton. Work was started today in tearing down the old shed in the rear of the armory and it is expected the new building will be completed about August 1" (*SR* 6/8/1909).

Beginning in 1907 the state of Michigan began the process of constructing purpose built armories for the Michigan National Guard. For example in 1908 the Ionia Armory design contract was awarded to Edwyn A. Bowd and in 1909 William T. Cooper was awarded the contract to design the Saginaw Armory. In Lansing it was decided to retrofit an existing building rather then build a new armory, why this decision was made is unknown; it may be that the legislators did not want to be seen as favoring Lansing. Therefore Moon's work was a little less glamorous. His task was to convert the Auditorium Roller Rink on South Capitol Avenue in to a functional building for the Battery A of the Michigan Light Artillery Company; Battery B formed in 1911 and occupied the same building. Both units would be part of the 119th Field Artillery and incorporated into 32nd "Red Arrow" Division in 1917. The unit would serve with distinction in the Great War. Besides the modifications to the hall, as outlined in the above newspaper articles, Moon also converted the home at 315 S. Capitol Avenue into club rooms for the battery's officers and designed a 'gun room' for the storage of the artillery pieces, connected to the main building at its rear. A stir was created in late 1909, when the state legislature passed a bill exempting buildings occupied by State Militia or U.S. Troops from property taxes. This deprived the city of the tax revenues from the properties on Ottawa street, the old Governors Guard Armory occupied by Company E and the Battery A&B property on S. Capitol owned by J.P. Edmonds and valued at $4,200.

From the Gould inventory of Darius Moon Buildings, listed as "Armory-Lansing, 1908".

FREDERICK SCHNEIDER HOUSE

726 Seymour, Lansing, MI

"Architect Moon is making plans for the remodeling of the residences of J.H. Wellings and Col. Fred Schneider, and the old Turner home on North street" (*LJ* 3/21/1902).

The above article places the work that Moon did for Colonel Schneider six years earlier then the Gould list stated. After a review of the property tax records for the city of Lansing in 1908, it can be asserted that Schneider owned no other property in the city, aside from Lot 9, Block 55, 726 Seymour. Joan Sheldon, the current owner of the home in 2014 states that Moon designed the back porch of the home.

Frederick Schneider, Civil War hero, died at his home on November 5, 1917. He was born November 24, 1840 in Saline, Michigan. Frederick enlisted in the Second Michigan Infantry, Company A. on April 20, 1861 as a private and mustered out as a Colonel. He was wounded in the arm at Petersburg, Virginia, June 18, 1864 and later at Hatchers Run, Virginia, October 27, 1864 he was wounded in the thigh. Frederick was captured by rebel forces after the action at Hatchers Run, but managed to escape. Unfortunately he was recaptured within sight of the Union lines at Remes Station, Virginia. Frederick was sent to Libby Prison, Salisbury Stockade and Danville; he was part of a Union prisoner exchange with the Confederacy and rejoined his regiment. After Appomattox he was sent to Washington and assigned to duty with his regiment as Provost Guard at the Capitol. Frederick remained in Washington until he mustered out of service with his regiment July 28, 1865, after four and a half years of service.

Frederick Schneider 1840-1917

In August of 1865 Frederick Schneider married Miss Elizabeth Strengson of Detroit, the daughter of Christian Strengson. The couple would have five children, three which would die in infancy, only Frederick and Helen would survive to adulthood. Colonel Schneider would work for twenty five years in the state abstract department and was an active member of the Charles Foster Post of the G.A.R.[254]

From the Gould inventory of Darius Moon Buildings, listed as "Camamel Schneider Hse, 1908".

FITCH R SAVAGE HOME

312 W. Hillsdale, Lansing, MI

---

254   *LSJ* 11/5/1917.

The Gould inventory had Moon designing a home for a person named Savage in 1908. The only home that matches all the requirements is the Fitch Savage residence at 312 W. Hillsdale.[255] The 1906 Sanborn map shows a completely different structure on the lot than the 1913 Sanborn map, which means Fitch's home was built between 1907 and 1912. The residence was a hip roof home with matching dormers on the front and back of the home. The dormers are an interesting design, the large soffit and the flaring at the base of the dormers is visually appealing. The dormers also have small pilasters that frame the window. The oversized soffit is repeated on the remainder of the home; notice how the bracketing at the front of the home mimics the positions of the windows. There are two oriel windows on the east and west ends of the home, which are in the Arts & Craft style. The wall is flared at the junction of the first and second floor an element Moon employed on the Lyons residence. The recessed entry porch is the only known example of Moon employing this feature on the façade of a home. Observe how the pent roof blends with the flaring of the wall when the home is viewed from the street. What is odd is the front first floor window on the left in the above photograph. Two windows or a larger single window would have provided for a stronger façade. This is one of the most intriguing homes the Moon ever designed.

312 W. Hillsdale, Lansing, MI

Fitch R. Savage was born in Dupont, Indiana on October 25, 1856 the son of Portus and Clarissa (née Raymond) Savage. Fitch was left as an orphan at the age of 14 and went to Portland, Michigan to live with his sister, Mrs. Mary E. Gibbs. After he graduated from Portland High School, Fitch opened a general dry goods store with William R. Churchill forming the Churchill & Savage Company; later the firm moved into men's furnishings and clothing. Upon moving to Lansing in 1891 he formed a business partnership

---

255   The property the West 3 rods of Lot 6 Block 147 was actually in Fitch's wife name, Anne C. Savage's.

with John D. Woodbury, the father of Chester D. Woodbury, and established the firm known as Savage & Woodbury Tailoring Company. Several years later Savage would buy James D. Woodbury's share of the business. On December 21, 1880 Savage married Miss Anna Cutcheon in Ionia, Michigan; they had one daughter, Donna. Fitch R. Savage would pass away at his home on February 27, 1925, survived by his wife, Anna and daughter Mrs. Donna Call of Richmond, Virginia.[256]

From the Gould inventory of Darius Moon Buildings, listed as "Savage Hse, 1908".

JOSEPH W. WOLFORD HOME

431 Cherry, Lansing, MI

The Gould list has Moon designing a home for a Joe Walfare in 1908 but there were no Walfares in Mid-Michigan. This should be Joseph Wolford a well known real estate man in Lansing. In 1908 besides his home at 431 Cherry Street, Wolford owned many other properties in Lansing, however none fit the criteria of a new home. It seems Moon modified the home at 431 Cherry into a two family dwelling, however between 1906 and 1913 the configuration of the residence changes and is split in to a large double house becoming 427 and 431 Cherry. The porch on 431 Cherry is reconfigured to be smaller while the porch at 427 Cherry is enlarged and an addition was added to the rear of the residence. Exactly what work Moon did for Wolford may remain a mystery.

---

256   *LSJ* 2/28/1925 and *Lansing Capital News* 2/28/1925.

The sunburst detail on the Wolford residence

The Wolford home was a Queen Anne style residence with varied roof lines and multiple gables. The wrap around porch had a striking pediment over the entrance which is shown in the above image; notice the step back feature on the dentils and the rusticated stones at the base of the columns on the porch. Just above the porch is a false gable which merges with the roofline of the large gable when viewed from the street. On the gable end there was fish scale siding and on the western gable visible in the first photograph there is a pentoid window with a triangular pediment.

427 Cherry, Lansing, MI

It is unfortunate that no complete image of 427 Cherry exist. The above photograph is pulled from a larger image. Little can be said about the home other than it had a clipped gable roof over the porch, it was a single story residence and had a one story rounded bay window at the north west corner. The home had seen better days when this image was taken. Notice how a section of porch from 431 Cherry was reused on 427 Cherry.

431 Cherry, Lansing, MI

Joseph W. Wolford was a resident of Lansing for 30 years before his death on June 15, 1913. Wolford was born in the state of New York in 1864 and served as a notary public in Clinton County in 1885. He was a prominent real estate agent in the Lansing area and had extensive property holdings. In 1907 Wolford was appointed executor of his friend's estate, Michigan millionaire William Cottrell; Wolford would be involved in a court case over the distribution of the estate for many years. At his death Joseph was survived by his widow Blanche, daughter Helen, two sisters, Mrs. Jennie Bates of Eagle, Michigan and Mrs. Marie Flagg of Aurora, Illinois, and one brother Daniel of New York. [257] Regrettably the site of the residence is now a parking lot. From the Gould inventory of Darius Moon Buildings, listed as "Joe Walfare Hse, 1908".

---

257   *LSJ* 6/16/1913 and *Lansing Evening Press* 6/16/1913.

EDDY ENGINEERING COMPANY

114 Chisholm, Alpena, MI

How did the Eddy brothers learn about the work of Darius Moon? There is no clear answer, however there is unwarranted speculation. It could have been a referral from either George T. Gordon or Thomas J. Shields; both were well respected Lansing plumbers who were involved in the state wide plumbing association and may have known the Eddy brothers. In 1908 Shields was secretary of the State Board of Plumbing Examiners. The Eddy Engineering Company was a plumbing and heating business and owned by two brothers Nelson M. Eddy and Henry G. Eddy. Both brothers were born in Cleveland, Ohio, Nelson in 1865 and Henry in 1868. In 1886 Nelson moved to Alpena and started a plumbing business and his brother Henry followed two years later. In 1890 Nelson married Miss Cora B. Coville; the couple had one child Winfred. Henry married Miss Maud E. Rose in 1892 and they had four children, Clara, Beatrix, Roy and Lomas Eddy. Henry died on August 1, 1941 on a visit to his class reunion. He was survived by his wife and four children. His brother Nelson died six years later on September 21, 1947.[258] Ignore the modern overlay on the first floor and examine the cornice with the oversized dentils, an architectural detail which Moon employed for the first time. The white stone banding over the windows not only acts as a frame to the windows but tells the passerby that the entire building belonged to the person whose name appeared on the panel, EDDY.

From the Gould inventory of Darius Moon Buildings, listed as "Business Block at Alpena, Mich For Eddy Engineering Co, 1908".

---

258 For Henry see the *Alpena News* 8/2/1941 for Nelson see the *Alpena News* 9/22/1947.

MADISON BATES HOUSE

427 W. Hillsdale, Lansing, MI

The Madison F. Bates residence on West Hillsdale is the only home that remains in Lansing from the city's automotive pioneers. The irregular hip roof ends with a flat top resulting in a home that has multiple dormers and gables. At the rear of the home on the third floor is a large dormer matching the one on the west side of the building. On the front of the home is a small open dormer and a large closed gable. Notice the unequal spacing of the brackets under the soffit. On the east side is an oriel window and a side entrance which was later enclosed. At the rear of the home is a single story garage that runs the length of the home. The wrap around porch with Ionic columns, delicate balustrade and pediment with motif over the front entry way is the most conspicuous feature of the residence.

Madison F. Bates 1869-1926

Madison F. Bates was a well know Lansing businessman and inventor. Madison was born in Clarendon, Michigan on November 7, 1869, the son of Benjamin D. and Betsy A. Bates. His early education was in the rural schoolhouses of Calhoun County and he was self-taught in many subjects. His father was a blacksmith and there Madison received his early training in metal work. In 1887 he invented an improved land roller for which he was granted a patent. Working with his father they built and sold hundreds of the improved land rollers throughout the state.

427 W. Hillsdale, Lansing, MI

After moving to Lansing in 1893, Madison F. Bates entered the employ of the Olds Engine Works where he became a master draftsman. Leaving the company six years later, he formed the Bates & Edmonds Motor Company, where they produced the well known 'Bulldog' engine line. Realizing that he could not compete with the large engine manufacturer Bates & Edmonds sold the company in November of 1910.

"Buy a Bates And Keep Your Dates" a great advertisement

The Bates Automobile Company (1903-1905) was formed on May 27, 1903. The investors in the new corporation were M.F. Bates, Bliss Stebbins and J.P. Edmonds. The initial capitalization was $60,000. The company, as stated by Mr. Edmonds, was entirely separate from the Bates & Edmonds Company. The Bates Automobile Company had an interesting history. The company produced a two seat runabout and later a four seat automobile. The plant was located in the 300 block of South Capitol Ave, in the old Armory building. The Bates Automobile Company only produced about 25 vehicles and ceased production in 1905. Other investors in the company were J. Edward Roe, R.W. Morse and H.A. Hayes. After he sold the motor company Bates then formed the Bates Tractor Company which manufactured tractors until 1918; during World War One the company manufactured machine guns for the United States Army. The Bates Tractor Company merged with the Joliet Oil Tractor Company to form the Bates Machine & Tractor Company of Joliet, Illinois. In 1896 Bates married Miss Celesta Thomas of Lansing and the couple had four children, Ralph, Louise, Harold and Viva. Madison F. Bates, one of Lansing's forgotten Automakers, died at his home on August 17, 1926.[259]

From the Gould inventory of Darius Moon Buildings, listed as "M.F Bates Res. –Lansing, 1908".

---

259   *Lansing Capital News* 8/18/1926 and the *LSJ* 8/18/1926.

DARIUS MOON PROPERTIES

1114 W. Allegan, Lansing, MI

In 1904 Moon purchased four lots on Allegan Street from Seymour Foster for $300. The home at 1114 W. Allegan was built in 1908. The residence was held by the Moon family until 1940 when Moon's daughter Princess Adams sold the lot for $3000. Darius had acquired quite a few properties over his life time. Homes built on these properties will be listed in the year that they were constructed as long as Moon still owned the property.

1114 W. Allegan, Lansing, MI

In the background of both images, just to the right, you can see Darius Moon's carriage house. The properties abutted one another. The house had clean lines which was typical of Moon's later work. There is an oriel window on the east side of the home and the side flares between the first and second floor. Notice on the side of the home how Moon used wood banding to separate the floors. The double columns along the face of the porch are tapered square style which complements the flared siding on the base of the porch. Unfortunately the home was torn down in 2011.

1110 W. Allegan, Lansing, MI

When Moon purchased this property from Seymour Foster in 1904 the land was vacant and by 1908 this home occupied the site. It is interesting to note that the home resembles several others that Moon designed for a variety of clients, for example Wilcox and Lacey. Unlike the other homes in this style that Moon planned, the structure at 1110 W. Allegan lacked some of the finer elements. There was no bay window and the porch is not as detailed as others he designed, although the panels on the piers are a nice element.

1909

WALNUT STREET SCHOOL

1020 N. Walnut, Lansing, MI

There is no record of the Walnut Street School being remodeled in 1909 as the Gould list stated. Lansing architect Edwyn Bowd designed the Walnut Street School in 1905 and it would be unlikely that the school would be remodeled after just four years. It is far more likely that Moon submitted plans for the new building in 1905 and his design was not accepted (*LJ* 4/20/1905). From the Gould inventory of Darius Moon Buildings, listed as "Walnut St. School Hse., 1909".

WILLARD WILCOX STORE

115 N. Butler, Lansing, MI

The Gould inventory of Darius Moon Buildings lists Darius Moon as drawing plans for a William Wilcox for a store and a home in 1909. Instead of William, Moon completed plans for a house and store for Willard M. Wilcox.

115 N. Butler, Lansing, MI

A purposefully designed building, the store was on the first floor and an apartment on the second with a side entrance as opposed to a center entrance which was typical in business blocks. Notice the side porch on the second floor, an interesting feature of this building when you consider this was rental space and adding this element would have been expensive. The structure was essentially a home built to accommodate a business, a style which fell out of favor in the 1950s. From the Gould inventory of Darius Moon Buildings, listed as "William Wilcox Store & Hse., 1909".

WILLARD WILCOX HOME

909 W. Ottawa, Lansing, MI

A resident of Lansing for over 67 years Willard Merritt Wilcox died at his home on December 5, 1949 at the age of 92. For 47 years Willard ran a grocery business on North Butler Boulevard in Lansing. He was born in Niagara County, New York in March of 1857, the youngest of six children, five boys and one girl. In 1877 he married Miss Addie Miers; the couple had two sons, Edward and Willard M. Jr., and two daughters Maude M., and Florence.

Willard and Addie Wilcox

Willard and his wife Addie retired from the grocery business in 1920; by 1926 Willard was back at work, this time with Oldsmobile where he worked until 1930. Willard's son, Willard M. Wilcox Jr., also worked at Oldsmobile, starting as clerk in 1915 and becoming Director of Material Control Department; he died suddenly on April 24, 1956. Addie who helped to run the grocery business and meat market at 115 N. Butler died at the age of 80 on Friday July 10, 1942. She was born in Oswego, New York in 1862 and came to Lansing with her husband in 1885.[260]

909 W. Ottawa, Lansing, MI

Something to consider about the Wilcox home is that it resembled a home Moon built as a rental at 1110 W. Allegan in 1908. One of the interesting aspects of the Wilcox residence is the stacking of the windows. On the left side first floor, there is a large single window that because of the placement of the mullions gives the impression of being a double window. Stacked above it on the second floor is a double window, which occurs again on the third floor. Combine that with the single entrance and the lone stained glass window above on the second floor provides an interesting symmetry when viewed from the street. There was a bay window on the east side of the home along with a single story porch along the rear of the home. The front porch is simple in design, tapered Tuscan columns and a delicate balustrade. From the Gould inventory of Darius Moon Buildings, listed as "William Wilcox Store & Hse., 1909".

---

260   For Willard senior's death see the *LSJ* 12/7/1949, Addie see *LSJ* 7/10/1942 and Willard junior, see *LSJ* 4/24/1956. An image of the new home being built for Willard Wilcox appeared in the *LJ* 10/9/1909. I would like to thank Amanda Sheets for the use of the photograph of Willard and Addie Wilcox.

RICHARD S. COLBY HOUSE

Onondaga Hotel managed by Colby

The Gould inventory has Moon designing a house for R.J. Colby in 1909. Extensive research revealed there was no one by that name in Ingham County at that time. There was however, a Richard S. Colby in Onondaga, Michigan who was an early pioneer in Ingham County and had extensive landholdings in Onondaga, Township. For over fifty years Richard owned the Onondaga Hotel. He also served as Justice of the Peace for Onondaga for over thirty years and was so well respected no candidate opposed him in an election. Richard was married to Mary Colby for over 65 years and had one son William C. Colby who preceded his father in death and a daughter Mrs. Charles Roberts of Detroit. Richard S. Colby was born in New York on September 9, 1822 and lived most of his adult life in Onondaga dying at his home on September 10, 1911.[261]

---

261   *LSJ* 9/11/1911, the *Leslie Local* 9/14/1911, the *Ingham County News* 9/14/1911 and the *Ingham County Democrat* 9/13/1911. The *Eaton Rapids Journal* 9/15/1911 gives Richard's date of birth and birth place as September 9, 1823 in Rutland Vermont.

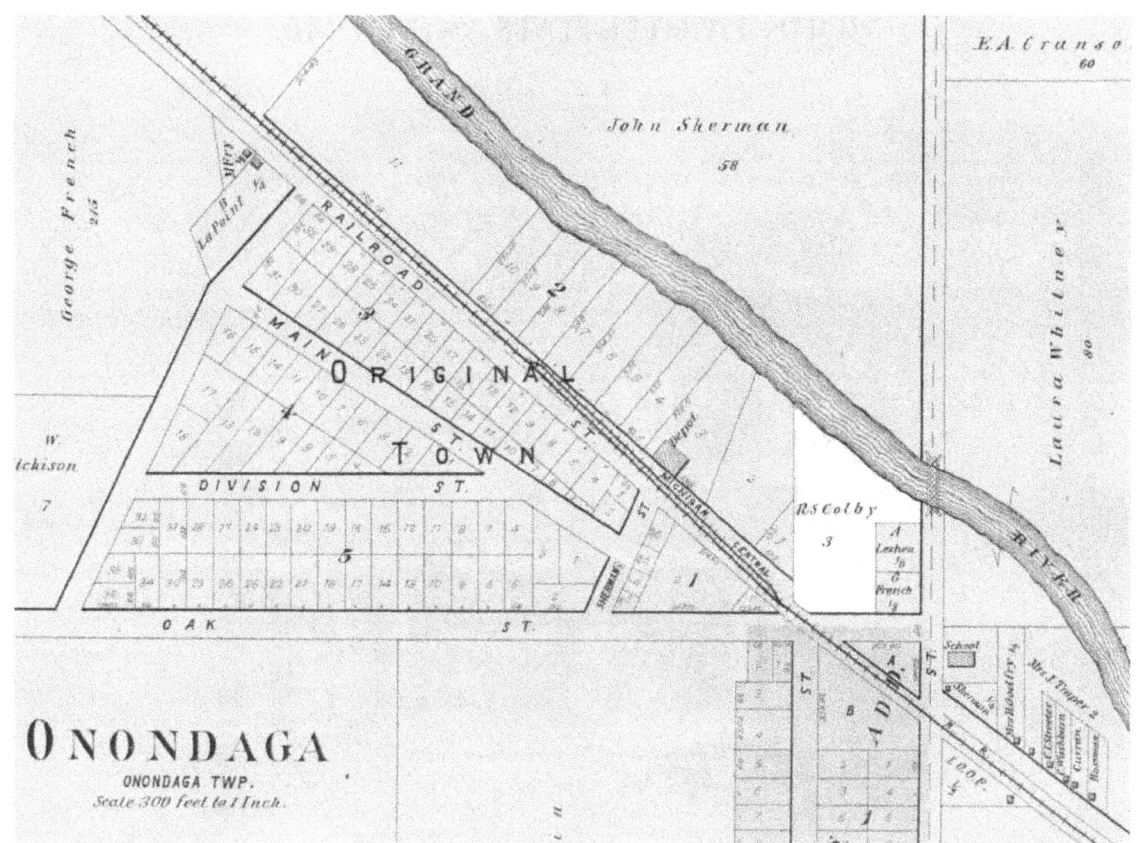

Onondaga Village

On the above map of Onondaga Village the Colby property where the Onondaga Hotel and the Colby home was located is in white. No image of the Colby home in Onondaga has been located, but it may have been damaged by the fire which occurred at the Onondaga Hotel in 1909 resulting in Moon's work for Colby. It undoubtedly was located on the same lot as the hotel. It is also possible that the Colby's lived in the hotel and that Moon redesigned their living quarters in the hotel after the fire. There is just not enough information to provide an answer. From the Gould inventory of Darius Moon Buildings, listed as "R.J. Colby Hse, 1909".

JOHN EICHELE FLATS AND HOME

608 (606) N. Capitol, Lansing, MI

"H.A. Prime (Henry A. Prine) has been awarded the contract for building a fine residence for John Eichele on Capitol ave n. It will cost about $3,000" (*SR* 5/19/1906). We know that John Eichele's home at 608 N. Capitol was standing in 1904. The work which Moon completed for Eichele was to build a set of flats for him at 610 N. Capitol and remodel his home at 608 N. Capitol into a set of flats. In 1908 Eichele's home at 608 N. Capitol is listed as a single address; after 1910 this would change, and two addresses would be listed for the structure. In the above image you can barely make out the second entrance.[262] By the time the above photograph was taken of 610 N. Capitol the home had changed. The original porch wrapped around the home while the enclosed area above the first porch did not exist; it was a small walk out porch.

---

[262] The address for 608 N. Capitol changes several times, it is listed at 606, 606½ and 608 throughout the years.

610 N. Capitol, Lansing, MI

In 1904 Eichele lived at 608 N. Capitol and Moon would convert this residence into a set of flats. Oddly Eichele would move to 610 N. Capitol by 1916. Notice the large window on the second floor and the oversized frame. This was done to draw attention to the fact that this was a main living area for 608 ½ N. Capitol. The recessed side porch was an expensive addition to the structure and it was meant to impress the visitor; notice the oriel window on the side. The separate entrances to the flats are framed by the Tuscan columns; the one column is hidden behind the tree in the first image.

John G. Eichele was born on January 18, 1855 in Bucyrus, Ohio the son of Jacob and Mary (née Funck) Eichele. At the age of nine his parents moved to Lansing, where his father worked as a salon keeper and manager of the Eichele House. John went into business for himself and owned the Eichele Grocery Store, located at 129 E. Michigan Avenue. The store was in the Newton Block which John operated for more then 40 years. The Newton Block was torn down to make way for the Priggoris Building after which Eichele sold his business and devoted his time to managing his real estate investments. John married Miss Helen Langenbacher on May 10, 1880 and the couple had two children, Helen E. and Andrew L. Eichele. John G. Eichele died in Detroit Michigan on April 6, 1924 while visiting his daughter Mrs. Helen E. Garner. Eichele was active in Lansing business affairs and was a member of the Independent Order of Foresters.[263]

From the Gould inventory of Darius Moon Buildings, listed as "John Eichle-Flats & Remodeled Hse, 1909".

---

263   *LSJ* 4/8/1924 and *Lansing Capital News* 4/7/1924.

DANIEL W. TUSSING HOUSE

226 S. Logan (MLK), Lansing, MI

Darius Moon had worked for Daniel W. Tussing earlier on the design of the Tussing Building and it was no surprise that Tussing would employ Moon to be the architect for his own home, in fact, they were almost neighbors. It is interesting to track the work Moon did on the west side of the city near his own home on Logan (MLK). The large front porch is one of the distinct features of the home, but the architectural elements that framed the small dormer were often overlooked. The petite columns in the arches that enclose the window are an understated aspect of the dormer that sets it off from its larger neighbor. Notice the little bump-out at the peak of each of the dormers, a subtle but classic detail. The larger dormer presents a problem because the second floor window seems too small; it is odd that a larger window was not employed in the design. The porch actually has an ell shape. It is recessed at the entrance and extended across the front of the home underneath the second floor with the finely turned balustrade connecting the Tuscan columns to complete the structure. Moon never designed another home which resembled the Tussing residence. It is a tragedy that the home was torn down.

Daniel W. Tussing 1861-1928

Daniel W. Tussing was born in Fairfield County, Ohio on March 6, 1861 to Daniel and Harriet (née Doty) Tussing. In his youth, Daniel W. Tussing taught in the local country school during the winter and in the summer he attended college. Later he became superintendent of the Ottawa, Ohio schools and at the age of 26 was elected president of the Ohio Central Normal College in Pleasantville, Ohio, where he remained for five years. Daniel Tussing came to Lansing as the general agent for the Union Central Life Insurance Company, a position he held from 1895 to 1905. In 1887 he married Mary J. Sager, who died in 1910. Mary was born in Fairfield County, Ohio on August 26, 1866 and attended Ohio Central Normal College where she met Daniel. There were three children from the marriage, Mabel, Edna and Emerson. In 1920 Daniel W. Tussing married Lillian E. Brown; the couple would have one daughter, Evelyn. Daniel W. Tussing was instrumental in forming the consortium which built the Tussing building in downtown Lansing, one of the first modern office buildings in the city. He was well known Lansing's business and political affairs and was a candidate for United States Senator in 1924 on the Republican ticket; he was defeated in the primaries by Senator James Couzens. Daniel W. Tussing would pass away at his home on Tuesday January 10, 1928.[264] The home was torn down in 2010. From the Gould inventory of Darius Moon Buildings, listed as "Hse for D.W. Tussing, 1909".

---

264   *LSJ* 1/11/1928. For Mary J. Tussing see the *SR* 10/3/1910 and the *LJ* 10/3/1910.

1910

BENJAMIN F. DAVIS HOUSE

528 S. Washington, Lansing, MI

"Mr. and Mrs. B.F. Davis have moved to 534 Butler street south, while their home on Washington avenue south is being remodeled" (*LJ* 5/17/1909 see also *SR* 5/18/1909).

"The home of B.F. Davis, which has been greatly remodeled, is now occupied by Mr. Davis and family" (*LJ* 10/4/1909).

Twelve years after the death of his first wife, Davis married Miss Sarah Day, on April 3, 1902. Sarah was born in Wauwatosa, Wisconsin, daughter of Dr. Fisk Holbrook and Frances A. (née Williams) Day. Fisk was a prominent physician whose home 'Sunnyhill' is a National Historic Landmark. After her marriage to Benjamin F. Davis, Sarah was active in many Lansing organizations. She was president of the Lansing Woman's Club, Regent of the D.A.R., member of the Y.M.C.A. Board and the principal organizer and first president of the Lansing Visiting Nurses Association. Mrs. Sarah Day Davis passed away on Tuesday February 14, 1950 at the Hotel Porter where she had lived since 1942.[265]

---

265   *LSJ* 2/15/1950.

After retiring from business life Benjamin F. Davis remained active in social affairs. He was a member of several Masonic organizations, the Lansing Country Club and an active member of the Michigan Pioneer Historical Society. Davis, before his death, committed some of his experiences in the Civil War to paper. In the work he recounts seeing the Grand Review of the Union Army in Washington D.C., where General Sherman and General Custer passed in front of President Lincoln. He also recalled how Edwin M. Stanton, Secretary of War, had publicly criticized General Sherman for the liberal surrender terms he granted Confederate General Joseph E. Johnston. Stanton reached out his hand to greet General Sherman who ignored Stanton and rode on as the crowd gasped at Sherman's action. Davis also missed the performance at Ford's Theater where President Lincoln was assassinated. Davis' roommate in Washington asked him if he would like to attend the performance at Ford's Theater on April 14, 1865 but Davis begged off because he was feeling ill. After the tragedy at the theater, Davis stood outside the Petersen House, where Lincoln was taken after the shooting, to hear news concerning the President's condition. Davis recounts that the City was near insanity, rumors were running rampant, General Grant was shot, Vice President Andrew Johnson was killed and some justices of the Supreme Court were dead. All of these rumors were untrue but they clearly demonstrated how fear outweighs reason. As Davis explains; "The very atmosphere seemed surcharged with fear, hate and murder. Everyone was overwhelmed, their energy spent. Treason had done its worst. I have seen published accounts of that tragic affair, but none that would give one, not present, an adequate idea of that night of terror" (*LSJ* 1/26/1934).

It is unfortunate that more of Davis' memoirs have yet to be discovered. Davis was active during World War I. As Chairman of the Ingham County Red Cross, Davis worked tirelessly to assure that the wounded men from the war which were sent to convalesce at the local hospitals and the M.A.C. campus received aNYThing needed to speed their recovery. Did Davis revel in the praise? No, he thanked the people of Ingham County for their support and donations.[266] Benjamin Franklin Davis, Lansing industrialist and humanitarian died at his home, 528 S. Washington on February 2, 1934 at the age of 85.[267]

It is interesting to see how Moon's former clients valued the work that he had done previously for them and employed him again and again on their building projects. There was no greater compliment for an architect than the approval of his clients. No image of the garage survives. From the Gould inventory of Darius Moon Buildings, listed "Davis Hse & Garage-Lansing, 1910".

---

266   *LSJ* 10/25/1918.
267   *LSJ* 2/2/1934 and Turner 442.

WILSON & KOPF SKATING RINK

Broad Ripple Park, IN

"Wilson & Kopf, proprietors of the coliseum on Ottawa st, will build a rink near Indianapolis, having leased ground for the structure at Broad Ripple Park. It will be open to the public May 20… Moon & Spice of this city are the architects" (*SR* 3/12/1910).

In 1910 John S. Wilson and Seigel D. Kopf decided to build and operate a skating rink at the new Broad Ripple Park located seven miles from Indianapolis. In 1908 the park, which was located on the banks of the White River, and then known as the White City Amusement Park, was almost completely destroyed by fire. The new owners, the Union Traction Company decided to rebuild the park and rename it the Broad Ripple Amusement Park. Wilson & Kopf engaged Moon's services to design a skating rink which was to be 64 by 150 feet in size. The partners moved the equipment from a skating rink they owned in Adrian, Michigan and transferred 200 pairs of skates from the Coliseum Skating Rink in Lansing to their new rink at Broad Ripple Park. The building and interior were to be of artistic design and opened for business on May 28, 1910.[268] No image has been discovered of the skating rink and the park closed in 1945.

---

268   See *LJ* 2/11/1910, *LJ* 4/10/1910, *LJ* 5/5/1910, *LJ* 5/19/1910 and Zeigler 79.

EUGENE A. HOLBROOK HOUSE

627 W. Washtenaw, Lansing, MI

The Gould inventory has Moon designing a home for someone named Holbrook in 1910. The best candidate is Eugene A. Holbrook. In 1908 Eugene A. Holbrook, a clerk at the Auditor General Office, resided at 211 S. Pine but by 1910 he had moved to 627 W. Washtenaw. The Stebbins' real estate record for the home at 627 W. Washtenaw listed Eugene A. Holbrook's residence as being built in 1909.

The Holbrook home had some interesting elements. On the third floor gable at the right in the above image there is no window but rather an extensive double "Λ" shaped motif. Notice the small dormer on the third floor. It has a series of small brackets along the soffit, fish scale siding at the peak and a stick work bracket on the side. The dormer is also set higher than the fish scale. The brackets under the soffit between the second and third floor are spaced over the second floor windows and the gable ends. Finally it is interesting to note that the windows in the left of the photograph are stacked three over two over one, matching the floors they were located on.

Eugene A. Holbrook was employed by the Michigan Auditor General in the Tax Collection office for more then 25 years. Born in 1848, Eugene would later marry Hattie E. Watkins in November of 1870; the couple would have one child, a daughter, Emma M. Holbrook. The family moved from Ypsilanti to Lansing in 1904. Eugene was an active member of Plymouth Congregational Church and of Lansing Lodge No. 33, F. &A.M. Eugene A. Holbrook died on Sunday, August 11, 1929 at his home after a long illness. His wife Hattie died in 1928. Eugene was survived by his daughter Emma, who cared for him during his last years.[269]

From the Gould inventory of Darius Moon Buildings, listed as "Holbrook Hse-Lansing, 1910".

---

269   *LSJ* 8/12/1929 and *Lansing Capital News* 8/12/1929. For Attie's death see *Lansing Capital News* 3/28/1924 and the *LSJ* 3/28/1924.

JOHN P. THOMAN HOUSE

217 N. Sycamore, Lansing, MI

In 1909 John P. Thoman engaged two local architects, Darius Moon and Edwyn Bowd to develop plans for the remodeling of his residence at 217 N. Sycamore. Both sets of plans still exist and they are held at the Forest Parke Library & Archives at the Capital Area District Libraries. In the end the contract was awarded to Darius Moon, but it is interesting to compare both sets of plans side be side. Bowd's plans contain far more detail than Moon's, but in the end Moon received the job.

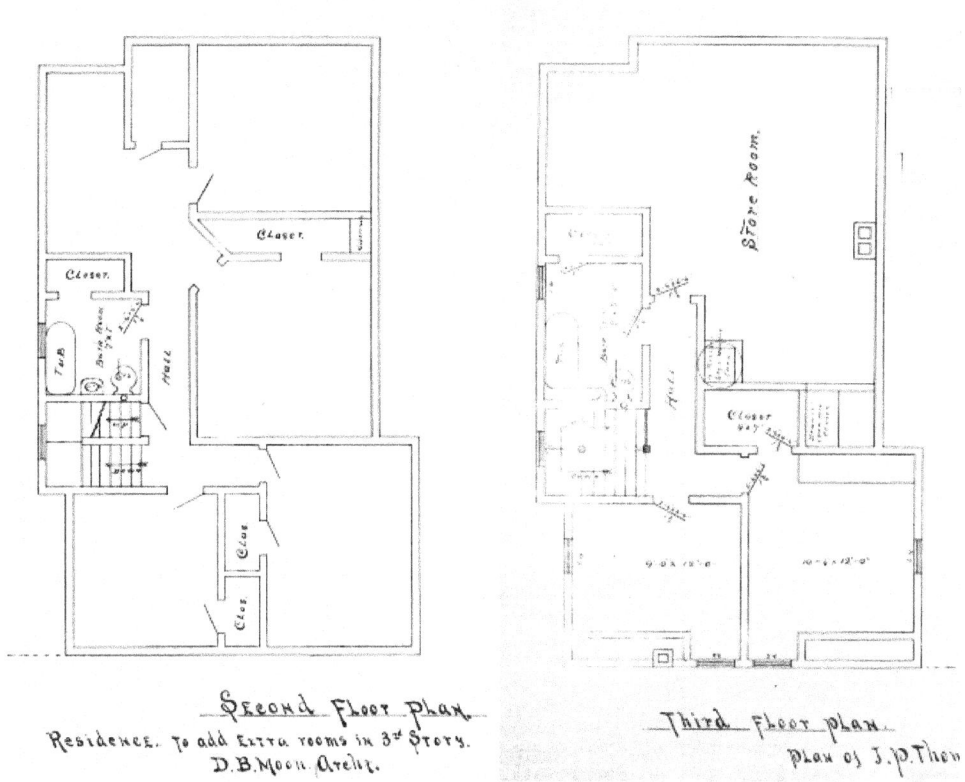

Second and Third Floor plans for the remodeling of 217 N. Sycamore

Born in Crestline, Ohio on June 1, 1853 John Phillip Thoman was one of the pioneers in Lansing's industrial growth. John graduated from Cornell University in 1875 and later attended Lehigh University in Pennsylvania. He would return to Crestline to manage a dry goods business. In 1883 John moved to Lansing and joined his brother, Frederick in the operation of the Thoman Milling Company, and continued as President of the company until his retirement in 1920. John also served as the Secretary of the Central Implement Company which was owned by A.B. Armstrong. On May 31, 1881 he would marry Miss Candace Paramore and the couple would have three sons, Frederick, Bart and Paul, and one daughter Candace.

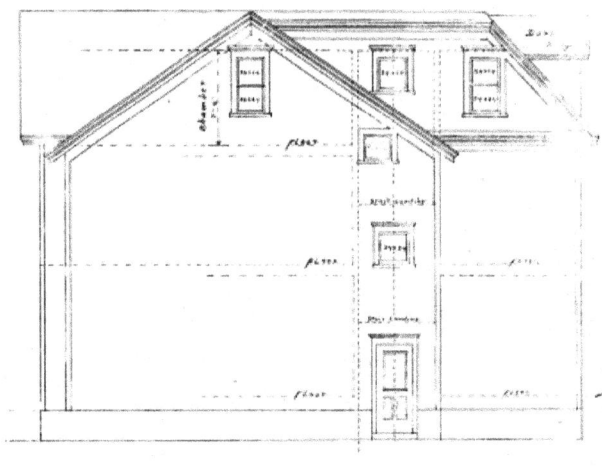

Drawing of the North Side Elevation of 217 N. Sycamore

Later John would develop a centralized steam heating system by using the exhaust steam generated by the mill. The steam produced by the mill would be used to heat several nearby factories by transporting the steam in crude wooden pipes surrounded with sawdust as insulation. As a result of this innovation John would serve for several years as Superintendent of the City Water and Light Board. John Phillip Thoman died at his home after a short illness on April 12, 1937 at the age of 83.[270]

North side, 217 N. Sycamore

---

270   Fuller 608 and the *LSJ* 4/13/1937.

There was no announcement in the local papers in regards to which architect, Bowd or Moon was awarded the commission for the remodeling the Thoman home. It is only when both architects plans are reviewed and compared to the present structure can it be determined which architect was awarded the contract. As you compare Moon's plans for the north side of the home to the photograph of the north side of the structure you can see that they match. Notice the position of the windows above the door and those on the third floor. The major change to the exterior of the home was the dormer added to the rear of the third floor; essentially it was added to expand the storage room at the rear of the home. From the Gould inventory of Darius Moon Buildings, listed as "Phil Thoman-Remodeled Hse., 1910".

WALDO HOMES

313-317 E. St Joseph, Lansing, MI

The Gould list has Moon building a home for Waldro in 1910 but this is a misspelling. There are no Waldros listed in the 1910 City Directory or the 1910 United States Census as residing in Michigan. It is possible that it could be that the residence was designed for Waldron or the Waldroms, however a review of the property records show that they either did not own property in the area in 1910 or the homes they lived in were not modified. In all likelihood Moon designed a house for the Waldo family, The Waldo name was well known in both Lansing and Delta Township at this time. There are two possibilities for this home, Alva N. Waldo who owned Lot 11 Block 155, 313-317 E. St Joseph, while Mrs. Elizabeth Waldo, his mother owned Lot 8 Block 174, 300 E. St Joseph.

The two homes located on Lot 11 Block 155, 313-317 E. St Joseph, owned by Alva were new construction built around 1910; the previous home on Lot 11 was torn down about 1909. Although not your typical Moon designed structure they would have been built by Alva as an investment. The two houses that were owned by Alva are typical American four square style homes. The residences are almost mirror images of each other; both homes had porches that stretched the entire length of the façade. The hip roof dormer was a typical architectural element for this style of house matching the hip roof of the home. Both homes at 313-317 E. St Joseph are still standing. The residence which Elizabeth owned, 300 E. St Joseph was not new construction; the structure was standing in 1906 and would have meant the house would have been a remodel. No image has been located of the home at 300 E. St Joseph and the structure is no longer standing.

Born in Oneida Township in Eaton County in 1839, Miss Elizabeth Nixon would marry Major Andre (Andrew) Waldo, on March 15, 1856; the couple would have two children, a son, Alva Nixon and a daughter Mabelle Annis. The family moved to Lansing in 1892 from Eaton County. Major A. Waldo would die at the age of 70 on April 5, 1904; Elizabeth N. Waldo passed away at her home at 300 E. St Joseph on July 15, 1912 and was survived by her daughter Mrs. Mabelle Annis Hunter of Lansing and her son Reverend Alva N. Waldo, pastor of the First M.P. Church in Saginaw, Michigan.

The Reverend Alva Nixon Waldo was born in Oneida Township, Eaton County Michigan on August 2, 1857. On November 14, 1877 he married Miss Alice Catherine Crossley in Delta Township. Alva would later move to Saginaw, Michigan where he became pastor of the Stephens Street Methodist Protestant Church. The Reverend Alva N. Waldo died in Lansing on September 23, 1918 while in the care of his sister and his wife. [271]. From the Gould inventory of Moon buildings, "Waldro Hse 1910".

MRS. LYDIA A. THOMAS HOUSE

515 (412) E. Grand River, East Lansing, MI

---

271   For Elizabeth's death see *LSJ* 7/15/1912 and *LSJ* 7/17/1912, for Major A. Waldo *SR* 4/6/1904 and for the Reverend Alva N. Waldo see the *LSJ* 9/24/1918.

"Plans are being prepared by Moon and Spice for Mrs. L.A. Thomas for a framed residence, which she is to erect in East Lansing" (*SR* 6/3/1910).

There is no listing in the 1910 East Lansing tax rolls for a Mrs. L.A. Thomas. The most likely candidate is Mrs. Lydia A. Thomas who was the sister-in-law of Charles B. Chase. Horace B. Angell and Charles B. Chase were business partners who developed the College Grove area of East Lansing, Michigan. Charles B. Chase had extensive property holdings in the East Lansing area in 1910; it is possible that the home for Mrs. Thomas was built on property that was owned by Chase.

A map of East Lansing from 1913, 412 E. Grand River is located in the bottom right corner of the image.

Mrs. Lydia A. (née Church) Thomas moved to the Lansing area after the death of her husband, Rev. Charles Gordon Thomas in 1900. After her husband passed away, Lydia lived with the Chases until she moved to 412 Grand River, East Lansing in 1914. The street numbering system used in East Lansing in 1914 had even numbers on the North and East sides of the street while odd numbers on the South and West sides. 412 E. Grand River was located at Lot 3, Chase Subdivision Plat of Lot 78 College Grove. Charles B. Chase owned all of Chase Subdivision which was bordered on the east by the alley way, on the west by Division Street, on the north by Albert Street and the south by East Grand River Avenue. For those familiar with East Lansing, the home was located west of the Peanut Barrel Restaurant. The address of the home would later change to 517 E. Grand River.[272]

The residence at 515 E. Grand River at first glance is a rather unassuming home, but the front porch displays something else. The original porch for the home also extended across the front of the home which would have dramatically altered the appearance of the structure. Notice how the windows on the façade are stacked, double window of the first floor, two separate windows on the second and a double window on the third. The corner window on the first floor which follows the ell of the porch is inexpensive but attractive feature; observe the detained casings on this window.

---

[272] The locating of the Thomas house was determined using the Sanborn maps for East Lansing and the East Lansing City Map by Chase Newman, Copyright November 1915.

507 (406) E. Grand River, East Lansing, MI

Oddly enough while researching the Mrs. Lydia A. Thomas residence I noticed that the home just west of her house 507 (406) E. Grand River bore a striking resemblance to several other homes Moon designed. Why? Well it was designed by Moon in 1914 for Professor Joseph A. Polson an Assistant Professor of Mechanical Engineering at the MAC. The home at 507 E. Grand River reminds one of the Murray residence built in 1904 and the home at 1110 W. Allegan built in 1908. The home at 507 E. Grand River was a larger version of the residences that Moon previously designed. The only major difference in this house when compared to the Murray home and the Moon structure at 1110 W. Allegan is the two large windows on the façade of the first floor. The other homes only had one window on the front of the first floor. The pattern of the upper windows and the style of the porch are almost identical to those elements of the home at 1110 W. Allegan.

Born in Napoleon, Michigan on October 11, 1849, Lydia was a member of the Baptist church, until her marriage to Charles G. Thomas in September 1872. The Reverend Charles G. Thomas was a well respected minister at the Simpson Methodist Episcopal Church in Kalamazoo, Michigan. On Sunday, January 7, 1900 he suffered a stroke while preaching a sermon and died the next day. Lydia maintained a cottage in Bay View, Michigan and in the winters stayed with her son, Fay W. Thomas in Chatsworth, California. On a visit to her son's home in California, she was taken ill and died on January 4, 1920. She was survived by her son Fay and a daughter Bertha had died earlier.[273]

---

273   *LSJ* 1/6/1920, *Minutes* 1920: 87, and *Minutes* 1900: 101.

WILLIAM T. BRITTON

In 1910, the Gould inventory of Darius Moon Buildings states that three homes were built and remodeled for William Britten with the notation that they were at the corner Butler & Ottawa streets. Just which houses these were presents some problems. William T. Britten was a contractor and a builder, in 1908 he is living at 817 W. Ottawa. The only homes built near corner of Ottawa and Butler streets between 1908 and 1913 were 909 W. Ottawa and 215-217 N. Butler. The home at 909 W. Ottawa was designed by Moon for William Wilcox and built in 1909. The homes at 215-217 N. Butler were built in 1910-1911, although 215 N. Butler is listed in the 1908 City Directory. The homes are almost carbon copies of each other except for the second floor porch on 215 N. Butler.

215 N. Butler, Lansing, MI   217 N. Butler, Lansing, MI

Both 215 N. Butler and 217 N. Butler were owned by Alfred Shuttleworth a pressman at the Wynkoop Hallenbeck & Crawford Company. Each of these homes are open gable structures with small facing dormers on one side. There was little ornamentation on either home. Except for the second floor porch on 215 N. Butler, the homes were mirror images of each other. Both homes still stand today and unfortunately the clean and simple lines of the original porches have been covered with siding.

817 W. Ottawa, Lansing, MI

The home at 817 W. Ottawa where William Britten resided is the candidate for the remodeling project that Moon carried out for Britten in 1910. Britten could have been updating the residence for his own use and later for resale or as a rental property. The Gould list is unclear as to whether it was three new homes and one remodel or two new homes and a remodel. If you include the Wilcox home then you have three homes that were new construction, 215 and 217 N. Butler and 909 W. Ottawa and one remodel 817 W. Ottawa. If you exclude the Wilcox home you have just the two homes on Butler and the remodeling of Britten's residence. William Britten's home at 817 W. Ottawa was an elegant Queen Anne style residence. The porch is simple with a delicate turned balustrade. On the left in both images there is a bay window which is complemented by the three sided window over the entrance porch. The circle top window on the front of the top gable coupled with the gable itself, technically known as a gable on a hip are two elements previously not employed by Moon. However it is unknown the extent of the remodel Moon did to the Britten residence.

817 W. Ottawa, Lansing, MI

William T. Britten was born in Fairfield, Michigan in 1868 to Thomas and Ellen (née Thomas) Britten. On September 2, 1891 William married Miss Pearl B. Crandall of Lansing, Michigan; the couple would have two daughters, Eva P. and Gladys. In 1923 Pearl Britten was a victim of murder in one of Lansing's notorious crimes. On the night of May 27, 1923 Pearl was at her family's home at 706 Britten Avenue with a friend, Miss Helen Powers. At about 2 am Mrs. Britten heard a noise and decided to investigate, she surprised an intruder who fired one shot in the dark, striking Mrs. Britten just below the eye, killing her instantly. Miss Powers screamed for help and Pearl's son-in-law who live across the street rushed to the scene. The intruder fled and later that morning bloodhounds followed the killers trail to the Grand Trunk railroad tracks adjacent to the REO Motor Car Company. William Britten was not in Lansing at the time of the murder, he was in Chicago on business. After an extensive investigation by the Lansing Police Department no motive could be found for the murder and no items were taken from the home. To this day the killer of Pearl Britten was never brought to justice. In 1952, Alfred Seymour, who at the time of the killing was police chief, and oddly lived directly behind the Britten home, stated that the case was the most baffling that he ever encountered. Seymour believed that it was done by a carnival worker, but no evidence was ever discovered.[274] Several years after Pearl's death, on February 28, 1925, William married Miss Ethelyn Alice Twiss, the daughter of Frederick M. and Alice (née Osborne) Twiss. William T. Britten died at the Masonic Home in Alma on Wednesday, October 30, 1946. He is best remembered as a former Lansing alderman and a contractor who built many Lansing structures.[275]

---

274   See the *LSJ* 5/28/1923 and the *Lansing Capital News* 5/28/1923. For Seymour's comments see *LSJ* 7/24/1952.
275   *LSJ* 10/31/1946. Ethelyn Twiss Britten died on January 12, 1979, see *LSJ* 1/19/1979.

AFTER 1910

After 1910 Moon according to the Gould list, built at least thirty seven additional structures and it is likely the number of structures was much higher then the Gould list records. It is left to another researcher to complete the inventory of Moon's work after 1910. There are many intriguing structures to be researched; Moon's work in Eaton Rapids is especially interesting, as well as his work for Lucien Driggs which demonstrated Moon's range as an architect. Alas I have run out of steam and only one other structure designed after 1910 and the family that commissioned Moon to redesign a home will be described.

MRS. RATHBURN HOME

229 State Street, Mason, MI, before the renovations

"Mrs. C.M. Rathburn has purchased the old homestead on the State Road and named in[t] The Meads. She will make extensive repairs to the house and yard under the supervision of an architect and landscape gardener and use for her summer house" (*ICD* 8/6/1913).

229 State Street, before the renovations

"Mrs. C.M. Rathburn, who has been making an extensive visit with her sister, Mrs. L.C. Webb, and making extensive improvements to her old home, The Meads, returned to her home in Atchison, Kan., Sunday morning. Mr. Rathburn met her in Chicago" (*ICD* 12/17/1913).

Moon would also renovate Lewis C. Webb's home at the same time, Mrs. Webb was Mrs. Rathburn's sister, but that is another story.

229 State Street, after renovations

The remodeling of the Rathburn residence was quite striking. Moon dispensed with the gothic features of the home. He removed the scrolled vergeboards from the gables and the eaves as well as removed the gingerbread porch. In regards to the interior of the house the after plans are available but there is nothing to compare them too, no description of the interior of the residence before the renovation exists. On the exterior, the window pattern from the original home remains, while the roof line has been changed and the porch has been extended. The porch is classical in style and has clean lines; the robust Tuscan double columns frame the entrance as well as the living room windows. The above image with the placement of the chairs demonstrates that the porch was used as a place where the home owners could sit and greet their neighbors. In the lower photograph you can see the details of the columns and the windows with pattern the of the muntins on the upper sash. As to the interior of the home, Moon designed an open floor plan with a large reception hall, the dining room and sleeping porch. It is interesting in that Moon located the dining room on the east side of the home with a bed room between it and the living room. The placement of the bathroom at the rear of the home away from the social area is a location that was typical in homes built at this time period; it removed the unfortunate odors that may have invaded the living quarters.

The porch after renovation

Helen Mead was born in Norwalk, Ohio on April 27, 1850 to George Graham and Minerva G. (née White) Mead. Helen was the oldest of the Mead's four children, her sister Delia was Helen's lifelong confident, while her brothers Ivan and Wilton S. Mead moved west at an early age. Helen left Norwalk as a child when her parents moved to Dansville, Michigan where her father was engaged in the milling trade. Later her father purchased the Phoenix Milling Company in Mason, Michigan in 1864 and the family settled there. Her father George also was for many years, involved in the clothing business with his son-in-law Lewis Cass Webb with the firm Webb & Mead. George G. Mead would pass away of pneumonia on February 15, 1892. George's wife Minerva died at the home of her daughter Delia Webb on March 18, 1913.[276]

Dr. William W. Campbell

Helen led an intriguing life. On October 12, 1870 Helen married Elias Culver in Mason, Michigan, and the union produced one child, George J. Culver. A few years after the birth of her son George, nasty rumors began to circulate regarding Helen's relationship with a young physician, Doctor William W. Campbell. The young doctor left Mason under a cloud of rumors in 1877. In the winter of 1878, Helen filed for divorce from Elias Culver which was granted by the circuit court. In September of 1878, Doctor Campbell retuned

---

[276] For George Mead see *ICD* 2/18/1892 and *ICN* 2/18/1892. For Minerva Mead see *ICD* 3/19/1913 and *ICN* 3/20/1913.

to Mason to marry the now divorced Mrs. Helen Mead Culver. Doctor Campbell was greeted by the citizens of Mason with eggs which were eventually tossed in his direction, but Campbell succeeded in marrying Helen. The couple left Mason for Atchison, Kansas where Dr. Campbell established a successful practice. Dr. William W. Campbell would die unexpectedly on August 11, 1902 in Atchison, Kansas while Helen was visiting her mother and sister in Mason.[277]

Charles M. Rathburn 1846-1935

Helen would return to Atchison, Kansas where eight years later she married Charles M. Rathburn, who was president of the Atchison Union Depot and Railroad Company. Born in Lower Horton, Nova Scotia on August 24, 1846, Charles spent his early years on his grandfather's farm. In 1860 Charles settled in Woburn, Massachusetts, where with the outbreak of the Civil War he would enlist in the 12th Regiment Massachusetts Volunteers, Company D, on June 26, 1861. The regiment was commanded by Colonel Fletcher Webster, the son of Daniel Webster. Charles mustered out of the 12th Massachusetts Volunteers on April 24, 1864 and entered the regular army as a hospital steward. After the war Charles worked for the Burlington Railroad, the Santa Fe Railroad, and finally the Atchison Union Depot and Railroad Company, where he served as president for 41 years until his retirement in 1930. In 1913 Helen purchased her parents old home on State Street, right next door to her sister's home.

Moon's elevation drawing for 229 State Street

---

277   For the Doctor Campbell saga see *ICN* 9/12/1878, for his death see *ICN* 8/14/1902.

From 1913 on Helen would return each May to Mason to spend the summer with her sister Delia or as was the case in May of 1917, the sisters along with their husbands would cruise to Alaska on board the S.S. Jefferson. The Rathburn's led an interesting life in Kansas; they were friends of William Jennings Bryant and Amelia Earhart who was born next door to the Rathburn home in Atchison. Oddly in 1922 Helen would sell her home in Mason, to W.B. Dean; the Rathburn's were building a large home on a bluff overlooking the Missouri River. Six years later the Rathburn's would purchase another home in Mason at 202 Park Street, where Helen would stay while visiting her sister. After Charles retired in 1930 the couple moved to Mason to live year round and spent time with Lewis and Delia Webb. Quite rapidly the members of this group began to die off, in 1934 after spending the winter of 1933/1934 at the Downey Hotel in Lansing, Lewis Cass Webb passed away, and he was followed in 1935, by his wife Delia. Charles M. Rathburn died on December 20, 1935 at his home in Mason. Helen Campbell Rathburn would be the last of the group to die, passing away at her home on October 14, 1936 while under the care of her son, George J. Culver.[278]

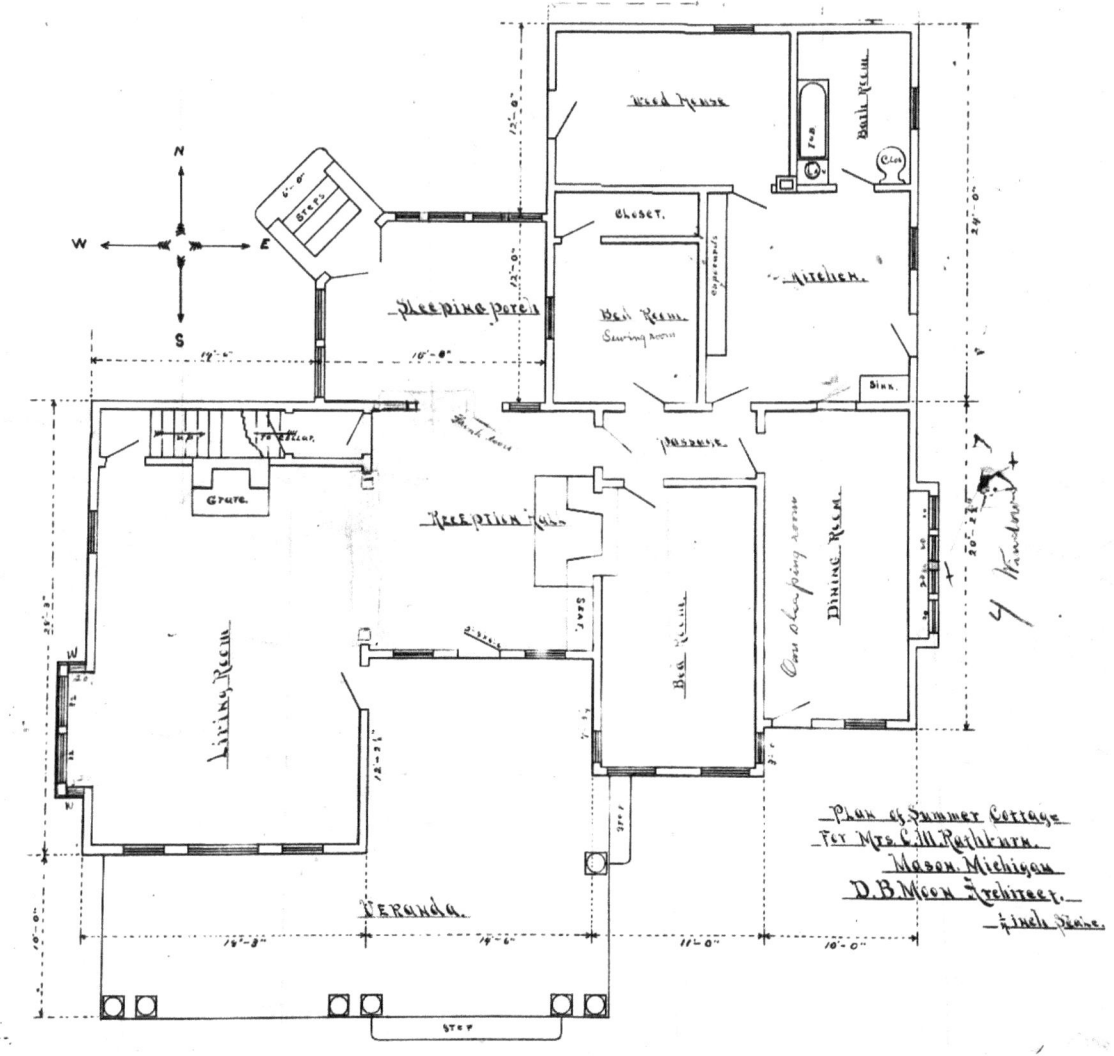

Moon's floor plan for 229 State Street

---

278 Charles Rathburn's death see *ICN* 12/26/1935 and *LSJ* 12/20/1935. For Helen see *ICN* 10/15/1936.

What became of Elias Culver the man Helen had wronged? His son, George lived with his mother Sarah in Atchison, Kansas, while Elias would become a prominent entrepreneur in Mason with a successful jewelry business. In 1903 he was elected mayor of Mason serving two terms. On September 16, 1880, Elias married Miss Nellie Barnes; the couple had one child who died at birth in 1890. In 1931 Nellie, suffering from ill health and concerned over the failed family's investments took her own life in February; Elias would pass away eight months later on September 28, 1931 of pneumonia, survived by his son, George Culver. There has always been a question in regards to George's paternity, was his father Elias Culver or William W. Campbell? The confusion arose because George used the names George M. Campbell, George M. Culver and George Culver Campbell throughout his life. George was born in Mason on August 23, 1871. George's parents Elias and Helen were married on October 12, 1870, so rough estimate is that George was conceived around November 30, 1870. Doctor Campbell did not arrive in Mason until August 1873. Simply Elias Culver was George's father.[279]

From the Gould inventory of Moon buildings, "Hse for Mrs. Rathburn (Mason) 1915".

Cheers

---

279 For Elias death see *ICN* 10/1/1931. For Dr. Campbell' arrival in Mason see *ICN* 8/21/1873. Nellie Culver's death was rather gruesome. Nellie secured herself to a chair after lighting a candle and turning on the gas on the stove then drank a bottle of chloroform. After the explosion Thomas Mclatchie broke into the home but was forced back by the flames, Ernest Parker a fireman carried Mrs. Culver from the building. Nellie Culver died the next day. See *LCN* 2/25/1931, *LSJ* 2/25/1931 and the *ICN* 2/26/1931

APPENDIX A

This is a copy of the Gould List which is mentioned many times in the text.

```
                SINCE THE YR. 1888
        ALL OF THE FOLLOWING BLDGS. I MADE PLANS FOR
```

Fifth Ward School Bldg.	1888
Millers Ins. Co. Bldg.	1890
Scofields Stores North	1894
Wilburs Store North	1890
B.F. Davis Residence	1888
Luthern School Bldg	1905
Luthern Parsonage	1905
Jacob Stahls Res.	1895
" " Barn	1895
Homer Luce Res.	1903
Hugh Lyons Res	1907
Frank Dodge Res.	1903
Tussing Block	1908
2 Hse's for Aldrich-E. Lansing	1916-1922
E. W. Sparrow Res.	1895
3 Hse's for C.D. Woodbury	1901-1907
Hse for C.E. Stabler	1916
Henry Kosichek Res.	1904
H.M. Rogers	1891
John Bissinger Res	1895
M.F. Bates Double Hse.	1905
M.F. Bates Res.-Lansing	1908
Mich. Screw Co. Bldgs.(3 Bldgs)	1911

Copied by Audrey Gould, granddaughter of Darius Moon from his papers - 1975

Jason E. Nichals Res. (3Bldgs)	1905
Mrs. Lacy & Abrams Hse - Leslie	1908
F. L. Dodge - Double Hse	1908
Dr. Ranney - Double Hse	1905
John Eichle-Flats & remodeled Hse	1909
Andres Eichle Remodeled Hse.	1914
Mrs. Fred Trastle Bungalow	1913
Clubhouse	1907
O. W. Ellis Hse.	1919
J. O. Black Hse.	1915
Fred Wood Hse-Bungalow	1904
D. N. Shull Hse.	1896
C. W. Crego Flats	1902
Mr. Murray Hse & Veranda	1904
Judge Person Hse	1904
Walter Pratt Flats	1885
Phil Thoman-Remodeled Hse.	1910
George McKenzie-Remodeled Hse.	1905
William Wilcox Store & Hse.	1909
Bea Davis Hse & Cottage	1907
Susie Stebbins	----
Hse for George Garden	----
Mrs. Lansing House	----
2 Houses for Mrs. Fred Bertok	----
House for Holstead, Hse & store	1912
Hse for Mrs. Rathburn (Mason)	1915

Hse for Lew Webb (Mason)	1915
Hse for Parkhurst (Mason)	1903
Bldg. for Farmers Bank (Mason)	1907
Risidence for R. E. Olds	1902
Most of the buildings Olds Motor wks.	1900
Business Black at Alpena, Mich.	----
For Eddy Engineering Co	1908
Cemetery Chapel at Eaton Rapids	1913
Hse for Dr. Stimposn (Eaton Rapids)	1912
Hse for L.J. Smith (Eaton Rpds.)	1912
Hse for Webster " "	1912
Hse for Bransly " "	1913
Hse for Crawford " "	1913
Hse for Dr. Canfield " "	1913
J.B. Nickle Hse at Sunfiedl	1902
Mrs. Smith Hse Lansing	1922
Paul Dunham Hse & Store	----
O.S. Care Hse Lansing	1908
Lew Driscoll Store-Lansing	1908
Lew Becks-Remodeled Store	1907
Hse for Fred Thomas	----
Glickman Store remodeled	----
Jake Stables office & Store	1895
J.W. Hicks Hse	1913
George Kneal 5 Houses	1902-1904

DARIUS B. MOON

Page 4

L. J. Driggs Store & apts.	1916
Alma E. Swanton Store-Lansing	1919
Fred Keith Hse	1908
J. W. Hagadorn Hse-E. Lansing	1904
C. N. Palmer Hse-Lansing	1921
R. J. Colby Hse-	1909
Calamel Schneider Hse	1908
G. W. Dennis Plans for Store-Leslie	1915
Ledercranze Clubhouse-Lansing	1903
L. J. Driggs Public Garage-Lansing	1913
William Britten Remodeled & Built 3 Hses. (Corner Butler & Ottawa)	1910
Edd Rectz home-Lansing	1901
Arthur Stebbins, Cottage at Roaring Brook, Mich.	1902
Bea Davis Cottage " " "	1907
C. D. Woodbury " " "	1902
William Brown Hse-Lansing	1895
Frank Moore Hse	1900
Sarah Wilson apts-Lansing	1903
Hatch Fleming-Lansing	1908
Armory-Lansing	1908
Arthur Stebbins- 2 houses-Lansing	1902
3 Bldgs for Lansing Co.	1902
School Hse at Gunnisonville	1907
Dr. Lameraugh apts-Battle Creek	----
Business Black for Dr. Ranny	1904

Page 5

Store on Washington Ace for Dr. Ranny	1896
F. L. Dodge Residence	1903
Hse for Edd Porter	1903
Hse for Ganuny	1906
Hse for Frank Hayes	1907
Hse for Levi Cottington	1891
Bauerman Residence (Country)	1892
Brown Store in Mason	1907
George Kneal store	1907
Hse for Ray Potter	1905
Hse for Ray Potter's father	1907
Slemmer Hse-Lansing	1902
Rietz Y Betts Factory	1903
Hse Ray Potter	1907
Stable & Piatt Richerd Mill	1903
School House (Columbia Park, E. Lansing)	1908
Savage Hse	1908
Judge McAlvery-Remodeled Hse	1908
Judson Hse-Lansing	1908
Union Bldg & Loan Assoc.	1908
J. M. Neal Remodeled Theater	1913
Mrs. Millbury Hse	1913
Mrs. Dennis-Mason	1913
Holbrook Hse-Lansing	1910
L. J. Driggs Bungalow(Biloxi, Miss.)	1906
Mich. Ave & Logan St. School	1915

Page 6

Walnut St. School Hse.	1909
Sparrow Hospital	1908
John Brooks Hse	1895
Joe Glaistac apts.	1891
Mrs. Emery apts.	1890
3 Hses for George Keith	1898
Harry Turner House	1900
Tom Shields hse.	1902
Store for Charles Porter	1896
Hse for D. W. Tussing	1909
Hse for John Wilson	1891
Frank Gadding apts.	1912
Frank Nice	1907
Hse for Dell B. Moon(my uncle) Main St.	1913
Lon Henry Hse.	1891
George Dayton apts.	1888
Bert Hansel Hse-E. Lansing	1912
Waldro Hse.	1910
Casgrove Theater	1906
John Rice Hse-Rogers Pl, Chicage, Ill.	1893
Emmet Thomas-Lake Bliff-Chicago, Ill.	1893
Smith apts.-Ravenswood-Chicago,Ill.	1893
2 Stores-Roger Park,-Chicago, Ill	1892
Sam Kilbaurn Hse	1889
Frank Moore	1887
George Wilson-Remodeled Hse.	1903

Page 7

Davis Hse & Garage-Lansing	1910
John Wilson Hse	1900
J. A. Palson Hse-East Lansing	1914
Furgersons Store-E. Mich. Ave.	1912
Joe Walfare Hse	1908
Sherman Hse at Banfraft	1904
John Vaisell Hse	1899
Charles Saier Hse.	1902
Levi Cottington Hse	1895
John Kneal Hse	1905
Driggs Apts.	1916
C. E. Stabbins Hse	1898
Armory for State Troops-Lansing	----
George Keith 2 Houses	----
Waldro-Remodeled Hse	----
Mrs. Hamilton 2 Stores	----
Dr. Wellings-Remodel Hse	----
Farm Hse-Henry Porter	1871
Church at Delta Center (Eaton Co.)	1872
Hse C. J. Olin-Lansing	1873
Hse Bill Matthews	1880
Hse Will Dan	1881
Hse Mark Garrett	1881
Philip Krause	----
D. B. Moon (1st Hse 23 yrs old)	1874

APPENDIX B

What follows are two odd little advertisements that refer to Darius Moon. The request for the "Play Ball" girl calendars is cool.

Letter to Mr. D.B. Moon, Lansing Mich.

Dear Sir: "Three quarters paint" is a good phrase for the best outside of Devoe.
Devoe is the standard: mark 100. The next best -there are several not far apart -are three-quarters paint; you may mark them 75 to Devoe's 100.
The bulk of the paints in the market are 40 or 50 or 60; a few better than 60; a few are worse then 40.
How do they act? They cover from one to three quarters as much as Devoe; and they last from one to three quarters as long as Devoe.
What are they worth? The same rule don't hold; it cost more to put on some paints then they are worth; they are not worth a*NY*Thing; the "put on" costs two or three times as much as the paint.
Yours truly
F.W. Devoe & Co
P.S. Freeman Hardware sells our paint.[280]

Richards-Wilcox Mfg. Co.,
Aurora Illinois.
Gentlemen- Would it be asking too much to send me some of your April calendars with the "Play Ball" girl picture? She is just as much of a peach as your door hangers.

Yours,
D.B. Moon, Architect.
Lansing, Mich.[281]

280	SR 3/23/1906.
281	From Richards-Wilcox Doorways catalog, January 1914.

BIBLIOGRAPHY

Works Cited

American Contractor. Vol. 31 No.27. Chicago: F. W. Dodge, 1910. Print

American Machinist 27.April (1904). Print.

American Machinist 47.10 (1917). Print.

Beal, W. J. *History of the Michigan Agricultural College and Biographical Sketches of Trustees and Professors.* East Lansing: Agricultural College, 1915. Print.

Beasley, Norman, and George W. Stark. *Made in Detroit.* New York: Putnam, 1957. Print.

Christensen, Robert O., *North Lansing Historic Commercial District Nomination.* Lansing, MI: Bureau of History, 1975. Print

County of Eaton, Michigan: Topography, History, Art Folio and Directory of Freeholders. N.p.: Bullock, Taggart & Morrell, Topographers and, 1895. Print.

Cowles, Albert E. *Past and Present of the City of Lansing and Ingham County, Michigan: Together with Biographical Sketches of Many of Its Leading and Prominent Citizens and Illustrious Dead.* N.p.: Michigan Historical Pub. Association, 1905. Print.

Creecy, John. *A Century at Harbor Point, 1878-1978.* Grosse Point Farms, MI: Madrus, 1978. Print.

Daboll, Sherman B., and Dean W. Kelley. *Past and Present of Clinton County, Michigan,.* Chicago: S.J. Clarke, 1906. Print.

Department of Public Instruction *Rural School Architecture Circular 28.* Springfield IL: Phillips Bros., 1901. Print.

Durling, Marion W. *Bancroft History.* S.l: s.n., 1977. Print.

Frazier, Richard, and David Thomas. *Let the Record Show: A Legal History of Ingham County.* East Lansing, MI: Michigan State University Press, 1997. Print.

Fuller, George N. *Michigan, a Centennial History of the State and Its People ...* Chicago: Lewis Pub., 1939. Print.

Haueter, D. S. *The Grand Ledge Works of Darius Moon.* N.p.: n.p., 1985. Print.

History of the Foster Parent Teacher Association History 1918-1942. N.p.: n.p., [1942].

Howard, Eller H.C. *North Western Reporter.* Vol. 54. St Paul: West, 1893. Print.

Howard, Eller H.C. *North Western Reporter.* Vol. 108. St Paul: West, 1906. Print.

Illustrated Souvenir Edition of Lansing Michigan. July 1903.

Ingham County, MI. Ingham County Register of Deeds. *Grantor-Grantee Index.* Mason, MI.: n.p., 1870-1940. Print.

Journal of the American Medical Association 73.14-26 (1919): n. page. Print.

Lake, D. J., H. E. Blakeman, and W. G. Hard. *Atlas of Eaton Co., Michigan from Actual Surveys.* Philadelphia: C.O. Titus, 1873. Print.

Lansing, MI. City of Lansing. City Assessor. *City of Lansing Tax Assessment Rolls.* Lansing, MI: n.p., 1900-1940. Print.

Larson, Erik. *The Devil in the White City: Murder, Magic, and Madness at the Fair That Changed America.* New York: Vintage, 2004. Print.

Livingstone, William. *Livingstone's History of the Republican Party. a History of the Republican Party from Its Foundation to the Close of the Campaign of 1900, including Incidents of Michigan Campaigns and Biographical Sketches.* Detroit: Wm. Livingstone, 1900. Print.

Lucas, Richard E, Elaine P. Davis, and F W. Beers. *Combined Ingham Co. Mich. 1874 & 1895 Atlases: With Every Name in Index.* Lansing, MI: Mid-Michigan Genealogical Society, 1988.

Michigan Federation of Labor Year Book (1906-1907): 233. Print.

Michigan Reports : Reports of Cases Determined in the Supreme Court of Michigan. Vol. 177. Chicago: Callaghan, 1914. Print.

Michigan Reports : Reports of Cases Determined in the Supreme Court of Michigan. Vol. 182. Chicago: Callaghan, 1915. Print.

Minutes of the Michigan Annual Conference of the Methodist Episcopal Church Sixty-Fifth Session. St. Joseph MI: A.B. Morse, 1900. Print.

Minutes of the Michigan Annual Conference of the Methodist Episcopal Church Eighty-Fourth Session. Lansing, MI: Wynkoop Hallenbeck Crawford, 1920. Print.

Moon, Darius B. "*Michigan in the Fifties. My Fathers Family and a True Story.*" 1932. TS F574.L2 M663 1968. Library of Michigan, Lansing, MI.

Moore, Charles. *History of Michigan,.* Chicago: Lewis Pub., 1915. Print.

Motor: The National Magazine of Motoring September (1906): 114. Print.

Munn, W S. *The Only Eaton Rapids on Earth: The Pioneer History of Eaton Rapids and Hamlin Townships with Reminiscences.* Ann Arbor, MI: Edwards Bros, 1952. Print.

National Cyclopaedia of American Biography. New York: J.T. White, 1892. Print.

The Northwestern Reporter: Containing All the Decisions of the Supreme Courts of Minnesota, Wisconsin, Iowa, Michigan, Nebraska and Dakota. Vol. 127. St. Paul, MN: West Pub., 1910. Print.

Past and Present of Eaton County, Michigan, Historically Together with Biographical Sketches of Its Leading and Prominent Citizens and Illustrious Dead. Lansing: n.p., [19-]. Print.

People of the State of Michigan vs Orpha Gilmore. 25 473. Circuit Court for the County of Ingham. 3 Oct. 1899. Print.

Portrait and Biographical Album of Barry and Eaton Counties, Mich. Containing Full Page Portraits and Biographical Sketches of Prominent and Representative Citizens of the County ... [and] the Presidents of the United States and Governors of the State. Chicago: Chapman Bros., 1891. Print.

Portrait and Biographical Album of Clinton and Shiawassee Counties, Mich., Containing Full Page Portraits and Biographical Sketches of Prominent and Representative Citizens of the County, Together with Portraits and Biographies of All the Presidents of the United States, and Governors of the State. Chicago: Chapman Bros., 1891. Print.

Portrait and Biographical Album of Ingham and Livingston Counties, Michigan,. Chicago: Chapman Bros., 1891. Print.

Report on the Cherry Hill Historic District. [Lansing, Mich.]: Lansing Historic District Commission, 1989. Print.

Turner, Frank N., and George N. Fuller. *An Account of Ingham County from Its Organization.* [Dayton, Ohio]: National Historical Association, 1924. Print.

Siebert, Philip A., *B.F. Davis Mansion.* Oxford, Ohio, 1971. Print.

Youngstrand, Charles O. *A Gallery of Pen Sketches in Black and White of Our Michigan Friends "as We See 'em,".* Detroit: W. Graham Printing Co, 1905. Print.

Zeigler, Connie J. *Indianapolis Amusement Parks, 1903-1911 Landscapes on the Edge.* Thesis. Indiana University, 2007. N.p.: n.d. Print.

Newspapers

Alma Record
Alpena News
Clinton Republican
Detroit Free Press
Detroit News
Detroit Times
Eaton Rapids Journal
Everett Daily Herald (Washington)
Georgia County Times (Georgia)
Grand Ledge Independent
Gulfport/Biloxi Daily Herald (Mississippi)
Ingham County Democrat
Ingham County News
Lansing Capital News
Lansing Evening News
Lansing Evening Press
Lansing Journal
Lansing Journal Weekly
Lansing Republican Weekly
Lansing State Journal
Leslie Local
Leslie Local Republican
Mt. Clemens Monitor
New York Times (New York)
Philadelphia Evening Bulletin (Pennsylvania)
Saginaw Courier-Herald
South Haven Daily Tribune
State Republican (Lansing)
Toledo Blade (Ohio)
Towne Courier (East Lansing)
Tuscola County Advertiser
Wichita Eagle (Kansas)

City Directories

Brown, C. E., comp. *Brown's Directory of Lansing, Michigan.* Lansing MI: C. Exera Brown, 1873. Print.

Lansing City Directory. Vol. 1-6. Detroit, MI.: R.L. Polk, 1883-1892. Print.

Lansing City Directory. Vol. 1-23. Lansing, MI: Chilson & McKinley, 1892-1923. Print.

Lansing City Directory. Vol. 24-34. Lansing, MI: McKinley-Reynolds, 1924-1935. Print.

Lansing City Directory 1906-1906. Marion, Indiana: The Inter-State Directory Co., June, 1905.

Mudge, Charles E., comp. *Mudge's Directory of Lansing City: Complete and Entire, Giving the Name, Business, Place of Business, If Any, and Residence of All Citizens ...* Lansing, MI: C.E. Mudge, 1878. Print.

Polk's Petoskey (Michigan) City Directory. Detroit, MI: R.L. Polk & Co, 1905-1906. Print.

Pryor & Co.'s Lansing City Directory, 1878. N.p.: Pryor &, 1878. Print.

Works Consulted

100 Turn-of-the-century House Plans. Mineola, NY: Dover Publications, 2000. Print.

Ann Arbor Architecture: A Sesquicentennial Selection. [Ann Arbor, MI.]: University of Michigan Museum of Art, 1974. Print.

Barber, George F. *Victorian Cottage Architecture: An American Catalog of Designs, 1891*. Mineola, NY: Dover Publications, 2004. Print.

Barber's Turn-of-the-century Houses: Elevations and Floor Plans. Mineola, NY: Dover Publications, 2008. Print.

Blumenson, John J.G. *Identifying American Architecture: A Pictorial Guide to Styles and Terms, 1600-1945*. New York: W.W. Norton, 1979. Print.

Christensen, Robert O., *Downtown Lansing Multiple Resource Nomination*. Lansing, MI: Bureau of History, 1980. Print

Christensen, Robert O., *Lansing Downtown Lansing Historic District, Ingham Co., MI. Nomination*. Lansing, MI: State Historic Preservation Office, 2009. Print

Eckert, Kathryn Bishop. *Buildings of Michigan*. New York: Oxford UP, 1993. Print.

Gottfried, Herbert, and Jan Jennings. *American Vernacular Design, 1870-1940*. Ames: Iowa State UP, 1988. Print.

Gottfried, Herbert, and Jan Jennings. *American Vernacular Buildings and Interiors, 1870-1960*. New York: W.W. Norton and, 2009. Print.

Griffin, Walter Burley, Mati Maldre, and Paul Samuel. Kruty. *Walter Burley Griffin in America*. Urbana: University of Illinois, 1996. Print.

Hardin, Evamaria. *Syracuse Landmarks*. Syracuse N.Y.: Syracuse Univ, 1983. Print.

Haynes, and Moran. *Mason Historic Survey Project*. N.p.: n.p., 1984. Print.

Henry, Irene J., and William R. Henry. *Lansing Architectural Survey II – Historical and Architectural Surveys of Selected Previously unsurveyed Areas*. Lansing, MI: Department of Planning & Neighborhood Development, 1998. Print.

Hill, Eric J., and John Gallagher. *AIA Detroit: The American Institute of Architects : Guide to Detroit Architecture*. Detroit: Wayne State UP, 2003. Print.

Historic Buildings in St. Louis County. Clayton, MO: St. Louis County Historic Buildings Commission, St. Louis County Department of Parks and Recreation, St. Louis County Department of Human Resources, 1985. Print.

Historic Structures in the Haslett-Lake Lansing Area. Okemos, MI: Friends of Historic Meridian, 2001. Print.

Kahn, Renee, and Ellen Meagher. *Preserving Porches*. New York: H. Holt, 1990. Print.

Keyes, Margaret N. *Nineteenth Century Home Architecture of Iowa City*. Iowa City: University of Iowa, 1993. Print.

Logan, Thomas H. *Almost Lost: Building and Preserving Heritage Hill, Grand Rapids, Michigan*. Traverse City: Arbutus, 2004. Print.

MacLean, James, and Craig A. Whitford. *Lansing: City on the Grand, 1836-1939*. Charleston, SC: Arcadia, 2003. Print.

McAlester, Virginia, and Lee McAlester. *A Field Guide to American Houses*. New York: Alfred A. Knopf, 1984. Print.

Meyer, Katharine M., and Martin C. P. McElroy. *Detroit Architecture: A.I.A. Guide*. Detroit: Wayne State UP, 1980. Print.

Miller, Whitney. *East Lansing: Collegeville Revisited*. Chicago: Arcadia, 2002. Print.

Phase III Architectural Resource Survey: Three Downtown Neighborhoods, Lansing Michigan,. Lansing, MI: Great Lakes Research, Consultants, 2000. Print.

Radford's Artistic Bungalows: The Complete 1908 Catalog. Mineola, NY: Dover Publications, 1997. Print.

Rodriguez, Michael. *R.E. Olds and Industrial Lansing*. Charleston, SC: Arcadia, 2004. Print.

Rural Meridian Township, Structures of Historic and Architectural Significance. Okemos, MI: Meridian Charter Township, Ingham County, 1972. Print.

Schneider, Robert, and Laurie Sommers. *Final Report for a Reconnaissance Level Survey of Historic and Architectural Resources in Lansing's Central Neighborhoods*. Lansing, MI: Prepared for the City of Lansing, 1986. Print.

Sinkevitch, Alice, and Laurie McGovern. Petersen. *AIA Guide to Chicago*. New York: Harcourt Brace, 1993. Print.

Skinner, Tina. *Radford's Artistic Homes 1908*. Atglen, PA: Schiffer Pub., 2002. Print.

Thayer, Laura. *Cincinnati Old House Handbook*. Cincinnati: Historic Conservation Office, Dept. of City Planning, 1984. Print.

Thematic Survey of Early Automotive History in Lansing, Michigan, From 1890 to 1930. Lansing, MI: Mannik & Smith Group, Consultants, 2003. Print.

Electronic Resources

Ancestry Library Edition. http://www.ancestry.com/

Family Search. http://www.familysearch.org/

Find a Grave. http://www.findagrave.com/

HathiTrust. http://www.hathitrust.org/

Interment.net. http://www.interment.net/

Michigan County Histories and Atlases. http://quod.lib.umich.edu/m/micounty/

Michigan Department of Community Health, Genealogical Death Indexing System http://www.mdch.state.mi.us/gendisx/search2.htm

Sanborn Maps Library Edition. http://www.sanborn.com/

Seeking Michigan. http://seekingmichigan.org/

INDEX

Abrams, David D., 334
Allen, Claire, 35
Alpena, MI, 114 Chisholm, 364
Altoft, Rose Evangeline, 157
Alton, Candace, 126
Ames, Charlotte (Mollie) E., 18
Angell, Horace B., 162, 391
Annah, Mary, 30
Appleyard, Anna, 199
Appleyard, James, 72, 84, 199, 201, 213, 228
Appleyard, William, 201
Armory, Battery A, Lansing, MI, 356
Armory, Governor's Guard, Lansing, MI, 142
Ashby, George William, 336

Backus, Alice A., 333
Backus, Helen A., 333
Bacon, Helen, 10
Bacon, John H., 10
Bailey, R. Arthur, 10, 87, 288
Baird, James J., 82
Baird, Norah, 338
Bancroft, MI, Sherman House, 260
Barnes, Louise A., 135
Barnes, Nellie, 402
Bassler, Barbara, 331
Bates & Edmonds Company, 178, 197, 366
Bates, Madison F., 1, 179, 268, 279, 339, 365
Baumgras, Elizabeth P. 38
Baumgras, Henry, 29
Beal, William James, 50
Beattie, Margaret B., 121
Beck, Louis, 317
Beilfuss Motor Company, Lansing, MI, 159, 161, 231
Beilfuss, Richard A.F., 232
Benjamin, Darwin J., 43
Bernard, Mary Parmalee, 95
Bertch, Fredrick W., 70
Bertch, Louise, 70
Biddecomb, Lizzie, 33
Biloxi, MS,
    156 Benachi, 300
Bissinger, John A., 104
Black, John O., 63
Blatt, Cyril, 8, 152
Boumann, Ida, 233
Bowd, Edwyn A., 61, 74–77, 80, 93, 116, 144, 149, 176, 193, 297, 327, 345, 357, 371, 386–389
Bowerman, Michael Hoag, 145
Bowser, Antoinette, 17
Boylan. William, 25
Britten, William T., 199, 398

Broad Ripple Park, IN, 347, 384
Brooks, John A., 107, 193, 292
Brooks, Laura, 308
Brown, Frederick J., 314
Brown, Henry L., 314
Brown, Lillian E., 381
Brown, Sarah, 64
Brown, William Clark, 67
Burchard, Louisa F., 66
Burgoyne, Anna B., 186, 190
Burnham, Grace, 220
Burns, Marie Teresa, 342
Burton, Ellen B., 354
Bush, John J., 120,
Butler, Charles W., 120

Campbell, William W., 399
Capital (Capitol) Peat Company, 267
Carey, Prelia E., 26
Carlton, Clarence C., 82
Carrier, Ralph, 91
Case, D.L., 14
Case, Florence T., 36
Case, Oscar S., 335
Caterino, David, 2
Cauthorn, Ailene, 10
Ceiles, Cora L., 264
Chapman, Charles H., 264
Chapman, Cora L., 264
Chase, Charles B., 391
Chase, John H., 8
Chicago, Illinois, 93
Churchill, Judson N., 297, 337
Clark, Helen J., 301
Cleveland, Margaret A., 68
Clinton County, MI,
    DeWitt Township, 1250 Clark Road, 293
    DeWitt Township, 1841 E Clark Road, 38
    Riley Township, Chadwick Road, 36
    Riley Township, Culter Road, 27
    Watertown Township, 4911 Clark Road, 25
    Watertown Township, 15
Clow, Sarah, 33
Colby, Richard S., 376
Colgrove, Philip Taylor, 157
Columbia Park School, Lansing, MI, 336
Cook, Rose, 263
Coors, Reverend D. Stanley, 14
Cottington, Levi G., 82, 122
Cottrell, William, 148, 363
Coville, Cora B., 364
Crandall, Mary E., 339

Crandall, Pearl B., 395
Crego, Ralph W., 167
Creyts, Joseph G., 47
Crosby, Louise H., 66, 197
Crossley, Alice Catherine, 390
Culver, Elias, 399
Culver, George J., 401
Cummings, Eliza S., 166 n123
Cutcheon, Anna, 361

Danforth, Elizabeth P., 323
Dann, John W., 24
Dann, William, 24
Davis, Benjamin F., 57, 119, 382
Davis, Bessie, 303
Davis, Clara M., 112, 348
Davis, Edith Eva, 303
Day, Sara, 303, 382
Dayton, George M., 60, 115
Delamarter, Sarah, 126
Denison, Frances, 323
Dickerson, Florence E., 45
Dodge, Frank L., 113, 182, 222, 339
Douglas, Clyde M., 9
Douglas, John M., 32
Driggs, Lucien J., 12, 300, 396
Driscoll, Louis A., 342
Drysdale, Elizabeth, 229
Du Betts, La, 339
Dubois, I.T. (Isaac F.), 36
Dunham, Paul Elmer, 262, 293, 311

Early & Fitzpatrick Contractors, 209, 349, 355

Early, Thomas, 351 n247
East Lansing, MI,
    229 Abbott, 244, 246
    104 Albert, 243, 246,
    323 Ann, 244
    215 Evergreen, 249
    335 E Grand River, 162
    507 E Grand River, 275
    515 E Grand River, 391
    110 W Grand River, 243
Eaton County MI,
    Delta Township, 3, 7, 11, 23–24, 26, 30, 66 n53
    Delta Township, 7146 E Mt. Hope, 38, 41
    Delta Township, Saginaw Highway, 46
    Delta Township, 5000 W Saginaw Highway, 47
    Delta Township, W Willow Highway, 40
    Oneida Township, St Joseph Highway, 39
    Roxand Township, 2463 Saginaw Highway, 168
    Windsor Township, Old Maid Swamp, 267
    6628 E St Joseph Highway, 30–31
Eddy, Henry G., 264

Eddy, Nelson M., 264
Edmonds, James Pelton, 179, 357, 367
Eichele, John G., 378
Ellis, Charles W., 12
Emery, Archibald M., 71, 73
Emery, Wesley, 73
Englert, Barbara, 340
Epley, Kate S., 139
Evangelical Lutheran Trinity Society, Lansing, MI, 270, 276

Fairgrove, MI,
    2106 Main, 228
Farmer's Bank, 312
Findley, Julia, 353, 356
Fitzpatrick, Martin Edward, 179, 233, 351 n247
Fitzsimmons, Fannie C., 25
Fling, Addella J., 352
Flitton, Flora F., 152
Flynn, Mary, 192
Foster, Joseph, 336, 340, 355
Foster, Sarah, 24
Foster, Seymour, 368, 370
French, John M., 20, 33,
French, Mary, 152

Ganung, Stuart F., 298
Garrett, Mark E., 23
George, Agnes, 335
Gibbs, Henry, 14, 54,
Gillett, Israel, 213
Gilmore, Orpha Wilson, 41
Glaister, Joseph C., 73, 84
Glaister, Orah, 73
Glicman, Israel, 140
Goodrich, May, 248
Goodyear, Carrie M., 157
Gordon, George T., 132, 364
Gorman, Harriet, 323
Governor's Guard Armory, 142
Grammel, Louise, 240
Grand Ledge, MI, 14
    326 Harrison, 34
    216 Jefferson, 35
Grant, Helen Therese, 121
Greenough, Estella A., 19
Gregory, Alice A., 296
Griffin, Walter B., 9
Griswold, Edward P., 35
Gunnisonville, MI, 30, 38, 293, 311
Gunnisonville School, 311

Hagadorn, Johnson W., 243, 246, 248–252
Hallett, John W., 64 n48
Halstead, Oliver W., 325–327, 355

Hamil, Benjamin F., 27, 49
Hamilton, Alvin N., 261–263
Hamilton, Robert W., 263
Hammond, Josephine Myra, 242
Harbor Point, MI,
    Bea Davis Cottage, 303
Harrington, Lillian M., 347
Hart (Hamilton), Isabella Elizabeth, 261–263
Hastings, MI,
    101-105 N. Michigan, 155–157
Hayes, Frank Henry, 184, 290, 315
Henderson, John L., 34
Henry, Alonzo Miles, 86
Hessert, Kate, 113
Hiesrodt, Lucy Ann, 168
Hildreth Motor & Pump Company, 230
Hildreth, Ned Elmer, 230
Hildreth, William W., 230
Holbrook, Eugene A., 385
Holly, Alonzo, 15
Holmes, Charles W., 45
Holmes, William J., 45
Hotel Ransier, 354–356
Howe, Fayette M., 8 n4
Howe, O. Friend, 1
Howell, MI,
    303 N. Court, 158
Hungerford, Harriet, 17
Hungerford, Mogan B., 16–18
Huxtable, John James, 46
Hyatt, Carrie M. Crosby, 66, 198

Ingham County, MI,
    Alaiedon Township, 2491 S. Okemos, 107 n80, 193
    Aurelius Center Cemetery, 14
    Onondaga Township, 14, 376

Jackson, Mary, 37
Jickells, Mary, 24
Johnson, Amanda C., 27
Jones, Fanny, 275
Jones, Neenah E., 180
Joslin, Abigail Cecelia, 24
Judson, Lorenzo, 39
Judson, Nathan, 353

Kalck, Fred R., 356
Kaltenbach, Simon S., 340
Keith, Clara Frances, 50
Keith, Fred C., 351
Keith, George A., 134–137
Kellogg, Mary A., 131
Kilbourne, Samuel A., 55, 65,198
King, George E., 15
Kirk, William, 134, 228

Kneal, George H., 163–166, 320
Kneal, John S., 286
Koons, Sarah J., 154
Kopf, Sigel David, 152 346–348, 384
Kositchek, Henry, 2, 253–256, 319
Krause, Defolia, 159
Krause, Philip T., 30, 38, 41, 47
Kroll, William, 121

Lacy, Philo E., 332
Langenbacher, Helen, 379
Lansing Wheelbarrow Company, Lansing, MI, 46, 186, 208–211
Lansing Wheelbarrow Company, Parkin, AR, 206, 292
Lansing, Garrett Y., 278
Lansing, MI,
    Allegan, 119 W, 329
    Allegan, 313 W, 154
    Allegan, 315 W, 134
    Allegan, 317 W, 134
    Allegan, 410 W, 238
    Allegan, 426 W, 302
    Allegan, 617 W, 286
    Allegan, 1024-1028 W, 167
    Allegan, 1110 W, 370
    Allegan, 1114 W, 368
    Butler, 115 N, 372
    Butler, 215 N, 393
    Butler, 217 N, 393
    Butler, 215 S, 136
    Capitol, 227 N, 186, 212
    Capitol, 514 N, 253
    Capitol, 528 N, 88
    Capitol, 608 N, 378
    Capitol, 610 N, 379
    Capitol, 624 N, 104
    Capitol, 319 S, 356
    Capitol, 501 S, 197
    Capitol, 620 S, 331
    Capitol, 711 S, 218
    Capitol, 717 S, 303
    Cedar, 603 N, 208
    Cherry, 427, 362
    Cherry, 431, 362
    Cherry, 609, 268
    Chestnut, 115 N, 138
    Chestnut, 623 N, 270
    Chestnut, 211 S, 134, 229
    Clubhouse, 309
    Fractional District #4 School, 19
    Grand, 536 N, 226
    Grand, 526-528 S, 69
    Grand, 532 S, 69
    Grand River, 200-202 E, 94
    Grand River, 204 E, 78

Grand River, 1221 N, 49
Grand River, 508 W, 265
Grand River, 523 W, 335
Hillsdale, 310 W, 352
Hillsdale, 312 W, 359
Hillsdale, 313 W, 292
Hillsdale, 427 W, 365
Hillsdale, 610-612 W, 196
Hosmer, 813 S, 291
Huron, 216, 97
Ionia, 200-212 W, 72
Ionia, 528 W, 122
Ionia, 602 W, 16
Ionia, 730 W, 32
Ionia, 734 W, 32
Ionia, 809 W, 159
Larch, 137 N, 52
Larch, 325 N, 18
Larch, 400-416 N, 60
Lenawee, 110 W, 315
Lenawee, 319 W, 256
Lenawee, 329 W, 125
Liberty, 515, 28
Logan (MLK), 104 S, 264
Logan (MLK), 108-110 S, 98
Logan (MLK), 116 S, 97
Logan (MLK), 210 S, 151
Logan (MLK), 226 S, 380
Main, 801 E, 289
Main, 903 E, 290
Maple, 326 W, 238
Michigan, 107 E, 342
Michigan, 121 E, 149
Michigan, 500-504 E, 259
Michigan, 1215 E, 345
Michigan, 600-614 W, 63
Michigan, 601-613 W, 62
Michigan 618 W, 64
Michigan, 1100 W, 33
Michigan, 1113 W, 66
Michigan, 1128 W, 21
Michigan, 1130 W, 20
Mill, 130, 203
Mill, 238, 178
Moores Park School, 297
North, 100 E, 221
North, 111-113 E, 339
Olds Motor Works, 150, 214
Ottawa, 115-117 E, 142
Ottawa, 120 E, 346
Ottawa, 106 W, 348
Ottawa, 120 W, 74
Ottawa, 320-328 W, 71
Ottawa, 613-615 W, 280
Ottawa, 706 W, 285

Ottawa, 712 W, 281
Ottawa, 817 W, 394
Ottawa, 909 W, 374
Ottawa, 1100 W, 42
Ottawa, 1203 W, 22
Pennsylvania, 610 N, 194
Pennsylvania, 612 N, 132
Pine, 300 N, 122
Pine, 310 N, 123
Pine, 207-211 S, 165
Pine, 208 S, 164
Pine, 210 S, 163
Pine, 214 S, 163
Pine, 512 S, 273
Pine, 516 S, 274
Race, 1131, 230
Saginaw, 701 E, 231
Saginaw, 423 W, 276
Seymour, 726, 358
St. Joseph, 112 E, 65
St. Joseph, 121 E, 199
St. Joseph, 126 E, 82
St. Joseph, 313-317 E, 389
St. Joseph, 117 W, 288
St. Joseph, 2123, W, 139
St Josephs & Waverly, 19
Sycamore, 201 N, 283
Sycamore, 209 N, 284
Sycamore, 216 N, 183
Sycamore, 217 N, 386
Sycamore, 200 S, 107
Townsend, 300, 237
Townsend, 332, 112
Townsend, 532, 351
Townsend, 606, 247
Turner, 1208-1212, 261
Turner, 1216-1218, 294
Turner, 1242-1246, 295
Walnut, 109 N, 184
Walnut, 1020 N, 371
Walnut, 1100-1104 N, 238
Walnut, 120 S, 37
Walnut, 207 S, 137
Walnut, 211, S, 110
Walnut, 232 S, 176
Walnut, 507 S, 124
Walnut, 830, S, 136
Washington, 112 N, 317
Washington, 117-119 N, 140
Washington, 213-215 N, 115
Washington, 220 N, 320
Washington, 230 N, 200
Washington, 602 N, 353
Washington, 716-718 N, 234
Washington, 720 N, 240

Washington, 915 N, 241
Washington, 929 N, 46, 152
Washington, 1003 N, 67
Washington, 1025 N, 322
Washington, 208 S, 127
Washington, 305-309 S, 325
Washington, 426 S, 298
Washington, 501-505 S, 84
Washington, 506 S, 116
Washington, 528 S, 57, 382
Washington, 619 S, 272
Washington, 700 S, 327
Washington, 713 S, 278
Washington, 720 S. 169
Washtenaw, 125-131 E, 354
Washtenaw, 118 W, 131
Washtenaw, 627 W, 385
Washtenaw, 709-711 W, 279
Laughlin, Mary, 344
Lazell, Minnie, 47
Leap, Charles, 1
Lee, Sophia (Sarah), 324
Lemon, Grace K., 265
Leonard, Sallie L., 314
Lepper, Olive, 40
Leslie, MI,
    Covert, 2230, 332
Lewis, Amy Rachel, 32
Liederkranz Hall, 226
Litzan, Alvina, 316
Longyear, John M., 121
Loughlin, Agnes, 91
Luce, Homer D., 218, 307, 352
Lyons, Hugh, 218, 220, 240, 305, 335, 360

Macomber, Georgia, 148
Madden, Ida M., 257
Martin, Flossie, 8
Mason, MI,
    Jefferson, 304 S, 314
    Jefferson, 322 S, 312
Maple, 229 E, 340
    Oak, 124 E, 107, 191-193
    State, 231, 396
Matthews, William W., 20
McAlvay, Aaron V., 331
McClina Kern, Mary, 196
McKenzie, George, 281-285
McKibbin, Frank, 329
Mead & White Architects, 340
Mead, Earl H., 61, 77, 181, 247, 248 n177, 303, 341
Mead, Helen, 278
Mead, James I., 16
Meridian Township, MI,
    Grand River, 1174, 145

Michigan Millers' Insurance Company, 74-77
Miers, Addie, 374
Miller, Stephen J., 40
Montgomery, Richard A., 86
Moon, David Sands, 7, 12
Moon, John W., 1 n1
Moon, Mary Wiltse, 7, 12
Moore, Earl V., 50
Moore, Frank I., 48, 152
Moore, Frank W., 49, 152
Moores, James Henry, 11
Moots, Helen, 68
Murray, Roanna, 34
Murray, Edward O., 264
Murray, George, 66
Murray, Jennie (Jane) Sutherland, 284

Nash, Charles E., 37, 237
Nash, Emily, 37, 239
Naylor, Jennie E., 158
Nice, Frank R., 2, 322
Nichols, Charles W., 42, 45
Nichols, Jason E., 272-275, 278
Nickle, John B., 168
Nixon, Elizabeth, 390
Northup Bill, Celia A., 161

Okemos, Chief, 65, 275
Olcott, Electra, 14
Olcott, Horace L., 14
Old Maid Swamp, 267
Olds Motor Works Lansing, MI, 150, 174, 179, 214-217
Olds, Ransom E., 11, 26, 107, 121, 169-176, 189, 265, 267, 278, 292, 327
Oliver, Peter, 33
Onondaga, MI, 32, 276
Opdyke, Charles J., 183
Otto, William B., 267

Palmer, Clarence H., 12
Paramore, Candace, 387
Parkhurst, Charles Ashel 340-342
Parkin, AR, 186
    Lansing Wheelbarrow Company, 206
Patch, Elmer A., 66
Peck, Emma Louise, 155
Peck, George Washington, 324
Perry, Anna C., 22
Person, Rollin H., 256
Pierson, Clara J., 32
Pope, Cora Lou, 299
Porter Rosserion, Sarah J., 329
Porter, Charles H., 131
Porter, Edgar, 166, 237, 301
Porter, Edwin H., 37, 237-239

Porter, Sarah L., 293
Post, Julius A., 130
Potter, James W., 57, 291, 327–329
Potter, Miles Ray, 288–293
Pratt, Mary J., 137
Pratt, Walter C., 42–45, 137
Price, Lawrence, 68, 194, 301
Prosser, Arthur D., 8

Ranney, George Emery, 127–130, 258, 280, 302, 339
    Prosser, Charles M., 8
Rathbun, Helen Campbell, 401
Ravenswood, IL, 94
Ray, Celia G., 328
Raymond, Dora, 252
Reedy, Diana, 2
Reitz, Elizabeth, 202, 232
Reitz, Edward N., 159–161
Rice, John, 94
Rikerd Lumber Company, 82, 154, 178, 203, 215
Rikerd, Arthur Randall, 205
Rikerd, Hiram W., 145, 205
Roaring Brook, MI, 186, 247, 303
    Stebbins Cottage, 187–190, 222
    Woodbury Cottage, 181, 222
Robert Smith Printing Company, 178, 198, 200–202
Robson, Albert M., 178, 199
Rogers Park, IL, 8, 93
Rogers, Herbert M., 88–91
Rohrer, Martin, 29
Rose, Maud E., 264
Rouse, Mary C., 324

Sackrider, Sophronia M. Revenaugh, 146
Sadler, Annie, 194
Saier, Charles, 196
Savage, Fitch R., 359–361
Schneider, Frederick, 221, 228, 258
Schroeder, Frederick C., 161
Schultz, Emma, 105
Scofield, Sylvester Green, 78, 94–96
Seely, Elizabeth, 327
Sellers, William S., 8 n4
Sever, Ada S., 109
Sharp, Edward C., 46, 47
Sherd, John, 14
Sherman, Edwin Porter, 260
Shields, Thomas J., 194, 196, 366
Shull, David N., 124–126
Slemmer, Henry, 176
Smith Apartments, 94
Smith, Angeline E. Haze, 18
Smith, Hiram H., 323

Smith, Quincy A., 73, 227,
Smith, Rhea, 344
Smith, Susan, 16
Sparrow Hospital, 120, 122, 293, 345
Sparrow, Alicia J., 119, 121, 278
Sparrow, Edward W., 57, 59, 81, 116–122
Sparrow, Eva (Delia Olivia), 59, 119
Sparrow, Isabella E., 119, 130,
Spice, Raymond W., 10, 75, 310
Sprague, Ellen, M., 7, 14
Sprague, Manervy, 14
Sprague, Molton, 14
Stabler, Christian E., 138
Stahl, Jacob, 64, 110–116, 203
Stansel, Augusta, 85
Stark, Byron Wade, 213
Stebbins, Arthur C., 183–190
Stebbins, Susan E., 212
Stowell, Rena, 186
Strengson, Elizabeth, 359
Stroud, Charles H., 305, 307
Sutliff, George E., 26
Sweazy, Adelia E., 268
Sweazy, Isadore, 268

Tarleton, John B., 52
Thenen, Charles, 8 n4
Thoman, Frederick, 160, 178, 201
Thoman, Frederick (Fred) J., 72, 150, 201
Thoman, John Phillip, 386–389
Thomas, Celesta, 367
Thomas, Charles Gordon, 391
Thomas, Emmet, 94
Thomas, Lydia A., 390–392
Tilden, Ella Gertrude, 86
Timmerman, Adelia, 19
Timmerman, James, 18
Travis (Traverse), Clara, 163
Truax, Cornelia W., 66
True, Orville, 193
Tuck, Ida May, 46
Turner, Abigail, 225
Turner, Harris B., 154
Turner, James, 14, 223, 225
Turner, Marion, 225
Tussing Building, 348–351
Tussing, Daniel W., 348, 380
Twiss, Ethelyn Alice, 395

Union Building and Loan Association, 329

Van Der Voort, Sarah E., 71–73
Voiselle, John B., 149

Voorhees, Elizabeth B., 32

Waldo, Alva Nixon, 389
Waldo, Andre (Andrew), 390
Waldo, Elizabeth, 389
Waldo, Mary Jane, 323
Waldo, Susan, 39
Walnut Street School, 371
Walter, Adeline E., 239
Watkins, Hattie E., 385
Watts, Francis C., 30
Webb, Lewis C., 397
Weil, Bella, 356
Welch, Mae C., 23
Wellings, James H., 154, 241
Wells, Charles E., 30
Wells, Emri J., 31, 41
Wells, Ida E., 83
Wells, Mary Nixon, 31
White & Butterworth, 345
Whitman, Charles W., 107, 191–193
Wilbur, Alroy A., 78–80, 82, 172
Wilcox, Myrtie B., 261
Wilcox, Willard Merritt, 274
Wilson & Kopf Skating Rink, Broad Ripple Park, IN, 384
Wilson & Kopf Skating Rink, Lansing, MI, 346–348
Wilson, George L., 237, 240
Wilson, John, 11
Wilson, John S., 11, 151, 239, 346, 384
Wilson, Lucius D., 235
Wilson, Sarah C., 234–236
Winters, Thomas Michael, 89–91
Wolfe, Sarah, 319
Wolford, Joseph W., 148, 361–363
Wood, Frederick A., 265
Woodbury, Chester Downey, 77, 181, 243–248, 361
Woodward, Metta Ursula, 175
Woodworth, Fred D., 340
Wright, Peter S., 7
Wyman, Fern Weldan, 107

Yeiter, Elizabeth, 79

www.ingramcontent.com/pod-product-compliance
Lightning Source LLC
Chambersburg PA
CBHW080527170426
43195CB00016B/2497